Octavia's Hill

Octavia's Hill

Margaret Dickson

Boston

HOUGHTON MIFFLIN COMPANY

1983

Library of Congress Cataloging in Publication Data

Dickson, Margaret.
Octavia's hill.

I. Title.
PS3554.I329O28 1983 813'.54 82–15830
ISBN 0–395–33159–5

Printed in the United States of America

S 10 9 8 7 6 5 4 3 2 1

For my dear husband, Pete,
and for Steve, with thanks

Surrender — is a sort unknown —
On this superior soil —
Defeat — an outgrown Anguish —
Remembered, as the Mile

Our panting Ankle barely passed —
When Night devoured the Road —
But we — stood whispering in the House —
And all we said — was "Saved"!

—EMILY DICKINSON,
"Of Tribulation — these are They," 1861

THE PERRYS OF OCTAVIA'S HILL

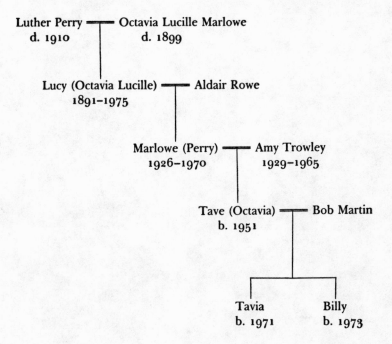

Luther Perry —— Octavia Lucille Marlowe
d. 1910   d. 1899

Lucy (Octavia Lucille) —— Aldair Rowe
1891–1975

Marlowe (Perry) —— Amy Trowley
1926–1970   1929–1965

Tave (Octavia) —— Bob Martin
b. 1951

Tavia   Billy
b. 1971   b. 1973

Tave

"... *H*OMELESS BY FIRES *which . . . warning to counties in . . ."*

Tave switched stations and, finding none, twisted the dial back. Most of her attention was on the road, on the car. Tuning the radio as she headed toward Octavia's Hill was always an experiment anyway: the reception from the nearest station, WAMD in Dover-Foxcroft, wasn't that good. Too many hills in the way.

But this afternoon she needed "the Soft Silver Sound of Ray Gray," as the smooth-voiced afternoon disc jockey at WAMD billed himself. He played Easy Listening, a kind of afternoon ironing music for the ladies, maybe, but Tave needed some soothing. She deserved that much, didn't she?

Now she turned the radio up and tuned again, somewhat savagely, until a voice exploded at her—not Ray's, a newscaster's— so loudly she jumped; the car even jumped a little. Fumbling, she turned the volume down. "*. . . advised to find shelter immediately . . ."*

She wanted music, not talk. With one disgusted twist of her fingers, she shut the radio off.

"I'll just go home then!" she mumbled to herself, making a turn and beginning to climb. "I'm in the damn car, aren't I?" She glanced at the speedometer; the dial had sunk too easily from forty to thirty. This damn car, this damn hill, she thought.

"If Bob doesn't do something about it pretty soon," she muttered as, pedal to the floor, she started up the brutal incline that would end at the summit of Octavia's Hill. The old green Ford station wagon banged from rut to rut. Its springs were shot, and you sailed high into the air with each bump and came down with jaw-jarring intensity, only to sail up again. And of course they had no money, and of course when this clunker finally went, that would be the end of it; she would be housebound once and for all.

Slam!

There. She'd hit it that time. After weeks of coming up the rutted road, each time managing to avoid that one really bad eight-inch rock—it would take more than a pickax to prize that beauty out of the roadbed—she'd smashed right into it, up, and over. But the car was still moving; she didn't dare to stop.

Front end alignment, she thought, and then, to hell with it.

The Ford would have to keep itself aligned somehow. In the 1970s Bob's salary at the district high school had seemed adequate; these days it barely fed them, clothed them, paid the mortgage, and put Bob into an old International Scout. But the salary didn't stretch to the running of a second batch of wheels, even this heap. Especially this heap.

A rumbling vibration sounded from the depths of the car, and Tave knew without looking that the speedometer had slipped below thirty. Whenever that happened the car trembled with a slow, deep quake, a rhythmic heave that said it wished, please, to throw a rod and die.

The trouble with Octavia's Hill, for which Tave was named, was that you had to get a running start to get up it. But in the Ford you couldn't go over forty; if you did, something—had Bob said the carburetor?—began to thump, like the unremitting countdown preceding some awful detonation. But if you went up too slowly, every minute seemed like a prelude to the last rites. (A slammed door, a kick, and a curse; the car dies, rolling slowly out of sight down the hill. Backward.) All of which made the road up Octavia's Hill almost impassable in winter or spring.

But today was summer, glorious summer for a change—high

[4]

time, Tave thought, it was the end of May—and the back of the station wagon was full of her paintings.

Seventy-five—count 'em—dollars, that was her highest-priced spread at the moment. But there were times when, if she'd sold just one of her canvases for any amount, she would have driven clear to Portland, checked into a motel, and stayed there until her money ran out or she did. There she would be, strolling down some long stretch of Maine beach, paintbox in hand, canvas under her arm, utterly content, until she collapsed from hunger and neglect.

Well, that was the trouble. Tave didn't think she'd be too good at collapsing on strange beaches.

The cosmic joke, she supposed. You didn't get what you wanted; it wasn't good for you.

All this foolishness passed through her mind in a matter of seconds. She was used to a kind of half-desperate, half-ironic spatter of thoughts that occurred to her like chain lightning, were not serious, and kept her entertained. Most of her attention was on the speedometer, which hovered at a blazing twenty-eight miles per hour. Come on, car! She pushed forward on her seat, as if the Ford would run on her own nervous energy.

Somehow it did run. The road continued to rumble toward the car, stones rolled under the tires. The hill road rose up before her. Pebbles bounced forward. The car pulled into the driveway and she turned off the ignition.

For a moment she sat and let the engine cool.

Tave squinted up at the white frame house on Octavia's Hill, at its long front porch (the metal porch chairs a little rusty now, with their once-red rounded seats and backs and no arms). It was a commodious old farmhouse with a long shed attached on the north side and beyond that a big white barn, emptied out in Tave's father's time. Tave and Bob still kept it painted and repaired, without knowing why.

Someday, when a four-lane highway passed by her door, maybe, or when she was a millionaire—one was as likely as the other—Tave had said she would hang out her shingle, TAVE

[5]

MARTIN, ARTIST, on the barn and display all her paintings there. No straw then, no redolence. Immaculate. Long white walls and track lighting suspended from the ceiling—on all three floors, of course. At the top would be the artist's studio. Utterly private; no number for it on the elevator. Her studio: the ceiling full of skylights, white walls. Central heating. Plumbing, of course. Paints. She'd go in there and shut the door, shut it all out.

Eight paintings. She'd sat all morning in the Tri-County Grange Hall and watched people look at her work. It hadn't been easy. She'd felt like a puppy with its tail beating, eager for a pat of approval, ready to slink if scolded. And that feeling had made her angry. In fact, she'd been mad for two days before the show, too.

"For Chrissake," Bob had finally blurted out the night before, running blunt fingers through his curly blond hair, "if you hate it so much, don't do it! Forget it! I don't care!"

"That's right," she'd yelled back at him. "Give us all a little peace and quiet around here!"

"Well, yes," he'd mumbled from the bed, turning his back to her and picking up a book.

Then she'd pulled her side of the covers open far enough so that a good-sized portion of his bare freckled back was exposed to the midnight breezes; even in May, Octavia's Hill could be chilly at night.

"Oh, God," she heard him mutter. "Anchorage, Alaska." That made her feel better.

She climbed in, turned her back to his, and picked up her own book, pulling the covers again so that cold air filled the space between them. She began to read.

Much later, when she reached up to turn off her light, she realized they were lying as usual, comfortably back to back. She shut off her light and went to sleep without acknowledging it. She wouldn't give him the satisfaction.

In the morning their little spat seemed so tangled into the knot of disagreements that she and Bob carried around that it seemed easiest to ignore it, act "normal." With frenzied cheer

[6]

she'd made breakfast for everyone, put up lunch pails, and packed Tavia and Billy into the Scout. Until the last moment, she had avoided the quizzical look in Bob's light brown eyes, but then she'd kissed him through the car window, a kiss that said, I'd like to be sorry, but I'm too upset. Pulling away, he'd given her a half-sided smile and a quick glance that said, humorously, So what else is new?

That was Bob, Tave thought meanly. Able to rise above every occasion.

They'd left and then, her paintings wrapped in old blankets in the back of the station wagon, a thermos and a paper bag of jelly sandwiches beside her on the seat, off she'd gone. And yes, she'd been the only painter there who ate at the exhibit; after her entrance fee, she'd had just enough for gas. Crumbs in her lap and on the floor.

She was also the only artist there not wearing what Octavia Lucille Perry, Tave's grandmother, would have called a Shelton Stroller—one of those flowered jersey, button-down-the-front dresses, belted, designed to fit anyone and go anywhere, with pumps and purse to match.

Art exhibits were hard to come by in Tave's part of Maine; you took what you could get. This was a Grange exhibit, and a pretty high-toned one at that. No young women were there. Tave decided that young Grange women didn't paint; their business must be "The Home." In Tave's mind "The Home" was spelled out on a sampler in gold thread. Those women were no doubt elbow deep in muddy-green canned spinach or, maybe, lengthy baking projects. They probably had plump children whose happy faces were flecked with flour as they gamboled in their mothers' fragrant kitchens.

Lighthouses. One hundred and fifty miles from the Maine coast, all the old women of the Grange sat in their back bedrooms painting lighthouses from picture postcards. But these paintings, Tave knew, would sell like crazy in the middle of the summer, when Moosehead was full of campers. And if not lighthouses, then kittens: formula "primitives." Acrylic fruit that looked as if

it had been through a difficult menopause: gray, wrinkled, be-
rouged. Horses. Flowers. Fence posts.

And in the back, Tave's paintings. Well, near a window at least.
Perhaps thirty people came during the morning. Tave could
spot their feet under the screens that had been set up to display
the paintings. It would have made an interesting study, she
thought: *Screens with Paintings and Feet.* More interesting were the
faces that finally made it as far as Tave's paintings. That bit of
shock on them. A sketch by Norman Rockwell called, say, *Oh.
Modern.*

In her early thirties, with two children and no formal art training, Tave felt it took guts to display her paintings. Most people
thought them bizarre, even sloppy, she could tell. Worse, Tave
herself never felt quite sure of what she was doing; she worked
by instinct, reaching for ideas, form. When people disliked her
work, she was often more than half-inclined to agree with them.
That, too, made her angry.

"I do enjoy modern paintings," one woman had said kindly.
"They let you see more than what's there, somehow . . ." Then
she'd replaced her glasses and moved on. Tave had brushed the
crumbs off her lap and started to smile, but it was too late.

She decided she'd like to paint a few people with metal hooks
in the backs of their necks, hanging on a wall . . .

So much anger, too much. She was tired, she was sorry, she
apologized to the whole world. Why couldn't she be content with
homemaking, and maybe a part-time job as, oh, a typist, even a
waitress, something? But without painting, nothing was worth-
while. She'd left the exhibit early, right after lunch.

Home again. In spite of herself, Tave was glad. She patted the
dashboard—good car—and caught a glimpse of herself in its
rearview mirror. Dark hair, the gray Marlowe eyes, her grandmother's nose; Tave wrinkled it, it was a little long. An oval face
and her mother's complexion, thank God—white, clear skin. She
no longer bothered with make-up, wouldn't, she'd told Bob, until
they made the kind of face you didn't have to take off at night.
Now she arranged her expression a little. She knew people

thought she was pretty, but she didn't care about that. What Tave cared about were all those long hours when she could find no reason to smile.

Tave opened the car door and climbed out. She was slender, even athletic in a tense kind of way. She knew she was built like her grandmother, too; slender females with girlish figures ran on the Marlowe side of the family. She was proud of her body when she thought about it at all; healthy and made for use, it served her well.

She stared off into the distance. It was as if the hill reached out and grabbed you, wherever you were. You couldn't stay away. The whole northern and eastern part of the State of Maine lay visible below her. Tave needed that view. The hill was like a mother making promises. How could you resist?

Moosehead Lake extended for miles to the north. Off in the blue distance, shining white, was Mount Katahdin. To the south lay a long plain of greenshag woods. And then the familiar contours of Octavia's Hill itself. The land at its foot as unpredictable as the road up it. A more distant road, this one badly tarred, meandered through woodlands; it was like a broken coil of gray wire, visible, not visible in trees, by stone walls. In the distance the road followed the Branch, which flowed into Moosehead Lake, then bridged it some ten miles away and went on into Monson; southeast, Monson was the only real settlement in a fifteen-mile radius of the hill.

From the top of Octavia's Hill, all you could see of the town was the tallest building on Main Street and the district school, where Tavia and Billy were students. Tave had driven through Monson today on her way home. One main street, two stores, a gas station, a firehouse, the school buildings. Some structures on Main Street boasted drooping square façades of wood that concealed sloped roofs. Today the town had seemed unusually quiet as she went through, no one out on the street to wave at. As she swung toward the hill the firehorn had begun to blow, not its usual long, hard, fire-alarm blast, but in a strange, wobbly way. A drill of some sort, she supposed. John Manders, at it again.

What a wail that horn had had, though, like the howl of a dying animal!

North, east, and south of Octavia's Hill were other, smaller hills, each of which had its residents, or had had them. At this time of year these hills were lovely; Tave couldn't go indoors without looking at them. Now she strolled to the edge of the driveway, where two forsythias finally bloomed, and looked across.

On one of the hills, tall elms had given out where a house used to be, and thick, old maples now betrayed the grassed-over space between them for what it once had been, an access road and driveway. This was Gould property, or had been briefly, years back. Now the jonquils planted one hopeful spring by old Ellen Gould at her doorstep ran across the grass and down the drive. From here they looked ethereal, all right. But Tave knew that if you went to pick them, the blossoms would be small, tough, and wild—and somehow more attractive to Tave that way.

Ellen Gould had died of consumption in the late twenties, and the little house out of town in the fresh air soon decayed, fell into its cellar hole. That hill, bought from Aldair Rowe, still belonged to the Gould family.

On the second hill, to the east, had been in Tave's lifetime a cottage, a little brown four-room affair that for several summers housed the dean of Union College and his wife and two daughters. No one knew them very well, although they did shop in Monson. The wife was thin and small, with curly light blond hair and light blue eyes, so that she'd reminded Tave—who was then a child—of ashes. The man was tall and slim, and once at some meeting he had been asked to open with a prayer. So he had, and had prayed for twenty full minutes in short, broken sentences that were more like questions. His dark eyes were set in dark sockets. Burnt umber, Tave now thought. He'd hung himself out of an attic window at the cottage.

"Grandma," Tave had cried that morning, "come here! What's —what's that thing, hanging, see, down there—"

Lucy Perry had come over with the indulgent little simper that she saved for Tave alone. But she'd taken one look at the dean's cottage and called for her son. "Marlowe! Marlowe!"

"Yes?" Tave's father came to the porch, his coffee cup still in his hand.

"Marlowe"—Tave saw that only her grandmother's thin lips were moving—"what does that look like to you?" Lucy pointed to the cottage. "Because it looks to me like a body, hanging from that window."

"Mother—"

"Marlowe, that foolish man has done it at last!"

Marl, Tave's father, had sweetly disregarded his mother, as usual. "Please," he said, sipping slowly, "not in front of Tave." Then he ambled down off the porch, stopped, took one careful look at the cottage, and caught Tave's wide-eyed, frightened glance.

"Come on, honey," he said to her quietly, "let's go back to the house." A few minutes later he left, in one of the ancient ancestors of Tave's present rattletrap, to help the dean's wife and family.

It had given Tave nightmares, four nights in a row.

"Look you, young one," her mother, Amy Perry, had said firmly on the fourth night, "you can spend your time havin' nightmares if you want, but it don't do no good."

Amy, Tave's mother, used the double negative advisedly. When she did it, it meant what it said: no, twice.

"Nossir," continued Amy. "Now, then, you don't plan to be one of them ladies who can't look at a poor dead man, do you?

"You can faint or fuss if you want, course." Tave could see the large round shouders in the dark, her mother's face with its still profile. "But seems to me some of us are made stronger 'n 'at. Now you sleep. Four shriekin' nightmares in four nights is enough. Don't you let me hear those screams again, now I mean it."

Tough words, but Tave knew you had to be tough to get rid of devils. And just as if her mother had invoked all those capable country people they'd both come from, and trotted them one by one in front of Tave, Tave had suddenly realized that looking a thing in the eye—even a dead shadow draped over the front of a distant cottage, looking that thing in the eye, the tired eye of the mind tired of questions—that was as much a part of her heritage as Lucy Perry, who had felt dizzy and spent that morning rocking and trembling on her porch chair.

On the fifth night Tave's bad dreams were gone.

The taxes on the dean's property were delinquent, but nobody wanted the land or bothered much about it. The cottage had been built up on posts, and now, except for the slant of a cracked and decaying shingled roof resting on split posts a few inches from the ground, there wasn't much left of it at all. Without it, the hill had a fine symmetry of old evergreens and wild yellow grass.

The third hill, a small one to the south, had never been inhabited and looked completely wooded and untouched, but Tave knew that it was crisscrossed with woods roads. Pulp for the paper company that owned the hill was harvested at intervals, and wood lay waiting at this moment in a row of logs higher than her head and a quarter of a mile long at the edge of the ridge, until the big pulp grapple could load it onto the long beds of several trucks. Later this summer, she and Bob and the children would probably go blueberrying in the slash.

Each of the hills had its own harsh history. But what you saw when you looked at them was a study of blue and white that in the middle distance became purple and then the gold-green and dark green and bright yellow and red of spring woods, bright ankle-high new hayfields, and stone walls like necklaces.

Except, of course, for that one other dwelling, near the bottom of Octavia's Hill, the crumbling house of Tommy Green. By mistake Tave spotted it and then looked away quickly. Tommy Green's big white Cadillac, so incongruous when you saw how badly the house needed repair, was not in the driveway. Quickly, so as to give it no more thought, she averted her eyes. People always looked the other way when passing Tommy Green's house, and if by accident they caught a glimpse of a tailfin, they wiped it and all thought of it out of their minds.

Tave left her paintings wrapped in blankets in the car except for the top one. This one she had called *Ghost of the North,* and it was, at the moment, her favorite painting. She pulled it out carefully and carried it inside, setting it on the table in the kitchen.

The table was maple and had once had a fine finish. Now it was very old, ringed and spotted. In Lucy Perry's time, each blemish had had a history, and if provoked, Lucy would recite these stories one by one, like a list of grievances. They might have been Lucy's own trials and tribulations: "I started out as a pretty little maple table, carefully fashioned and finished by the best people. Over the years, however, the children and the grandchildren who were too careless, the hot, heavy pans of food I carried . . ."

Lucy must have had a long memory, because once Tave's mother came to live on the hill, Lucy Perry had never again carried anything heavier than a teacup.

Once, in an overzealous attempt to bury herself in domesticity, Tave had tried to refinish the table; she found its pores so full of history, kitchen grease, and old, gossipy, damp air that even after sanding the wood wouldn't give up its stain. So then she'd left the top as it was, washing it after meals and occasionally coating it with oil. It looked like what it was—an old farm table, spotless but scarred. It could hold anything, from books and crying babies and pans of hot baked beans to this painting (if you could call it that, Tave thought).

On the table right now, as always at this time of the year, was a pitcher of poppies. On the high shelf of the black kitchen stove was another. Along the north wall of the kitchen were cupboards and the sink, and a window over this through which budding lilacs could be seen, and a bird feeder, active now as it was all day long throughout the year.

Bob had long since insulated the wall under the sink, but Tave could remember childhood mornings when Lucy Perry paced the kitchen, one hand pulling at her straight white hair, the other curled tight as a wound spool in front of her, while the kettle came to the boil on the back of the wood stove. Then Tave's mother, Amy, poured the boiling water into a basin under the sink so that the steam could rise and help to thaw the pipes. It was hothouse hot and freezer cold then by that north wall; all the washcloths in the kitchen were laid in the water and pressed one by one over the pipes. Amy Perry did the work. When it was done, old Lucy Perry would sit by the stove and look exhausted.

Tave never came into the kitchen even now, twenty years and all that insulation later, without a visceral expectation of those extremes of temperature. Besides that, there were times when Lucy Perry still seemed to pant in her warm, comfortable rocker by the stove, and Amy Perry moved unhurried around the chilly periphery of the room, doing the kitchen work. They were both dead, but Tave could see them almost as if they were still, truly, living. At times her memory was so sharp that she could see details of her mother's face and how her quiet mouth would move almost imperceptibly toward humor as she glanced at Lucy Perry, sitting and rocking exhaustedly in her chair. And just as it had so many times during Tave's childhood, the kitchen would become cooler in Lucy Perry's warm corner, and the warmth would locate itself in the imagined wake of Amy's forthright footsteps.

Tave shook her head now and twisted *Ghost of the North* to a better light, staring at it. That was the trouble with inheriting the family house on the family hill, she was thinking idly. There were too many "ghosts of the north," as vigorous and fiery as her mother's poppies.

Then quickly she looked away from the painting. But just too late.

"Damn," she muttered.

It was happening again, this time to *Ghost.*

Tave began to pace about the kitchen, staring from different angles, stalling. But no matter where she stood, she had to see it: the unavoidable. At last she stood still, covered her face with her hands. Her next audible words fell into the room as softly as if she had spoken them in her sleep. "My head hurts," she said. "My head hurts."

Sliding down, moving away from her—optimism, hope, something. It wasn't the headache that hurt so much, it was the painting. Suddenly, somehow, the light had changed and it seemed to her—as it had in the past, to how many of her other paintings?—that *Ghost* was no good. She knew it, she could see it.

The worst of painting for Tave was this: her best work—what seemed at one time or another to have the most potential, the one painting she counted on, her favorite—that painting could on the twist of a glance change, become nothing at all. Now it had happened to *Ghost*; she couldn't bear to look. The lines of the painting blurred, shifted, became no more than, say, your early morning snowstorm on the television set.

She fought, of course, as she always did. She pushed at the picture in her mind, pasting in new lines, putting old ones where they should be, or where she thought, or maybe, or no. Trying to retrace, retrieve: there, that's not so bad, is it? Running ahead of herself, to see if it would be, or not be, so obviously bad.

Her fingertips moved from her temples and covered her eyes. Faulty eyes; with blinders, she'd read somewhere, and you didn't know it until you became accustomed to them. Then, suddenly, the blinders were lifted, and it was all a big joke on you. There you were, queen and fool.

She mustered up a little satirical snicker and then forced herself to look again, hard, at *Ghost*. At last, however, she reached out and gently turned it to the wall. Tomorrow, maybe, thought Scarlett O'Hara, it would all look better. But Tave Perry knew it would not.

She found herself a towel and mopped at her eyes. Standing around in a deserted kitchen, weeping at four-thirty in the afternoon. Typical.

"Is that my good tea towel?" the dead Lucy Perry asked her.

"Oh, shut up," said Tave, and blew her nose on it.

Bob would be home soon. Bob taught Civics, Government, U.S. History, and senior Sociology at the district high school in Monson. Three afternoons a week, in addition, he coached junior varsity baseball—or basketball or football, depending on the season. Tave wouldn't tell him about *Ghost*, couldn't. Not that he wouldn't try to understand, but that she couldn't bear to be the object of sympathy. He was so successful—a good teacher, a good coach, an excellent father; his projects always came out right.

She saw before her the pattern of their evening, so predictable, and felt helpless. She would be withdrawn, *Ghost* well hidden in a closet somewhere. Bob would ask her questions about the art exhibit, about her paintings; she would reply in monosyllables, too upset to do more. At last he would give up, the hurt look she dreaded in his brown eyes. He would turn his attention to the children. She would sit across the table in a widening shadow, unable to share, miffed and distant.

Later the children would go to bed and Bob would disappear into the cellar; she would be left to nothing, too proud to call him back. At ten he'd come up cheerful. They would go to bed and perhaps find themselves in an embrace, if they were lucky. Maybe they would cling together before they slept, as if the arguments they had were problems of timing in a mechanism that was basically sound. But some corner of their hearts they would keep to themselves, Tave thought. Not dare to give it all, always a bit on the alert for some new battle.

Today Tavia, aged ten, and Billy, eight, had been told not to ride the school bus home but to go to the field after school to watch the practice, and then come home with Bob, because Tave didn't know exactly what time she'd be home from the exhibit. Tave knew that Billy would sit as though his pants were nailed to the bleachers, watching the baseball, and that Tavia would spend the time glumly, hand on skinny hips, asking everybody she saw what time it was and pushing her glasses up on her nose. Then going back to her book. For two years Tavia had carried a book with her wherever she went, one finger stuck at her place so that she could slap it open at a moment's notice. The books were like an appendage at the end of her fingers. Well, if you had lanky black hair, freckles, and spectacles, you would need some security at the age of ten, Tave supposed.

They would all be home soon, and hungry for supper. Making

a wide circle around the disgraced painting, trying to pretend that it didn't exist at all, Tave turned on her electric wall oven and took a casserole out of the refrigerator. As she did, Lucy Perry moved restlessly in the corner. Lucy Perry had never approved of casseroles.

Tave threw the casserole into the oven with a bang and dumped some frozen broccoli into a pan and set it on the back of the stove. It would thaw while the casserole was cooking, and after the family came home she would turn on the burner. Her private rule of thumb: when it boiled over, it was done.

She snickered at herself and moved past the cellar door, her glance falling as she did so to the floor. She was not a fussy housekeeper, but now she noticed a small, dry spot there. She scrubbed at it with her toe. Maroon, underneath. Paint, probably. Now who had had red paint in the kitchen?

The phone rang. Three-two-one, a series of short rings that could mean only one thing on this line: fire. It was the prearranged signal. When there was a fire, every able-bodied man and boy in town was expected to volunteer. At first Tave thought she wouldn't pick up the phone, since Bob wasn't at home. Then she realized he'd be home soon and she'd better. Three-two-one, the phone rang; three-two-one. She ran into the dim living room and picked it up.

"John, Bob's not here," she said hurriedly into the receiver.

"Tave? Tave, it's Bob."

"Bob? But—"

"Listen, Tave," she heard him say. But her mind was sorting: what was Bob doing at the fire phone?

"I've got a lot of calls to make," he said. "This isn't a fire call. You hear me?"

"Of course I can," she answered him, somewhat crossly. "But what are you doing? Why aren't you home? I've put the casserole in—"

"Tave, please!" His quiet voice had that little hitch in it that she recognized: Bob under pressure, his lips working to form the right words. Something, she suddenly realized, was quite wrong.

[17]

"There's no fire, Tave," he said. "It's an air raid alert."

"It's a—what?" Tave's mouth fell open. "Bob, this isn't funny. Where are you?"

Suddenly, sternly, his voice interrupted her. "This is not a joke! Please!"

"What is it, Bob, what's wrong?"

"Listen to me, honey." Still arguing, when he knew he didn't have to. "Turn on the radio and listen. This is an air raid alert."

"You mean there's no fire?" Queer how the brain functioned at one level, and the tongue at another.

"No! No fire! Turn on the radio. Do what it says to do. Don't worry about me. Don't worry about the kids. John's down at the basement shelter at the school, opening it for the kids. Tavia, Billy, and the others are with him. I have to keep calling—"

"John Manders?" A picture of the bewhiskered John, who slept at the firehouse, came to Tave. The only time John seemed to wake up was when there was an emergency. You give him something dangerous, Bob always said, you couldn't find a steadier hand. "What?" She couldn't help her confusion. "I don't understand—"

"Tave, there's been an explosion, the real thing. I mean it. I got fifteen more places to call. Tave?"

"Turn on the—the radio?"

"Right. One more thing. Tave, the generator, you know how to work it?"

"I know."

"All right, then, turn it on. Then go right downstairs, the way they tell you to. Do everything they tell you to, all right? Everything. Promise me!"

"Yes, all right—"

"Promise?"

"Why, yes, I promise—"

"I love you, Tave." This wrung from him, she could tell. He'd never been one to say it easily.

"I love you, too," she said, surprised.

He hung up.

Tave stood quite still. She allowed herself to think how quiet it was, here in the living room. Was there anything like the repose of empty furniture?

Turn on the radio, Bob said.

At once, dark into light, she was in the kitchen and at the end of the counter and the radio was on, at the only station they ever received at the top of the hill, WAMD in Dover-Foxcroft.

"... *run this list, and then run the warning again.*" It was Ray Gray, but no longer smooth-voiced. "*'The shelter should contain absolute necessities: water, food, sanitation supplies, and any special medicine or foods needed by family members.'*" It was obvious he was reading. "*'Milk, canned meat, poultry, fish, items in your refrigerator, ready-to-eat cereal, sugar, coffee, tea, cocoa, salt. Sanitation supplies include a metal container with a tight-fitting lid . . .'*" The list continued.

Tave frowned, blinked, tried to concentrate. What had happened? Oh, Lord, was it war?

There was a rattling sound, as if fingers fumbled at papers.

"*We'll continue that list in a moment . . .*" Ray Gray's voice, barely recognizable, taut, with a businesslike edge to it. "*Concerning the present emergency, the latest information we have is this: contrary to previous reports that there was an earthquake or other seismic happening in the Vermont area, it has now become apparent that a nuclear explosion of some severity has occurred there, possibly at the air force base at Lessing. There are fires throughout a wide area at this moment. The reason for the blast is unknown at this time. However, all counties downwind have been officially warned to take shelter. All of New Hampshire and the State of Maine have been declared to be under air raid alert. Latest reports are that fallout can be expected in all areas. At this moment we are not, however, at war.*"

Tave found herself holding on to the radio knob so tightly her fingers hurt. She made a conscious effort to loosen them. Fallout? Shelter—the cellar?

Obviously a mistake, but now two voices were transmitted briefly from WAMD:

"*Chrissake, have them tune to the bunker! We been on this all afternoon—*" A voice Tave didn't know. "*Time's runnin' out—*"

[19]

"They can't get the bunker." Ray Gray, arguing back. *"I know they can't! Some of them only get us!"*

"Ray, we have to get out of here! There's goin' to be radioactivity—"

"I don't care! The bunker's clear the hell over in Milo! Mount Katahdin's in the way and every other damn thing—"

"Okay! Up to you! But I'm goin', Ray, I got to. I got kids—"

"I got kids, too, damnit!"

There was a slam, an abrupt click, silence.

Tave knew that WAMD was only a one-room brick building set on a hill in Dover-Foxcroft, not even in the town, really, but out in the middle of nowhere. Just a little one-man station; when the disc jockey went out for coffee, the janitor took over.

As if in a dream, Tave looked about her darkening kitchen. Air raid? Explosion? Fallout? What she could remember about radiation she hadn't really thought of in so long that—

But here, blessedly, was Ray Gray again. *"Folks, I'm going to ask you to bear with me. It's been a long afternoon. Listeners who are able to do so should tune to WAZQ-FM, in Milo, for the best radio information. WAZQ in an emergency bunker fully hardened to withstand the effects of radioactivity. For the rest of us"*— here his voice hesitated, sounded again in a quiet, broken way— *"I don't know just what to do. No one has given me any instructions about this. I hope my family will forgive me, but I've decided to stick it out here, at least for now. I guess the essential thing is to tell you that if you haven't taken shelter, you should do so immediately. I have some materials here that may help, but please do take shelter, if you haven't already done so. This is Ray Gray—"* Silence.

Tave began to move, slowly at first and then faster and faster, tearing things out of cupboards and dropping them in a heap beside the open cellar door. From her radio came muffled scraping sounds, as of furniture being moved, and then Ray was back, obviously reading.

" 'Move to your basement or fallout shelter,' " he read, *" 'or into a public shelter. Home shelters will need to be stocked, if they are not already, and as quickly as possible. Close off all possible access to the home shelter. Once in the shelter, it is imperative for you to remain there until government authorities inform you it is safe to leave . . .' "*

Tave glanced toward the cellar door. Although she did not remember opening it, the door reached into the kitchen. She viewed the dark space beyond it with distaste. She would have to go down there, make herself stay down there, she knew. The problem was, of course, that you never could be sure what you might find, what you might step into at the bottom of the cellar stairs—

"Don't be foolish," she told herself. But once again, just for a moment, she thought she heard the wailing call of that Monson siren. Did it really howl like an animal? Was the sound coming from Monson, or from somewhere deep inside that black cellar opening?

Ray Gray shuffled his papers again. *"Here is the latest bulletin from our wire service,"* he said. *" 'Civil defense authorities ask that the following instructions be carried out with all possible speed. Go to the nearest shelter. If none is available—' "* Tave thought his voice became huskier, just for a moment. He cleared his throat and continued. *" '—t-take cover in the nearest underground protected place, preferably a basement, cellar, or crawl space. Calculations of the weather service indicate that within a matter of minutes, fallout danger will be at more than fifty percent in the State of Maine . . .' "*

Tave caught back a desperate little laugh. Fifty percent chance. Just like predicting rain, or snow.

Ray Gray continued, but now he was not reading. *"The news we have had after a long afternoon of conflicting reports indicates—"* But he didn't go on. There was another scraping sound, a silence, as he seemed to pause for breath.

Tave stared into the shadow of the cellar door and her stomach began to fizz. She heard Bob say "I love you," as if it were a farewell, and her legs began to tremble. Her head was pounding. She felt terror, suddenly, as if it were statewide, all of her State of Maine, in surprised, agonized confusion.

Then she heard Bob again—he'd made her promise! To bury herself—that was what it amounted to—in the cellar! And then another thought occurred to her: the mother of children should not be afraid of her own cellar! She should keep her promises, make every effort to survive! And she should not, under any circumstances, ask why.

The dark cellar reached for her; the door hung open. With a cold hand Tave felt inside the jamb and flicked a switch, flooding the stairway, at least, with light. Well, she would have to have light, she thought.

Now Ray Gray's voice continued, stumbling once again over that awful, somehow final, word. *"We are not at war,"* he said.

"That's what you think," muttered Tave, staring into the cellar.

Lucy

*T*HE RUG WASN'T RICH and Oriental, nearly perfect and full of figures, but Momma's long, pale hand dragged elegantly toward it on the floor. The sofa on which Momma lay was not of gold brocade, although Momma's family, the Marlowes, had had a gold brocade sofa in their Boston sitting room, a sister to the light green one of polished cherry they kept in the parlor (the one in the Marlowes' sitting room had been hollowed out comfortably, but the one in the parlor was so smooth and slippery, you felt as if you were climbing when you sat). No, in this dark little room off the kitchen the rug was only a braided one and the sofa a hand-me-down Momma had covered somewhat clumsily with flowered chintz.

Momma's hand dragged toward the floor, and Lucy, aged six in 1897, knew that if she were to touch that hand it would be cold and blue. Momma was sick. The child studied her mother, the little narrow form, a figure hardly womanly. The look of Momma was enough to remind Lucy of their one trip to the Marlowes' in Boston, they'd gone just last year.

Momma's exhausted little-girl shape had fit so well into that protected atmosphere: translucent china and polished andirons, embossed leatherbound books, and a man who came into the house especially to polish the brass candlesticks and the pendulum on the big clock. Momma had spent her mornings upstairs resting and her afternoons, when she began to feel better, receiving visitors. Lucy, named Octavia Lucille after her mother, had done everything just as Momma did it: somehow she knew, even at that age, that her mother had narrowly missed death. Now, she might be dying again.

Blue-white eyelids closed, Momma lay hardly breathing on the thick sofa. A child knew enough to be frightened at this. That other time, the Boston time, young Dr. Sapley had come and said, "You must get away from him, Octavia, go home for a rest, can't you?"

Momma had sighed, little lines like parentheses (Lucy had been reading for three years) around her mouth. "I don't want to be a burden," she said.

But young Dr. Sapley, never known for his tact, snorted, "Octavia, do you want to be dead? Get away from him, I tell you! For a little while, until you recover. For God's sake, get away from here!"

Her mother's eyes, open and full of tears, had found Lucy where she stood in the doorway, and she'd whispered, "John, please—"

"You don't want to ask him? Well, if you don't, I shall do it myself!"

"Him" was Luther Perry, Lucy's father, she knew that. He was Dr. Sapley's distant cousin. They'd grown up together in this tiny Maine community: Luther the tough poor boy, quick with his fists, good at tools, ambitious, and John Sapley the bright one, who made it to Boston to school, and who understood Octavia Perry—for whom Octavia's Hill was named—far better than Luther Perry did.

Abrupt, terse, strong, Luther Perry had single-handedly dug out the foundation and placed the stones for the house in which they lived. By himself he had fitted out the fireplaces and planned the kitchen and the bedrooms and all the windows, views, spaces. The house was full of wishes and dreams, Lucy thought. Sometimes she felt she could see some of them—happy people at the fireplace, cups of tea beside the french doors, girls in pretty dresses walking down the hall. Her father had built this house.

Then he'd gone to Boston to get himself a wife; he'd brought her home like a trophy and named the hill after her.

Momma talked fairy tales to Lucy: Luther Perry had driven up in a black carriage drawn by a pure white horse. Lucy was the result of that particular fairy tale, brought forth in agony and love. Since then Momma had had three miscarriages, whatever they were—Lucy was not supposed to know about them at all.

"Mother is indisposed," Momma would say, lying back on her pillows, her face a peculiar color, not white and not gray. "Tell Sybil, have her go for the doctor, Lucy—"

Dr. Sapley had come again yesterday, but now Momma lay so still. That one pale hand, blue around the fingernails—

"Momma?" Lucy cried suddenly. "Momma?"

Not for anything would she awaken her mother from a normal sleep, but Lucy would fight with all her little strength to waken her from death.

But she didn't run to the sofa and fling herself upon it, as she would have liked to do. She didn't dare. You had to take care of Momma, not jump on her, not jostle her. Just waken her.

"Momma?" Lucy cried again, very softly this time.

There came from the little body on the sofa a tiny sound, an inhaling. Then the eyes opened. They were a quiet color, as pale as the early morning mists that rose from the valley and reached toward Octavia's Hill.

"Lucy?" Her mother's lips trembled a little, but she spoke bravely. The voice was that of a wounded child.

Lucy crept closer. "Momma? Are you—" All right, she wanted to ask. But the question presupposed that there might be something wrong, and this was against Momma's rules.

In the rules that governed Momma's world, Lucy's mother was now in the process of living happily ever after with the knight who had carried her away behind, if not on, his white charger. And somehow Momma still managed, too, to believe that Luther Perry, that rough man with all his demands, was her white knight. Or if not to believe it, exactly, to convey the impression that one had to believe it.

"Why, Lucy," she said now, weakly, "whatever is the matter?" This in the barest of whispers.

Against Momma's rules Lucy was helpless, but she wanted to be, too. Momma's world was so much more beautiful than her own—a fairly humdrum place where she roamed around empty rooms or played with Sybil's doll. Sybil was the slow-witted girl who came to cook and clean in the mornings and to make the dinner at night. Good, solid Maine fare, too. Beans and hot biscuits with plenty of baking powder in them, although Momma chided Sybil gently. "These quick breads, these chemicals—they cannot be good for the digestion, Sybil." But Sybil merely tapped one flat foot and kept on cooking what she pleased.

Lucy was not the only one charmed and ensnared by her mother's vision. What company they had loved it as well: the women who came to call on Octavia Perry because she was ailing and delicate and "stuck up there on that godforsaken hill, not a soul around."

The women came because what Octavia Marlowe Perry provided for them in their own lonely lives was an element of romance. No ladies from the town ever wished to say to Octavia Perry's face what they might have whispered behind her back: "For God's sake, why don't she tell Luther Perry to sleep in the front sitting room?"

No. On the strength of the rules of Octavia's charming game, they could not, and didn't want to. Because her dream had to be believed in, had to exist somewhere, else why dream?

"Momma," Lucy said now, "tell me the ring story." It was the only way she knew to keep her mother alive.

Deathly ill, perhaps, but not sick, not at all, Octavia Marlowe Perry closed her weary eyes for one frightening moment, but when she opened them again, they were full of the light of humor and behind that the almost fanatical gleam of her romanticism. She could barely force her lips to move, but she was all right, yes.

"I was a young girl," she whispered.

"What color was your hair?" Lucy demanded, but softly.

The corners of Momma's lips lifted a little. "Chestnut brown," she whispered. "Very like yours, my dear Lucy."

"Where did you first see him?" "Him" again Lucy's father, that silently demanding man who never spoke at meals anymore and expected Lucy to do likewise.

The faraway look: where mists rose over the Charles and there were cabs and the theater and you could go to Stearns and order a half-dozen pairs of fur-lined white kid gloves. "I was at the parlor window," her mother said, "sitting there by the diamond-shaped little panes. I had on a blue dress with a blue satin ribbon here—" Momma pointed to her thin lovely neck.

"And you knew who was coming—"

"Oh, yes. For he had come, my dear, every day, for two weeks. Handsome, Lucy! So tall, full of energy! Dressed so well—your father knows how to dress—" Here her mother's voice began to fade again; these days it was most difficult to keep up this particular pretense. Recently Luther Perry had given up his town business and now ran the farm on Octavia's Hill. He'd done it, he'd told his wife bitterly, to keep the hill from falling apart behind his back. "That's what happens, Luther," Octavia Perry had replied, "when you want everything just your way."

At any rate, these days Luther Perry clumped around the house unshaven, very often unclean and smelling of the barn.

Lucy searched her mind for something to say, to keep the story going, but then Momma continued it for herself.

"Your father knows how to dress!" Octavia said it again, firmly. "He drove up and jumped out of the carriage and took the stairs two at a time and was inside before Colin could get to the door." A glimmer of a smile touched her lips. "Well, now, you may believe, I was not going to have any caller know that I had been looking for him all that time. Even though, of course, I had." Here a hint of dimples. "So he found me sitting on the green brocade sofa with a book in my hand—you remember that sofa, don't you, Lucy?"

Lucy nodded.

"Good," said Momma. "If you remember that your mother was

sitting on a green brocade sofa when she waited for your father to propose—" But here the tale broke off, and once again her mother seemed to forget how to breathe.

"Momma?" Lucy prompted quickly. "He came into the room and he put his hand in his pocket—"

"Yes, Lucy. You do remember, don't you?" She sighed. "My dear, he came into the room with his hand in his pocket, and there ensued the strangest proposal a girl ever had! For he stood in front of me and said not a word, but took his hand out of his pocket, and then, Lucy, do you know what I saw?"

Oh, yes, she knew, she couldn't hold herself back. "Rings!" she shouted. "He had rings!"

Momma looked shocked. Immediately Lucy controlled her voice. "Is that what he had?" she whispered. Momma's brow smoothed.

"Indeed, yes," she continued. "Three diamond rings. They were beautiful, Lucy! One was three diamonds wrought in gold, one a diamond set between two sapphires, and one was a diamond solitaire.

" 'Choose,' he said." Lucy liked this part.

"Oh, indeed," whispered her mother. "That is exactly what he said. 'Why, Mr. Perry!' I said, 'Whatever do you mean?' 'I want you to choose the one you like best, and when you have, I intend to propose to you and place it on your finger. The other two,' he said, 'I will save. And if you accept my proposal, you shall have one on the birth of each of our first two children.' "

This must have been a cruel irony for Octavia Perry, but not a quiver of that passed her lips, she was by now wrapped up in her story. "Well," she said, "I looked those rings over. And I chose the single diamond, which is on my finger to this day, Lucy."

Sure enough, there it was, on the quiet hand that held the book. A cruel stone, with two dagger-sharp points set at an angle from the hand. It was an ice blue diamond; but on her mother's thin hand—white skin, blue nails—it seemed to belong.

"And then when you were born," continued her mother, "true

to his word, he gave me this." And there, on the hand that had reached toward the floor, was the diamond set between two sapphires. "And someday," Octavia Perry went on, "we shall have the third ring, I'm sure."

"Where will you wear it?" Lucy asked. This, too, was part of the story, and once again Octavia Perry, far off in her gray mist, seemed not to tremble at what she said: "I shall have a golden chain made for it and I shall wear it around my neck!"

Lucy laughed and clapped her hands, and Momma reached out to her. They had a small, careful hug, and Lucy knew she was dismissed—that was one of the rules of this game. So she left the room and went to sit in the kitchen and watch Sybil for a while.

*

Lucy's mother lived until Lucy's ninth year. During that time she continued to play her make-believe game and Lucy continued to believe in it; it seemed to be the only way her mother could survive. Octavia Perry kept to her little room, and Sybil took care of the house, coming and going on her flat feet.

By this time, Lucy had begun to realize something more about their household. When her father came into the house, it shrank. The very doorframes tipped and tightened, and there seemed to be no place to go to get away from him. Her mother would weaken and, if she had been sitting against her cushions, would suddenly lie down at the shock of his entry. Sybil, whose crossed eyes were the mirror of a star-crossed intelligence, would begin to breathe in gasps and to talk in a chuffling whisper.

"Here, he's home, here is his supper. I got to feed him, ain't I? Octavia certainly ain't gonna be able to get off her bed and do it, now. Biscuits, some of them, and some ham to slice—"

Her eyes would twist and she would stumble from sink to stove, marring her endless succession of flowered cotton dresses with stove black and sink grease, because when her eyes turned in in that way, she couldn't see at all.

Luther Perry would enter the kitchen, Sybil would inhale quickly and throw him blind, sidelong glaces, dishes would begin to ring and clatter. Octavia Perry never allowed Sybil to touch the good Marlowe china, and Lucy could see why. Not a meal she and her father ate together that Sybil didn't serve on old china with new cracks and chips in it. Lucy's mother took her meals where she lay, in the little room off the kitchen.

Luther Perry didn't have to say a word. When he came into the house he took it over, it was his. And his, too, a kind of disruptive and ironic dissatisfaction with everything he had. He would look Sybil over from head to foot as she passed the heavy, chipped plates with their sloppy, mismanaged helpings. He would look past Sybil toward the little room where his wife lay blue-fingered and limp on the sofa, he would look at the none-too-tidy, ill-used rooms, and he didn't have to say a word. He just sat and looked; it was comment enough. And sometimes he looked at Lucy.

Lucy didn't have the least idea what was on his mind or why he was dissatisfied with everything he had. There was no way her child's mind could fathom it. All she saw was her silent father, pushing the women in the house around without so much as a word, hating them until the whole house seemed to inhale and expect punishment. When Luther Perry was in the house, the rules for Lucy became different, even more exacting than Momma's. If there was any game to it, it was the game of survival.

Never make a noise, never speak unless spoken to, never seem to be talking to Momma when Father came into the room. Because if you did any of these things, Father would stare at you.

"Lucy," he would say, dangerously, quietly, "what are you doing?"

If Lucy did not immediately become still, anything might happen. Once a dish flew across the room and crashed on the floor, causing Octavia to cry out and Sybil to come running, while Lucy simply sat in her place and shook. Once she was thrown from her mother's room and the door slammed. From behind it came the sounds of a struggle and then her mother, weeping. Once Lucy's clothes were torn open and she was spanked and spanked, crying helplessly, piteously, while Momma cried right along with her. So the cardinal rule was this: as much as possible, hide.

Lucy did. She tried to hide most of the time. But she also

needed comfort. So sometimes she would finish a meal opposite her father and then slip quietly away, creep for refuge into Momma's room. Momma, deep in her own reveries, hardly seemed to hear her. That didn't matter. Lucy would tiptoe in and sit in an armchair pulled up to a bookshelf. There she would read, near Momma, until her father's shape appeared in the doorway. When he entered the room she would slip out again quietly, behind his back.

"Well, it's time," he would say to his wife.

He would go to the sofa and lift her up, carry her down the hall and up the stairs to the big bedroom where they both slept. Lucy's mother wasn't allowed to take the stairs, so Luther Perry insisted on doing this for her. It seemed to please him to pick something up, carry it, put it down just so, and have it stay.

But one afternoon, Lucy hid in her chair by the shelves and did not read. Instead she watched her mother, who seemed more agitated than usual. Octavia Perry sat up, for once, on the sofa, her usually pale cheeks pink, one foot tapping on the floor, her hands wrapping a handkerchief round and round her fingers. Her eyes were on the door. Once again, she didn't seem to know Lucy was in the room. It was Lucy's father she waited for, but when suddenly he appeared in the doorway she was startled enough to gasp.

"Well, it's time," Luther Perry said. He stared at his wife. Lucy prepared to slip away the minute her father crossed the threshold. She watched him closely; when he spoke, nothing on his face moved except his lips and jaw.

But then Octavia Perry raised her chin. "No," she said.

"What?"

"No," said Octavia again, her hands digging into the sofa cushions and gripping them tightly. "I'm not going upstairs. Not today. I'll sleep here tonight." She quivered.

With the force of an explosion, Luther Perry slammed the door to the little room shut behind him. "Where I come from," he said, "wives do not tell their husbands what they will and will not do."

Octavia still trembled, but she replied with a challenge: "Your goods and chattel, sir!" She paused, then said very gently, "But Luther, what you think is yours will never stay with you—it will slide away." Her face was sad.

"Octavia!" Lucy's father's angered voice. "You've had a whole hill named after you! A whole house you didn't lift a finger to build!" He approached the sofa. "You're not so bad off—"

"No!" she cried, pushing herself away from him. "Go away!"

Lucy saw her father take hold of her mother's shoulders. He dragged them forward until Momma had to look at him. "Dream, and then spin right off the top of it," he said. "That's what I did, what you'll do, damnit!"

"But you didn't dream," Lucy heard her mother gasp. "You laid traps, Luther! That's the difference!"

He looked as if he would shake her, but then, abruptly, he lifted her to carry her out.

"No more pregnancies!" Lucy's mother cried. "Please, Luther. No more sicknesses!"

But it only made him laugh. "A wife's body is a place a man hides in. He climbs in and covers himself—"

"No!"

"Don't fight me! You have always made every lovemaking a rape!"

Now Momma began to sob, but Luther Perry muttered, "Who gives a good goddamn? What in the world does it matter if a man makes love to you, or to a post, or—" He swung his wife around. It was then they both spotted Lucy.

Immediately Momma remembered her dignity and put it on like a queenship. "Lucy, my dear," she managed, "your father is taking me upstairs now. You run along to Sybil."

Run away, far away, that politely edged voice meant to tell her.

But Lucy didn't move. Her father was looking at her; she didn't dare.

"Lucy . . ." Octavia, more weakly.

"It just doesn't matter," said Luther. "Way out here in the country, we're not quite so high class."

"Run along, child!" Now, at last, Lucy heard her mother. She turned to run.

"Yes," said her father as she did. "Hell, it's time."

Then he carried his wife up the stairs.

*

Not long after this, Lucy's mother suffered a series of hemorrhages, none of which in itself was fatal. Young Dr. Sapley came daily. Quite often Momma lay white and still on the bed and Lucy wanted to go and speak to her, touch her, but did not dare. At a touch, she felt, Momma would die.

It was during this time, too, that she watched at the window one day and saw Luther Perry towering over John Sapley. They stood nose to nose. For a moment Lucy wanted to run out and warn Dr. Sapley, tell him to ride away and not to come back, to save himself. But the doctor seemed to stand his ground. At last it was Luther Perry who turned away.

From that time on, her father never went near Momma, never even went so far as the doorway of her little room.

"Look what life has given me," he seemed to say. "I worked hard! I deserve whatever I can get."

For months Lucy's mother lay listlessly against her pillows, too delicate, it seemed, for any human touch, withdrawing far into some dream of childhood in which she was back at the Marlowes' and her father was bringing her presents in his briefcase; or where she lay among gold and green brocade pillows and read fairy tales while Mozart was played in the music room below. But whatever the dreams of Octavia Perry, so rarely did she come back to the dismal little room with its dull braided rug and knobby homemade quilt that she seemed hardly to see Lucy, who came into the room on tiptoe and stood the prescribed two feet away from her, yearning toward her.

But now the rules of her father's game shifted again, and in the dark of night Lucy had reason to be afraid.

Sybil went home in the evening, having cleared up the supper dishes and laid out the breakfast things and made Momma as comfortable as possible. So after dark there were only three people in the house: the sick woman downstairs, the little girl awake at midnight upstairs in her room, and the man, who had taken to roaming the halls.

Night after night Lucy, hardly daring to breathe, heard her father walking up and down the hall. With one squinted eye she watched her doorway, and sure enough, sooner or later every night he would appear at her door. His large shape would loom out at her from the doorframe. Lucy by now knew a good many rules, so she obeyed the most obvious. At nighttime, people slept. She pretended to be asleep because she was afraid, deeply, shakily frightened, of what might happen.

Lucy knew the rules, all right. She lay still. But night after night, something taught her to stay awake until she heard the footsteps cease, and then to open one eye a very little. And there he would be, standing in the dark doorway, sometimes no more than a dark head rising out of the darkness. What did he want? Why was he there?

On one level she did not know, she could no more understand him than understand anyone she knew in the adult world. And there were rules for dealing with adults. If you did thus-and-so, you would be safe, that was what it amounted to. Rules were dear to her and necessary.

On another level she did know that even this simple rule—you could escape punishment by going to sleep at night—even this rule was not going to work anymore. It unhinged Lucy. Because now there was no way to escape punishment, no way at all. One night the pacing stopped, and Lucy opened one eye to see her father not in the doorway but leaning over the bed. It startled her so that she forgot to breathe evenly for a moment, and he knew she was awake.

In the next moment he had opened her covers and crept into the bed beside her. "Lucy," he breathed, and the breath was hoarse and quelled. He pulled her little body close to his.

Lucy lay still. What else could she do? She who had never been embraced by her father before was now drawn into the curve of his body, and she felt his breath on her neck. This was a new game—she knew no rule for escape. His two hands, with one quick twist, could break her body in two—that was all she did know. How bad would it be? Her mother's daughter, she knew no "facts of life," but she knew what was proper.

She was wearing her usual nightgown. It had three tiny buttons at the top. In a moment his thick fingers were fumbling with the buttons. In the next moment they gave this up, realizing that a nightgown could be lifted, and then the fingers were searching at her thin chest.

What did Lucy know? Only that she was deep in a game that she did not understand and that she was not Lucy Perry, specifically, to her father, and never had been. She was an object— something to use or abuse, to play unexplained games with. Finally she knew, as his fingers fumbled with the strings of her drawers, that he was playing a game ladies did not play—that much she had been taught. His fingers crept down her stomach toward the thin-lipped tender place she would not admit to anyone that she herself occasionally touched, and she knew he should not be doing it, that he had no right.

But she did the only thing she could do: she waited. Lying board-stiff on the bed, waiting for the fingers to be done; stiff as a ruler, waiting and measuring. The thick fingers that grasped and tried to open her straight thighs could not do it easily.

And then the fingers seemed to sense somehow that while Lucy waited, she was taking the measure of this game, that she was helpless but full of utter outrage and disapproval. For a moment it seemed that the thick fingers on her thighs would break her apart, like a ruler made of balsa wood.

What happened? Lucy would never know. But at the moment when she was about to break, the house sighed. Or the hill, Octavia's Hill, moved. Or something seemed to speak so loudly, so silently. It might even have been Octavia Perry herself crying out for help in the sickroom below. It was some disappointed and disapproving noise, some sigh, some shifting in the silence, and Luther Perry's hands suddenly dropped from her thighs and he lay back board-stiff himself, ruler-stiff, listening. It was as if something occurred to him that he had long ago forgotten.

And then, suddenly, he was out of Lucy's bed and gone.

Lucy didn't move until she was sure he had left. Then, trembling, she got out of bed, stole to the door, and shut it. Silently she set a chair in front of the door and on the chair she put a tower of books. But it would never be strong enough, she knew, to keep him out. So, on top of this, she put a glass vase. If the chair moved, the vase would fall onto the polished wood floor with a crash. This was more than crafty on her part—it was an instant adaptation to new rules. After all, if a noise was all it took to keep her safe, very well then, they should have noise. And then, still in the arms of the breathless house, of the upright hill she would never understand and always fear, she lay awake and listened, drowsed and listened, for all of that night, and for the nights that followed.

Once she heard the doorknob turn, and once the door came open enough to find the chair, to realize the chair. But the vase never fell.

In the next weeks, Lucy grew thin and pale and more than ever tried to shrink into the corners of the house and keep to herself. Now she only went as far as the door of her mother's room. Nor could she look her mother in the eye: she felt she was to blame. It seemed to her that she must have done something or said something that had made her father play this bad game with her. And if so, her mother would guess it. One look and her mother would know how guilty Lucy Perry was, how unclean. In those golden castles in the air her Momma built—that Lucy helped her build—how could Momma cope with the knowledge that Lucy hid inside? Momma had to be protected. Night after night, therefore, Lucy lay awake, and only the hill knew what she dreaded, or why she grew thin and pale about the lips.

But one day Dr. Sapley saw her. Lucy had been avoiding him, too. Doctors, she felt, saw everything. One glance of the diagnostic eye and her awful secret would be known. So she had slipped around doorframes and avoided him until one day he happened to find her reading.

"Lucy?" he said gravely. "Is this you?"

What John Sapley saw was a tiny child behind an enormous book. She was even emaciated; there were shadows under her eyes and in the hollows of her cheeks. When he came toward her she stared and blinked; her forehead was hot to his touch. When he spoke she shrank away and wouldn't look at him.

"Lucy?" he questioned as he took her pulse, which was faint and rabbit-fast, and examined her hands, as blue around the nails as her mother's. "Aren't you feeling well, dear?"

The child could have borne it if it hadn't been for the kindness in his voice. She was a pitiful, ugly little thing, and now her long nose reddened and tears gathered in the gray Marlowe eyes and rolled down the thin little cheeks; and she held on to his hand and rocked and bawled, like the hurt, lost child she was, not like the grown-up she had been forced to become. She wept all the rage and outrage, all the dirtiness and helplessness she felt, and all her hope in the possibility of good, as well, for there was the something that had saved her—who knew what vagary?—and there was young Dr. Sapley.

Dr. Sapley was shocked. Why should the child look so, cry so? It was obvious that he now had not one patient but two. The child was suffering, from nervous exhaustion, possibly. He saw that she was on the point of collapse. "Lucy, you tell me now, what is it?"

Lucy would have given anything in the world to tell him then exactly what had happened, she wanted to tell him. But she didn't have the courage and she didn't have the words. She couldn't tell him. All she could do was rock and cry, the tears falling down her cheeks and sliding off her nose.

He asked again, "What is it now? What is bothering my little Lucy?" But he felt a bit helpless, she could see that through her tears. Maybe he wasn't good at little girls who cried. Or maybe Dr. Sapley, too, had to be protected.

"Lucy," he said gently, "are you sleeping at night?"

At this she only cried harder, hanging on to his hand.

It seemed to John Sapley that there was only one answer to the child's problem: to get her away from her mother. It was obvious to him that Octavia Perry's condition was exhausting this remarkably controlled but high-strung little girl; they had to be separated. But first he would have to waken Octavia out of her dreamland long enough to get something done about it. "Dry your eyes," he said to the child at last. "Come on. We're going to fix this all up."

He scooped her up and carried her—she had lost weight and seemed no heavier than thirty or forty pounds—into her mother's room.

"Octavia," he said to the still, white form—Momma—on the bed. "I want you to look at me now."

"No, Luther," whispered Octavia Perry. "Please. No." She said it so listlessly that it might have meant yes. It might have meant anything.

"Octavia, it's John," Dr. Sapley said. "And we have a problem. Wake up, now. Listen to me."

"John?" Now the white-gray eyes opened and the pale woman blinked. "Did Colin—" She began and then stopped. Lines of intense pain suddenly wreathed her mouth—she had recognized where she was. Quickly, however, she covered her dismay, supplying the requisite polite little tale. "My goodness, John," she said to Dr. Sapley, "do excuse me. Colin . . . I believe I was dreaming of Boston, again. How these dreams stay with us." She blinked and looked, but for some reason she hardly seemed to see the little girl in his arms. "What is it, John?"

"It is your daughter." If Dr. Sapley spoke a little grimly, he tried to soften it as much as possible. "Octavia, Lucy needs a rest."

"A rest? You mean in the afternoon?" The woman said this a trifle dazedly. "Why, when I was a girl, an afternoon rest was essential. I had a little feather pillow and a little lace coverlet, and Mother would read to me."

"No!" This to call her back from wherever it was she was going, far, far away again. It was a small explosion, but it was enough.

"I believe," Dr. Sapley began again, still more gently, "that the child needs a change of scenery. She is overwrought and, if I'm not mistaken, too thin, undernourished."

Octavia Perry moved her head slowly to the right and blinked feebly. "Why, Lucy," she said with some surprise, finally focusing on the child in Dr. Sapley's arms, clinging to his arms, "are you ill?" There was the old note of mother-concern in her voice.

Again it was a kindness that was more than Lucy could bear. She began to weep, this time silently, hiding her smudged face in her hands and rocking back and forth.

"Why, Lucy," said her mother. "What is it?" The hurt mystification in her voice was unbearable. And it was also unreal, as if the girl in the castle room had been found weeping. It was straight out of a book.

Dr. Sapley heard it, too. "Octavia, the child must go to Boston," he said firmly, "to your family. She must get away from here."

"She must?" For a moment Lucy's mother seemed to search for a framework to put this in. Then she sighed and lay back on her pillows, it was all she could do. And then she had it. Oh, yes. A change of scenery was good for delicate children. They went to the Alps and grew to be healthy and strong. "By all means," Octavia whispered. "To the country."

"No, Octavia!" said Dr. Sapley. "Tonight I will take her into town with me. She can stay with my mother. Then, with your permission, I shall wire your family in Boston. Lucy can go there for a rest, for a change."

"To—to Boston? Perhaps I could go with her."

"You aren't strong enough, Octavia," said John Sapley. This was true. But he was also convinced that Lucy's problem was her dying mother.

Lucy, who understood this, could not say what the real difficulty was. Forever afterward she felt she had denied her mother the one thing that would have made her most happy: to go back to Boston and to live there comfortably with her parents, like the protected child she was, until she died.

Somehow Lucy was provided for, dressed in her outdoor clothing, set beside John Sapley in his sleigh, with her little satchel close by and the blankets tucked up about her so that her eyes

could barely peek above them. Then it was a silent flight, down
Octavia's Hill and through the town to the other side, to the
Sapley house.

There Lucy was taken in like the orphan child she was, given
egg drinks made with milk and molasses, and put in a big cradle
by the parlor stove to keep warm while the Sapley family, which
kept appearing in all sizes and shapes, stared down over the
railing at her. The youngest children, stout and strong and imp-
ish, could not believe that this little girl was really eight years old.
Or that she could read out of the big books that Cousin John
showed them to silence their derision.

In the Sapley home Lucy wasn't afraid; there was too much
going on. After a while the mesmeric action of the rocking cradle
that swayed and squeaked every time she moved, her comfortable
stomach, warm limbs, the brisk coming and going all around her,
put her to sleep. She drowsed while the Sapleys had their supper
and awakened much later, as her habit had now become.

Around midnight, she opened one eye, anticipating the looming head and shoulders that had terrified her so. She woke and
saw, not her own room, but this place near the sitting room stove,
a little lamp burning in case she did awake and not know where
she was. And off the sitting room an open door to the small
bedroom where John Sapley's mother slept, the woman with the
water-swollen hands and the good egg drinks. It was all different.
For a long while Lucy simply lay there, thinking how it was all
blessedly different, thinking how warm she was, how safe. It was
like heaven, tucked in here.

After weeks without an appetite, she found she was hungry.
The sitting room was next to the big kitchen, where everyone ate,
and from there came the seductive smells of the evening meal.
Lucy stirred and sat up in the cradle.

It swung dizzily and creaked a bit, and there was an ear in the
house finely tuned to its sound, an ear that had listened to two
generations of Sapley children. While Lucy tried to decide how
she would get out, since the cradle was suspended about two feet
from the floor, Mrs. Sapley arose from her bed with a certain

automatic, fatalistic sigh she had developed years before. The cradle had squeaked. That meant that some child was hungry or had had a bad dream or needed the chamber pot. She often said that when she was on her way to heaven, the squeak of the cradle would bring her back from the dead.

She came into the sitting room and saw the wide-eyed, frightened look of that impossibly thin little girl. But if the big eyes worried her, she didn't let on. "Well," she said comfortably, "you 'wake, I see."

Lucy nodded.

"Hungry, I bet. Missed your supper?"

Lucy nodded again.

Mrs. Sapley had expected it. "Come on, then." She lifted Lucy out of the cradle and patted her hand and took her into the kitchen.

"Put some oatmeal on the back of the stove, just in case," she said. "Nice and smooth, now. You'll have some." She set Lucy at the table. "Don't know but what I'll have some myself."

In a few minutes there was a bowl of steaming oatmeal cooked smooth as baby cereal in front of Lucy, and brown sugar and milk. Then Mrs. Sapley helped herself to some. Lucy had two helpings, not so much because it tasted good, although it did, but because Mrs. Sapley, who was really quite an old woman, her face lined, her hair gray wool, her eyes snapping, seemed to enjoy the baby cereal so much.

"Good, ain't it?" she said. "Now you come here to me."

Lucy pushed her empty bowl away and obeyed. The next minute the strong old woman had carried the little girl close to the fire and sat with her, as she had sat with innumerable children and grandchildren, in the rocking chair. They sat and rocked; for the first time in Lucy's memory, she sat and was rocked in someone's arms. Soothed, comforted, she fell asleep again, not awakening until midmorning. She was again in the cradle, and all the Sapleys were passing by and peeping in and grinning. The sun shone on everything white outside and in, on all the white woodwork in the Sapley house. She wanted to live there forever.

[43]

Mrs. Sapley insisted that Lucy was not even well enough to set foot outside, "say nothin' of goin' clear up to Boston," despite what her grown-up son said. She was used to winning in these things, and John Sapley finally agreed that Lucy could stay with them for a little while. He didn't tell Octavia Perry, however; it didn't seem worth the trouble it might bring her. It wouldn't be long before Octavia Perry died, he knew, and to send the child to Boston and then to bring her all the way back for the funeral seemed frivolous to him.

Within three weeks, Octavia Perry did die peacefully in her sleep. Dr. Sapley was called and the body taken to the town undertaker. Lucy, in later years, had a dim memory of the funeral service, held in the Perrys' parlor, with some of the town present and especially the Marlowe grandparents and cousins, come from Boston to attend the funeral and to take Lucy home with them. When Lucy contrasted their genteel look with the louring, unhappy face of her father, there was no contest. She would go to Boston, as soon as possible.

Old Mrs. Sapley let her go with a big hug and a loving pat. She herself was getting on in years, and although she would have liked to keep Lucy with her, she thought it better not to start something with a child that she couldn't finish. Also, her son had told her how well off the Marlowes were, how richly Lucy would be clothed and fed and educated; it was far more than the Sapleys could ever do for her. Everything seemed for the best.

The next thing Lucy knew, she was on the train to Boston with that little, bent-over couple, Grandmother and Grandfather Marlowe, the Marlowe cousins, and Octavia Perry's imposing older sister, Aunt Etta.

It was time to learn a new set of rules.

Do not make friends with the gardener; do not bother Cook, who is temperamental and likely to save herself for big occasions. Do not fidget when Grandfather begins one of his long discourses on the history of the railroads. Do not touch anything in the house without asking permission. *Never* mention Momma. Be ready at a moment's notice to run and fetch: Grandmother's handkerchief, Grandmother's book, Grandmother's sewing box. Do not skip in sight of the house. Go to school and study hard, but do not invite friends over or go to their houses; if they weren't of precisely the right class, it might make Grandmother or Grandfather uncomfortable. In short, act like a grown-up.

Grandfather Marlowe was an old man, now retired and somewhat broken. In his lifetime he had managed to lose a good portion of the Marlowe wealth, and his health was failing. Grandmother looked after him with a truehearted, single-minded devotion, the upshot of which was that when he died, she soon after sickened and died herself. There wasn't much time or sympathy for the new child in the house.

At first Lucy thought Momma might still be alive. When she was downstairs, she thought all she had to do was run up to her mother's room and there she might be, smiling, her hand reaching a welcome to Lucy. Or if Lucy were upstairs, she would seem to see Momma just down around the corner, just by the window, or passing out of sight in the front hall.

But when Lucy ran to these places, they were empty.

The pain Lucy felt she could not cry away, and her good manners would not allow her to try. Her health improved, but she became, if anything, quieter than ever. After a few weeks, she was placed by Grandmother Marlowe in a country day school in town. There she was for the most part a solitary little figure, conscientious in her studies, polite to the other children, but never particularly happy or friendly. She could not make friends, she felt. Besides the stricture and responsibility of being a Marlowe, there was the pain she carried with her—it made her fear close contact. She didn't want to depend on anyone, not ever again.

While her grandparents were alive, however, there were big Sunday dinners and family friends came in for tea; Colin opened the door for them. The man still came twice a week to polish the brass. It gave Lucy a secret inner satisfaction to watch him make andirons and fenders shine like gold. Cook reigned in the monstrous and drafty green kitchen with its big black sink and its brand-new gas stove—eight cooking units and two large ovens. Once a week the laundrywoman came in and filled the kitchen full of steam and then went to the laundry rooms in the basement, where she washed the clothes and then ironed everything, right down to Grandfather's underwear, which she placed carefully and neatly into flatly organized piles in the drawers of his bureau.

Lucy didn't talk much to any of these people, but she watched them closely, and what they did gave her some small pleasure. She liked their routines, and it pleased her to open a bureau drawer and find every article in it placed carefully, even artistically, in its own neat place. Order strengthened and soothed her, so that as she grew she came to thrive on it and to expect it. She managed to put on a little weight; Grandmother bought her nice clothes. Occasionally Lucy would watch herself as she got dressed in the morning before the large mirror in her room. Chemise, petticoat, stockings, garters, dress, belt, buttons— every item immaculate, the finished product so neat, so precise-looking. She was pleased, she discovered, to grow up in an orderly way. As she matured, she developed rituals of dressing. She bothered with none of the usual adolescent self-consciousness; it would have been wasted on the tiny bust she hid beneath layers of white cambric.

At school Lucy came to be accepted, even respected, if not liked. She was withdrawn, yes, but from an excellent family. At graduation time she was voted "most courteous," which greatly pleased her grandparents. They were proud of her, they said. She was a true Marlowe.

Encountering her own reflection in the mirror day by day, Lucy tried to make this so. Her father's long nose—could she minimize it by holding her head a little to the side? Her father's thin lips—she pursed them and imitated what she could remember of her mother's sweet expression. She had her mother's eyes, but they were unfortunately obscured by glasses. Aunt Etta Marlowe frowned and said Lucy had spoiled her eyes by too much reading. "Far better than to have spoiled my outlook with too little," Lucy would have liked to snap back, but she did not. Aunt Etta was imposing in every sense of the word. She bossed her parents and obviously felt that Lucy was fair game, too. In fact, the whole household lived in fear of Aunt Etta's tongue. Lucy learned early that it was best to make a wide circle around her and go on your way. But sometimes she found it within her to think that which she did not say.

Soon after Lucy entered Miss Winsor's School, a girls' college preparatory school in the area, her grandparents died. Aunt Etta was left in charge of the household and the Marlowe inheritance, whatever there was of it. Aunt Etta claimed there was very little. She said she had to cut back on spending—it was just possible that she did have to. "My parents were unwarrantedly extravagant," she told everyone. "Father lost a good deal of money and frittered away more." The upshot of what Aunt Etta said, Lucy discovered, was that they had money, but they didn't have any money.

Money for church, but none for extra salad. Money for the laundress, but could Lucy, please, polish the brass? They would depend on the aging Colin to keep driveways and walks clean, with the result that in the winter, very often there was little more than a solitary foot-wide access to one door for the huge house that sported five separate entrances. Even that task was beyond Colin. In the middle of the first winter he left. Then Lucy did what shoveling was done.

Cook stayed for a little while, but there was no longer any company to cook for, and Etta interfered with her budget. The laundrywoman requested her yearly raise and was denied; she left. Soon Lucy was doing her own laundry, but ironing every last speck of it. Her clothing was always immaculate, she saw to it. It was a way of holding her life together.

Daily she expected Aunt Etta to tell her she must drop out of Winsor and attend the public high school. Weeks passed, however, and when this didn't happen, Lucy was happy. Her teachers were excellent, and she was a bright pupil. Studying, especially in the Marlowe household, came easy. And the school itself was a place where order—blessed, immutable—reigned. School rules were simple: you learned and you were rewarded. Astonished at Lucy's dedication, her teachers took an unusual interest in her. They saw to it that after three years at the prep school she was enrolled at Boston University. And she would have gone gladly.

But in the late summer of her nineteenth year, following her last year at Winsor, Lucy received a letter from Luther Perry. It was the only correspondence she had had from him since she left Octavia's Hill.

"Daughter," his note began. The look of that big, scrawled hand frightened her. She felt a quiver of horrified remembrance in the parts for which Aunt Etta had provided a second washcloth. (Two washcloths a week was the ration, and they were strictly segregated as to use.)

"Daughter, three years ago I received a letter from Etta Marlowe in which she demanded that I pay for your support and education. For the past three years I have done this, but now I find it is no longer possible."

Lucy, staring at the writing, blinked. Evidently Aunt Etta had made this arrangement with Lucy's father after her grandparents died. She, Lucy, had known nothing of it. Perfectly fair, when you thought about it, but why, then, did Aunt act as if Lucy were using up the Marlowe money, even taking the very food out of her mouth? Unless, of course, Aunt was trying to run the whole household on what Luther Perry sent. Could she do that?

"I have had to sell off a good many cows in the last few months," the letter continued, "and find, as my health is declining, that there are more demands upon my funds than I can attend to. Over the last three years I have sent what money I could, with never a word of thanks from you, but always through Etta Marlowe. She has continued to ask me for more. I do not know if you have received this money, but I sent it because Boston was the best place for you.

"Now, however, the doctor informs me that I must have a nurse. I have no money to hire one. Alden Green is here, but he is the hired man and cannot keep house for me. Therefore I must tell you to come home at your earliest possible convenience, as I am confined to my bed. Luther Perry."

Lucy, who had opened the letter at the lowboy in the parlor, dropped the envelope back into the shining silver dish on which Aunt Etta always placed the mail, much as Colin had done. Then she picked the letter up again.

She went to sit on the gold brocade sofa, which Aunt Etta had caused to be covered with dark green rep, to save it. Lucy no longer knew quite why, or for what. She sat on the dusty green and felt that her ordered world was falling away from her. When Aunt Etta came into the room with her big apron on and a hand full of dustcloths, Lucy didn't move, the letter still dangling from her fingers.

"Lucy? What is this?" Although of course Aunt Etta must have known who it was from—one look at the handwriting could have told her.

Aunt stood tall and thin in her apron and scanned Lucy's face. Lucy somehow knew that she had already read this letter and that she didn't care. Lucy would be going home—this was in her aunt's eyes—so it no longer mattered if the child knew where the money for everything had come.

"It's from Father." Lucy stood up, not that that helped much. She was tiny beside Etta Marlowe. Lucy's head was tilted to one side, a habitual placement now. With her dark hair and her long nose and her spectacles, she wasn't particularly pretty. She resembled a small cornered animal, or a bird preparing to fight. She stared up into Aunt Etta's gray Marlowe eyes. They matched her own, she suddenly felt, for pure hardness and despair. "He wants me to come home. He says he has no more money to pay for my living here or my education."

"Oh?" said Aunt Etta. "And when will you leave?"

This reply only showed Lucy how tough she would have to be.

"Why, Aunt." In spite of her small stature, Lucy suddenly seemed to look at Etta as in a mirror. "As soon as possible, I would imagine.

"And," she added as she made her way past the woman and

toward the dark stairs in the too-large foyer, "you may check my packing, to be sure I've taken nothing of yours when I go."

"Why, Lucy!" Aunt Etta was plainly shocked; it was as if a bird had turned suddenly and nipped at her.

*

Lucy had a mink muff; Grandmother had given her that. It was brown, with a fine sheen. On one side were two mothholes: bare, eaten-off places about the size of two quarters. Lucy held that part toward her so that no one would see. Grandfather, with all the insouciance of long custom, had once bought her expensive dark brown leather luggage in a great variety; it was the substantial luggage to which Marlowes had always been accustomed. Along with this she had a box of schoolbooks and a box of beautifully bound books that had been given to her as presents. She had packed all her things with careful precision, and she went over them again and again in her mind as she boarded the train and it moved away from all that she had known of civilization, toward Maine.

Trees! That was what she saw, miles of them. The towns were small, the stations dirty. For the most part Maine people didn't impress her. What a collection of downtrodden types! She saw lame legs, puffy fat sallow skin, chilblained fingers. The other passengers on the train stared at her, too. She clutched her muff. Too dressed up for them, she supposed. Too clean.

The people who stared seemed like the devil's henchmen to her; the train moved out implacably beyond her control, soon she would see the devil himself. She would be buried alive in these forested hills, she felt; there would be no escape. Truly, if there were anything beautiful in Maine—one of Lucy's day school acquaintances had had a summer home on the coast somewhere—Lucy didn't see it.

By the time she arrived at Bangor, she was tired, worn out, frightened. Exiled back to that imposing hill where she would once again be powerless. But this thought she concealed far beneath a highly civilized exterior. She stood at the station and saw a man waiting on a wagon of the kind that left milk and eggs in Boston, and it didn't occur to her that soon she herself would be riding on that vehicle.

Slowly the man on the cart turned, stared at her. Bewildered, half-fascinated, Lucy tried not to stare back. He was huge and frighteningly slack-jawed; instinctively she feared him. He wore a knitted cap and his dark hair stuck out around it. His face was ill-shaven and dark. Lucy drew herself up within her tailored coat and continued to search for Alden Green.

But the man on the cart—that awful man, she said to herself—lifted first one heavy boot and then the other, climbed off the wagon, and walked toward where she stood with the mink muff clutched tightly in one hand.

"You be Lucy Perry?" he asked.

Involuntarily Lucy shuddered, controlled it. So, she thought; he can speak. "Why—why yes," she said. In Maine, it was obvious, tradesmen knew no manners.

The man didn't even nod. "Luther sent me," he said.

His eyes were a peculiar shade of violet, "rheumy" was how Lucy described them to herself. His nose dripped, and he wiped it on one unraveling mitten.

Lucy's lips settled into a straight little line. "And who are you?" she asked coldly.

"Green" was all the reply.

The hired man? Well, there was only one way she knew to handle him. "Alden," she said—it must be that he was a little like Colin—"if you would be so kind as to see to my luggage—" It lay around her, boxes and bags that had not seemed like so very much in Boston, but that now, she felt, under the gaze of this "hired man," took on the lineations of a small mountain.

But if she expected Alden Green to bow and tug at his forelock—that expectation was certainly in her voice—she was surprised again. He gave one long, wet snuffle, picked up what he could, and took it to the dairy cart, where he climbed on and sat, waiting.

After one confused moment, Lucy picked up more luggage and carried it, placing it with difficulty onto the high body of the cart.

Then after a moment she went back for a second trip, a third. Colin she could have ordered to do this for her, but not Alden Green. Alden Green, she somehow understood, was not a man she could order to do anything.

"Don't disturb yourself, Mr. Green," she said in a voice that dripped icicles and hid well her fright and dismay. "Pray don't." But some of the good of that was lost as she pulled herself up awkwardly onto the cart to sit beside him.

She did not want to sit there. Alden Green cursed at the horse in a way that unnerved her. Also, she observed that he was unclean, his long, dark coat stained and torn. One finger stuck through his mitten. Lucy saw it, looked away quickly. That thick begrimed knuckle, that long, black-rimmed fingernail, made her feel ill.

Then they were off on the cold ride through Bangor, past Kenduskeag, through Dover-Foxcroft, and out to Monson. It was a silent ride during which Lucy clung as much as possible to the outside edge of the seat. Alden Green said nothing, but from time to time he moved his blank face to stare at her. Once, by mistake, she met his gaze. It was, she felt, a personal kind of sizing up from a man who quite obviously respected no one and nothing. As if he knew something about her that she didn't know herself. As if he would take advantage of that, if he could. She clutched the cart seat and looked away.

Finally they approached Octavia's Hill. It was a long cold ride, by now mid-October. As they began the long incline of the hill, Alden Green got out and led the tired horse, but Lucy, as befitted her station, stayed seated on the cart. From there she could stare down at the dark-haired man whose dark coat flapped behind him in the wind.

Past the fields she remembered, past a new ramshackle building up on posts, up the hill proper they went, until they were at last pulling into the driveway of Lucy's old home.

Lucy was by now not only frightened, tired, and numb with cold, she was depressed. Her back ached, as did her head. They pulled up at the front porch and what she saw was the clutter on it, its peeling paint.

"Luther's upstairs," Alden Green said, and spat. "I got to milk."

Lucy climbed off the cart and watched as he casually tumbled her luggage from the back of it and then led the horse away. This time she carried every last bag and parcel into the house herself, and it was all heavy. Finally she stood alone in the kitchen.

Dark. The pumphead in the sink could only be called primitive, the wood cookstove a monster. The room was in an utter chaos of unwashed dishes and slopped food. The smell! Dirt? Manure? Leftovers moldering in chunks on dishes. The Marlowe china— Lucy remembered it, suddenly—lay about on the kitchen table, chipped, broken, covered with grime. Sybil, it seemed, hadn't been there for some time. "Oh, good Lord," muttered Lucy. "Oh, my good Lord."

There was a groan from the room above her head, then a pounding on the ceiling. "Alden!" roared a heavy voice. "You home?"

Lucy at that moment began to understand the fairy tales her mother had spun long ago. For there were two levels of life: life in Boston and life here on the hill. And from the hill, even Aunt Etta could begin to look angelic.

She stared at her precious possessions, the last evidences of her Boston life. Then, from them, or from somewhere deep inside herself, she summoned up strength, a kind of wiry, stubborn strength, and picked up her skirts. It was 1910 and there weren't so many of them, but she managed to make it look like more. Head high, she went to the stairs. She didn't touch anything on her way up.

At the top, however, she paused to make last, desperate plans. If her father was sleeping upstairs, she herself would have the little room off the kitchen downstairs, Momma's old room. And she would close the door every night, she promised herself wordlessly, and she would somehow manage to lock it, too.

Slow steps toward the doorway; then she opened the door.

At first she could see nothing at all. The shades were drawn; there was only one kerosene lantern lit. Then her eyes grew used to the dim light and she saw on the bed a huddled form with the face that she remembered. It was her father, but much changed. This face was jowled, the skin slack and gray. The hair was now pure white and very thin, the cheeks hollowed, the nose a long, gray-yellow beak.

"Lucy?" His voice rumbled. "Is that you?" His eyes searched, found her. They were as sharp and ironic as ever. She stayed by the door.

"Yes, Father," she whispered.

"Come here."

She still held the muff. The fingers of both hands crept into it as she moved toward him. The man on the bed looked her up and down.

"You know what ails me?" he said at last. She shook her head.

"Tumors." The ghost of the old voice Lucy remembered, but it still said, "This is all life has ever handed me, what did I do to deserve it?" She wouldn't reply.

"Come closer!" he demanded. Lucy stood so close that her skirts brushed the bed. He reached out one hand, its fingers raking at the muff. "How do I look to you?" he asked.

Lucy blinked. "Why, quite . . . well, Father," she managed to say.

"Quite well? Hah!" He grabbed at the muff and hauled her close to him until they stared at each other, Perry nose to Perry nose. "What do you think this is, girl, a tea party?"

With a gasp, Lucy wrenched herself away.

But only a jerk of her frame and he'd let her go, she realized this with surprise. Why, she was stronger than her father, now! He would die, yes, but at least he wouldn't come stealing down to her bedroom.

"Father," she said, finding her voice again, "I am quite tired. The kitchen is an unspeakable mess. But if you will be patient, I shall try to clean it enough to fix us a meal."

It was a close-clipped, polite little speech.

"Oh, you shall?" Luther Perry looked startled. Civilization, catching up with him at last, Lucy thought, daring to walk away.

"Is Alden doing chores?" he called after her, almost begged, as she left the room.

She barely turned. "He has said so."

"All right, then." The man pulled his covers up about him. "Get to it!"

It was an order, but Lucy felt she had won—something. What had she won?

Octavia's Hill was a shambles. Every room filthy, every corner filled with clutter, mildewed clothing, broken furniture. The rugs were ragged and begrimed, the curtains sticky and limp. Once back in the kitchen, Lucy went directly to her mother's old room and opened the door.

The room was cold and musty, even dank. The wallpaper that Octavia Marlowe had chosen, light blue with tiny strips of peach-colored flowers on it, had long since started to peel away at the corners. The bed must have been made up by Sybil before she left; it had her mother's white damask spread upon it. Lucy approached, touched. No, the men had not come in here. The spread was tight and smooth, the room uncluttered. In the center of the bed Lucy saw three faint, rusted stains. She knew at once that these were blood, probably her mother's.

In the bookshelf beside the bed were the books that Lucy remembered: dropping from the long blue fingers, or lying across the thin, white-nightgowned breast. Now she stood in the center of the room and it seemed to her that her mother had just left, that she was a lost wraith, wandering somewhere alone; that her mother was a child weeping, eternally unhappy. It seemed to Lucy that she wanted to find her mother, gather her up in her arms, and hold her and soothe her and tell her not to be afraid. She wanted to apologize to Momma and beg for forgiveness— for what she wasn't sure, and maybe it didn't really matter. She wanted to say that she loved her, would take care of her forever. But of course there was nothing left.

Only the rusted stains on the bed where Lucy herself would now sleep. They frightened her past the tears her throat ached to shed. Suddenly she didn't know which one was the wraith wandering, searching for comfort, or where the comforting one had gone. She sagged onto the bed, hands to her throbbing throat.

But from this bedroom she could see into the filthy kitchen. How could she possibly manage that? And then, sighing wearily, she called once again on what stubborn strength she possessed and began to make trip after trip across the kitchen floor with her bags and parcels. In the next minutes she searched out an old cotton dress and wool sweater she had worn in Boston when she cleaned the brass or worked in the kitchen. The house was chilly. She shivered, but she changed.

And she managed.

*

Over the next few days, Lucy quickly learned more rules for survival. Alden Green did the barn chores and was expected to keep the woodbox full. This he did after his own fashion: a few sticks when he felt like it. Rather than ask her father or dare Alden's leering stare, Lucy became quite adept at going out to the barn herself and picking up chips of whatever she could manage from the woodpile. Once she let the fire go out, and that was disastrous. She had to ask Alden Green to start it again, but all he did was stare at her. After a moment he shook his head and left and did not return for two hours. By that time Lucy was shivering, thoroughly tired out and upset, her hands black from the stove soot of many attempts to start the fire herself.

When Alden did come in to start it, she watched his filthy hands on the dampers, how he emptied the ashes, placed the paper, chips, and small logs. She would never have to ask him to do this for her again, she promised herself. She didn't want him around her, for any reason. He took his time starting the fire; he was in control and he knew it. Lucy felt as if some unreasonable animal were threatening her while he was in the kitchen. She kept a hold on her dignity while he was around. If you lost that, she felt, you might easily fall prey to someone like Alden Green.

The house she took on single-handedly, working from room to room, rising early in the morning and going to bed late at night, outdoing, overdoing, herself in order to make it clean enough for her to live in. When four days had passed, she took up the matter of finances with her father, who informed her that their only income at the moment came from the dairy milk and the eggs that Alden sold for them.

"Father, do you pay Alden," she asked on that morning, "or does he keep the money?" She wanted to replenish the larder. They had eaten scrambled eggs three nights in a row, there was no flour, little sugar, and there were no vegetables or fruit of any kind in the house.

The violence of the old man's reaction shocked her. "Who the hell sent you to question me or Alden?" he shouted, half rising from the bed. "Who gave you the goddamn right?"

Shaken, Lucy waited, steeled herself, tried again. "I'm not questioning you, Father," she said carefully. "I merely thought—"

"My arrangements with Alden Green are private, do you hear?" Now his voice was under control. "And no one, not even you, is allowed to question them!"

Lucy, exhausted from days of cleaning the filth out of this man's house, almost lost her temper. "Do you think I care?" she wanted to cry. "Lord in heaven, Father, do what you want with that—ox! It's no difference to me! But for three days I have been scrubbing this house and now I am out of soap! There is no food! How can I learn to cook for you? Give me money and tell your ox to take me to town! And I will buy soap! And potatoes and what vegetables I can find! No wonder you're sick! You need oranges! I need tea! Money! That's what I want—for food!"

But all she said was: "Can't you ask him to buy some things for us to eat?"

There was a silence in which her father seemed helpless. But then he smiled a crafty smile. "Bring me the lamp on the mantel," he said.

"Get it yourself!" trembled on her lips, but she bit them and held on to her pride and did as he said. It was an old-fashioned kerosene lantern, similar to the one he kept burning by his bed. The chimney was black, the base oily; some kerosene still slopped inside. She took it to him and then stepped back.

Carefully the man lifted the blackened chimney and laid it

aside. And there, resting against a metal prong, were two rings. Lucy gasped. She remembered her mother's words: three small diamonds in wrought gold, that was one of the rings. The other was the diamond between two sapphires that her mother had worn since the day she, Lucy, was born. The third ring, the single diamond that had been her mother's wedding ring, was not there.

"Now, my girl," said Luther, and there was even a chuckle in his throat, "I'll give these to you. If we eat or not—hell, that's up to you. I don't give two shits one way or the other." And he held the rings out to her.

Mesmerized, she closed her fingers on them. She stared especially at the sapphire ring. "You took it off Momma's finger?" she wanted to ask him. But such a detail was beneath all she had left to cling to. So instead she spoke in a carefully clipped voice. "Go to sleep, Father," she said quietly. "And I shall remember that Mother is where she never has to see you or hear you again."

Then she turned all of her small form around and left the room.

"Bitch!" he wheezed after her.

The next day John Sapley came for his weekly visit. Dr. Sapley was approaching forty, and it was obvious from his ample girth that his wife was an excellent cook. His face was lined with the years of getting out in all weather, coming too late in cases of fatality, attending women in childbirth, farmers in pneumonia, children with scarlet fever, old people with consumption. Stitches, broken arms, stomach ailments—approaching forty he seemed closer to fifty. But he held Lucy's hands.

"Well," he said. "All grown up, I see."

"More or less, Doctor." Lucy tried to smile.

"And not eating and not sleeping again?" The hand on hers crept to her pulse. "Cleaning this place up by yourself?" He smiled his weatherbeaten, trustworthy smile. "Come now, I don't need two patients on this hill, Lucy." His eyes missed nothing. "Is there anything to eat in the house?"

Lucy shrugged, a little ladylike shrug. If she'd done more, she would have wept.

Dr. Sapley's eyebrows went up and he looked her in the eye. "Sell the goddamn rings, Lucy. Go ahead, do it."

Lucy's eyes widened.

"Oh, I know all about them," Dr. Sapley said. "He tells me, every time I come. You sell them. Your mother wore the one in her dream world, and as for the other—well! He didn't care for her at the end, she knew it. Luther has cared for just two things in his life: this hill, and what he thought he deserved. Mostly, he cared about what he thought he deserved—lost everything, and look at this hill now." Dr. Sapley nodded. "The rings meant nothing, Lucy. They mean nothing now. Just dreams, that's all. Sell them. They ought to go someplace where you'll get a good price."

To keep from collapsing, Lucy kept a tight hold on her veneer. "I shall consider it," she said vaguely.

But John Sapley had watched Octavia Perry die. He'd seen what happened in the house afterward. How much the girl knew he couldn't tell; he himself had no illusions. "You think about it, but don't for God's sake go into a decline over it. I believe I know a man who would help you sell them, if you need it. I think you do, Lucy. Remember, you'll live on, long after your father's dead."

Lucy gave the rings to Dr. Sapley that afternoon in return for an IOU and a little money to buy food with. She also gave him a list, and he gave it to Alden Green, who went to town and brought groceries back without comment. So at least they had food.

What the association was between her father and Alden Green, however, Lucy could not figure out. She discovered that the Green shack was built upon Octavia's Hill property, down there at the foot of the first incline. Green did chores, for what wages Lucy still wasn't sure. But he did seem to keep the small amount of money that Octavia's Hill made—at least she never saw any of it. In fact, it began to seem that Alden Green owned the farm, and that her father had given it to him.

Every morning Green came into the house and stood first on

one foot and then on the other, staring at her. As if I were a word in the dictionary he couldn't quite make out, Lucy sometimes thought. But then, of course, Alden Green probably didn't know what a dictionary was. What he did seem to know were bodies — hers, and how it was put together. Lucy kept her arms wrapped tightly about her chest when he came into the room, and she practiced her Boston manners on him.

"Well, Mr. Green, what a surprise," she would say. "Do come in." She would open the shed door to him; he always came through the barn, wearing boots stuck up with straw and cow dung. His hair hung in a shag about his dusty ears and greasy collar. "You've worn your dancing shoes again, I see," she would say, managing a small, distant smile.

Somehow Luther Perry always knew when Alden had come into the house. He would roar from his bedroom, "Lucy! Octavia Lucille! Show him upstairs. What ails you?"

Lucy would lead the way through the house with Alden Green lumbering behind her. In fact, Show Alden Up! developed into a game Lucy dreaded. He would follow her so closely that she could feel his breath on her neck as she arrived at her father's bedroom door, and he would shamble into the room on her heels, so that she sometimes found filth on the edge of her skirt from the brush of his boots. She would try to get out of his way, but Luther Perry found this infinitely amusing. "What, is he chasing you, Lucy?" Luther would rumble. "Now don't be scared, nobody ever gets away from a Green, do they, Alden? What's the matter, Lucy, isn't he pretty enough for you?"

Green would laugh with a wet snuffle and stare at her until Luther grew tired of watching it. Then he would roar, "Lucy! Get out of here, girl! Alden, chase her out for me!"

Alden would turn to do so; he ran the farm and Luther Perry ran him, perhaps that was it. Or they ran each other. Lucy couldn't understand it, but she knew that the game called Chase Lucy Out was also one both men enjoyed. Just out of reach of those ghastly fingers she would leave the room, while her father roared with laughter.

Alden Green would be upstairs for two hours, sometimes longer. During that time Lucy heard nothing; no conversation came from that room. It was probably quite difficult to have a running conversation with Alden Green in any case, she thought. But to lie there and look at him, for two hours at a time?

He came every day. It was a kind of private daily trial for Lucy. "Come in, Mr. Green."

He would clomp into the kitchen.

"I see you wore your dancing shoes . . ."

His boots were becoming the curse of her life, now that the house had begun to be clean.

But the worst was this: sometimes Lucy went into Momma's room and found Alden Green lurking outside the window, as if he'd been looking in and had moved away just as she entered. When she saw him, Lucy always closed the curtains with grim, sharp movements. Once their eyes met, and the insolent threat in his almost made her gasp.

In less than a month's time Alden Green came to represent for Lucy all that was unclean, unprincipled, restless. He frightened her. Whenever she caught him lurking just beyond a window, she felt she was in danger of losing—what? Something so vital that without it she would be only a small, naked thing, shivering in a corner.

One morning after Lucy had been on the hill about three weeks, she forgot to give her father the medicine Dr. Sapley had prescribed. She'd been distracted by housekeeping chores and the usual morning pantomime over Alden Green's boots, that ragged ritual that enabled her to keep some distance between them. So she picked up the bottle, mixed a teaspoon of medicine in water, took the glass upstairs to the old man's room.

The door was closed. Lucy knocked and opened it, all in one motion.

The curtains were shut as usual, and beside her father's bed his soot-blacked lantern glowed so dimly that at first she couldn't see. But her delicate nose was instantly sensitive to the smells in the room: of sickness and spilled medicine, kerosene, of Alden

Green's boots, and of something else Lucy could only identify as personal filth. It was very quiet. Almost at once she saw the cluttered mantel, a side chair with a rumpled blanket upon it. On the floor beside the bed was a heap of tattered clothing, yellow in the light and unfamiliar.

Then she realized that on the bed was the shape not of one man but of two, that the long, shining surface thrown over the hump of her father's lower body was the bare leg and flank of Alden Green. Both men were naked. In the dim light she saw her father's flesh-roped protruding stomach, his skinny arms and legs, and in the yellow light, the round upper half of Alden Green's hip and bare buttock.

Instantly Lucy moved out of the doorway and shut the door tightly behind her. Hardly knowing what she did, she fled down the stairs. Then she stood still in the kitchen.

It occurred to her that perhaps the two men didn't know she'd been there. They'd appeared to be asleep. She listened. No one bounded out of bed or made any move to come after her.

She looked around the kitchen and suddenly didn't know where to lay her eyes. Should she run? Where would she go? She'd never hitched up a horse in her life. What could she do? Should she confront them? Be ill? Faint? Run? Everywhere she looked, everything she touched, went bad. Where could she go?

She ran into her room, Momma's room, and closed the door behind her, still clutching the medicine. Dr. Sapley—no! She could never discuss—this—with him. "Momma!" she cried silently. She touched her mother's wallpaper, her books now side by side with Lucy's own. "Momma!" she cried again, without a sound.

And then, without knowing it, Lucy Perry took her mother's way out. Not in fairy tales, precisely. But suddenly Momma's genteel life became the only kind that Lucy would believe in or fight for. Momma's life in Boston—what were its problems now? —took on for Lucy an aura of respectability, ease, authority. And God knew that at this moment Lucy desperately needed authority.

She put down her father's medicine and sat on her bed, Momma's bed. She touched the three rusted spots there. Momma had been out of her head, Lucy knew that, and Lucy wasn't crazy, no. But Momma had believed there were ways of doing things amongst civilized persons, ways that did not involve pain, filth, degradation. One had to have ideals and pursue them. Always! Momma had believed that, hadn't she? Every detail of life was a symbol, in fact, of how life should be lived, with decency, forethought, restraint, self-respect. In Boston Momma had learned to live this way, and now Lucy resolved to do the same.

Her father was weak in spirit, as he had always been. He'd built this house—that had taken strength. It took another kind of strength to live beautifully in what one built. She would have rules, manners, as strict as those she had learned at the Marlowes'. If it killed her, she would!

After a while the old man roared for her, banging on the floor. She sat and let him roar. She was suddenly tired of being screamed for, she would not have it. None of her Boston acquaintances was addressed in this manner; why should she be? Then he quieted. Alden Green's boots came clumping down the stairs, through the kitchen, past her door. She heard the back door slam.

"Lucy! Octavia Lucille!" the old man roared again. "Come here! I want you, Lucy!"

She let him yell. She let him scream for her until his voice ran out. Then, when he was quite still, she moved.

She stood, picked up the medicine again, went back up the stairs. She opened the door and entered the dim bedroom, a small and quite ugly girl with a bird's beak of a nose and a steel rod for a spine.

"Father," she said in a quiet, carrying voice. "I do not enjoy being yelled at. From now on, if you scream for me, I shall not come."

There was a silence. The sick man looked this girl up and down, missing only the little light of fanaticism beginning to flicker in her eyes.

[63]

"What's that?" he sputtered. "Speak up, girl!"

"If you wish to call me," Lucy continued, "you may ring." She set the medicine down and reached into her apron pocket for a clean medicine spoon. "All you need to do is tap the glass lightly," she said, "and I will hear you and I will come. Otherwise, I shall not come."

"Otherwise you shall not—" he repeated, his lips trembling. His covers were pulled up to his chin. Lucy found herself wondering if he'd dressed himself or not. Immediately, however, she banished this thought. This was her father and of course he was dressed. In civilized life, real life, fathers always were.

"Today," she said with that same ramrod-stiff determination, "I will clean your room." And then she went to the window and opened the draperies.

By hanging on to the furniture, Luther Perry was still capable of getting himself in and out of bed and onto a commode if he had to, but he certainly couldn't move fast enough to stop her now. He gasped and shut his eyes, moaned.

Sunlight poured into the room, for the first time in years, perhaps. In one corner, Lucy saw, there was an old woodbox, not too large, and empty. The fireplace in this room had not been used for some time. There was a grate cut into the floor so that heat from the kitchen could rise to keep the bedroom warm. Quickly she moved the woodbox to the center of the room. One by one, she cleaned articles of every sort off all the available surfaces. Into the woodbox went rags, old newspapers, long-forgotten remnants of food moldering in corners, pieces of tools left where they fell, glasses and dishes of all descriptions. When the box was full, she carried it down the stairs and emptied it, then went back up and filled it again.

She had been treating her father's room as sanctum sanctorum, into which she should not intrude, was too frightened to intrude. But now that was over. Luther Perry didn't say a word until the room, except for its unpolished large furniture and unclean bed, was completely empty.

Lucy brought the empty woodbox back up the stairs for the last time and dumped it in the corner by the fireplace. She stared at the man on the bed. His eyes were closed, but she knew he wasn't asleep. "Tomorrow, Father," she said softly, "I shall scrub this room from top to bottom. And I shall take the draperies down and burn them. Then you won't need a light in here in the daytime."

"Bring me back my lantern!" It was a small, dreadful whisper. "And shut the curtains, damn you!"

Lucy continued to stare. "I'll bring the lantern back tonight. Perhaps it's about time you looked at yourself by daylight."

"Lucy!" he roared.

But she had already headed down the stairs.

"Lucille! Octavia Lucille!"

He roared until he was out of voice, but the thin bird of a girl kept moving, down the stairs and out to the kitchen, busying herself with plans for supper, using up the last of the flour because tomorrow, when Dr. Sapley came, she would get the money for more. And not until she heard the jingle of spoon handle on glass did she move to go back up the stairs. By this time her knees were buckling under her, and her eyes were filled with weary tears. But up the stairs she went.

"Yes, Father?"

"Look at me."

Lucy looked. The face was yellow and lined, the lips suddenly pitiful and small between the two cheeks. There was a certain delicate line about the mouth that Lucy suddenly disliked.

"Yes," she said.

"Shut the curtains," he begged, whispering. "No one should see me like this."

She almost pitied him. Then she saw his eyes. They held a kind of native shrewdness, the innocence of a wild animal full of savvy and trapped.

"No," she said. It was almost involuntary.

Then the thin lips opened again. "Lucy, did you come up here earlier?"

This was the question Lucy had been answering all day, her

body strung taut, her senses sick. But now she pretended to mis-understand it. "Earlier? Why, Father, I cleaned out your room—"

"Before that!" He waited.

For Lucy it was like the silence that comes between the first and second blows of a whip. She had an instant's vision of genteel poverty at the Marlowes', all pretense. She saw the church they attended, the ornate gold of the communion table, the cup en-crusted with amethysts and rubies. Then she opened her Mar-lowe mouth and said firmly, "No, Father."

He knew she was lying—she felt that. The lie bubbled up between them. It was a necessary Marlowe lie, a Boston lie, even a high church lie, for without it, how could you believe in Boston, Marlowes, or, indeed, in civilization? But it was a lie; they both knew it. For different reasons, they now let it float unburst be-tween them, a fragile camouflage.

At last Luther Perry turned and stared at the ceiling. "Oh," he said. "Because I thought I heard a knock while I was with Alden Green. I thought I heard the door."

"No, Father. I was in my room."

"You had my medicine in your room?" It was because he both needed her lie and hated it that he catechized in this way, she knew. It was almost like a challenge: come on, you filthy blue-stocking, the real truth is cleaner than this pretense, let me see your lying tongue.

"I moved the medicine," said Lucy clearly, "and then went to my room, knowing that you and Mr.—Mr. Green would not want to be disturbed."

"Mr. Green takes care of the farm in return for the land at the foot of the hill. I have deeded it to him."

He said it as if at the highest level, the long, bare flank of Alden Green and the parts and connections protected by it did not exist. It was her own pretense, shoveled back at her. Lucy felt sick. But she kept her spine straight. Very well, she thought, so be it.

"Take your medicine," she said, careful to hand it to him without touching him in any way. He lifted his head and shoul-ders and put the glass to thin lips. Then she took it, not touching the places his fingers had touched. He saw this. "Mr. Green will be coming tomorrow as usual," he said.

"Yes, Father," she replied formally, and went to the door.

"Lucy." She turned. He was still staring at the wide expanse of gray-nothing ceiling. "I guess you don't want to kill me, Lucy," he said. It was more like a question.

"No, Father." But when she replied, her back was straight as a ruler, and the implication was: you can do that for yourself.

Then down the stairs, white hate flaming, sickness between her ribs. She fled and vomited off and on all that night, at last bringing up something sticky and greenish and thin as egg white. But the next morning, pale and proper, she took her father's breakfast up and laid it before him without comment.

At ten o'clock she let Alden Green in. He stood before her, and she felt faint and placed her father's medicine on the counter. "I am not well, Mr. Green," she said clearly. "Will you take Father's medicine up when you go?"

He nodded and took hold of the medicine glass, and Lucy saw the black fingernails and the grimed knuckles of that dirty fist closing, as it might have been, around the part of a person, around her ankle, her neck. She covered her mouth and ran to her room and blocked the door with a chair, not emerging until Alden Green's boots had clumped down the stairs and back out the door.

That afternoon John Sapley visited. Lucy told him nothing, but he saw how ill she looked and arranged it with Alden Green that a grocery list be taken and filled at the general store in Monson immediately. Dr. Sapley wanted Lucy to go to bed and rest, but she refused. "Let Alden Green go and get the things and leave them outside the kitchen door," she told the doctor. "I'll be all right. Let him leave the groceries outside the door from now on." And that was how she avoided having any more to do with him than she needed to.

She couldn't have told John Sapley—how could she? In a way it was like being eight years old all over again—helpless, preyed upon. Once again she kept quiet. She had made her decision: life worked best on a polite level; on this level she would live. She would never admit to the kind of curiosity that begged to examine just what it was the two men were doing up there, and why.

*

By the end of the third week after Lucy had found Alden and her father together, she had managed to delude herself quite completely. The house was now as clean as soap and wax could make it, and what she hadn't discovered about housekeeping, she was learning. If she had to run this house, she was determined to do it the way Aunt Etta ran hers: the laundry on Monday, the downstairs on Tuesday, and the upstairs (including her father's room, now curtainless and immaculate) on Wednesday, the mending on Thursday, and the baking on Friday. All above reproach. If there was a wrinkle in a kitchen towel, she would lift her hand to take it out: this was how things were done in civilization. Her tiny frame undertook it all; she would change the world.

Soon she managed to accept Alden Green on a new, polite level, too. She would open the shed door and there he would be, a tall, dirty man in a flapping, black coat, his hair in sweaty points about his face, his eyes passing over her like dark hands.

"Mr. Green," she would say, as if from a great distance. "Do come in."

But she no longer led him up the stairs. She nodded and up he went, taking the medicine with him.

Two weeks more, and Luther Perry had taken a turn for the worse. It wasn't anything Lucy did by the work of her hands; if anything, he was receiving better care than he had had since he became ill. His room was spotless, his clothes were regularly laundered, his meals balanced and served on time. Perhaps it was Lucy's pretense that made him sicker. If so, it was her only weapon or defense, and she used it.

Eight weeks more, and her father was in great pain from his tumor. He took by John Sapley's order laudanum mixed with water several times a day. The visits from Alden Green became shorter until at last he only clumped up the stairs to stand in the bedroom doorway and holler "Yup," "Nope," to her father's half-gasped, half-yelped questions.

In three months' time, Green was coming only as far as the back door.

"Father says, sell the heifers and bring the money. Father says, buy more hay. Take this to town and fill it for me and leave it at the door." He did what Lucy told him to do, but she was never sure he would.

John Sapley came once a week as usual. He had managed to sell her rings for a sum that would last her two or three years, maybe more, if she were careful.

Soon, however, there came a time without leisure of any kind, when Lucy ran on instinct in the whirl of her father's helplessness and pain. She fed him, washed him, cleaned up after him. Despite her constant scrubbing, the smell of his sickness dominated the room, the house. He communicated in gasps of pain. "Octavia!" he would cry, for his wife.

Lucy couldn't ease him. For days he spoke in words that were mostly gibberish, alternately begging for medicine and swallowing medicine, clawing at the bedcovers, out of his head. The last week of his life, Lucy slept outside his door on a cot. He had lapsed into a coma, and she spent hours listening to him breathe.

During the day she did the washing; she couldn't keep him in sheets. His back was covered with bedsores he had hidden from her until he could no longer take care of himself at all. She treated the sores at John Sapley's direction, but in all the time of caring for her father, she never touched him with her bare hands. It was as if she felt they would convey a blessing she couldn't give. If she touched the man by mistake, the sick feeling came back and she vomited in secret. No, she kept a washcloth between them when she could, or a piece of old sheet.

For two days before her father died, Alden Green didn't come to the house at all.

Late one night, Lucy fell asleep and woke the next morning to the smell of soiled sheets, and found that her father was dead. His flesh was already quite cool, gray-blue, and he lay stiffening in the mess he had made. Without touching him, she cleaned him up for the last time, placing one of her laundered sheets over him. Then she put on her coat and walked down Octavia's Hill to the Green place.

It was cold, early spring, but there were two children playing barefoot in the yard at the bottom of the hill, one a little girl with brown hair and a faded cotton dress, the other a toddler in a ragged shirt and diaper.

Perplexed and shaken, Lucy stood in the Greens' yard for a moment. An immaculate corpse and a filthy child, she thought; now where was the sense in that? She stared back up the hill, but its abrupt incline seemed to move in front of her eyes. March was a difficult, muddy time. The road seemed flayed; it bled brown down the sides. The hill itself was yellow and brown and ragged with last year's hay. Ravaged, torn. If she had gone very close she would have seen, tucked inside the soggy, wild network of old grass, the new bright green of shoots not an inch high. But what she saw was dirt and mud, and she was afraid.

She turned from the hill, and there was the toddler. His dirty little feet, she saw, were blue with cold.

But then, Boston straight, Lucy took his hand. Why, this was a disgrace. She would have a talk with the child's mother! She led him through the yard covered with trash and worse and up onto Alden Green's splintered, stained front porch. She knocked on the door.

She could, of course, have hitched up Becky, the Perrys' horse, and gone for Dr. Sapley herself. But Becky had a mean streak, would kick as soon as she would look, and Lucy was terrified of her. So there she stood, clasping that filthy child's fist in her gloved one. The porch was strewn with mildew-damp bedding. She knocked again—there was no doorknob on the door. Behind her, the little girl in the cotton dress burrowed under some quilts.

No rules here (but there had to be rules, else Lucy wouldn't survive). Here, she saw, there was nothing: no guidelines for washing, dressing, sanitation. No rules between people; flesh without mind was putty, and one piece as good as another to work out designs of flesh. Abruptly, she knocked again on the door.

A woman answered. She stood against the jamb dressed in something ragged and pink.

Lucy's tongue was between her teeth. What she thought was, Do I address this person as Mrs. Green? The compliment will be dubious.

But this woman didn't care what she was called, obviously. She stood and stared. She at least belonged in that doorway. And she might have as much mind or spirit as a can of tallow on a shelf, but there she stood.

"Yuh?" she said.

"Your—your baby was out," stammered Octavia Lucy Perry. "I—I know how hard it is to w-watch children, but he's cold and w-wet—"

She held the baby's fist toward his mother.

The woman stared at it. "What?"

"I brought you your baby," said Lucy, again.

Just then, however, Alden Green dug his arm into his wife's side and shoved her out of the way; she moved like a cow against a prod. Lucy caught a glimpse of the cluttered interior of the house and then Green stood before her in a pair of pants he had not yet buttoned.

Lucy dropped the baby's fist and stood with her hands clenched together in front of her. "He's dead," she said. She could barely speak past the scorching sickness she felt.

"Dead?"

"Yes, he is. Sometime—sometime in the night."

Alden Green's face didn't move. "You want me to go?"

Lucy nodded. "Get Dr. Sapley. And whoever the undertaker is, we'll need—"

"Have to take your horse," the man said. "You bring it?"

"No," said Lucy. "As you can see, I—"

"Got to get my shoes." His feet were bare, the nails long and yellow-green.

[71]

"Well, I'll start back now." Lucy turned and picked her way out of the driveway and back up the hill.

She was almost at the doorstep before Alden Green caught up with her. She turned suddenly, out of breath, and found him walking not two paces behind her, staring at her laconically. His eyes once more passed along her body and met hers with that look of careful calculation, as if he had some secret he were waiting to share with her. But Lucy jumped and ran into the house and slammed the door behind her. She thought for a moment she had seen, not only Alden Green, but an animal, untrained and unreasonable, measuring and wild. Some instinct made her slam the door for herself, and also for her father, lying dead upstairs.

Of course, Green came and banged on it.

"Go away!" Lucy cried out at him through the latch. "Go to the barn!"

But the beast would not. "Can't," came the reply. "Ain't got my pay."

"Pay!" Shocked, Lucy took a step backward. The door opened and he was in, staring at her.

"Luther said I was to get my pay."

"What pay?" Lucy cried. "What—what about the income from this farm?"

Green snorted. "Couldn't keep a fuckin' chicken alive."

"You are to go get the doctor," Lucy cried. "Go now!"

But he walked toward her, past her, up the stairs.

Lucy ran after him. "Don't you touch him! Don't lay a finger on him!" she cried crazily.

He went into her father's bedroom and knelt by the bed, reaching under the corpse. In among the ropes of the old-fashioned mattress support the dirty fingers clawed. In a moment Green brought out to show Lucy the third ring, her mother's wedding ring, the cold blue diamond set on a slant. It flashed in his hand.

"He give me the farm," Green said, "but I said I didn't want no farm. So he give me this. Said, 'You take care of this hill, Alden, and the day I die you take this ring.' "

"Momma's ring," Lucy whispered.

"Mine now," said Alden Green. He stayed on his knees, watching her, to see if she would fight him for it. It was clear that he thought he could win a fight.

"Take the ring!" she whispered. "It's your—pay! Go for John Sapley, and when you have told him about Father, go away! And don't ever come back here again."

Green rose and stuck the ring in his pocket. It seemed to Lucy that the hill was moving or that the floor of the house suddenly slanted under her feet. Still, she clung to an equilibrium of sorts. After a moment Green moved past her, too near. Then he was by. She followed him down the stairs and slammed the door after him.

"Goin' now," he said to her, as if the two inches of proper Christian wood weren't there at all and he knew she would hear him. If he hadn't been so like an animal to her, she would have guessed he was snickering. Then he was gone.

Lucy sat in the kitchen and didn't move until John Sapley and Jack Holt arrived. She opened the door for them. Outside, the hill rocked, moved toward her, tried to speak; she fainted.

Luther Perry was buried without his daughter. Lucy was ill, out of her head with exhaustion, John Sapley said. He found one of his young cousins, Jane Sapley, to move into the farmhouse to take care of her. Jane was no more than fourteen, but Lucy herself was only approaching twenty. Another Sapley cousin came to tend the few neglected animals left on Octavia's Hill.

*

Like all the Sapleys, Jane was capable. A small, quiet girl, brown-haired and dark-eyed, she had the curious, mischievous twitch of the upper lip and the grin that all true Sapleys possessed and that Lucy half-remembered, in her delirium, from her days in the crib at the Sapley house, now nearly twelve years ago. All those faces with their merry eyes and mischievous smiles, coming to grin down at the little girl in the cradle. In fact, there were times when Lucy awoke and thought she was back at the Sapley house, for there was Jane, merry-eyed and smiling, leaning over her bed. When Lucy saw her, she felt comforted immediately. For days she woke just long enough to see that face, then slept again.

Gradually she began to recover, unhurriedly. She saw how sensibly Jane managed the house. John Sapley said that Lucy had not been meant to work as she had up until her father's death, and Lucy came to agree with him. Under Jane's hand, the house seemed to have lost some inner, secret dirt that for the life of her Lucy had been unable to scrub away. Perhaps it was just that Luther Perry was no longer there. But the house was shining, and there were groceries in the cupboard. Alden Green had lit off somewhere, Jane told Lucy, but one of the Sapley boys would come to get their grocery lists and bring their wood and do the barn chores. Lucy was more than happy to hear it.

Jane stayed. She was bright and good company and just enough younger so that she deferred to Lucy in most things. Octavia's Hill was quiet. Lucy heard no more from the Greens; the whole family had disappeared. She found it necessary to sell off the cows; the farm was simply beyond her to run and did not, she discovered, pay for itself. A few months later, when money became tighter, she and Jane were asked to take over the little one-room schoolhouse at the foot of Octavia's Hill, about a mile from the Green shack.

"You won't come to want." That was how Jane expressed it one day while serving Lucy's breakfast, as she always insisted on doing—wasn't she working out her room and board on Octavia's Hill? "They need a teacher, the young ones around here," she said, "and it's a good job."

Lucy regarded across the table this little person who, at the age of fourteen, seemed ready to gather under her wing all the children in the area as well as Lucy herself. "A teacher," Lucy said. "It's what I thought I would be, when I finished the university . . ."

"All them books," Jane said, nodding at the shelf in the dining room. A room without books was a room without a soul, Lucy believed this.

"All those books," said Lucy tentatively.

Jane grinned at her. "All of those books," she said.

In a way, the teaching job had come like an answer to a prayer, and Lucy accepted at once, for both of them.

Lucy taught reading, spelling, mathematics, geography. Jane, whose own formal education was limited, taught handwriting, singing, and artwork. She took the children outside at recess and supervised their play. With Jane they went after the sweet-scented mayflower, the trailing arbutus that grew in a dense mat in many sun-dappled, wooded areas on Octavia's Hill. The flower bloomed for only a few days in May, but Jane seemed always to know those days. Then the classroom would be fragrant with a woody, apple blossom smell and colorful with the children's drawings. Each drawing would bear a careful inscription composed by Lucy: "The Trailing Arbutus, *Epigaea repens.*" With Jane the children brought back colored leaves in the fall, tied on their skates in winter, and untied them to the tune of Lucy's bell.

At the end of three years, Alden Green brought his family back to the shack and left them there, but Alden himself didn't stay in town. His boy, Cone—the toddler Lucy remembered—began to attend Lucy's school, and somehow Lucy, with Jane's gentle mediation, found it within herself to try to teach the boy.

Cone was not shoebroken when he came to school for the first time, and he had very few clothes. There was no agency in town to help the poor in those years, and he and his mother and sister were dirt poor. But Lucy wouldn't have a child without proper shoes and clothing in her classroom, so in the back of the school Jane set up some charity boxes. Soon the more well-to-do families were dropping into them what they could spare, and it was these boxes that supplied Cone Green at the age of six with his first pair of shoes. Then Lucy and Jane spent one whole winter in the little ten-by-twelve schoolroom teaching him not to take them off.

He learned to wear shoes, but not to read or write. He just couldn't, Lucy and Jane finally decided. By the third grade, he was much older and at least a head and a half taller than the other children in his class and far behind them scholastically. After he'd been in the fourth grade for several years, he dropped out of school entirely. By then he was sixteen years old.

All this time passed quite gently for Lucy and Jane. Despite Cone's failure, there were some successes in the classroom. Two of Lucy's pupils eventually made their way to the district high school and then to the state university. In a town with one college graduate—John Sapley—this was quite remarkable. It was due, people said, to good teamwork. Miss Lucy was the brainy one and she taught the literate, but you had to have fun in school, too, and it was Miss Jane who supplied that.

The town approved. In fact, as the years passed, Miss Lucy and Miss Jane came to be known as their old maid schoolteachers, although neither of the women was so very old. They "ran a good school," townspeople said. Parents from outlying districts often pooled their resources to get transportation for their children to attend at Octavia's Hill. In 1920, two two-holers were built onto the schoolhouse, one for boys and one for girls—just as drafty, but at least closer. In 1922, a wall of blackboard was provided, and a new set of windows. What books there were in the area came to be concentrated in the schoolroom as well; Lucy kept them on a table set over the hand-me-down boxes in the back of the room.

The money from the teaching kept Lucy's and Jane's household going, and Lucy constructed an immutable routine for herself, which Jane laughed over and softened gently when she could. Lucy instructed Jane in the proper ways of ironing, polishing, bedmaking, acquainted her with her preference for tea towels and the evening perusal of the writings of Mr. Emerson. Jane seemed always at pains to indulge Lucy's likes and dislikes. In this she was like a young mother with a bright, high-strung child. It was perhaps one of the few times in her life when Lucy felt safe.

*

At age thirty-three, Lucy's form was a familiar one in the schoolroom. She was small-boned, thin, and stood very straight. Her face was severe: the complexion clear, the nose large, the mouth

[76]

a thin, straight line. Her eyes were a sharp, cool gray; if there was any lurking shadow in them it was obscured by her spectacles. Her hair was brown beginning to streak with gray, and Lucy was one of the first women in town to have it cut short; with Lucy, you could not have called it "bobbed," everyone agreed. She wore it straight to her ears and pulled back off her forehead with a pin, simple and shiny clean. In fact, there was an extreme cleanliness and delicacy about her person: the white lace at collar and cuffs, the carefully pressed clothing, the spotless gloves, the polished shoes. She was elegantly immaculate and unusually dignified, altogether a person one might respect, if not love, and about whom one might never suspect hidden weakness, loneliness, or fright.

Jane alone knew the real Lucy, and she tried as best she could to answer Lucy's constant, silent cry for help. It was an instinct with Jane to nurture, to answer the calls of children. She did it without thinking, treading with an easy smile the thin line between mother and handmaiden in Lucy's household.

In 1924 Jane was twenty-seven and had blossomed. Her hair grew long and dark, and she wore it braided round her head in a shining halo. Her eyes were dark and clear and merry, her complexion browner than Lucy's, but full of bright-cheeked color. Her figure was fuller than Lucy's, temptingly full, but for some reason she kept the young men in town at arm's length. The mischievous Sapley smile could become an appealing pout or magically radiant. None of the pupils in the school could resist her.

After a time, she and Lucy opened up Luther Perry's room, scrubbed it once again from top to bottom, threw out the old bed and brought down one that had been in the attic, rearranged the furniture, sewed new curtains for the windows. To Lucy, who had begun this project somewhat dubiously, it seemed that Luther Perry was now gone, forever, from the house.

At home, the two women shared the work as they did at school, the heavier things falling to strong, plump little Jane, who eventually took over the wood carrying, the snow shoveling, the cooking, the scrubbing. Lucy, remembering her delicate frame, did the laundry and the lighter chores, the bill paying, dusting, and shopping. They sold mean old Becky and bought a small, competent pony. With Jane's help, Lucy eventually overcame her fear of four-footed beasts enough to learn how to hitch the pony to the buggy or the sleigh. Then Lucy and Jane would drive into Monson, Lucy to shop, Jane to visit her relatives.

So they settled into a routine of days and nights, shopping trips and teaching, seasons that drove snow into their faces as they plowed through drifts down the hill to the schoolhouse or that welcomed them with unexpected warmth and buds bursting into fine-pointed leaves of red-veined green overnight. In the little schoolroom Jane was quick-witted and practical; she often avoided open confrontation and punishment of children simply by inspiring them to work and then noticing their best. In a time when school whippings were common, this, too, was remarkable. In those years, a country teacher was more often chosen for the stoutness of her whipping arm and the distance she could throw a farm boy than for any other qualification.

Small, slim, and elegant, Lucy stood in front of the classroom and gave the children a sound basic education and some background in the classics. Plump and loving, Jane Sapley hovered in the back and smiled and watched. The children learned willingly, as they were able.

The rhythm of the two women in the classroom was a thing of beauty, and many late afternoon cups of tea were consumed, feet up on the stove lip, laughing over this one or that or plotting how to reach so-and-so. These were their teachers' conferences.

Lucy might say, "Jane, that little Grover boy has a mind for figures, but no geography." Jane would nod.

"Well, that's right, too," she would say. "He's got his chin on his hand, and there he sits during the geography lesson, having a nap, like. It's his imagination we've not caught, and he's off somewheres—"

"The minute I open the map—"

"That minute."

A silence, while they sipped their tea. Then Jane might stand up and peep into the stove, see if it was down far enough to bank and leave. But they liked sitting by this stove, for the morning-banked fires up on the hill would be low by now, the house dead cold. When they got home, there would be no warm place to talk; it would be time to scurry around, warming things up, doing chores, setting out supper. The schoolroom always seemed that much cosier at the end of a day.

In these moments, a few wisps escaping from Jane's neat, shining hair—Lucy never saw it down but once, and then it was long enough to sit on—a little flush on her face from the fire, and the brown eyes crackling with enjoyment, Jane Sapley was beautiful. The suggestions that she made were useful; they always seemed spontaneous, and she offered them as if she'd never forgotten who owned Octavia's Hill and who had the real book learning in this team. In later years Lucy Perry spent time wondering and eventually convinced herself that Jane had had suggestion down to a fine art. But in the midst of these comfortable times, Lucy was content to listen to her. "Do up your hair, Jane," she would say, and Jane would pat the runaway strands back into place.

Then, attractive and thoughtful, her face as homey and sweet as applesauce, she would say, "Perhaps James Grover needs to be made of, Octavia. Perhaps"—and Jane would dimple irresistibly—"James Grover should lead the expedition, next time we go to darkest Africa."

Lucy would have to smile; it was, of course, the very thing. The next day at school, there James Grover would be, in a captain's hat made of paper, leading the expedition to darkest Africa. He would learn, as if by the way, its deserts, rain forests; he would discover diamonds and the Congo.

As the years passed, the dialogue at the school stove became a time for Lucy's problems and Jane's practical solutions. In the end, perhaps, Jane was really the head teacher, although Lucy still gave the lessons, because it was Jane's imagination and ingenuity that made the dull material unforgettable.

Lucy reached the age of thirty-four. It seemed obvious to her that what most women had—marriage and a family—would not be for her. There were, of course, eligible men around from time to time. The truth was that Lucy was too high-hat to be interested in them, and they were too scared of her to try. Lucy immersed herself in books, teaching, and the changes of the seasons.

*

Aldair Rowe had got out of the service after ten years with a good deal of back pay in his pocket and one sole and ultimate plan in his mind: he would be a farmer. Not only that, he would be the best and biggest farmer in Monson. Although he and Jane Sapley were first cousins, they didn't look much alike. Aldair was tall and white-blond, with blue eyes that subsequently reminded Lucy of a lake at certain times in the sun. He was big and funny, and when he laughed, the wind picked up a million droplets on the lake and turned them to pure sparkling gold. He didn't know much about books, but somehow Lucy Perry didn't like him the less for that.

The army had worked a sort of toughness into him, too. If he couldn't have what he wanted, he would take it. He wanted to buy Octavia's Hill, but Lucy Perry couldn't leave her school and wouldn't sell it to him. At last he bought the hill opposite instead, what later came to be known as Gould Hill. But then he laid his eye again on Octavia's Hill and wanted it any way he could get it.

Lucy knew this, but it was the tough quality in Aldair that intrigued her. She felt dominated by his instinctive reach for what he needed, captured by his drive and energy. And there was the felicity of the buggy rides they went on, and the sudden, disarming sparkle of the big laugh and the light across windy water. Of course, that light was all reflection, not penetration, a kind of decoration of the ripples; Lucy saw this, too. In fact, years later she came to see the laugh and the sparkle in the same light as she saw Jane's rising to peek into the stove or to straighten the broom: a delaying tactic, a manipulation.

She felt it at the start or wouldn't have had it to think about later. At the time, though, she was thirty-four years old and had been a girl for a long time. She was sensitive to the male restlessness in Aldair, the urge and search in his every movement, and it opened what she had kept locked. She felt vulnerable, she was afraid. She didn't look him square in the eye very much. Later she told herself that this was probably why she never saw him looking at Jane Sapley.

In that part of the country you didn't marry your first cousin: it was uncouth and unclean and a little like marrying your brother. And while unions of cousins or even of siblings did occur from time to time along isolated country roads, this was always hidden from the neighbors; more often than not the participants hid it from themselves as well. Occasionally babies grew up among aunts and uncles as among mothers and fathers, but it was all concealed in a kind of smudged innocence.

Jane Sapley's people were plain and clean-living. Over the past ten years, John Sapley had become a patriarch of sorts. The antiseptic, solid manner of his settled life spoke for all the family: no half-breeds, no weak stock. Jane and Aldair had grown up as brother and sister, and it was assumed that they would marry strength and bring it into the family.

The urge to have, almost predatory in Aldair, made Lucy helpless and blushing and heedless at the age of thirty-four. Behind much of Aldair's acquisitive restlessness was his searching for Jane, but at the time, how could Lucy have known?

Jane rode on the outside of the buggy seat, and Lucy next to Aldair. The touch of his sleeve on hers created a throb in her arm and all along her body. If he lifted Jane down first, he did it quickly and waited for her to go into the school or the farmhouse. When she was gone, he turned to Lucy with all the world's want in his eyes and lifted her thin frame high in the air and set her on the ground with such personal care that it was all Lucy could do to keep her legs beneath her. All that spring, he lifted her up and set her down morning and night, at first too polite to hold her long, at last allowing his fingers to linger about her waist, so that in mid-April she could feel them through coat, sweater, dress, and underwear. It was as if those fingers reached right through her skin and touched sweetly somewhere in the center of her, all in a moment's hesitation before he let her go.

By the end of that school year, Aldair had begun to come into the schoolroom at the end of the day, and at last even sat for a cup of tea with them. Jane would hand him his cup and then make herself busy at the far end of the room. He would turn from her and look at Lucy, and Lucy would grip her teacup with cold fingers and feel herself vulnerable; air would ripple over her body as if she sat naked with him.

That summer Aldair hired himself to cut the hay on Octavia's Hill for a price he dictated to Lucy and she accepted at once.

"I'll cut what there is of it," he said, "and store it in your barn and buy it back from you at so much a bale."

In those days, great sworls of loose hay were forked up and bound in big, round bales. Aldair's price was generous, but Lucy would have said yes to anything. So there he was, cutting hay at the side of the house one day in late June.

School was out. Jane Sapley was standing by the ruffled curtain in the front sitting room, watching him.

Lucy came into the room softly and saw her unmoving form and profile.

"Lovely day," she said.

Jane turned. Nothing on her face moved. "Well, it is, isn't it?" she said, picking up her dust mop and setting to.

In the way events have of impressing themselves on the memory, so that if you wish to remember you often forget, but if you think a thing is unimportant you are liable to remember it forever, Lucy remembered three pictures from that one afternoon: Jane too still at the window, Jane turning with a face like nothing at all, Aldair.

While Jane dusted the floor, Lucy went to the window and there he was, working a little way down the field in the sun, laying the grass in swaths neat as a shell pattern on a plastered ceiling. He was moving swiftly and seemed to be whistling a little.

"He's done a good deal, hasn't he?" Lucy said, but there was no reply; Jane had left the room. So Lucy stood, gripping the windowsill, a little gray bird. Watching Aldair.

He was naked to the waist and tanned chocolate, his hair bleached bone white. Now she saw his back, now the curly blond hairs of his chest, the symmetry of active muscles, the smooth skin.

It was part of the haying bargain that Aldair went home at nightfall, washed and changed, then came back over the cricket-chirruping firefly fields to have his supper with Lucy and Jane. Often that summer they ate on the screened porch, to catch the cool breeze, with the hills facing Octavia's Hill looming up in the distance: vague, dark shapes. They talked about the price of hay or the price of land for the kind of farm Aldair wanted. Jane and Lucy served. If something was needed, one or the other of them would spring up and go to the kitchen for it.

Night after night, Aldair's beautiful eyes were on Lucy. Lucy blushed and talked harder, to cover the melting inside her. They were in love with each other, she believed, and Lucy was glad. Deep in her woman's tissues she wanted to get rid of that ghost of her father's fingers. If Aldair proposed, she would accept. But in any case she would give him what he needed. Proper Boston on one level, on a more basic one she was still angry, ravaged, deeply curious, and now, wanting.

One evening in July she went to the kitchen for something and came back to find Aldair and Jane engaged in conversation. This was so unusual that Lucy paused in the doorway to listen.

"It stands to reason!" Jane was saying. "The best farmland is never located on hillsides!"

"Like to see you grow melons anywhere else," Aldair retorted, but softly, looking down.

"Muskmelons!" Jane hooted in a way that reminded Lucy of the bond these two had: they had been children together. "So now you're going to live on muskmelons? Well, how about your cows? Graze on your hill, they'll have to have two long legs and two short ones!"

Aldair flushed. "My cows'll do just fine, damnit; best milk in town, good Jersey milk, none of your downtown Holsteins."

"Buttermilk!" Jane cried. "By the time they get over your hill

and into your barn! Half buttermilk and half whipped cream!"
Now she was arguing as if her life depended on it, her cheeks dark
red, her brown eyes snapping, hair escaping from the halo of
braids.

Unexpectedly, Aldair pounded on the table until his glass
slopped lemonade. "Good Jersey milk, goddamnit, and hay that
ripes up early and cuts easy, and a good garden on a south
slope!" he cried.

Lucy entered and picked up a napkin. "It's all right," she said,
"I'll get it," and she began to mop at the spilled lemonade.
Neither Jane nor Aldair moved. They were glaring at each other
as if over some longtime feud.

"Just because you can't have what you want—" Jane cried.

"I have what I want! And there's never anything else I wanted,
either!"

For answer, Jane snatched the napkin out of Lucy's hand.

"Octavia will walk you across the field," she said.

"Anything to cool an argument." Lucy spoke as if the whole
discussion were—as it was—beyond her.

"Fine," said Aldair. He stood up. In a way that said she'd
wanted to do it for some time, she stepped up to him and took
his arm.

"Come," she said gently. "It's been a long day, you've worked
hard in the heat, you're tired. We're all tired. I'll walk you a little
way; you'll go home and sleep. Two farms of hay for one man is
too much, perhaps. Don't you think so?"

They walked out into the noisy dark, away from the light of the
house. Without a word, they started down the north slope of
Octavia's Hill, toward Aldair's new little house. It was still warm,
almost damp with heat in the field. Hand on arm was not enough.

"Octavia!" Aldair's voice, muffled with want.

She went to him and held him, gave him her whole body in a
desperate flowering of pain. She was hurt as a child, and made
her love half-crippled with a limp: not freely, but fighting. Take
this, Father. Take that.

When it was over she wasn't sure. Had she won? It was more

as if you were chalk on a board and bucket after bucket of warm water poured across you and washed you away and left you wondering. Only a trifle mussed, she quickly got up off the ground and assumed her usual elegance in a way that must have puzzled Aldair.

"You're ready to go back?" Still pulling on his clothes.

"Yes." Even her lace collar was on straight, and all the tiny buttons down the front of her bodice had been locked tight once again.

He offered his arm and she took it; he walked unsteadily back to the house, but she moved with her usual precise, little steps. Then they were on the porch. Jane had cleared everything away; the porch was in its usual good order and the house was dark, save for one lamp burning in an upstairs window.

Aldair turned to Lucy and kissed her hungrily. He put his hand back on the difficult bodice, but Lucy hushed him, saying "Jane."

He heard it, turned, and left.

In August, Jane made the wedding dress and helped Lucy with all the arrangements. Lucy and Aldair were married on the front lawn of Octavia's Hill. The schoolchildren brought flowers and sang. Well-meaning parents came to the wedding; so did all the Sapleys. John Sapley was best man, and Jane, in a quiet, gray dress, bridesmaid. A minister and his wife drove all the way out from the First Episcopal Church in Bangor to perform the ceremony. There were finger sandwiches and tea and punch and small cakes—all the things you might find at an afternoon high tea. After the ceremony Jane went to Monson to visit relatives. Lucy and Aldair, who didn't want to leave the farm during its busy season, had the whole of two hills to themselves.

Whatever Aldair wanted, Lucy Perry Rowe gave. During the two weeks they spent together, he exhausted her with lovemaking. It was as much as she could give him—her whole body, she felt. But he wanted something more. His hands possessed her in a way that never seemed to satisfy him. When he entered her there seemed to be something more that he had not found, that he needed. Lucy's curiosity was put to rout. She was tired. At last her need for proper restraint took over. Too, by the end of August she was sure she was pregnant. But they seemed to be happy. Aldair woke and went to sleep loving her.

In mid-September, Jane Sapley came back to the hill. Lucy had insisted on this, though both Jane and Aldair objected. Jane, Lucy said, was a member of the family. She had lived on Octavia's Hill for fifteen years, and it was her home. Lucy and Aldair slept in Momma's room downstairs. Without Jane, the whole upstairs was empty and unused. Lucy hoped Jane would now take over the big room up there, and Jane eventually did; she had always slept in one of the smaller upstairs bedrooms. Lucy wouldn't have admitted it to Aldair, but she'd grown used to Jane's domestic arrangements, her cooking, and the way they shared the chores in the house.

But with Jane's arrival came the onset of a number of illnesses that plagued Lucy's pregnancy to the end. In the first three months she was ill morning and night. The sound of Aldair's whistling in the morning made her think "breakfast," and that was enough to make her sick. She lived on crackers and tea and occasionally the breast of a chicken. She couldn't teach, she couldn't even ride in the buggy. At last Jane had to take over the classroom completely. She also did special cooking for Lucy, all without a murmur.

Lucy thought of herself as a lady in delicate health. After all, there were Momma's pregnancies and all her blue-fingered delicacy for a precedent. If the bed jiggled or Aldair turned over in his sleep, Lucy lay hanging on to her stomach and sighing or, worse, vomiting. At last they moved Lucy to the front sitting room. It was Momma's lying-in room, away from the kitchen smells. Aldair took to sleeping on a cot in the front parlor. It might be less comfortable, he said with a smile, but it usually turned out to be neater.

Dr. John Sapley shook his head over Lucy. Even in delicate health, ladies were supposed to get over morning sickness after the third month. By the end of November, however, Lucy was still very ill and all the doctor could prescribe was bed rest. At last he concluded that the baby was pressing on Lucy's gallbladder. Bed rest, four vegetables a day, no salt. Jane, cooking separate meals for Lucy, never seemed to tire.

It was in January, her sixth month, that Lucy's sickness began to become confused somehow. Or perhaps it was her mind that became confused. All around her, suddenly, she sensed an elaborate coolness. Although she could hear Jane and Aldair speaking in quiet tones elsewhere in the house, conversations beside her bed had stopped.

What had happened to the old, foot-on-the-fender school talks, the cups of tea? Did Jane need any help in the schoolroom?

But when Lucy asked, Jane blinked her cooled brown eyes and said, "Oh, no, Octavia. I simply repeat the lessons word for word after you! Nobody seems to know the difference. In fact, those children probably think Jane Sapley has left and Lucy Perry is running the classroom single-handed."

"Lucy Perry Rowe," Lucy corrected her quietly.

Jane smiled. "Lucy Perry Rowe."

Aldair, too, was the soul of polite concern. He came in to see Lucy often during each day, straightening her pillows, fussing with the curtains, bringing her her lunch. He patted her hand and kissed her with cool lips. But there was no more lovemaking or laughter.

"What is it you and Jane talk about?" she asked him fretfully one day as he was leaving the room with her lunch tray. "You're always talking, and I never hear what you say."

"Jane?" His face didn't move at all. "Why, I don't know. Nothing much. Get some rest, now. Don't worry." He left the room with a new kind of extinguished smile—and he and Jane began to talk in whispers.

Lucy became convinced she was dying.

She was sure of it. Confined to her room, she lay back against the pillows and confronted death. For days. After all, what else could cause so much out-of-earshot conversation?

She tried to speak of it.

"Feeling a little down today, Jane," she would say.

"Oh?" Opening the curtains, bringing hot tea, forever busy.

"It's been so long . . ." Eyes on the quilt, ashamed to speak.

"You're doing well, though. Doctor said you were." Setting the bureau to rights, plumping the pillows on the chaise—could she never stay still?

"Well, he did, but—Jane?"

"Yes?"

"If there were something wrong, really wrong with me, you would tell me? If—if I were going to—to die, Jane, I would like to know it."

Jane stared down at the bed, and Lucy thought she'd never seen the kind of cool appraisal that now she saw. "The doctor himself—" Jane began.

"You'd tell me, though?" Lucy interrupted. "I would have so much that I would want to do, if I—" Half frantic, picking at the covers, which lay like lead on the creeping lump of her stomach.

But Jane seemed—was it possible?—amused. "Octavia, you are not going to die," she said abruptly. "Why, you're going to have this baby and take up life as usual." A smile, concealing— what? Jane pressed Lucy back down and pulled the sheet and blankets up and tucked them in until Lucy felt like a captive.

"Sleep now," Jane said, staring into the panicky Octavia Marlowe eyes. Then she left the room.

Jane was not herself anymore. Lucy thought about it for days, and then, deep in her nightmare of dying, she turned to Aldair:

"Aldair, please, what is wrong with me?"

Why did he look so surprised? "The doctor said—"

"Don't tell me that! What do you say, Aldair? Tell me the truth."

"Lucy, it's nothing! You'll have this baby and then we'll all live happily ever after!" Why, he was laughing, Lucy saw! And why did she want to apologize—for what, she didn't know?

"Aldair, I'm so sorry for the trouble I've caused—"

"Now, Lucy—" He seemed embarrassed.

"Aldair, do you still love me?" she begged him. "Even after all of this?"

And am I dying? Suddenly she wanted to dance on his skin until he told her the truth, to twist her fingers in his hair and torment the truth out of him. She wanted to be held and comforted, told that everything was all right . . .

But Aldair did nothing. "Of course, Lucy, dear. I love you as always," he said. But those blue eyes were cold, light on lead.

She *was* dying!

It was the middle of February, well into her seventh month. Lucy created for herself a space full of horrors. She no longer tried to communicate with Aldair and Jane; they didn't listen. In fact, she began to think that she should protect them from the nightmare that lurked in every corner of her room: death.

One night she heard them whispering and could stand it no longer. She got out of bed and, holding on to her stomach, felt her way down the hall.

As she went toward the lighted kitchen, however, what she saw was Aldair's back and, between his pant legs, matched toe to toe, the dark-stockinged feet of Jane Sapley. Jane and Aldair were kissing.

Lucy reacted as she had at eight, at eighteen. She remained absolutely still. After a moment she went back into the bedroom, shut the door carefully, and got into her bed. And there she sat, absolutely still, until they came in to say goodnight.

Aldair offered one of his cool salutes to her forehead. Lucy watched the approach of his lips and thought Jane was still printed on them.

"You have everything you need now . . ." Jane was scurrying around as always, never once, Lucy suddenly noticed, looking anyone in the eye.

The next day Lucy looked into Aldair's extinguished eyes and knew that he had had Jane; he was no longer hungry. He was, in fact, on his way to becoming ordinary.

She loved him! One part of her loved him until she died. But she was no longer carried away by him; suddenly she was no more in love with him than she was in love with being sick and pregnant. She waited. She waited for him to say, "Lucy, Jane and I have given in to temptation, and we ask you to forgive us. I am sorry."

Because she loved him and because of the baby, she might have forgiven him.

But Aldair only went whistling about the house, did his chores, tucked his wife into her convenient bed. Days passed, and he didn't seem sorry for anything.

Lucy became angry, and the angrier she got, the more she began to think that Jane and Aldair were laughing behind her back. Oh, their faces were straight enough when you talked to them, but what went on amidst the clatter of pans in the kitchen? Or in the evening silences when Lucy was left to sleep? What was happening when the house creaked and the hill moved in the middle of the night? There were times when the house itself seemed to speak to Lucy, telling her she was a fool.

"Get up!" Octavia's Hill whispered to her on those nights. "Be angry, be something!"

Lucy no longer worried about dying.

*

"Octavia, shall I pull the shades?"

"Thank you, Jane."

"Mother? Anything you want?"

"No, Aldair, not at all."

"There's nothing wrong?"

Lucy looked into his ordinary blue eyes and past him at Jane's now lightly flushed and well-loved cheeks. "Nothing that a thin stomach wouldn't cure," she said. Everyone laughed.

At night the house laughed. "Get up, Lucy," it whispered.

At last she did.

A little more each day, a little longer; she ignored the pain in her legs. She began to sleep during the day and to prowl at night. Anger made her strong.

One night she went to the front parlor and found the door open. It was very dark. She had learned by this time not to breathe heavily when she walked. She found her way into the room where Aldair should have been sleeping, and went toward the cot he had set up there. But it was flat and cold, empty.

She listened. There was no sound in the house; it seemed to hold its breath, waiting for her to scream. But Lucy did what she had always done: she went back to her room and hid. She couldn't face it. That night the house sighed and resumed its whispering.

The next day Lucy learned to take the stairs.

It was hard. But she planned to see Jane and Aldair together, to catch them, maybe even to accuse them and have it done—if she had the courage. They would be in her father's old room, of course, but it had changed a good deal, she saw when she at last made it up there. The bed was a new one, the room painted and papered, with white ruffled curtains at the windows and a white Bates spread on the bed. It was now a pretty room, with all of Jane's things in it, some new things Lucy didn't recognize: a knitting basket up on legs, a set of tortoiseshell brushes, a white robe on a hook. Under the bed was a pair of Aldair's shoes.

Lucy stared. Then with a little muffled sigh she moved slowly to the bed, leaned over with difficulty, and touched those shoes —his creases across the instep, his laces. Then she stood still, a small, swaying, front-heavy form in a loose nightgown, and she hung on to the bed, gripped it in her fists, and made no sound at all.

That night, over her supper tray, she watched Jane and Aldair, the very great care they took not to show signs of their attachment: when Aldair handed Jane a pincushion, he did it in a way that proved they were not touching. And the two never once looked at each other. They were both, elaborately, ordinary.

Lucy was furious but still she waited, watching for the signs of breaking, the wave of decency that she still hoped would force these two to their senses; anything would be better, she felt, than open confrontation. She waited for signs that they were getting done with each other or had become ashamed. But during the days that followed, it suddenly occurred to her that in any case neither Aldair nor Jane would ever care about her, Lucy Perry, again. And all that time Aldair was casual and Jane bland as a peach beginning to blush.

One night Lucy had had enough. She heard Jane go up the stairs and shut her door; she felt Aldair's cool kiss and his quiet look that said nothing personal. Then she saw him shut the door to her room, heard him move across the hall to the front parlor, heard that door open. But she didn't hear it close. After a while Jane's light—she could see its reflection on the snow—went out. It was near midnight. Lucy got out of her bed. She was thinking, In all this time I haven't heard a footfall, not one. She stood on the cold floor, shivering.

Little, thin, and in pain—at times the baby seemed to be suspended from cords around her neck—barefoot because slippers might shuffle, and in a bathrobe that wouldn't button across the front, she went to her door. She was listening to the house, to the hill. There was no sound. Silently she lifted the latch on her door and started into the hall. Now, she said to herself, if she were strong enough, they would have it all out in the open. And they would talk about what was, for a change, instead of what wasn't.

Her head was full of pictures: Aldair and Jane as children playing together, toddling together, bathing together when they were too little to know they were learning about each other. Aldair and Jane walking to school in Monson, stopping at the general store: who liked mints, who had spice drops? Blue sky and children playing, Aldair and Jane half grown, grown. And then their faces turned to wood.

Lucy went up the stairs, dismay like a sharp finger in her chest, splitting heart from supporting muscle. Eyes closed in the dark she reached out, opened Jane's door. Eyes open she peered in. There they lay. Jane, a shadow surrounded by the white of sheet and pillowcase, her body all dark, without clothes. Lucy blinked, her eyelids scraping at her eyes, and there was Aldair, his shadow complicating the lower body of Jane's, his light hair across it. There was no sound at all but their breathing, normal quiet breaths, like a pair of kittens asleep in a basket.

The house held its breath. She opened her mouth. She was a small, burdened, desperate figure; she was shaking.

Nothing happened. She struggled with herself, but it was no good. She'd never spoken up before; she couldn't now. She took one more look at the two on the bed. How Jane's hair spread and flowed—longer than she, Lucy, could have imagined it—across the pillow and down over the side of the bed. And there Aldair lay, as innocent in his way as a baby.

Lucy stood in the doorway. She was crying, but she didn't make a sound. She wept silently so as not to disturb the two on the bed, went out of the room weeping, down the stairs to her own door.

Then a pain came that was too much for her, too cruel to ignore, a deep, gripping pain. She sobbed aloud, moaned—she couldn't help it. The house rang with the sound she made.

Aldair came running down the stairs dragging on his pants, saw her, knew she'd seen him. Sobbing, she watched him come toward her, but even then she couldn't bring herself to refer to what he'd been up to.

At the moment Aldair reached her her water broke and she began serious labor. Twenty-four hours later her son, Marlowe Perry, was born.

Dr. Sapley attended the birth. The baby was small, weighing not quite five pounds. Lucy couldn't nurse him—too weak, thin, overwrought. A woman came in and cared for the young one, fed him. After a week or so, Aldair and Jane left together.

*

For the rest of that school year Lucy and the baby lived almost all alone on the hill, except for the woman who came in by the day to take care of the baby. They supported themselves on what was left from the old rings, which had been prudently saved all these years.

Aldair and Jane had been seen driving through town together. Dr. Sapley had said publicly that he was ashamed of them. So during those hard months, Lucy did have the sympathy of the town behind her. She was Octavia of Octavia's Hill School, the best school for miles around. By contrast, Jane Sapley and Aldair Rowe were beneath mention.

When Aldair sent money for the baby, Lucy returned it, and

when she was able to drive out again, she went into Bangor and started proceedings for a divorce, one of the first in that part of Maine.

"Damn right, too," was the sentiment in town. And she took back her original name. In the eyes of the town, so ingrown that a twenty-year resident was often known as a newcomer, this was fine; they'd "never really stopped callin' her Miss Perry anyways." Lucy also took back her old teaching job—it was how she supported herself and the baby. She took little Marlowe to school with her. The townspeople didn't mind; they were sympathetic. For three years she taught with the baby balanced on one hip, and Marlowe grew up with twenty or more brothers and sisters of all ages. He became a welcome guest in homes all over town.

But Lucy Perry kept her distance. She was a creature of distances now, of separations. The town called her Miss Perry or Miss Octavia Perry. But as for the "Octavia"—Jane had always called her that, for status—Lucy thought of it privately as her school name now, her scolding name. She was Lucy Marlowe Perry, not the Octavia of Octavia's Hill. That would have to be some other person—not her; not, surely, her mother. But somebody who could take the hill on its own terms, somebody, maybe, who was not such a coward.

Tave

*Y*OU'LL BE TAKING me downstairs, I presume?" The old woman, the ghost in the corner.

"Food, aspirin, my paints—I have no time."

"Time for your grandmother, though."

Tave turned her back on the empty rocking chair. "You I leave upstairs," she said.

"We'll see."

That was the trouble with Lucy's ghost; these days it always talked back.

*

Octavia Lucille Perry, dead several years, had been born in this house in the front sitting room, although she'd always referred to it as her mother's "lying-in" room.

Once Tave, age seven, had searched all over the house looking for that room, and hadn't found it.

"Mumma?" she'd asked, back in the kitchen. "Where is the lying-in room?"

"What room?" Amy Perry looked at her daughter with that glint of humor that came nowhere and everywhere on her face. "For heaven's sake, Tave—"

"I can't find it!" Tave persisted. "Grannie says we have one, but—"

Amy stood there for a moment, perplexed, which gave Lucy

Perry, alive then and too apt to hear everything in the house from her corner by the stove, a chance to speak up.

"In Boston," she croaked with the remnants of the highly cultured accent she'd used all her life, "one always referred to the lying-in room—when we referred to it at all!"

"Why, I believe"—Amy's low voice—"that there ain't any such room in this house. I believe, Tave, your daddy has told me your grannie was born in the old front settin' room."

"She was?" Tave could hardly believe it. It seemed far more likely that there was a secret and holy white room into which Lucy Perry had been born. Or not born so much as handed out, as from a carriage. Tave stared at her grandmother's wrinkled, sharp face and then back at her mother's round, flat, truthful one. "The front bedroom? With no special bed, nor nothin'?"

"Oh, illiterate!" Lucy cried in a frenzy. "The child is doomed! Country talk!"

She would never realize, as Amy did, that Tave had learned both her language and Amy's very early, so that it was equally easy to speak Lucy's Fine and Proper or Amy's Incorrect Emphatic.

"I'll take her off this farm, yes, I will!" Lucy raved on. These were old promises. She stood in front of Amy Perry and looked old and thin, wobbling slightly on her pins.

"Now, now," said Amy Perry soothingly.

"Bringing her up here? Nowhere! Send her to Boston, I have people in Boston—"

"Now, Mother Perry," said Amy.

"Coming out of the Maine swamp, never make it out of the mud—"

"I'm goin' to clean the living room." Amy shrugged and turned her back.

"Left to this!" Tave's grandmother burst into tears. "Someday . . ." She subsided, sniffling, into a corner.

Tave and her mother looked at each other; no words were necessary. Amy reached into her apron pocket and found a clean handkerchief and handed it to Tave. Then she picked up her mop and bucket and left the room.

Slowly Tave went to stand in front of the weeping old lady, but Lucy Perry, ever one to press an advantage, continued to cry. Tave stood helplessly, staring down at the clean man's handkerchief in her hand. It was folded but unironed: utilitarian; her mother all over again.

"Grandmother," Tave said, taking care to speak quite properly now, "please don't cry."

A little at a time the weeping subsided. At last Lucy sat still, her hands covering her face.

"Here's a nice handkerchief, Grandmother," Tave said softly. "You can wipe your eyes—please."

Lucy dropped her hands and took from her breast pocket her own handkerchief, a tiny cambric square edged with an inch of crocheted lace. "I never used to cry, you know," she said. "I don't know why I do it now. Nobody loves an old lady." She dabbed at her eyes and then stared at Tave from the red old rims. "Do you know how old I am?"

"Only sixty-seven," said Tave promptly.

"Correct," said Lucy Perry. "Where is this handkerchief you've brought me?"

Tave handed it to her. Deliberately the woman shook it out to its full size and turned it to one side and then to the other, as a magician might. Tave looked at it and then into her grandmother's eyes; they were bird-sharp and missed nothing.

"This?" said Lucy Perry, now playing the duchess to Tave's page. "You brought this, for me? You must think I have a very big nose." Lucy reached out and grabbed Tave's arm and pulled her close. The old woman smelled of Evening in Paris, having lately bought a lifetime supply through a Ward Brothers catalogue. Of course the Ward Brothers catalogue wasn't good enough, but like much else in Lucy Perry's life, it had to do.

"My nose," she said now, "isn't as large as all that. Is it?"

Tave was made of sturdy stuff. She gazed at the nose, which was long and sharp as a chisel. "You have a noble nose, Grandmother," she said.

It was from an old catechism. Lucy looked surprised, then pleased. Tave tried to pull away.

[99]

"Wait! I have something for you!" From deep inside her dress the old lady produced a small blue bottle tied around the neck with a string and suspended within her underwear. Evening in Paris was then dabbed liberally behind both Tave's ears.

"Thank you, Grandmother," she said.

"Dress you in overalls if they want to," said Lucy Perry. "You're my granddaughter all the same. Give me a kiss now." Tave did. "Good girl," said Lucy. "You love me, if they don't!"

Once again Tave struggled to get away, but Lucy hung on. "Where are you going now?"

"To the front sitting room," said Tave, adding—she couldn't help it—"to look it over."

Lucy gasped, her hand slacked for a second, and Tave was out of the kitchen and down the hall before the old woman's howl of outrage reached her. By the time it did, Tave found herself look-ing directly up into Amy Perry's face.

"Oh, Tave," said Amy, sighing, "couldn't you do no better 'n 'at?" But then she paused, sniffing air, and bent over and sniffed at Tave. "Well, you must have tried," she said. "You stink."

There was the beloved humor. Intoxicated by it and by the cloud of scent that surrounded her, Tave moved on into the front sitting room—which after all looked as it always looked.

*

"You'll take me with you," insisted the ghost in the corner by the stove.

"Not a chance," said Tave, wiping sweaty palms on her jeans.

Ray Gray was still talking.

" '. . . should take shelter,' " he was reading in a tense voice. " 'Go to the corner of the basement farthest below ground. Stay in this protected part of the house until advised by radio to leave . . .' "

"Aspirin." Tave muttered against the sound of his voice. "First aid kit—" She rushed upstairs. Jeans, underwear—what would those children wear? They were going to be awfully dirty when they got home—when would they get home?

Again she was downstairs, a bundle of clothing under one arm and, as a defiant gesture, paints and easel under the other.

" '*Matches.*' " Ray seemed to chide her. " '*Candles, baking soda, paper towels, heat sources such as an electric hot plate . . .*' "

"That's downstairs," Tave told him. Beside the cellar door was a growing heap of things that had to be carried down, but they had always had a hot plate in the cellar. "Oh, the generator!" Crazily she rushed through to the shed, flicking off one switch and turning on another, so that there was only one instant of darkness in that dark little room.

Inside the house the black box on the counter continued its bleak litany: "*If you have not already done so, you are urged to move as quickly as possible to a shelter now . . .*"

That was the cellar, strong, well built, blocked off. Dark. "There will be plenty of lights," Tave whispered to herself, for courage.

She took a deep breath. Then she unplugged the radio, went to the cellar doorway. The dank cement-and-stone smell of the place rose to meet her. It was a smell like old blood. Dizzy from it, Tave clutched the radio, forced herself to move, to load her arms with groceries. Then, one step at a time, she descended.

A peculiar chill lurked at the bottom of the stairs. Cautiously she stepped into it, moved toward Bob's workbench. With some relief she touched a light switch there and plugged the radio in again.

The reception in the cellar was not good. Ray Gray's voice fought through static that was at first very loud and then settled to a kind of constant background noise, like the sound of marching feet.

"*This explosion,*" he was saying, "*in the area of one megaton in strength, was not an incident of nuclear war. The latest report is that it was accidental, and originated from a secret storage facility in the State of Vermont. Most of the State of Maine has taken shelter at this time . . .*"

Tave went upstairs again and then, one step at a time, down; then up again. It was like being in a swing, she thought. Close to Ray's voice, far from Ray's voice. "*Radiation is most dangerous to the very young, very old, or to sick people,*" he was saying.

The children! Tave took one last trip for supplies. She would not allow herself to worry, she thought. After all, at any moment Ray Gray would announce that there had been a mistake and everybody could come up now . . .

"The President will speak soon," he was saying. *"I have no way of patching his voice to you, but will see if we can receive him here, and then relay the contents of his message . . ."*

"I don't care about that!" It was a cry. Tave bit her tongue. Suddenly, wildly, she had wanted to be patched in to her children, look into their faces, touch their hands, and make sure they were all right.

Her lips clamped themselves into a grim line. She trudged back up the stairs and slammed the cellar door shut. Then she was back down by the heap of supplies and clothing. While she listened to the radio she was, she saw, automatically sorting things out and placing them in strange, neat little organized piles.

" '. . . *large doses of radiation will cause death.'* " Now Ray was reading apologetically. He stopped, cleared his throat, continued. " '*But if you receive small or medium doses, the body will repair itself and you will get well—*' " Silence.

Tave's hands paused, she listened. She wondered: was Ray going to leave that little booth at WAMD? It was probably unprotected.

"Come on, Ray," she urged him. But she wouldn't have blamed him much if he'd left.

At last his tense voice made a rather grisly comeback. *"The worst fallout damage is expected to occur in the State of Maine within the next twenty-four hours,"* he said. *"Radiation is falling now in a cigar-shaped plume more than one hundred miles long. The plume will be driven by the prevailing winds—"* Once again, silence.

Restlessly Tave fiddled with the tuning knob.

When Ray spoke again his voice was hollow and echoing: *"More bad news is—that our teletype machine here at WAMD, Dover-Foxcroft, is now dead. I don't know why—maybe—well, they say electromagnetic pulses from nuclear explosions can wipe out machines. Somewhere, down the line—"*

Quiet. Tave held her breath. Then Ray spoke in a grating, hoarse whisper: *"What am I doing here?"* he said. His Silver Sound was completely gone.

Silence.

Tave stared down at her foolish little piles of supplies and felt a lump at the back of her throat. At that moment, if she could have lifted a hand to comfort Ray Gray she would have done it. Was he going to leave the station? She waited. All over the state, she thought, people who had never thought about it were probably making decisions like Ray's. Who would stay? Who would go?

"We'll keep on as long as we can." He resumed, suddenly, quietly, *"This is Ray Gray, broadcasting from a crawl space beneath WAMD in Dover-Foxcroft. I urge listeners who can do so to tune to WAZQ-FM, in Milo, one of the two broadcasting facilities in the state hardened for nuclear incidents. For the rest of us, we will continue along here as best we can. This is an emergency. Please take shelter. The news at this hour is this: radioactivity of potentially harmful levels is beginning to fall within the State of Maine at this moment as a result of what has been reported to be a nuclear accident. A detonation in the one-megaton range . . ."*

So there was one brave man out there. Bravery was a mystery to Tave. Relieved by it, however, she looked around her as she listened. Her eyes took in the contours of the cellar, plane surfaces, beams. For an instant the place seemed to her to float, exist on a cloud—

The casserole!

"Oh, my Lord," said Tave, "I've left it in the oven!" Without thinking, she started up the cellar stairs once again, then realized that perhaps she should let the food burn.

But wouldn't that start a fire? It might. She would make one last dash, she decided; she would have to. But it was slowly, as if each foot were a brick, that she approached the stairs once more, climbed them.

As she entered the kitchen and shut off the oven, she was remembering a picture from some civil defense pamphlet she'd seen long before. The picture was of a man's silhouette, a big red

X drawn through his face. The man was saying, "I don't see any fallout!" You knew he was going to die.

Tave turned, but there was a movement at the birdfeeder outside the sink window. Automatically she identified two evening grosbeaks with flashing yellow feathers. Beyond, in the budding lilac bush, a mourning dove waited. Involuntarily Tave pitied them: ignorant things, caught.

It was a thought she could hardly bear.

Hurriedly she lifted the casserole, which was dark but not charred, out of the oven, and, holding it with potholders, took one last look around her kitchen. Table, woodstove, poppies. A nice kitchen. She had always been fond of it. Now there was nothing she could do.

Then she was down the cellar stairs for good, the door shut firmly behind her. She was in the cellar, she told herself, and here she would stay until somebody said different.

Ray Gray was still talking. *"WLBZ in Bangor is broadcasting, but under difficult conditions,"* he said. *"Apparently the governor of Maine has already issued a statement from underground civil defense facilities in Augusta. New information in his statement is that some areas of the state are without electrical power at this time. According to the governor, this emergency could last from two days to two weeks—"*

Two weeks! It was far too long . . .

Tave's generation had grown up with the threat of nuclear holocaust, mostly in horrific rumors. The world could be blown up one hundred times over—everybody knew that. But in your daily life you couldn't take it too seriously. If you did, Tave supposed, you'd spend your time in a corner, crying. Nuclear disaster was like the weather: you learned to live with it, joke about it, even ignore it. Caught in a nuclear explosion, you were vaporized on the spot; one kid not over his stay in Vietnam had told her that the first thing that happened was that your eyes fried in your skull like eggs in a skillet, and then you were cooked to bursting, or you died later of some strange internal disease. Stories like these—you almost had to ignore them.

But—two weeks in the cellar? Tave felt helpless, betrayed. All these years she'd been half-expecting the worst without any idea of what it might mean. Two weeks in the dark?

Well, if you planned for it, you accepted the possibility, maybe. Maybe, even, the responsibility. And who could accept a nuclear holocaust?

Not Tave. Red flower children—that was what she had come to call the hippies of the past who advocated defense spending in the present. She had even painted a picture of them once, faces in petals like Carnation babies, but each petal like a drop of blood, and each baby with one eye staring left, the other eye looking right.

That picture was at this moment up in the attic, turned to the wall. Tave had liked it—for a little while. Now it was covered with dust.

Dust that killed?

She shivered. There were, she suddenly saw, cracks around the cellar door. They would have to be blocked—with what? Plaster of Paris, maybe, she had some of that down here. Or clay. There was a tub of it under the stairs, dug this spring from the Branch, perfect for modeling. Probably she should plug the leaks as well as she could and then stay away from the door altogether. And from what might drift under it . . .

Ray Gray was reading once again: " '*The present emergency is reported to be the result of an accident in Lessing, Vermont . . .*' "

Tave got some clay from the tub under the stairs and worked at the cracks around the door, wedging the stuff in piece by piece until every niche was filled.

When she was finished, she saw that the clay had made her hands gray, so she moved down the stairs to the old pump in the soapstone sink, something her father had put in for her mother years before. Grasping its cold handle she cranked, but nothing happened. She cranked again, harder and longer. Needed priming, no doubt, but what Tave remembered about priming a pump you could put in a thimble. She looked around. There was no other water downstairs.

"Great," she muttered. "Now what?"

There was a pot of coffee left from breakfast over on the work-table. This she sloshed into the opening at the pumphead and cranked. The pump gurgled, swallowed, quit.

Suddenly Tave panicked and began to pump like crazy—she wasn't going to be stuck in this cellar without a drop of water! She pumped until at last she had a tiny stream coming from the pumphead. Some of it she caught in a basin, but clunks of rust fell in, too. She strained out the worst with her fingers and then sloshed the basin of water into the pumphead opening as well. All at once, too, she was angry at Bob. It was typical of him, just typical, to have fixed every damn thing in the house but the one she would need the most! "Water, Bob!" she taunted him, while her arm engaged in a new panic of up-and-down motions. "Most basic to life! Forgot it, did you? So here I am, clayed into the cellar all alone, not a drop of water to drink—"

It wasn't Bob's fault and she knew it, but she couldn't help herself; she was scared.

Suddenly the pump coughed and shuddered and a clear, even stream burst from it. Tave kept on pumping even after she'd filled a basin and a pan. She didn't apologize to Bob in her head, either. Well, she'd been frightened! Not a soul around for miles except, she supposed, Tommy Green, if he was at home at all.

Her hands were cold from the water drawn from an underground river she'd never even seen. She realized this, and then was angrier at herself than anybody else. She guessed she'd been wrapped in a cotton bunting all her life. She thought a little viciously that she should paint her own picture. *Self-Portrait: A Woman Muffled in Comforters.* You'd have to put a hand coming out of the quilts, too, though. Five fingers reaching in panic through a newly discovered hole, and maybe a half-awakened look in the eyes. The surprise in that splayed hand as it reached through the comforter and found nothing at all! Yes, she could paint that in a minute. Well, as soon as her heart slowed down. As soon as she figured out a way to paint by lightbulb.

A basin and a pan full of water. She'd be all right with that, wouldn't she? Yes, she would.

Tave shook her head at herself, washed her hands, found a plate, and put a little of the hot casserole on it. She ought to eat it now, she knew. She had no oven down here and it would probably never be uniformly hot again. But she couldn't eat. Instead, plate in hand, she nerved herself to take a tour of the cellar.

The walls were of thick stone. Tave remembered tracing the patterns they made when as a small child she'd followed her father around.

"Your great-grandfather laid these stones by hand," he told her.

Such big stones, Tave remembered thinking. How could he lift them?

Unwittingly he'd built a fortress of a cellar: a twelve-inch-thick underground walled shelter. A fallout shelter, without knowing it.

Tave's father had been fixing the cellar for her mother, filling in cracks around the stone with cement he carried in an old bucket. Her father had done a lot of things for her mother when Tave was quite young. Amy wanted a place for her canning, she said, a place to wash things like canning jars and muddy boots, so Tave's father had put in a new sink. Along the walls, suspended from the old upstairs floor beams, he had hung shelves that still divided the long, low space of the cellar into a series of cubicles for storage.

No matter how neat they made it down there, though, in her childhood, the cellar had seemed to Tave like a musty dark mouth that swallowed her mother periodically. And it was always a surprise when Amy Perry emerged from that hole safe and forthright, her arms loaded with canned food, a lit lantern swinging from one elbow. Sometimes Amy wouldn't even bother with the lantern. The dark didn't scare her none, she'd always said.

It was Tave's husband, Bob, who had cemented in the old dirt floor. It would never be level, but at least they would be able to keep it clean, he said. Bob had put the electricity down here, too. He seemed to think that all he needed to do was clean the place up and put lights in and Tave would stop worrying about it. But it hadn't worked. She'd been afraid of the cellar all her life.

Bob did have a way of going quietly about his business, though, come hell or high water. Once he'd made up his mind to the cellar project, nothing Tave could say would stop him. Perhaps that was what Tave resented, that he could come up with a plan and then carry it out. Hers was a less decisive nature, doomed to misgivings, attempts, and subsequent self-criticism. Bob made up his mind and then let the rest take care of itself. She supposed if she were honest she would probably admit that this was lucky in a way —he'd decided on her, hadn't he?

Maddening to have good and bad so mixed up together in people.

Now she stood staring down the long cellar. Dusty but livable, it would have to do. The shelves divided the large area into spaces, with a center passageway about five feet wide. At the farthest point was a little room under the bulkheading: that was the only really impenetrable part. Tave walked down toward it, careful to switch on electric lights as she went. Then she peered in. Musty, damp, cluttered; the only dark spot in the cellar. She could see a broken sled, a wheelbarrow without a wheel, somebody's hip boots, a box of children's puzzles, parts of an old sink —these piled together with a number of shapes of junk too dark to name, all covered by a heavy layer of dust and spiders' webs. The bulkheading was still shut and blocked off as it had been during the years that Tave was growing up. For the children's sake, for their safety—at least, that was what Tave had always said.

Walking back toward Bob's workbench, Tave made herself stop and look over each little area with its shelf boundaries. In the first was stored an old stove, a coal hod, a set of fire tools and an odd screen, a few small pieces of asbestos, and a box of ill-scoured pots and pans that Tave had brought down here years ago when her wedding presents arrived to take over the kitchen. Some of those wedding presents stood on the shelves, too, a couple of tall, ugly, green vases, an electric knife that had never

worked right, a set of bowls, a silver plate done up in plastic—
Tave didn't polish silver by choice. She wrinkled her nose at it
and moved on.

In the next area were canning jars, jelly jars, a canner, and
apparatus; they had belonged to Amy and now all sat empty,
except for two or three forgotten jars marked only "July 1965"
and containing some nameless brown sludge that if opened, Tave
didn't doubt, would probably mean instant death. Ought to
throw those out someday, she thought.

Next came a cubicle that Bob had turned into storage bins for
root vegetables, complete with the sand to store them in. If he
put them there and brought them up the cellar stairs for her,
Tave had told him, she would cook them. But Bob was interested
in building, not in food storage, and as a result the bins were full
of wizened vegetables with long histories. Tave skirted by this
cubicle quickly.

On the set of shelves nearest the stairs was where Amy had
once put her canned vegetables, fruits, jams and jellies, relishes
and pickles. Tave wasn't afraid of these shelves—at least, not
precisely. The cellar just wasn't her favorite place, that was all.
But it was silly, she decided, not to look, see what was there.

What the shelves now held were a set of old encyclopedias, a
bunch of cleaning tools for a vacuum cleaner that Tave had long
ago given up on, three sneakers in a small size, Bob's softball
mitt, a sprung tennis racquet, and an old box of raisins. On the
nails where Amy had hung her strings of onions there were some
slickers and a discarded evening dress of Tave's, which Tavia had
had a spell of wearing a few years back, along with her mother's
high heels and make-up.

Tavia! Billy! Those children would never get to sleep tonight,
Tave thought. Not in a strange place. They'd be up until all hours
probably, impossible to live with tomorrow. Tave ran distracted
fingers through her hair. After all, she might not see them tomorrow, either. Oh, she didn't like this—any of it! After a minute she
went back to the workbench, where the radio was, and sat and
listened.

"... *the explosion was the result of an accident and in no way an act of aggression upon our country* ... *New England has been declared to be in a state of civil defense emergency. There is widespread damage in Vermont* ... *All possible aid is being given to survivors. Residents in New England are urged to keep to their shelters* ... *and follow the instructions of their local civil defense authorities* ... *the President asks for our prayers—*"

The radio was silent for several minutes.

Then Ray Gray, with curious formality: "*Ladies and gentlemen, the President of the United States has finished his short address with a warning to countries abroad. Our armed forces are at this moment at battle alert. However, we are not at this time at war. The President has declined to make known the source of this afternoon's explosion at this time. However, he will speak again tomorrow morning, after further talks with his advisers—*"

The President, Tave thought. Where was he? In his million-dollar bombproof mansion underground, surrounded by family, friends, and all the comforts of home? Still, you had to have a President, you had to be able to take care of yourself.

"*If there is anyone out there,*" Ray Gray said, "*who, like me, was hoping this was somehow a hoax or a mistake, it isn't. Please keep to your shelters. We will continue to hear the news as it is broadcast through WLBZ in Bangor. This is WAMD, Dover-Foxcroft, Ray Gray speaking.*"

He went back to reading what was obviously a blurb with a civil defense history. Tave wondered how long he would hold out, how long he could keep broadcasting, keep talking. Long enough, she hoped. She got down off the stool and shut off some electric lights, except for the one bulb by the furnace and workbench area. Well, they were stuck where they were, it looked like. She hoped to heaven John Manders knew what he was doing with those children; she supposed he did. It was town legend that he could loll down at the fire station day after day, unshaven, looking up at passers-by through lowered eyelids and slurring his "gooddays," until people swore up and down they'd seen him drinking. More than once Bob had come home after a late night fire call, shaking his head in wonder at him. "You never saw the beat of old John," he'd say. "He was all over the truck! Good thing, too. Rest of us didn't know what to do."

He would go on about how John Manders had unsnarled the pumpline or repaired a faulty nozzle or some other such tale.

The man was indispensable in an emergency, and many people in town were grateful to him for the saving of family or property, but he was such a disreputable-looking geezer, sitting outside in the summer sun or feet up to the firehouse stove in winter, that each emergency came like a revelation. People would just get to the point where they were feeling the least bit impolite toward old John and whatever it was he did on town time, and then something would happen and they were glad they had him.

Once Tave had sketched him, head back, arms spread, shirt unbuttoned, drunk on peace and quiet. Now she hoped he knew what he was doing.

She remembered the town meetings when John had stood up and asked for this or that for the air raid shelter he was constructing in the basement under the school building. One year it had been folding cots; another, special medical supplies; and once a transceiver for the radio. People said this last item was little better than town support for John's private hobby, and they had refused. If he'd been given the transceiver, of course, Tave and others out in the country could have heard what was happening with their children in Monson; she thought of that ruefully, now. Very often, however, when John asked for little things, when he stood up and held his ground, they had given him what he wanted, mostly to keep him in a good mood.

Tave was glad the town had given John as much as they had. If the children were going to be stuck in that shelter, at least they would be comfortable. But she realized guiltily that she herself had never inspected the shelter and she had no idea what John had been able to provide. Well, Bob was with them. Or was he? She would have to hope so, that was all.

Tave stared past the workbench and out into the rest of the basement. It was completely dark except for this one lightbulb near the bench. She was grateful to the farm generator, one of

Bob's improvements. Town bred, he couldn't bear to be without electrical power for more than a few moments, but there had been some winters when Octavia's Hill was out of power for long stretches of time.

"Come on now," Tave had said when she first realized how he felt. "We light up a few candles, we wait, we remember not to flush the toilet." But he didn't think it was funny. Soon after he came to live on the hill, he'd gone out and tinkered with the old generator Marl Perry had put in to keep his milking machines going in an emergency.

When the lights went out on bad days in winter, Marl had always said, milking thirty cows by hand was not what he had in mind. But then Tave's mother had died and Marl had begun to fade and the generator had been forgotten. One by one, he'd sold off the cows, and then who needed the old generator anyway? Marl hadn't needed anything after Amy died.

Bob had tinkered with the generator and "refined" it, he told Tave proudly. Now he switched it on as a matter of course at the beginning of every bad storm. Tave, standing in this warm, lit part of the cellar, was grateful. Staying alone in this place was bad enough, but at least it was lighted. The furnace would keep her warm. The cellar windows were still banked with the hay bales and sand they'd put on last winter. She wondered for a moment if radioactivity could get through that combination. Deeply, viscerally, she was afraid of radioactivity, for herself, Bob, the children. It was a treacherous killer, the more deadly because it lurked unseen. But in a situation like this, she felt, you couldn't panic. You almost had to ignore the possibilities, make yourself ignore them, to survive.

She began to figure out how to make her bed; she'd have to have a way to sleep. Inspiration had led her to throw the mattress part of a small open-out sofa down the stairs. Now she dragged this near the furnace. On top of the mattress she spread blankets that smelled of mothballs, which she'd torn out of an old blanket chest upstairs. On Bob's worktable she made a place for her paints. Then she looked over the food she'd brought from upstairs. Never, by any stretch of the imagination, she thought, would the groceries she had last for two weeks. One week. Maybe, if she skimped, ten days. The emergency would simply have to be over by then.

Aspirin, Band-Aids, an Ace bandage, soap—these went onto the shelves beside the food. A few dishes and utensils were set into a dishpan beside them.

When you thought about it—Tave was making herself be optimistic—an emergency like this could be useful. Maybe somebody would figure out something about coping with nuclear explosions? Or was that a naive thought? As for her, it looked as though she was going to have some time for uninterrupted painting. She was always angry at her family for interrupting her work. Well, here was her big chance. As long as the lights held, of course. Tave had no idea how long the generator was good for. Once it had lasted for four days in a particularly bad storm. Bob had said, proudly, that he guessed it would have lasted forever. Now they would see.

She decided that just to be on the safe side, she would hunt up matches and candles. In case. On a shelf at the top of the stairs she found a box with three small dinner candles in it and in her purse, a penny box of matches. Underneath Bob's workbench she located his battery-run lantern, the light in it still very strong, and a set of batteries for a flashlight. She examined the flashlight she'd brought downstairs and found it dead, so replaced the batteries in it. There was also a set of batteries for the radio if the generator failed.

There. Not much, she supposed, between her and the dark, but it would have to do. She stared for a moment at the flashlight lit and then snapped it off. This cellar with its blocked-off windows would be very dark, she knew, without electricity. She placed the flashlight carefully beside her mattress: she didn't intend to be without some light, not if she could help it, not all by herself.

Finally she took *Ghost of the North* out from under the cellar stairs, set it up on Bob's workbench, and stared at it. She was hoping that if she looked at it from time to time she might discover what was wrong with it. What it showed was a tiny square on a curve that might have been a house on a hill, and around it huge clouds, gray on white, like layers of fog, falling away from the curve in loops, like banks of snow. It was Octavia's Hill; she'd done it this past winter and thought it pretty good, abstract enough to please the artsy types, representational enough to make an impression on the inevitable traditionalists in this part of Maine. Perhaps that was why she hated it now. That is, for a picture minus any human creature, it seemed to have a lot of people in it. She left *Ghost* and sat on her mattress and listened.

Night reception. Ray Gray's voice wove in and out of static. *"Some loss of electricity due to the absence of protected facilities, some also due to a force known as EMP . . ."*

She heard the sound of shuffling papers, then Ray again, reading. *" 'A nuclear detonation emits electromagnetic radiation. This radiation can affect several thousand square miles of electrical wires, even several states could be subjected to EMP . . .' "*

In and out, more shuffling. *" 'During post-attack periods, it would be advisable to protect all electrical lines . . .' "* he read.

Tave was so exhausted, suddenly, she could barely hear him, and too tired to try to understand what he was reading, anyway. She realized all at once that she'd made no provision for a toilet, then decided that Amy's big old canner with its lock-on top would have to serve.

" 'Intensity of fallout radiation . . .' " She heard the words, but they were making little impression. She washed her hands and face and tried again to listen, but the washing hadn't helped. At last, leaving the one light on, she climbed under her blankets and lay down. Almost immediately she was carried away, marched off into a fitful doze. Ray's voice shook, faded. Tave went with it, very far away from the cellar, only stopping now and then to make sure the light over her bed still burnt.

*

A long march. When she awoke again for good, she found to her surprise she'd slept more or less—mostly less—for ten or eleven hours and she was rotten with it. It was six A.M., and she felt grimy and hungry. In the last of her dream, she'd forgotten to check on her light and had found herself frightened in the dark, waiting for something or someone to come after her. But what the thing was, beast or human, she could not tell.

Only a dream. The light was still on. Sighing deeply she rose, found the coffeepot, and turned it on. The radio emitted a kind of soft general static with which Tave was familiar. A noise like a fog, it came on on misty days sometimes when the reception was bad. She touched the dial, tuned, found Ray farther along.

"... *fifteenth hour of air raid alert.*" Now he was speaking in a soft tired voice, hardly more than a whisper. "*Residents of the State of Maine are urged to keep under cover until further notice. Latest reports are that storm winds to the west may create a rain pattern across the state in the next few hours, and considerable amounts of radioactive dust may be washed to the ground with the rain, especially along the coast.*"

Tave groaned. When the smell of coffee began to fill the cellar she poured herself a cup, scowled at her painting on the workbench, then went back to sit on her mattress. Ray Gray's voice became a kind of background noise for her own worrying. Were those kids all right? She hoped that between them Bob and John Manders could come up with food. She wished there were some way to call and ask. A little quiver passed through the muscles near one eye. It was hard to be separated from your husband and children. You felt it like a physical loss almost, as if you were suddenly without a limb. And the idea that they might be hurt in any way, or that she might not be able to help them, or that she herself would be too hurt to be a wife or a mother anymore—

"Be positive," she reminded herself. "Think of it as a—as a—" But by no stretch of the imagination could she call this a vacation. Once again Tave quelled a kind of lurking horror.

Too energetically she spread a slice of bread with margarine and ate it with her coffee. Then she opened a book; she hadn't had a chance to read in a long time. Today, she resolved, she would read until seven. You couldn't begin painting before seven o'clock in the morning, it was too uncivilized.

A schedule, that helped. Get yourself organized, it was good distraction. She sat back on her mattress. Ray continued to broadcast in a kind of reassuring, if weary, undertone. She opened her book. Lucy Perry would have approved of this reading, she thought. Amy Perry wouldn't have cared one way or the other.

She was thinking back, remembering her mother, when all the lights in the cellar dimmed, flared, and faded out. It was pitch black and very, very quiet.

"Damn," said Tave.

Her voice sank into the dark, into nothing, like a stone thrown off a mountain in fog. At once she felt for the flashlight.

"God's sake." Amy's voice. "Get some light around here, why don't you."

"Countrified speech." Lucy Perry fretted. "Oh, Octavia, don't listen to her."

"Leave me alone!" Tave whispered. She couldn't find the flashlight. With desperate fingers she again felt along her mattress in the dark.

Marl

*T*HIN LIKE HIS mother, but brown-tanned and blond like Aldair Rowe, Marlowe Perry sat sweating in the hot, dark house on Octavia's Hill, reading to his mother from *Sartor Resartus*.

Lucy Perry had spoken to him sharply time after time that morning. "Marlowe, you're wandering! Pay attention, now!"

Fidgeting at the dining room table, Marl would feel bad and begin to read again, but it had been a long morning.

" 'For the rest, how-however'—however?" Now he looked sideways at her. She sighed.

"Yes, yes, 'however.' Continue."

" 'It cannot be un-unint—' "

"Uninteresting, Marlowe."

" '— that we here find how ear-ear—' "

"Early! You know that word!"

" 'The significance—' " He pronounced it *sine-off-ants*.

"Marlowe!"

" 'Of cloths—' "

"Clothes!"

" 'Clothes—' "

"All right, all right, be done!"

It was what in all the world he'd been waiting for. He leaped from his chair and dashed through the house just to let off steam. He had no idea what the sine-off-ants of clothes was. The best and only thing about clothes that he could think of that hot summer morning was getting them off.

Of course, *Sartor Resartus* was too difficult for him. Often he went over whole paragraphs without understanding a single sentence. His mother made him read it to enlarge his vocabulary, she said. He wished she wouldn't bother.

But Marl forgave his mother; he had forgiven her long before. At age eight he knew already that she was scared, a woman bringing up a son alone, and not some backwoods country woman either. His mother was Octavia of Octavia's Hill and she wanted him to take after the Boston Marlowes for whom he was named.

She was always after him. His manners and his schoolwork had to be perfect. She made it obvious that there were two levels of achievement: one for Marl and one, considerably lower, for his classmates. Marl didn't let this bother him, or bother the other children either, for that matter. It was lucky he'd grown up in the schoolroom, he thought, so that he knew how kids were supposed to act, how to get along, for God's sake.

Marl squirmed through lunch, which he ate with his mother in the darkened dining room. They used silver, china, napkins, and all, because Lucy was bound that when her son finally made it to a place called Harvard, his manners would be impeccable. But Marl thumped at lunch, he rattled. He couldn't help it; he twisted in his chair restlessly until at last Lucy gave him an angry glance and let him go.

Often during the summer he was invited to other farms in and around Monson to visit and play, but today had not been one of those lucky days. For either of them, it seemed.

He stuffed deviled eggs into an old towel when Lucy wasn't looking and, with one last glance in her direction as she lay back wearily against her rocking chair with her eyes closed and her little wire spectacles sliding off her nose, he sneaked down off the porch.

It was no life for a boy, alone with his mother day in and day out. He knew it and she knew it, which was why she so often let him spend summertimes with his cronies. People in town approved of this. Octavia Perry, they said, was trying to bring her son up right.

But days like today were hard for them both. When Lucy looked at Marl, he knew she didn't see him exactly. She saw a piece of putty, and for some reason she was desperate to mold it into something she saw in her head. It was because she was desperate that Marl went along with it.

Now he scooted out across the field with the deviled eggs in a moist package under one arm, then doubled back to the road far down the hill out of her sight. He didn't want to risk her spotting him, which she could sometimes do, even in her sleep. Then he was free!

The first order of business, of course, was to take off his shoes and socks. These were required in Lucy's house, but all summer, far from her sight, Marl Perry had gone barefoot. In fact, he thought, as he stowed them by a big stump halfway down the hill, this pair of shoes would probably last him, for a change. He took out his package of deviled eggs, munching as he made his way toward what he thought would be bubbling water, a little tributary of the Branch that ran beside the road. It started at a spring about halfway down the hill. The water was clear and good to drink and Marl's eggs were salty, so he could hardly wait.

When he got there he saw that the spring was bubbling all right —one bubble every five minutes. Marl stood and stared. Why, just the other day that brook had been a regular stream! Suddenly his whole body felt itchy and unclean; he was sweaty and decorated with the grime of half-ripe field grass, and he was thirsty.

He'd wanted to take off every last stitch of clothing, right down to the foolish underdrawers he had on. Lucy counted underwear, so he had to wear these at least a part of every day, but he hated them and tried to give them a maximum amount of wearage in a minimum amount of time. Lucy made his underwear herself, and the drawers were of an embarrassing variety, baggy, a yard of material to an inch of flesh, and held up not with an elastic, as Sears Trowley's were, but with—of all things—strings. Ribbons, practically. It made Marl blush just to think of it.

The particular underdrawers he had on today he'd worn all morning, which was long enough. He wanted to get them off, get all his clothes off, lie jaybird-naked in rippling water, and not go home until the sun was even with the Goulds' across the way.

He looked down at the tiny trickle of water in the streambed and he was unbearably thirsty.

His mother was what he would call a doubtful cook. She made him strange things to eat, including what she called blonk monge, an evil, white vanilla pudding that she was apt to forget to stir. He would come into the kitchen and find her deep in some book or other while the pudding on the stove thrummed and hollered. Oatmeal was never the same two days in a row, one morning gummy, the next water-thin. On weekdays they often had meat sliced and cold, or Lucy would put it into what she called a chafing dish recipe, mixed with vegetables until it was a sticky and undistinguished mass. It didn't matter. Marl would have to eat it.

The deviled eggs were very salty. His mother had made lunch today as if she were having an argument with someone. She had wagged her head and talked under her breath while she cooked. "It is insupportable," Marl had heard her say, and then other long words. Talking to no one—the kitchen sink, maybe. But the eggs—oh, my. Marl, always hungry, burning all the fuel he could pack into his thin body, had eaten four of them by the time he reached the brook. He was very thirsty.

Dejected, he stared down into the mud. The beginnings of the spring were half-obscured by fallen twigs and grasses. It looked hopeless, but he took off his shirt to investigate, finding himself a pole and sticking it into a wide, flat piece of mudbed that was as shining and moist and brown as so much baked chocolate. On this pole he hung his shirt. The mud, he saw, extended for about four feet beyond where the tiny spring still bubbled feebly.

Without a shirt Marl felt better. There was no breeze, just pure air on his back. He could hear his mother now. "Marlowe Perry, how did you get so brown, have you been going without your shirt?" "Well, ol' Sears and I—" and then his mother would sigh. "Boys," she would say. "I don't pretend to understand them. But in my presence, Marlowe, you will wear a shirt." "Yes, Mother." He obeyed her, but the pure air on his skinny brown back was better than the shirt any day.

He put his bare feet into the mud. It oozed up through his toes nicely, and underneath the sun-warmed surface it was quite cool. It made, he decided, good footprints. Diverted for a moment, Marl paced with infinite care the length of the brown chocolate, until the soles of his feet were actually quite cool and the mud dotted with prints facing in various ridiculous directions. They were pretty good; he wished his friend ol' Sears could see them. But he was still thirsty, his tongue thick as a dry sponge.

He stooped over the spring source and gently pulled away what sticks and grasses he could, but it was no use. The source of the water was still obscured by a small grassy bluff and the roots of some bushes. There was only this little bubble, this inch-wide faint trickle, and now it was running muddy because of the stirring he'd given it.

Squatting, Marl waited. He stared out across the smoky blue of the horizon. Not a soul, it seemed, for miles. Idly, he wished again that good ol' Sears were with him. Him and Sears, boy, they'd dig out this old stream, he thought. Him and ol' Sears—the phrase had a satisfying, ungrammatical sound. Him and ol' Sears, they'd find themselves some water! They liked to swim, in the farm pond in the Trowley pasture, if they had to, or down in the Branch, if no one knew about it. Sometimes Mr. Trowley took the whole family to Deer Pond, the local swimming hole, and then they had some fun. Oh, that cool water! Him and ol' Sears, yessir.

Marl sat beside the mudbed and watched the pitiful trickle of water, and in spite of himself he began to fume. He began to fuss. Here he was, hottest day of the year, practically, so thirsty his eyes were hanging out, and all he could do was sit, and all he had was that tiny bubble of water, wouldn't fill a thimble.

After a while, however, the spring did run clear, and he stooped over and cupped the water as well as he could with his hands. He tried to drink, but it wasn't enough—it would never be enough, he felt. There wasn't enough water in the world.

Suddenly it seemed obvious that in order to get a good solid drink, why, he was going to have to lie right down in that mud and put his mouth to that old water-run-through-your-fingers.

He never even hesitated; there was no one anywhere near. He skinned off the hot pair of trousers his mother had bought for him in Monson, then he took off the voluminous drawers. God, he thought, in full sail the things billowed out almost to his knees. Quickly he slung them up onto the dry, grassy bank, glancing around him again as he did so. In Lucy's household you grew up modest, even if good ol' Sears said what the hell did it matter anyways. Good ol' Sears. Just thinking of him made Marl grin a little.

"Yeah," he muttered to himself. "What the hell." (Lucy didn't allow swearing.) And then he lay down flat on the warm chocolate mud and put his mouth to the stream.

Thanks to Sears Trowley and his water hole, Marl was well tanned in places Lucy hadn't looked since he turned five; the sun on his back, buttocks, and thighs didn't bother him at all. He lay there, a pencil-slim arrow of heat in the warm mud, his tongue the nether tip. It was an odd feeling but a good feeling, hot from the sun, cool in the mud; the heat of his body and then, flowing in a line like the mercury in a thermometer, the narrow, cool trickle of that water down inside him as he swallowed.

In fact, that mud felt so good underneath his stomach and arms that when at last he had drunk enough, he continued to lie there, just worming his way down into that cool damp. With one hand he grabbed a chunk of mud and brought it to his nose. It had a peculiar smell, rotten but somehow friendly. Idly, he began to build a little wall, about a foot long by the time he finished it. And by that time he had made this discovery: if you dug down into the mud far enough, why, you got to water. Not clean water, course, he told himself. You couldn't drink it, hell, no. But it felt good when you dribbled it on your neck, around your ears, and in places where the grass chaff seemed to stick. It felt good on your face, too.

The implications were very far-reaching. If you dug enough,

you'd have water to sit in! Excited, Marl began to work, heaping the mud to one side. A little messy, sure, but the mud was really pretty cold when you got down a few inches. Matter of fact, that nice cool mud underneath felt good on your back, which got awful hot stuck out to the sun while you worked. Every now and then Marl would reach up and pat a handful of that trickling aromatic black stuff onto his shoulders. "What the hell," he mumbled.

Pretty soon he had scooped out a basin about six inches deep and two feet long. Then he moved back and for a moment regarded his handiwork. Sure enough, the water had risen about an inch. Marl sat in it. Then he turned and eased himself into his mudbath the way a pig wallows, going down belly first and covering himself by rolling from side to side in the cool, damp grit. After a minute, he raised himself enough to make a pillow to lay his face on.

He rested. Then he turned and lay on his back and, inch by inch, while the muddy water coursed in a scarcely distinguishable rivulet around him, he covered himself up with mud until he looked like a root vegetable at the end of a long season. His head showed; the blond-white hair, however, was no longer shining. It was a gray and brown color that trickled down the sides of his face and into his ears, and it was drying at strange, stiff angles all over his head. From a distance it even had the faint greenish cast of worn-out vegetation.

"What the hell," he muttered, and settled once again. He closed his eyes, patted a little of the drier mud on them. Jeez, this was good. This was great. You could take a little nap.

Sure he was getting dirty, but so what? he wanted to know. Hell!

To date, Marl had never sworn so you could hear him except in the company of good ol' Sears. Now he practiced. "What the hell," he said tentatively, but that sounded a little too quiet. "Goddamnit, what the hell!" he roared.

After a while, however, he looked down his length and realized that it had turned a strange gray-brown all over. The old mud was drying, he guessed, getting pretty stiff. Time, he supposed, to move on. But he didn't, he thought, seem to be all that dirty, considering.

Once again he dug out the spring as well as he could and managed to wash his face after a fashion, not so much in the interest of cleanliness, but it was nice to be able to move your mouth if you wanted to. The rest of his body didn't feel too bad. Mostly it had a nice powdery smoothness. Here and there, course, a clump of dry mud; he scraped these off as well as he could, and trickled enough water onto his skin to make a kind of pattern that interested him. Black and gray, sort of like watermarks on his mother's silk dress. At last, however, he picked up his pants and moved toward the woods with them slung under his arm. The drawers he would not wear; he stuffed them into a pants pocket. The shoes and socks he forgot entirely, the shirt likewise. After a moment he turned off the road deliberately into ferns and underbrush and, coming up to an ancient stone wall—a fortress of other days—he sat upon it carefully because his bottom was bare.

The wall was lichen-covered, its crevices turned to rich humus and scratchy rock crystals that were almost like beach sand. It was in dark, comfortable shade, because this wall went right through the pine forest. Marl sat and stared off into the soundless, sun-dappled, fly-whirling woods and chewed a piece of sweet grass. He could have used his shirt now, maybe, to keep the bugs off, but he didn't care. The whole hill was his to play on, and he guessed he could go down and get that old shirt whenever he wanted to. He was happy. Under the wall, his old fortress, the hill breathed and moved with things to do on other days, but for now he was like a baby settled on its breast, so close to the heartbeat of it that it sounded like his own.

For a little while he thought about the men who had built this wall. They'd slung those old stones day after day to build these rock piles that meandered along the sides of their fields. Then they'd grown old or moved away and left the grass to turn into woods again. It was as if the hill knew something they didn't.

Somehow Marl knew you had to listen to the hill if you wanted things to last.

Marl dug one bare foot into the crevice of a rock that was as familiar to him as his own skin. Someday this woods would be his. Ol' Sears's dad was a farmer, so were most of his other friends' fathers, and Marl had long ago decided for himself what his future would be. Oh, he would go along with his mother's fancy ideas for now, to keep the peace, but someday . . .

Just then Marl's eye was caught by something moving on the road. A horse and wagon—it was the Trowley wagon, and there was ol' Sears's father, Bill Trowley, and there, sitting right beside him and scanning the fields, was ol' Sears himself! What the hell!

Marl was immediately too excited to sit still. Ol' Sears had come to get him—oh, boy! He looked again through the woods at the wagon. There, sitting on the back, was thick-shouldered, square little Amy Trowley, age five, and beside her, her mother. Why, the whole family was out for a ride—no! They had a picnic basket with them! They were going on a picnic—and coming up onto Octavia's Hill first! Why, that must mean they were going on a picnic and they had come to get—of all people!—him! Marl Perry!

"Yahoo!" yelled Marl as he stood up and pulled on his pants. He raced across the soft pine-needle floor of the woods, with the pair of drawstring drawers flopping and flapping forgotten from his back pocket. It would take too long to catch up with Sears by going out to the road, so he took to the fields, skimming deer-fleet over them. Why, the day wasn't lost after all, he was thinking. All that good mud, and now this!

In the distance across Octavia's Hill he could see the Trowley wagon pulling in at the farmhouse, and yes, there was his mother, still rocking on the porch. Marl's adventure with the mud couldn't have lasted more than an hour, then, although he felt he'd been gone for hours, all afternoon. No, the sun was still very high. There was Mother standing up on the front porch, and there was ol' Sears hopping down off the wagon and staring out toward the fields, his hand up to shade his eyes. Yes, there was

Mother talking and nodding from the porch, and there was Mrs. Trowley, with broad, square Amy on her lap, nodding and talking back. And then Marl was in the driveway and he was approaching the porch.

"Sears!" he yelled, a high-pitched, excited treble. "Hey! What you want me for? Hey, Sears!"

The adults turned toward Marl, then froze. What they saw was a little mud man about three and a half feet high, with blue eyes and gray-brown hair sticking out like the roots of a beet, in all directions.

"Oh, my Lord," said Lucy Perry. "My good Lord." And she sat down in her rocking chair quite suddenly.

Only Sears saw nothing out of the ordinary about his friend. "Mackerel!" he yelled—this was his name for Marl—and his brown eyes lit his whole broad, pink and white face. All of the Trowleys had a well-nourished look, and Sears was no exception. "Hey, Mack! We gonna go on a picnic! You wanna come? Goin' over to Deer Pond, and I made 'em come to get you."

"Deer Pond!" Marl cried. "Oh, boy! Just a minute, I'll get my bathing suit."

Turning from where he stood with one arm over Sears's shoulder, Marl grinned excitedly at the three too-quiet adults and at little Amy, who promptly hid her head in her mother's shoulder. What ailed her? he wondered. Perplexed, he looked from his mother, whose face combined shock, embarrassment, and shame, to Mrs. Trowley, who simply looked surprised. And her nose twitched a little, as if she smelled something she didn't quite like. As for William Trowley, Sears's father, nothing about him moved except his eyes, which winked and blinked. Come to think of it, Marl saw, his shoulders were shaking a little, too. "Why, Marl," he said gently, "been real busy today?"

"Oh, my Lord," said Lucy Perry, "I must apologize—" She sat forward a little in her rocking chair, then lay back again. "Marlowe Perry, I wasn't sure it was you!"

"Me?" said Marl uneasily. He was beginning to wonder if this meant he couldn't go on the picnic. "Course it's me!"

"I knew it was," said Mrs. Trowley loyally. But she was hanging onto Amy and rocking—with laughter, Marl saw. "Don't think Amy did, though." The little girl was still hiding in her mother's bosom.

"What is it?" cried Sears, now beginning to be anxious, too. "What's the matter?"

"Look at him!" Lucy cried. "Marlowe Perry, I am surprised! I am ashamed! Look at you!" She stood up and advanced upon Marl, waving her hands in little helpless gestures around his gray-dried hair, his mud-caked shoulders. "What have you been doing? Why, you look as if you'd been—lying in—in—" but she couldn't say "cow patty." It wouldn't have been proper, and it certainly wouldn't have been adequate. "Oh, Marlowe! No shirt! No shoes and socks—"

She circled him. Marl stood stock still. He was beginning to be alarmed. Sure, he was a little dirty, but for the life of him he couldn't see what all the fuss was about.

"Marlowe," his mother was raving, "you smell! You smell awful! You smell like a—a swamp! And what—what, why, your drawers! You haven't got on your—" Now his mother seemed to have forgotten herself completely. She pulled his underwear from his back pocket and waved it in the air accusingly.

"Them drawers," muttered Bill Trowley, "is the cleanest thing about him, if you ask me."

"Bill!" said his wife. "Now, Octavia—Miss Lucy—" Under the circumstances Mrs. Trowley didn't know how familiar she should get. "Don't let it get you down on our account! We seen bad's this and worse, you got to expect it from boys," and all the while she was wiping tears of laughter from her eyes.

Lucy was oblivious. "Marlowe Perry," she cried at him, sorely distressed. "Do you mean to tell me that you have no underwear on?"

This was serious. By now Marl was so afraid he wouldn't be allowed to go on the picnic that his thin, dirty frame began to quiver. But he told the truth. If you could depend on Marl Perry for one thing, it was that. "They're too big," he said briefly.

Behind him Bill Trowley snorted and let out a big "Haw! Haw!" Mrs. Trowley laughed, too. She'd never seen Octavia Perry so out of control. It was worth the price of admission.

Hearing the Trowleys' laughter, Lucy seemed suddenly to realize she was waving a pair of homemade underdrawers in the air. Quickly she rolled them into a ball and hid them under her apron, at the same time visited by a powerful rose-maroon blush that heated her face from dainty collar to hairline in one rich movement. After all, you wouldn't catch the Boston Marlowes raving in the driveway and flapping a pair of underdrawers in the breeze! "I am terribly sorry," she whispered to the Trowleys, who were by now weak with concealed laughter once again. "Please, forgive me."

"Oh, hell," said Bill Trowley, whose vast stomach rolled and trembled with his mirth. "Get him on up here. We'll take him to the pond for a good swim, and bring him back clean as a whistle. It'll save you carryin' the bath water."

"Looks," said Mrs. Trowley, blowing her nose and wiping her eyes, "'s it would take quite a lot of carryin', too."

"Oh," said Lucy faintly. "How—how very kind. But he certainly can't go like this." She stared at Marl. "Merciful heavens, no. I couldn't allow it! No one in our family has ever—" As if for evidence, she looked down at her own spotless dress.

Marl was in agony. It looked like she wasn't going to let him go. In spite of himself, two tears fell down his cheeks, making their way like raindrops down a grimy window.

Mrs. Trowley saw the tears and realized it had all got a little past joking now. "Octavia—Miss Perry," she began, "please, he wouldn't want to miss a picnic. Would you, now, Marl?"

Marl shook his head somewhat pitifully and looked down at the gravel. Since he'd already cried, he tried to make as pitiful a picture as possible, mostly to hide the quick-leaping hope in his eyes.

"Oh, you let him come now," said Bill Trowley. "After all, got to give our best schoolteacher a rest from kids in the summer anyways. Why, you just set back up there on the porch and rock and we'll take care of this youngster."

"Oh, I couldn't," said Lucy, the blush still upon her. It came and went. "He's so filthy! And how could you sit beside him, considering how he—how he—"

"Stinks," said Bill Trowley. "Well, put him up here beside me. No, better still, put him on the tailgate. He'll be downwind all the way, we'll never smell a thing. Come on there, young Marl. Hop up! Five miles to Deer Pond!"

"But he has no bathing suit," said Lucy. Marl was already climbing up onto the tailgate.

"Oh, don't give it a thought," said Mrs. Trowley. "We've brought a bunch of clothes. We'll have something to fit him."

"You are too kind," said Lucy. "Marlowe, you be polite now! You remember to say please and thank—Oh, Marlowe! How could you?"

But Marl was happy. He was blissful. He and Sears sat on the tailgate with their arms over each other's shoulders and grinned for all they were worth. He waved at his mother while Bill Trowley turned the wagon around.

"We'll keep him overnight!" called Mrs. Trowley. "Save us a trip up the hill after dark. Don't worry, he'll be fine. We'll clean him up all right." Then they were off down the hill.

Inside Marl was singing. Deer Pond, a picnic, ol' Sears, and a night at the Trowleys'! And to top it all off, he realized as he watched his mother's neat little figure diminish in the distance, he'd managed to get away without the dadblasted underdrawers. Yessir, dirt and all, for once he was comfortable in his pants.

*

When he was clean, Marl was a handsome boy—not that he cared. Feature by feature, his face was ordinary, but he had a sort of happiness about him. Whether he was going to bed or rocketing snowballs or sitting and daydreaming in the quiet classroom, there was something lighthearted in his face. He was not a joke-teller but he loved a good joke and, hearing one, would sometimes give up and roll on the floor, giggling and holding his stomach. But it was more than humor, it was an optimism, even a kind of joy, that made Marl so attractive.

[131]

Thanks to Lucy's home tutoring he was very bright in school, and she often set him to helping the slower ones puzzle out their arithmetic or memorize their geography. These children could have resented it, but a word from Marl Perry, a grin and a tilt of the head, and even the slowest kid perked up and began to hope. "Come on now," Marl would say. "You can do it." And even if the kid finally proved he couldn't, at least he felt better about it, thanks to Marl.

Beside the schoolhouse the winter that Marl and Sears turned nine, the children had spent some weeks organizing a system of snow buildings. Everybody worked on them, and they had rooms for eating, sleeping, farming, animals, airplanes, jails, fire department. It had, in fact, become such an elaborate means of play that Lucy never gave it a thought when she sent the children out to recess.

One day after a huge new snow she sent all the children outside after lunch as usual while inside she made a tour of the schoolroom, picking up a mitten here, someone's arithmetic assignment there. She had put on her warm coat, gloves, hat, and boots to go on her usual tour of duty outside, however, when something strange caught her eye. It looked like a big bird or some kind of animal, but it was traveling so fast past the little window in the back of the schoolroom that she couldn't tell.

"Good heavens," she said to herself, straightening and moving rapidly to the schoolroom door, "that wasn't a child, was it?"

*

Marl had left the classroom that day grinning like a monkey, and the other children had immediately ignored snow buildings and all and clustered around him to find out what his big secret of the day might be. Marl had only grinned and led them slowly past the winter fortifications they had worked so hard on, and to the back of the school, where he stopped and stared up at the schoolroom roof. Following his gaze, they all looked up.

It had been a good year for snow and now it was heaped against the schoolhouse on all sides, but especially toward the back. In fact, snow ran in a continuous curved bank down the top of the little building, over the lilac bush in the back, beside the one small window on that side, and into a big fluffy drift beyond it. Marl gazed for one more instant and then turned to the group. "What we need," he said, "is stairs."

In five minutes willing engineers had made snow stairs, and no sooner made them than at least half of the school—there were twenty-four children enrolled at the time—were perched, with a little help from Marl Perry, atop the ridgepole of the school building—or what would have been a ridgepole if it hadn't been so snow-muffled.

Below, a dozen children watched with their mouths open, because you could slide, shoot slick as a whistle down that roof, over the lilac bush, and into the snowbank—*poof! thud!* Why, it was the best thing Marl Perry had thought of yet, and he slid first, to prove it. Oh, it was fine, he told them, to feel yourself leave that roof, sail into the air, and land in that big, soft bank underneath! You had to slide, course. Climbing up the roof was easy, but climbing down was impossible. It was too slippery and there was nothing, nobody, to hang on to.

Shuss, poof, thud! One by one the children tried it. Why, Marl was right, they told each other joyfully. You could fly right off that roof, pass the lilac bush so fast all you did was scare a little snow off it, and there you were, landed in a bunch of fluff! It wasn't long before even the smaller children were clambering up, and in a few moments the whole school, jabbering excitedly, was climbing ten feet off the ground and lining up on the roof peak for the airplane ride of the century.

There was only one problem, of course, and it was rounding the back corner of the building. They all clung to their seats. "What *are* you children doing?" Lucy Perry gasped from below.

Marl spoke up. "We made a slide," he said, and grinned. "It's awful fun—"

"You children get down off there immediately!"

She meant business. Marl gazed down at her. She was mad, was what she was. And here they were, just keeping busy. Hell, he thought, she was always after them to keep busy.

Down on the packed snow his mother tapped her foot. "Marlowe, do you hear me?" she cried.

"We'll have to slide down, Mother." Marl's cheerful voice was now somewhat subdued.

Lucy, staring up into all the cherry-cheeked faces above her, saw anxiety, but also secret delight. What the children were thinking in that instant was all too obvious: sure, their teacher was mad, but that Marl Perry, he was something else, wasn't he?

It made her furious. "You climb down! Right now! Don't you dare slide! And you be careful!" Her voice fluted angrily.

The children appeared to consider this. Marl called, "But it's too slippery to climb down!"

"What do you mean?" Just about beside herself, Lucy stamped her foot. Above her on the roof, twenty-four throats clicked back tears or giggles, some weren't sure which. "You children could hurt yourselves!"

"Oh, don't worry!" Marl called out reasonably.

"All right!" Lucy cried, stamping again. "All right, slide down, if you have to! But I'm warning you, when you get here—"

The children all thought that was enough to make you want to stay right where you were. Nobody moved.

Then Marl stood up, ran lightly along the ridge of the roof, and stood at the head of the sliding-off place—it was like the irresistible cry of a leader in battle: "Charge!" Marl was their captain. One by one as he pointed to them the children took their places on the runway and boomed down off the roof, over the lilac bush, and into the snowbank: stormtroopers landing in enemy territory.

But the enemy, it seemed, prevailed. One by one as they landed in the snowbank Lucy grabbed them by available appendage and hauled them out. Marl was last. Him she took by the ear. Then they all marched back into the schoolhouse.

Never was there a quieter entry. There were sheepish looks that barely made it by sogging mittens and boots.

At last everyone was seated. The children rubbed runny noses and waited. Lucy sat in front, scowling because she had been honestly frightened—and angry.

When all were seated she spoke in a dangerously quiet voice: "Whose foolishness was this?"

But the word *foolishness,* designed to make them crawl, tempted them instead to laugh. Here and there eyes rolled to the left or the right in an effort at control. No one said a word; not a single soul moved.

Right then, in that instant, Lucy knew who was to blame; if it had been anyone else they would have told her.

"Marlowe Perry," she rapped out, "step forward."

Up he came to stand at the front of her desk, his face serious but not frightened. He knew he was going to catch it, but at that moment the price seemed cheap.

"Was this your idea?" his mother asked.

"Yes," said Marl clearly, looking her in the eye. It was, had his mother but known it, this sweet economy of the truth that made even the big kids follow him around.

His mother closed her eyes. "Didn't you know how dangerous it was? Didn't you stop to think that someone might get hurt?"

"No," he said.

Now there was nothing funny in that. But suddenly someone giggled; someone else picked it up. Then all the children were laughing, right out loud.

Marl's mother didn't laugh. She sat very still and waited. But in spite of her stillness, or because of it, maybe, laughter rose in wave after unquenchable joyous wave—the classroom was ringing.

"Take out your notebooks," Marl's mother cried at last, pounding her desk.

But if she had expected silence to fall immediately, she was dead wrong. Even Marl couldn't stop giggling, although he felt sorry for her and wanted to. He was bent over, holding his ribs: nothing like a good joke.

"Open your notebooks!" his mother shouted furiously. She picked up a piece of chalk and turned to the blackboard. "All of you!" she cried. "Five hundred times!" And on the board she wrote, "I will learn to play in safety, with care and wisdom."

Then Marl's giggles began to subside. Some children, he saw, were swallowing, looking anxious. He was sorry for them.

"Five hundred times today!" his mother cried. "Five hundred times tomorrow! Five hundred on Friday! This will be done along with your regular schoolwork. I shall keep the schoolroom open tonight until you finish! Marlowe Perry, stand up!"

He'd gone back to his seat to get out his notebook. Now he stood.

"Marlowe Perry, you will write the same sentence, but you will write it one thousand times per day. Is that clear?"

Marl nodded and sat down. He was stunned. Once he'd had to write "I will not whisper in school" twenty-five times. And once, fifty times on the blackboard, "I will not draw pictures during class time." (Only a picture of Octavia's Hill, with cows on the lower pasture and a garden growing. And a sketch of the garden, corn here, beans there. Strawberries, pumpkins.) The labor of those writings had been difficult enough. Now Marl quelled panic. A thousand times! Hell, no one could ever write that much! If you wrote for six years, you could never write—

But if he didn't do it, he knew, his mother would look stupid. That was what it amounted to. Well, he would do it then. Somehow.

The schoolroom was kept open until six o'clock three nights in a row. It was excessive, parents agreed, although most supported Lucy in her punishment: no telling what kids would do if you didn't squelch them. But some mothers and fathers felt bad, especially since Marl Perry was there at least two hours after all the other children had left, to finish his sentences. Some parents, in fact, shook their heads over that child's punishment. Among his schoolmates, however, it raised him to the stature of folk hero.

Marl stuck at the writing without a word of complaint, and even Lucy couldn't remain angry at him forever. On the third night, pale and tired, he handed her that day's sheaf of papers and tried to grin. "I'm sorry, Mother," he said.

He wasn't the only one. Lucy was so glad he was done with it she could hardly speak. "But Marl, your ideas, and all those children—"

"I know. It just seemed like it would be fun." He shook his head regretfully.

"But a leader has responsibilities, Marl." She lectured so as not to say she was sorry she'd lost control, that it was the sound of the laughter, so much like laughter she had imagined years before, like the hill itself laughing at her . . .

"I know," said Marl, and he did, somehow. "Look. My hands are worn out." White and swollen with the grip of the pen.

Lucy was inclined to shed tears over those hands. "I should have worn you out in another location," she said.

Marl thought this over. "Would have been faster," he said.

"But would you remember it?" Touching his blond curls.

"Naw. Too busy proving I'm not a damned panty shirtwaist."

"Marlowe Perry!"

Now he really grinned. "But we were steaming, Mother! D'you see how fast we came down that roof?"

"I saw. You won't do it again, will you?" Trying to be severe, failing, begging.

"No." That tilt of the head, the sweet truth. "I wouldn't go through this again for anything. Come on, Mother, let's go home."

*

She kept the papers in a stack on the front bookshelf in the schoolroom. Now and then the children looked at them, just to see how much they had written. And Marl had done twice as much! That Marl Perry, boy! And if there was ever mischief again that year, they all stayed quiet about it and Lucy never found out.

Now and then when Marl was much older, a big, thick-shouldered farmer with a wife and thirty head of cows, when Lucy was old and narrow with her chin grown to a hook, she would stand before him as he sat, say, at the supper table, and hold him by the shoulders and look him in the eye. "Now you tell me, Marlowe Perry," she'd say, "you tell me truly. What mischief did you do at that school that I didn't know about?"

Then Marl would set down his coffee cup and lean way back. "Couldn't say, Mother." And he'd grin. Or, "Who, me?"

"But you're too big to whip!" she would fret. "I'd break my fingers on you! Come now, tell this old lady before she dies." Lucy's death was imminent for twenty years before it happened.

"Mother, I never got into anything else I couldn't handle."

"Oh, you!" And she'd slap his arm. "You!"

And then you knew that he was always the flower of her heart.

*

The spring that Marl Perry was eleven, Cone Green came back to town. Cone was Alden Green's son, the toddler that Lucy had taken to his mother the day Luther Perry died, the little boy she and Jane had spent a winter on, trying to teach him to wear shoes.

With his mother and sister, Cone moved back into the little white frame house up on posts built into the foot of Octavia's Hill, and for a while no one heard anything from them. But then the rumors began.

Cone Green was trying to buy some farmland and he was trying to pay for it with a diamond ring, the biggest solitaire diamond you ever saw in your life. Nobody knew where Cone had gotten the ring. Some said he'd robbed a jewelry store in Portland or Boston or wherever it was the Greens had been for the last years.

No one would sell Cone any farmland; no one wanted to live beside the filth that seemed inevitably to follow the Greens wherever they went. Soon more rumors had begun to fly. It became known that Cone Green, age twenty-seven or more, owned not only a diamond ring, but one of the few plows and harrows on a horseless motor in the town. When asked point-blank in the general store where he'd come by his new tractor, he'd merely said "Weldin'," then scratched himself in an embarrassing location.

Of course "weldin' " was immediately expanded upon. Some said the tractor was stolen. Some said Cone had struck it rich down there to Boston. Some said he and his father had been on a welding job on a bridge and Cone had the ring from his father, who got it no one knew where and would rather not say. Then —so the rumor went—Cone had given Alden the tiniest shove, see, the littlest push, and Alden's clothes had caught fire and he'd flown like a huge, flaming bird down off the bridge and into the water and died.

The truth was that Cone had gotten the ring from Alden, who had saved it for years, no one knew why. Maybe against a bad spell, maybe for luck. But when Alden Green was in the Massachusetts General Hospital, suffering from third-degree burns he got welding, he gave the ring to his son to pay off the doctors with. It never got that far, however, because Alden died soon after, and Cone, who had won a tractor in a poker game, moved his mother, sister, their claptrap, himself, and the ring home again, right on the back of it. It wasn't comfortable, of course, but not too bad if it didn't rain. Too, by the time the Greens arrived on Octavia's Hill, they'd given all their bill collectors the slip.

So he had the tractor, but no land to speak of except the half-acre that the Green shack was on.

Marl knew a lot more of this than his mother did. Lucy didn't gossip and she really didn't have any friends. In the Trowley barns Marl heard whatever was going on. There were a lot of things a boy didn't talk over with his mother, and Cone was just one of them. But—and this was almost more than Marl could bear—Cone Green had that tractor.

A tractor! The farming you couldn't do with one of those!

At last Marl decided he would have to speak to Cone.

It was afternoon, the third week in May, and almost warm enough to swim. The brook on the hill was running hard. The dirt road was a little dusty, a nice warm dust, so Marl kicked at it a little. Things were beginning to bud out and he felt glad and at the same time restless.

It was planting time! He wouldn't let it go by another year— he couldn't! It teased him, the idea of manured moist soil and all the little things in it that would grow if you just set a hand to them. Hell, he thought, all they needed was a little help! Someday, boy, he'd have cows and pigs, fields and pastures. But for now, if he could only get the damned garden in (Marl still didn't swear out loud much, except with ol' Sears).

For some time he'd wanted to ask Bill Trowley to come up and plow; Bill also owned a brand-new tractor. But Marl knew Bill would feel it necessary to discuss this with Lucy, and that's where it would all stop. She saw no point in gardens, Marl had asked her before. A kid could get desperate, he thought.

The Green yard was littered with rotten boards, pieces of old furniture and broken glass, and Marl was glad he had kept his shoes on. Mrs. Green was asleep on the front porch. Her feet and ankles were swollen and puffy in old slippers and her wrists were thick with grimy rings of fat. She lay snoring, her mouth wide open.

Marl might have been a little afraid of her, but he reached up and knocked on the porch railing. "Mrs. Green?"

The old woman on the porch didn't move. Was she alive? For a second Marl wondered. Could a corpse snore? Of course not. He rapped on the porch again.

"Hell." An unexpected voice spoke. "She won't wake up."

Marl jumped. Then he squinted up at the porch, toward the windows of the house. He couldn't see anybody. "She won't?" He said it tentatively.

"Hell, no." The voice spoke again. "She come home, slep' till noon, ate some, had enough beer to last her till seven. Then she'll go down to the schoolhouse, clean that fuckin' place up after all them beshitted kids."

Marl felt an instant's admiration for a disembodied voice that could swear like that. He searched the windows again, but they were either broken or blank.

The voice spoke again. "You the schoolteacher's boy?"

"Yes," he said. His crisp hair caught the sun as he nodded.

"Well, bugger a teacup." There was the sound of spitting, then a snicker. "Bet you wonderin' where I am."

"Yes—"

But then Marl jumped back, because right in front of him a part of the porch underpinning opened up like a door, and there, squatting in the opening, was Cone Green. All Marl could see was his face. Thin and unshaven it rose out of the dark, pale as a fungus on a tree root.

That porch, Marl thought—when he had grown a bit used to Cone's appearance, like a dirty ghost in the unexpected doorway —that porch was one hell of a place to hide. He peered past the man's head. Looked like he lived under there, too, stove and all. Now wasn't that something? But, Marl had to admit, he felt a little uneasy.

Cone Green didn't move. He waited for Marl to finish looking. After a moment the boy stood back with his head a little to one side. "Cone Green, that you?" he said at last.

For answer the man stood up. He was tall and lanky, dressed in a dark, stained shirt and filthy jeans. His hands and face were pale and grimy, his eyes a peculiar bleary dark blue. He swaggered a little out of his doorway, as if he were a man who owned things and liked people to know it.

He could scare you, Marl thought, if he tried.

"Yep." Cone snickered. "I am that person."

Marl gulped and nodded. "I—I wanted to talk to you," he began. But then he saw something that made him forget to be uneasy. "That your machine?" Down inside the porch opening he could see the big wheels of the coveted plow.

Cone nodded. Hell, Marl thought, a man's got a tractor, you forget where he lives and what he looks like. "Can I see her?" he asked.

Cone turned without a word, leading the way around the porch to where a garage hole had been cut in the foundation at the far side of the house. There was the tractor, a thin, high-wheeled contraption with all its insides in plain view. Marl gaped. "You know how to work this thing?"

Cone didn't move. "Just like fuckin' with your legs up," he said.

Marl's eyes were as big as flapjacks. "You been plowing with it?" He'd seen a few plow marks beyond the half-acre of Green property.

Cone began to mutter. "Went to every shittin' landowner this whole goddamn end of town. I says, gimme ten acres—woods on it, I don't give a shit, anythin', just land—and I'll pay you—"

Cone reached into his pocket. "I said, you see here—" And sure enough, he held out the diamond solitaire ring.

"Holy old—" Marl began. But Cone set it under his nose in a beam of light, and the prism-split rays that ring gave off stopped speech altogether.

"This here's worth a thousand fuckin' dollars," said Cone. "But you try to buy land with it. Hell, like gettin' the pants off a pregnant bitch."

"That's one hell of a ring," Marl whispered. He stared up at Cone. "I don't want to sell any part of Octavia's Hill," he said. "It's going to be mine and I'm plannin' to farm it. I want to fix up the barn, have cows, pigs, I dunno. But you can plow what you got plowed up already, free, if you'll come and make a garden for me, in the old place that used to be, out on the south slope. Have to be harrowed, too, course, and it'll need a load of manure."

It was a lot to say. Marl's pulse was pounding. His mother didn't know it, but he'd already spent every red cent of his Christmas money on seeds.

Cone put the diamond ring back into his pocket. He looked Marl up and down, and for a moment Marl had the uncomfortable feeling that Cone might even like him. "I don't give a devil's shit for farmin'," Cone said. "Just want the town to see my plow works."

"Well, plow it!" said Marl. "Take a couple of acres, plow it over and over, if you want to. Just so's I can have a garden." His voice rose a little; he hated it when it got out of control.

In the half-dark, Cone Green slouched against a post and appeared to think. "You gonna tell your fuckin' friends, right?" he said after a moment.

Marl didn't understand. "Tell—"

"As Cone Green's plow works good, they should hire him, for Chrissake!"

"Oh," said the boy. "Sure, sure thing!"

Cone nodded. "Be up Sat'dy, I guess," he said.

"You—you will?"

Cone grinned wetly. "Right up there in your asshole," he specified.

[142]

"Oh—oh, yes! I'll—I'll see you Sat'dy!" Marl stood still. He gaped from Cone to the tractor. After a second Cone shifted his hips from left to right and leaned forward so he breathed on Marl's face.

"You better go," he said softly, "before I have to chase you."

"Oh—right!" Marl left, fast. Behind him there was a little snickering sound.

Once out of the yard, however, he was triumphant. All the way up the hill he jigged in his bare feet; he'd taken off his shoes and tied his shoelaces together, and the shoes swung from his hand.

When he got home, Lucy bawled him out for his dusty tracks in her house and he didn't tell her anything. It didn't seem like a good time to.

The next day he did talk to Sears.

Sears Trowley was still as wide as he was tall, and a better-natured boy you couldn't find—everybody said so. Down in the barn at the Trowley place, Marl told him all about Cone Green.

"Jesus," said Sears, now eleven, the same as Marl. "And he's really goin' to plow up at your house?"

Marl nodded, affecting a Cone Green slouch. "Sure as your asshole," he said casually.

There was a sharp intake of breath from ol' Sears. "You never," he said.

"Yep," said Marl. "I said, what the hell. Might's well try the fellow out, now he's had a chance to practice. It ain't, I said, like bugger in a teacup."

"Jesus," Sears said—it was more like a whisper. "Come on, Mack—"

"And he said," Marl kept on, "he said he could do it, easy as fuckin' with your feet up. Shit, he's got to get some work, wants to hire himself as a plowman. Money to live on. But it ain't easy —like gettin' the pants off a pregnant bitch."

He left Sears a quivering lump of adoration.

After Marl left, Sears began to do some practicing, but that was when his father caught him. Then what his father said was: he'd had five sons, he said, and four of 'em worked good as you please, but one of 'em was always in trouble and he, Bill Trowley, didn't know what he was goin' to do. One of his sons, Bill Trowley said, just wa'n't cut out for anythin' but trouble. Well, one of his sons was goin' to cut it out before he had his stern whipped bright blistered blue. Then Bill took his fifth son by the scruff of the neck and held him under the pump till he was clean. He didn't know, he said, where one of his sons picked up the language, but if he ever found out . . .

It didn't cross his mind that ol' Sears could have got it from the son of the schoolteacher.

But the upshot was twofold. Sears got cleaned up a little, and his father learned that Miss Perry was having Cone Green plow her out a garden. It was news he talked about, down in his barn, to whoever happened to be around. Miss Perry certainly did seem to throw a different light on Cone.

It wasn't long before Cone began to pick up odd jobs plowing out gardens from people in the neighborhood. The women stayed indoors while Cone was around, of course, and never invited him to the big farmer's dinner that was most often served at noon. After all, they said, Cone Green, wa'n't he dirty?

*

The next Saturday morning Lucy fed Marl early, as usual for that day, and then set pots of water to boil for the laundry. The washing was hard, hot work that always exhausted her, and she planned to have it done before the heat of the day.

Instead of running off about his business, however, Marl sat around the table. Literally. He moved from one chair to another in a circle, eyeing his mother all the time. On the sideboard was a small, closed box that contained seeds. Radishes, Red Globe, Early. Nantes Carrots, Big Boy Beets. Marl had read the packets over and over again. He loved the shiny feel of the labels, the sound of the seeds inside, and the pictures of the vegetables on the front. He'd even bought some flower seeds, and these were contained in two packets with children on them, sweet little children watering blooms ten feet tall. That was how Marl felt, at once the big farmer and the little child. He'd begged for a garden so often—he had to have one!

From the time he could remember, Marl had spent long hours by himself roaming the house and the grounds on Octavia's Hill. He thought the place had a kind of mystery about it. It had been laid out and built by his grandfather, that much Marl knew. His mother, when he asked her, got a closed look on her face and would say no more than that. Sears's grandfather Trowley was a few years older than Marl's mother, and had a vague memory of Luther Perry. "He was awful stubborn," the grandfather said once. "Awful attached to that hill, as a young man."

Marl knew why. He himself felt that Octavia's Hill was waiting, crying out for someone to care for it. The land rolled away to fields, woods, other hills, Mount Katahdin, Moosehead Lake, and it was like a promise, Marl felt. Something that kept you going, that whispered to you, "Someday you might own this, it might be yours, and it might be more beautiful than you have yet imagined."

Then a wind would blow, grass would bend, a needle drop from a pine. Marl would wander across the lawn, through the empty barn, out over the south slope of the hill to where his grandfather's hopes lay forgotten, and he would think that not only the land called to him, but all the hopes of a man. What his grandfather had tried to do, Marl felt, should not have failed. It made a personal wound in him to see such a good plan go bad.

A garden was a beginning; it touched the closest edge of Marl's want for the hill. It was a start, and proved you didn't have to wait forever. Sure, he was a little doubtful about Cone Green. Hell, who wouldn't be? But in this case, he felt, the garden itself would be so much more important than how he got it.

There was only one small problem. His mother didn't know. For four days Marl had tried to tell her. Marl of the singing truth was not in general given to crises of conscience. If a thing was so, he usually said so. But on this one issue he was afraid. What if she got mad and said Cone couldn't come? That would be the end of the garden.

He'd left the box of seeds in plain view in the dining room. He was hoping she'd pick it up and open it and then the conversation, the dreaded one, could begin.

So he went round and round the dining room table, rattling silver and pulling the tablecloth awry, while his mother cleaned off the breakfast things and got out her laundry soaps and tubs. He went faster and faster—sit, spring, sit, spring—until at last he managed to send one of the chairs crashing to the floor.

"For heaven's sake, Marlowe!" his exasperated mother cried. "What is wrong? Find something to do! You could help me with this—"

Marl's mouth, which had been open to explain everything, shut. He skinned out of the house with his box under his arm. Maybe he could catch Cone on the road and get the garden all plowed before his mother knew what was happening.

It was a great day to be alive, he couldn't believe his good luck. The air was full of warmth and moisture. It was a spring and a summer rolled into one day. Marl thought the sun looked different, even seemed to shine from a new angle; it looked good on the ground. The grass by the house was suddenly too thick for the scythe, the pasture was full of bluets, some trees were blossoming, and the forsythia, more lemon than yellow, was full of sun. Just the kind of day for a plowing! Just the day for Marl Perry to be out getting his pant legs soaked in the grass, running in three directions at once! He paused only to intone, to the beat of the approaching tractor, "Radishes, Red Globe, Early."

Sure enough, Cone was coming slowly up the hill on his machine; the plow was hitched to it in a raised position. Marl began to do a jig in the roadbed. Soon Cone was alongside and Marl was directing him to the garden plot. Luckily this was on the south side of the house, out of Lucy's earshot as long as she stayed at the scrubboard.

Cone drove over the field, stopped. Marl stood in the middle of the garden: it had once been about half an acre in size, far too big for one eleven-year-old boy to manage. But Marl planned to. In fact, he could hardly wait. The box of seeds still clutched in his hand, he went to Cone. "Is it all right?" he asked.

Cone ran one hand through his uncombed hair, twisted in his

seat, and stared down at the boy. "You tell your friends?" he said slowly.

Marl nodded. "Told Sears Trowley. It'll get around, he'll tell everybody."

Cone seemed satisfied with this. "I'm gonna keep plowin' the lower land till I get some fuckin' jobs," he said.

Marl nodded.

"All right, then," said Cone. "Let's get to it."

Cone plowed. Lucy, oblivious to the sound of the tractor, began her business at the washboard, scrub-rub, rub-scrub. She worked until she was quivering all over, until her arms were red to the elbows, wringing the clothes until she felt wrung out herself; then she was ready to hang the first load on the line. Unfortunately, Lucy's clothesyard was to the southwest of the house, in full view of Marl's garden.

*

Marl saw her coming, the sharp look on her face, the neat little line between her eyebrows, and he knew he had trouble. He ran to her.

"Marlowe Perry," she said, "what is going on here?" She was in a flap—her apron, her skirts, even her hair.

"Well, you see, Cone is plowing—"

"I can see that!" she cried, stopping in midstride to face him. "What I want to know is, why?"

Marl gulped. "W-why?"

"You heard me!" Staring at him with a strange, hard look in her eye.

"I made—a deal with him."

His mother's hands wrapped into fists, she banged her flapping apron with them. "You what?"

"I—I went to his house. I told him if he would plow us a garden, I would tell my friends so he could get plowing jobs."

"Plowing . . . jobs?"

"That's what he wants!" Marl was beside himself. Cone's plowing was nearly done, but there would be harrowing, and the manure. If his mother said no . . . "He just wants plowing jobs, to use his equipment on." Marl tried to be reasonable. "So much an hour, you see."

"I don't believe it." Cone had finished, he'd begun to raise the plow and secure it with chains. "Mr. Green," said Marl's mother, walking in a gingerly way across the uneven field toward the plow. "Mr. Green, I'd like to talk to you."

Cone turned.

He didn't speak. There followed one of those inexplicable pauses that now and then occurred in Marl's mother's communication with those whom until the end of her life she called "country folk," the "locals." She was never able to understand these pauses, but when they occurred she never waited them out, either. She should have known, Marl thought, that the cliffhanger of rural life was who would begin the conversation first.

She had never understood, as Marl did instinctively, that conversation between adults was made for a polite purpose. It gave you time to discuss the weather or the road conditions. Business was never meant to be carried on as his mother would always have it, straight out and done. Perhaps it was because life in Maine was bald, hard, often dirty and without excuse, and talk brought ease, but politeness demanded that you state your business in a fine rolling curve of conversation that included just about everything and everybody. In each curve would be a hint of your reason for the conversation until, in half an hour or so, the business lay between you and your neighbor in a neat series of spirals, as well placed as the ovals in a handwriting primer, laid out where you could admire it, or rewrite it, or begin a new exercise.

"Nice day, ain't it," such a conversation might begin. I call it a nice spring, s'far. You got plenty of roo-bob"—"rhubarb," Lucy always said, rolling her fine Boston *ah* in the second syllable —"down here? Gosh, I got it growin' like a weed all over my back lawn. Limit to how much pieplant anybody can eat, ain't there? Hell, help yourself, you want some. Almost time for the garden, got to get that plowed. Had frost up on the hill last night, you have any, no? Sick a seein' my breath and puttin on my shoes

[148]

'fore I can get to the backhouse in the mornin'." And so forth.

"My son says he made a bargain with you," said Lucy Perry, breaking into the pause and laying her business out—like a wriggling snake, Marl thought.

He watched Cone grab the snake by the tail. "Said I could plow your lower land till he got me some goddamn plowin' jobs."

Marl's mother scowled. Marl sucked in breath. "So," said Lucy acidly, "it seems the bargain has been completed."

"What the fuck," said Cone.

Marl rolled his eyes heavenward. "Are you quite finished now?" he heard his mother ask Cone starchily.

"Got the harrowin', course," said Cone. He wiped his dripping nose on the back of his hand.

Now Marl was begging at the feet of God Almighty, but he'd been around farmers enough to know what was coming next. "An' can't," said Cone, "have no garden without some cowshit."

"Oh, my Lord," said Marl's mother.

Cone stuck one hand into a deep pants pocket that must have had a hole in it to the inside, because you could see his hand wriggle through it and up into the inside of his crotch. He began to scratch.

"Oh, God," muttered Marl, horrified and fascinated.

"Mr. Green," said Lucy, "we will arrange for the rest of our garden work at some other time, perhaps!"

Cone pulled his hand out of his pocket. "Brung this," he said.

Marl heard his mother gasp. "Mother's ring," she whispered. Suddenly she was ash-pale, swaying a little. "Where did you get this?"

"M' father," said Cone.

"It belonged to my—my mother." Suddenly Lucy looked little and broken. "Taken off her finger—"

"Hell, Luther give it to m' father," said Cone. "You c'n have it back, you give me some land to plow."

"My father—" Marl thought his mother was speaking in a child's voice.

"Old whores, the both of 'em," Cone broke in, a look of dull humor on his face. "You want it?"

[149]

But Lucy took a step back. "No!" she cried. "Oh, Marlowe!" Hand over her mouth, she turned and ran for the house. Marl went after her, found her vomiting at a basin in the kitchen. After a while he put her to bed. Cone had left long before.

"Well," Marl said to himself as he closed his mother's door, "that takes care of that."

He might, of course, go down and put the seeds in the ground, hoeing the heavy turf as best he could. But that dirt was stiff. It needed manure, too, a good solid dose. He hated to dump precious seed into unworked dirt. What a waste!

He kicked at the doorframe and went back out to the kitchen. It was hot out there, the stove still going full blast; pans of steaming water awaited Lucy's second washload. Marl was sorry Cone had upset his mother; he felt bad for her, he felt to blame. He hoped she would feel better later. Rolling up his sleeves, he poured some of the hot water into a washtub and rubbed the scrubboard with yellow laundry soap. Then he set to work. When the washing was done, he hung it carefully on the line.

The next morning he got up early and built the fire in the stove to make breakfast—the day before he'd cooked for himself; his mother would take nothing but tea. Then, because he couldn't resist it, he went out to see how his garden looked. Sure enough, black in the early morning light, twenty-odd rows lay before him of the toughest old clods you ever saw in your life, full of weeds and grass and roots. Marl thought a harrow could break them up maybe, raking its steel tines down into the sods and giving them what-for, tearing them into workable pieces. But it would take days of labor to do the same thing by hand, and it would never be as good. Marl reached down, lifted a monstrous sod, dropped it. It shrugged off a little dirt as it fell, but that was that. He'd have his breakfast and check on Mother, he guessed. If she was all right, he'd set to work here.

But when he got to the house there she was, up and dressed and stirring the oatmeal. She looked better.

"You've been in the garden?" she asked.

He nodded.

"From now on, Marlowe," she said, "if we have garden work to be done, we will ask the Trowleys."

"We will?" Marl stared.

But there she was, lace collar and all. "I shall speak to William Trowley about it, or you may ask him. Even a gentleman, Marlowe"—and she looked at him over her spectacles—"needs an outlet."

"I'll ask Bill Trowley!" Marl cried. "Why, I'll hike down there and ask him today, and—"

"Fine," said his mother. "But you must promise me never again to have any business with Cone Green."

Marl saw that hard look, that secret, frightened look. "I promise," he said. "And I'm sorry it upset you, Mother."

"It's all over now," she said composedly. "I should appreciate it if the whole subject were closed. We need not discuss it further."

"Yes, Mother, thank you! And just leave everything to me!" Why, he could do chores for the Trowleys, to pay back for harrowing and manure! And he would put in his garden.

Off he went, never guessing what had changed his mother's mind: the sight of her son, out on the hill all alone, a small, skinny boy wrestling with a clod of dirt that weighed almost as much as he did. In a figurative sense, Lucy knew how that felt. And she wouldn't have it for her son Marlowe, not ever.

*

That year they had garden produce to eat and to store and their own vegetables for the winter. Marl did everything, and even his mother was impressed. Gardening, she said, could be Marlowe's hobby. The next year Bill Trowley did their plowing, and for many years thereafter. Just waitin' to be asked, he said. Amy, stocky and bright-cheeked, often rode up the hill with her father on their new tractor. She was a farm child—so Lucy thought. Sears and Marl didn't give her much thought at all.

The hill was a joy to Marl. He spent early mornings and late afternoons hoeing, transplanting, weeding, or just walking over it.

A half-acre became too small for him as he entered high school, and he bargained with Bill Trowley: so mamy hours of chores for so much use of the Trowley farm equipment up on Octavia's Hill.

Vegetables grew so well there that Marl often had extra to take in to Monson to sell to the summer people. In the quiet of his bed at night, he planned how he would set one field to alfalfa, another to winter rye, what would be pasturage for cattle; how to turn Octavia's Hill into a profitable piece of land. Sometimes, lying in the dark, he would hear the house settle and it seemed to be whispering to him, the whole hill whispered, "Farm, farm." As far as he could see, his only problem would be his mother, and so far, in one way or another, he'd been able to manage her.

*

Perhaps because he was so caught up in farming, Marl didn't spend too much time thinking about girls. Oh, he looked them over. But until his senior year, he never saw one he really liked better than he liked the looks of a good green garden row or a bucket of Jersey milk.

When he did find the girl he liked, it was Amy Trowley. But she was three years behind him in school, and when you were eighteen, that was a big gap. And she was ol' Sears's sister; for years he and Sears had been practically honorbound to ignore her. Still, though Marl didn't for a second want to get involved in all that soppy love business, he did like the looks of Amy.

She'd developed into a tall girl, not slender, maybe, but with fine brown-black hair and white skin. She could draw. Her scenes were in demand for school circulars and they illustrated the front and back covers of the school's annual literary supplement and the school yearbook. She was a quiet girl—Marl liked that, too. If you looked at her closely, you could see her reactions in her eyes, a kind of humor or warmth or dismay in them, if nowhere else on her still face.

On the other hand, she was the girl Sears had been known to call Old Pigeon Head.

On the day of his high school graduation, Marl sat sweating up on the platform. He had won some school prizes and a scholarship to the University of Maine. After he delivered his valedictory address, he was awarded the Monson High School Trophy, given each year to the student who had made the greatest all-around contribution to the school.

Now the trophy was beside him on the floor. Marl could see his mother, sitting down near the front of the crowd, so proud of him her nose was pointing straight at the ceiling. He knew what she was thinking, that it wouldn't be long before her son would be off to Harvard. He had been accepted there, and she'd written to the Marlowe cousins. Aunt Etta was now dead, and they'd written back to say that Marl could live with them in return for the odd jobs he could do around the house. There only remained the matter of a scholarship, and Marl was on the waiting list for one of these. His mother was sure that any day now a notification would come that the money he needed was his.

But Marl and Sears had other plans, had had them for weeks. Marl stopped looking at his mother; he hadn't told her yet, and he knew he would have to.

Row by row he went over the crowd, seat by seat. Amy Trowley wasn't there. He was half-ashamed to be looking for her anyway. When his name was called, he stood up to receive his diploma. And then he spotted her.

The principal of Monson High was a man of some polish and always held out his handshake hand first to the big boys. He had no doubt that Marl Perry would get it right: right hand to the principal, left hand over it for the diploma.

Marl walked across the stage, dragging his eyes away from Amy, and, all appendages, grabbed the handshake hand improperly with his left and swung it and blushed and let go, then took it properly with his right. The principal stifled a sigh; he might have known. But a laughing murmur washed over the crowd of parents and well-wishers. That Marl Perry, they thought affectionately, he was something else. Take all the prizes and then muff a little thing like that. Marl clomped back across the stage and sat. Sears sighed. That Marl, boy . . .

The graduates marched out into the hot June day and across to the school building, where they took off their robes. Parents joined children and there was plenty of laughing and a few tears. Then all went in to the senior banquet. Lucy was bursting with plans for her son.

The tables were laid out in the largest schoolroom, and there the graduating class of thirty-five youngsters and their parents ate a cold meal of sliced meat, chicken, salads, and pie. Marl and Lucy received plenty of congratulations, which Lucy accepted with pride. Marl just grinned. At one point Lucy turned to Marl, frowning slightly, and said, "Who was it you were looking at out there, Marlowe?"

Marl shrugged. "Who, me?"

"It wasn't some girl, was it?" she asked.

She was afraid it was, Marl knew. She'd never mentioned Marl's father; it wasn't a subject you could discuss with her. But over the years, Marl had pieced together the story. He guessed his mother was afraid that some junior version of Jane Sapley would eventually run off with him.

"Who, me?" he said again, grinning.

But Marl's mother embarrassed him in some ways. She made him private and modest. Now that he had someone who'd caught his eye, his mother was the last person he could tell about it.

That evening Marl went to the graduation dance. Lucy approved of this dance because it was called the Senior Reception, and she liked the sound of that. He was tall and handsome enough, he thought, in his new gray suit and the new outsized-looking shoes that made his mother say that even at six feet, she feared he was not done growing. He wasn't in love with himself, but he felt optimistic. At eight o'clock he got into the rattletrap truck he'd earned with chores and garden produce and went to pick up ol' Sears, who hadn't asked anybody to the reception either. That was the custom: some had dates, but a lot of people didn't, too.

The gymnasium had been cleared of chairs and its walls banked with lilac and apple blossoms. It was wartime, but the girls were

[154]

dressed in formal gowns, and that night at least there seemed to be no shortages of any kind. The senior class lined up and friends went through the receiving line to shake hands and wish them well, and then the dance began.

Marl stood beside ol' Sears and shook hands and received kisses from some of the girls. Far down the line, he could see, was one large figure in light-colored cotton. Out of the corner of his eye he watched her make her way toward him, and then she was in front of him, her hand filling his. It was a hard, blunt-fingered hand, yet somehow a good fit. She looked at him with the quiet eyes in which something seemed to light and flicker. Her dress, he saw, had a sort of ruffle around the neck. Her skin looked soft. Would she kiss him, as so many other girls had taken advantage of the occasion to do?

"Congratulations," she said. Marl held her hand. Ol' Sears looked over.

"Hey, Sis," he joked, "give him a kiss and let's move it along."

"Congratulations," Amy said again, loosed her fingers and moved on. Marl was disappointed.

He didn't see her again until the dance began. By that time he was hanging back against a wall. "That Marl," dancers murmured. "Look at him over there, cool as a cucumber. He ain't goin to no college next year, di' you hear that? Ol' Marl . . ."

After tomorrow it'd be all over anyways, was what Marl was thinking. Tomorrow he'd be on a bus, going to fight for the hill —that was how he thought of it. Him and ol' Sears had enlisted together, and tomorrow was the day.

Marl could see Amy sitting near the back of the hall, not dancing, either, but she was only a sophomore. He wondered if she would write him letters if he asked her to. Somehow he doubted it. A girl like that wouldn't do any of that sweetie-pie stuff.

"Look, Mack." Ol' Sears, now with a pretty senior girl named Linda on his arm.

"What?" Marl took his handkerchief out of his pocket and mopped his forehead.

"Mack, this is pitiful," said Sears. He opened the eyes in his round face very wide. "You think we don't see who you're lookin' at, but we do. It's pitiful."

So Sears didn't approve. Well, that was no surprise to Marl.

"Go on," said Sears. "Look, I say if she can make you shake hands backward in front of two hundred people, it's all right by me."

"What?" said Marl.

"So you'll go over and ask her to write to you—"

"She doesn't write letters," said Marl.

"Christ," said Sears, "you want me to take you over there, I will."

"I can manage on my own," said Marl. Linda and ol' Sears laughed together, a musical sound.

Casual to an extremity, Marl took a circling route, but at last landed beside Amy. Her dress, he saw, was more gray-white than blue. It enclosed a full breast in a soft wide ruffle. Her neck was strong and wide, with three soft wrinkle marks like tiny necklaces around it. Her profile was plain: wide nose, generous lips, deep-set eyes, high forehead.

"You're not dancing much," he said.

"Never really learned to," she replied. "Mother and Father can dance, you see them over there?"

Bill and Mary Trowley were dancing at the far end of the floor, stepping faultlessly to the music. Mary was dressed in polka dots, with a wide, white collar, he in the pants to one suit and the jacket to another. The end of his tie flapped negligently out of his breast pocket. They were having fun—they'd worked well, loved right, and didn't mind showing these young people a thing or two about how to dance.

"Didn't they ever teach you?" Marl said.

"Oh, I can dance with my father," she said. "But I get swished up with boys."

"Swished up?"

"Two left feet."

"Then you wouldn't want to dance with me?" He said it very softly.

"I might."

The floor under their feet, the feel of her dress, the movement of her body beneath it—she came to his shoulder. Her hair was very dark and soft, her hand was strong, her fingers touched laughing spots on his palm, and he held them curled in his to keep from grinning out of pure enjoyment. After a time, in some quarter of his brain it occurred to him that the music had changed and the band was playing a new song. His hand fell to her waist and urged her closer. She came slowly, almost thoughtfully.

The music stopped too soon. There was Bill Trowley at Amy's shoulder. "Well, Sis," he said, "pack 'em up, time to go. Up early tomorrow. Mack, you'll be going up to Bangor with Sears?"

Marl nodded. Amy and her father left.

Not a word from her. Well, if she could turn away from him in that way, why, hell, Marl guessed he could do the same to her! He climbed into his rattletrap alone and clattered the ten miles home up Octavia's Hill. Sears was still with Linda, had made arrangements to walk her home and then get a ride with someone else.

His mother was in bed when Marl got home. Good thing, he thought. If she'd been up and asked him how the dance was, who knew what he might have said? "I picked up three girls, Ma, and now two of them are pregnant." That would fix her. Women. He'd had enough of 'em. Tomorrow he'd be gone.

The next morning at breakfast Marl told his mother he'd enlisted and was due in Bangor at noon, him and ol' Sears. From there they'd be shipped out, he wasn't sure where.

It was more of a shock than he'd thought it would be. His mother sat at the breakfast table with her hands over her mouth. She looked stricken.

Marl was tired, he was impatient. In the night he'd dreamed that he'd made love to his high school trophy, and it hadn't worked out very well. After all, he was thinking, a lot of guys left high school to enlist, and if they were too young they lied a little. But he'd stayed in school, him and ol' Sears, too; he, Marl Perry, had done it because he knew it would kill his mother if he didn't graduate.

"For God's sake, Mother." Now he tried to reason with her. "I stayed in school, didn't I? I graduated! But probably I'd be drafted anyways—"

"You enlisted?" His mother moved her head backward and forward.

"You knew I would! You can't be as isolated as all that!" But of course she was and he knew it. "You must hear things! Nobody sits around going to college when the whole country is at war."

Now she was crying. He felt sorry for her. But without meaning to, he struck the final blow.

"I've written to the university," he said. "I told them my situation, and they'll defer my scholarship up there till after the service—"

"Harvard!" Lucy began to sob aloud.

"What? Oh, now." Marl looked down at her bent gray head, her quivering shoulders. Then he went to her and lifted her face. Tears rolled down her cheeks from the frightened gray Marlowe eyes. "You write to them, down at the Marlowes'," he said gently. "You tell them I've enlisted in the army and that after that I plan to go to the university and major in agriculture. I plan to farm. You know that, Mother. You tell them I have things to do with my time."

He smiled at her. "Why, we got better things to do, Mother. You tell them that. All right?"

The tilt of his head, the singing quality in his voice. It was all so simple for him, everything was simple for Marl. His mother stared at him helplessly. Eventually she dried her tears and let him go. She couldn't have prevented it, he was too big. And it was typical of Lucy to take the blow and not once speak out against it.

*

It was only much later, lying in a boot camp bunk, that Marl realized how hard he'd been on her. He didn't write her letters very often; he was too tired. But one night, he began a letter.

[158]

Dear Mother,

We're all dead tired as usual and we still don't know where we're going. Probably we couldn't stand it if we did know, but there is quite a bit of speculation. We spend our free time eating and sleeping, too tired to think too much. But I remember the hill all the time, and how I went off and left you to cope with everything. I was being kind of high-handed, maybe. I had to go, and I hope you understand that high-handed was the only way I could do it.

I should have told you about enlisting sooner, when I did it. It wasn't fair to wait until the last minute. I guess I was afraid you'd try and stop me. Big guy like me, I had to join up.

Mother, if I get into the war and out of it again, I don't want to spend any time in Boston, I want to come home. I hope you can understand this. I want to farm Octavia's Hill and always have. I'll learn what I can at the university, but summers I'll spend at home with the gardens. I want to fix the barn, too, and have some animals. There used to be cows, and there ought to be again—I've always thought so. And we'd eat well and have plenty of milk, use the land as it was meant to be used.

Mother, you've always given me everything I needed, everything you could give. You've raised me and supported us both all these years. I'm thankful for everything you've done. I only hope that now you've finally got me raised, you'll be able to live with me. But I plan to care for you, always, if you'll let me.

> Love,
> Marl

P.S. Would you ask Bill to put more fertilizer on the garden this fall, and plow it in? That'll keep it going for next spring. You'll have to plant, I guess, but he might do that for you, too.

Bill Trowley did take care of the garden for Lucy, out of affection for Marl and out of grief for Sears, who was reported missing in action soon after he and Marl were shipped overseas. Bill planted the garden in May, harvested it in August and September. At last, in May of 1946, Marl came home. He'd grown two more inches, his face was square and mature, he missed Sears, and he was quiet. He never talked about his war experiences, and if asked would shrug and change the subject.

That spring he planted his garden again and spent the summer toiling long hours on Octavia's Hill. He also worked for Bill Trowley in exchange for the use of Bill's tools. Marl worked—overworked, really—until he'd worked all the poison out of his system, or that was how it seemed to his mother. In the fall he enrolled at the university, and Lucy was almost happy to have him do it. He would be home sometimes, and he wouldn't work so hard. The university agreed with him. After a few months he had become his cheerful old self again.

*

Marl could see that his mother had changed, too.

During Jane Sapley's time, Lucy Perry had been known as a fine, progressive teacher, and after Jane left, Lucy had ridden high on a wave of parental support and town sympathy. "Poor Octavia Perry," the line had gone. Someone had seen Jane and Aldair riding through town the day they left, Jane sitting close beside her first cousin on the wagon seat, with her hand through his arm. Shocking! So no one blamed Lucy for getting the first divorce in town. "Don't she do a good job with them schoolchildren, though?" That was the line then; as a little boy Marl had heard it often.

By the time Marl was fourteen and had been graduated from her little school to go on to the high school in Monson, however, the schoolroom had changed again. By this time Lucy had carefully weeded out every evidence of Jane she could find. The trips to the fields had stopped, the Christmas projects had ceased. The art projects, the math games, the fairy tales for reading, and at last even the boxes of clothing were no more in the schoolroom. "Don't she make them kids hop to it." That was the line then.

Now it seemed to Marl that his mother had begun to believe that education was a matter of a child's discovering the teacher's level, instead of the other way around. One day in June, Marl brought Lucy her lunch and found ten children—out of the eighteen she now taught—standing up, trying to work at the front of the classroom. What worried Marl even more was that his mother seemed to know to a nicety the flushed cheeks and shaking hands that meant a child had been driven almost to collapse. When this point was reached, she allowed the child to sit.

By the time Marl was graduated from the University of Maine in 1950, Lucy Perry was fifty-eight years old. Her hair was more white than gray, her eyes magnified astonishingly in very thick lenses, her contours those of an old woman. Her face, too, seemed to be twisting in on itself: her nose longer than ever, her chin more hooked, her mouth twisted into a tight little bow to one side of her face. She looked old and angry. Marl still heard things around town about her, but now they were grimmer than ever. "Had twenty years livin' off the town's good humor," some exasperated parents said. Or, more charitably, "Gettin' old, time for a change."

It didn't surprise him much that when the new school building in Monson was finished and the mechanism of school centralization in place, Lucy Perry was out of a job.

*

At Marl's graduation, Lucy deeded Octavia's Hill over to him so he could begin to farm. "That Marl Perry," the town said affectionately. Mother and son, it was obvious, had been cut off two different bolts of cloth altogether, people agreed. She'd barely say hello in the street, but he'd stop and help you if you needed it. Tinker and talk. Spend an awful lot of time down to the feed store, reading up on everything he could get his hands on.

And looking at the new clerk in the store, who happened to be Amy Trowley.

*

It wasn't that Marl had forgotten Amy precisely or even that he'd ever made an effort to forget. But she'd gone off to art school after Monson High and he hadn't seen her for years. During that time she had stayed in a lit-up back corner of his mind. Maybe he didn't know she was there precisely, after a year or two had passed, but he felt her imprint in his mind.

Marl could have had his pick of girls at the university, and for a while after he'd left the army, he did pick and choose. He was handsome, and he pressed a girl so politely it was like being seduced by a down-home version of Prince Charming. For Marl it was all easy, simple. He was just being himself. None of the girls seemed to mind. A few, in fact, spent time waiting for the telephone to ring, wishing it would.

In his senior year at college, Marl picked up a girl who was hitchhiking from one end of the campus to the other. Her name was Betsy Thomson, and she was beautiful.

"Where are you going?" he asked as she climbed into the car.

"Lord." She hauled a black case into the car with her.

"Your machine gun?"

"My violin."

"Music major?"

She nodded. "Going to the practice rooms."

"Awful cold night." They arrived at Lord Hall. He looked into her open music bag and saw sheet music. "My mother would like you," he said.

"Oh. How nice. Well, thanks for the ride." She began to clamber out of the car.

"How long you going to be?" said Marl.

"Why do you ask?"

"I could pick you up later, take you back."

Her eyes opened wide. She looked like an elf, he thought, a bright wisp of hair, big blue eyes. She didn't seem that interested in him, either. Somehow this made her more attractive. "Please?" he said.

She squinted, as if measuring him. "All right, it's cold. I'll be about an hour."

She sprinted off toward the door of Lord, music and violin bobbing. In a minute she was inside and shaking off the hood of her coat. Her hair, he could see, was bright blond.

*

Betsy Thomson was not in the habit of hitchhiking, or of being picked up by strange men. Perhaps that was why, on this particular night, she did it. Betsy was restless. Now and then, she felt, you had to go against the goads—not that she'd ever encountered a painful goad in her life. That was just it, she thought. Everything in her life seemed to move too easily in what her mother would have called "channels foreordained." Betsy had always done the right thing, and for the most part she enjoyed doing it. She liked the comfortable home she'd come from and her gentle, unassuming parents. Her studies in music satisfied her. Her whole life was laid out for her: after four years of general college education, majoring in music and teaching methods, Betsy would go on to Boston to study music at the New England Conservatory.

The University of Maine, in Orono, in the northern part of the state, was a long way from South Portland, however, and lately it had begun to occur to Betsy that there was a world out there she knew nothing of. She was growing up, perhaps, but there was in her an uneasiness, a feeling of delicacy. She was like a small boat in an easy stream, tenuously afloat, looking for obstacles. Muscles she'd never used suddenly were demanding to be stretched. She wanted something different, to dare, risk, find out; the truth was, she didn't know what she wanted.

She'd shocked her roommate by going out unattended this particular night.

"Betsy, please—"

"Oh, just leave me alone, will you?" And she'd flung up her hood and stalked out. She would, she supposed, have to apologize later.

But where was life? Had she ever really lived it? She was tired of being a good little girl!

Standing outside on the dark road, however, her thumb had felt cold and exposed, and she'd had an instant, opening Marl's door, when she was utterly frightened and almost ran. Strange men: hadn't she been warned against them since she was old enough to walk?

Marl picked her up at Lord when she was finished practicing, and took her back to the dormitory, asking if he could call her soon. Betsy studied his face and said yes. A few days later he did call her, and then his calls became a regular thing. They went to the movies, or to Orono for supper, or to college dances. He liked Betsy fine. He liked the fact that she had to be wooed and won, that she was a strange mixture of dedicated, unswervable artist and warm-blooded, restless half-woman. It piqued him and made him all the more attentive.

He coaxed her, and Betsy sometimes gave in and made love, feeling liberated. If she had stopped to think she wouldn't have recognized herself. She didn't even know if she loved Marl Perry; he was very nice to her and she liked him. She listened with one ear when he talked about his farm. "Old childhood plans," she said once, faintly amused after listening to a long spiel of his farm talk. She didn't know that he felt the same way when she talked about music. As the weeks passed, she began to believe that with gentle patience, she could help him see the mistake he was making, unaware that Marl sometimes thought she might be an interesting wife to come home to at the end of the day, if she gave up some of her practicing and got up a little earlier in the morning. If they were married, Betsy sometimes thought idly, they would go off into the wild world together and do something unpredictable . . .

After thinking that, Betsy would turn hungrily to her violin and practice harder than ever.

*

By the middle of his senior year, Marl had begun to suppose he would marry Betsy if she would have him. Maybe this was because she said she didn't want to marry anybody, and he knew she could be coaxed.

"What is it?" Marl asked one night, with her cool kiss on his lips. She sat within his arms in the car, but drawn into herself, a quiet, little, separate person.

"Marl," she said, "after graduation, I'm supposed to go home."

"I know that."

"Next year, supposedly, I'm going to Boston to study."

"I know that, too." Trying to kiss her, but she sat too still.

"Marl," Betsy said softly. "We have to figure this out."

Instinctively, like an animal whose prey is about to escape, Marl held on and nuzzled. "I don't want to break it off," he said.

She shook her little shoulder at him. The front of her dress moved as she did so. He knew the tiny white breasts inside, he'd seen them before. In his mind's eye they moved when her shoulder moved.

"Be sensible," she said.

"Marry me," he whispered, thinking of those tiny breasts; he could hardly wait to get this settled. Occasionally Betsy could be gentled into making love, and tonight he planned to try.

"What?"

"I don't have a ring, I just this minute thought of it. But you'd better marry me, don't you think?"

Betsy blinked. "Why, do you want me to?"

"Of course."

"Then I will!" she whispered slowly, in her voice equal measures of triumph and determination.

As Marl had hoped, they lost themselves in lovemaking.

Betsy wrote home, informing her parents that she was engaged, although Marl hadn't had time to give her a real ring yet. "His high school class ring," she wrote, "is what he gave me until we can shop together. You'll like Marl. I think he and I will have an exciting life together."

Her parents wrote back gentle, cautionary letters. Betsy tossed these aside. If she felt remorse at the surprise they expressed, she didn't show it. Her roommate, Joanne, said, "He's very nice, and good-looking, too, Betsy, but isn't he planning to farm somewhere out in the country?"

"Just be quiet!" Betsy cried at her. "You're not my parent, you know!"

On graduation day she introduced her mother and father to Marl with a charming and determined smile.

It was, in fact, a day held together by her charm. Marl and her parents had little in common. He seemed to tower over them, uncomfortable in his unaccustomed suit, full of suppressed energy. Her parents huddled together in their quiet, well-cut clothes, doing their best not to seem bewildered either by Marl or by his severe-looking mother, a tiny woman who when introduced offered only the tips of her gloved fingers.

Betsy smiled. The more she worked at charming everyone, the more determined she became, and the more insecure. With Marl's mother she was deferential and smiling, with her parents, smiling but firm. She took Marl's arm possessively. That bewildered him a little, she could tell. But she kissed him in front of everybody, told him to write soon. Smiling, she got into her parents' car, waved, and drove off.

But all those smiles cost her. By the time they reached South Portland, Betsy had vowed to herself to write to Marl immediately. She needed his reassurance. Her engagement: was it so tenuous, to have needed so many smiles? Had Marl's regard for her been created as, say, a child might construct a house, one block on top of another? If so, she was afraid. Any vagary might upset the balance and bring the whole fragile building tumbling down around her.

She resolved that she wouldn't allow it to happen.

*

Marl said goodbye to Betsy and drove his mother home from Orono quite contentedly. Betsy had made a good impression on his mother. "A cultured voice," Lucy had conceded. It was a start.

Marl was relieved. He had finished the last class and the last examination he would ever have to take. His mother had put the farm in his hands. Tomorrow he would go to the bank and the next day begin to find animals to fill the barn. During spring vacation he'd cleaned the barn and repaired it so it would be ready. Spring vacation. To be allowed out of school for one week —to play? Not when Marl knew that the real work of the world waited for him the minute he got outside those walls.

The next day he did go to the bank, and on the next he began to stock the barn. By the end of the first week of his summer he was at the feed store, and there was Amy.

[166]

The store was a long, low warehouse, its air thick with the smelly dust of grain and shavings and baled hay. One whole end of the building was put to floor-to-ceiling stacks of grain in fifty-pound sacks. Up in front was a small room with the counter, where the clerk kept track of sales. The end of the warehouse was lined with small dusty windows, not unlike those you might find in a henhouse. A potbellied stove in one corner glowed all winter long, and beside it were two orange crates full of the latest circulars from Carter and Blue Seal, grain distributors. It was a place to stand around and find out about grain prices and nutritive mash, and the whole field of chemical additives. You could buy an agricultural newspaper and sit and read it. Opposite the warehouse was a little shed with garden tools in it, and in the spring, tomato plants, peppers, onion sets, and potato sprouts for those too lazy to start their own were all sold there, too. Besides the clerk, there was the old man who owned the store, Paul Wright. Amy Trowley's job was to keep the accounts straight and tend to the mail and the tools.

If Amy Trowley was all bowled over by Marl Perry, or if she even remembered the night at the reception—now some six years past—she wasn't letting on. Marl only knew that the minute he saw her his feet began to function like wheels. They rolled him up to that old counter without any particular effort on his part.

She was very busy with a stack of cash register receipts. These she laid flat, one by one, on top of each other, binding each stack with elastic. She was husky and strong, as Marl remembered, made square, with the same full hips, full breasts, the fine skin. Her hair was a shining brown, and she wore it in a soft knot at the back of her head. She had on a cotton dress, a sweater, ankle socks, and brown oxfords. Marl thought she looked beautiful, and was just able to drag his eyes away from her before she looked up at him. Then he pretended to notice her for the first time. "Hello." He cleared his throat. "You mindin' the store today?"

He saw immediately that that was a silly remark. She didn't bother to answer, and he didn't blame her. He looked away and squinted at the feed list tacked on the wall in back of the counter. Then he cleared his throat again.

"Better give me two fifties," he said. "It'll do for a week or so."

Without a word, she moved from behind the counter, past a knot of men arguing road-scraping in one corner. Marl watched her; it seemed to him she knew how to use the big parts she'd been given. It didn't occur to him what her errand might be, however, until he saw her push a dolly with two fifty-pound sacks of grain on it past the doorway and out to the garage door at the end of the warehouse. Then he went after her.

At the end of the ramp she stopped and looked at him. "Two fifties," she said quietly. "Anythin' else?"

"Amy, I would have gotten that for you," he began.

"You got a truck?"

"Yes."

"Drive it around. I'll put the grain right in there."

"You?"

"Who else? Paul is off today. You want to pay, or put it on a slip?"

"There may be other things I'll need," he said. "I better start a slip. And I'll take care of the grain myself."

He followed her back into the store, watched her reach for a new receipt book, open it, slide in the carbon. It was the way they kept slips on all the farmers in town, anybody who asked, really, so long as you knew them.

"Marlowe Perry," she wrote at the top. "Octavia's Hill, Monson."

"You remember me, then," he said. "I didn't know if you did."

"Oh, yes."

"How was art school?"

"Glad to be home. I remember you." Now she looked at him directly.

"Danced with you once," he said. "Only thing I remember about the whole damned affair. We danced, and then you turned right around and went off with your folks."

"I did?" she said.

"I miss ol' Sears," he said. "Still."

"We all do. I—I remember how you used to be together all the time."

"My good friend. He was a good guy."

"Queer how separatin' makes people into strangers. Sorry I didn't say hello before."

"It wasn't all your fault."

Amy wrote out the slip and handed a copy to Marl. "Thanks," he said and turned to leave, but then turned back. "You remember that dance?" he asked.

"I don't recall it too clear." But Marl saw a blush rise from her neck and touch her cheeks and even her forehead bright, clear pink. She remembered more than she was telling. Well then, he thought. Well.

The knot of men at the stove had stopped arguing, and they were listening in on Marl's conversation. No worse gossips than a bunch of idle men, Marl thought. He guessed he hadn't lost his wits enough to forget that, in any case! So then, very casually, he nodded at Amy and left.

Thinking about her began to occupy his time. The next day he received a long and closely written letter from Betsy, but he hardly read it seriously, putting off answering it from day to day, even after he had received two more letters from her.

He was trying to think how soon he could return to the feed store. Five days later, he went back.

*

Having glimpsed the essence of what we have been seeking, we keep after it, discarding all the old husks of our life. Thus it was that Marl approached the steps to the feed store with Betsy's latest letter stuffed unread in his back pocket. Betsy he could attend to any time. Amy, on the other hand, was pressing business.

He didn't walk to the steps, he sprinted. Then, urgent hand on the door, he made a conscious effort to slow himself down. There was no rush, he reminded himself. He opened the door slowly and walked in without so much as a glance at Amy's counter, walked to the corner by the stove and pulled up at a bench next to the orange crates. He sat. For a few minutes he did an impersonation of a busy office manager at his file cabinet, shuffling through the latest circulars. Finally he came up with one about mash, which he opened and read. That is, his eyes felt along each capital letter, tumbled across the line, and stopped at each period. And as each period came up, so did his look: Amy.

The men at the feed store were out in back at the warehouse: it was cooler out there. As Marl's eyes swung behind the magazine, his peripheral vision told him that no one else was in the store area. There Amy stood, behind the counter, with a checklist in one hand and a pencil in the other. Her dress was sleeveless, her arms tan against the light-colored body of it. Her hair, pinned loosely at the back of her head, made her neck look bare and cool, he thought. Around that neck were the bracelets of tiny blue wrinkles; he remembered them. Of course, you had to know where to look. Took Marl half an hour.

Meanwhile the men's voices out in the warehouse droned on. Occasionally there was a burst of laughter, and then the talk resumed in a low monotone. Whatever they were talking about out there, must be good. Marl made sure of this. He made sure of Amy. When her back was turned he stood up, walked to the counter, and squinted at the feed list again.

She turned quietly and waited for him to speak.

But this was Marl Perry; he was sick of deception. "I'm sorry you don't remember the senior dance," he said. "I remember it very well. I wanted to dance with you all night that night, but I was too damned shy to ask. When we finally did get together, it was the best thing that happened to me, either before or since. I like you and I'd like to take you out, some night, if I could, if you wanted me to."

The talk in the warehouse had stopped and the men out there were listening in. Somebody had jabbed somebody else with a sharp elbow. Didn't I tell you? someone's cocked eyebrow said.

[170]

Didn't I say he'd come back and speak to her? That Marl Perry! No one snickered, not yet. That would come later, when the whole story was down pat. Meanwhile, this was too good to miss.

But Amy and Marl were oblivious. "I don't know where we'd go," Marl was continuing. "Anywhere you want."

Her eyes were on his. The two of them might have been dancing on the moon, for all they knew where they were. Marl waited quietly for her answer. Amy opened her mouth to speak.

But the sounds that came next were not hers.

"Found you at last," another female voice said. Behind him, small and pert and pretty, in dress-up heels and a town-cut bouffant dress, stood Betsy Thomson.

With awful surmise Marl wheeled, spotted her, glanced back at Amy.

The men in the warehouse doorway stood openmouthed. After a second, Amy pushed past them in her quiet way, but not before Betsy had planted herself in front of Marl, reached up, pulled his face down, and kissed him full and hard on the mouth.

Then those men gaped. "Jesus, you see her kissin' ol' Marl?" they said later. "Just like nothin', right in front of everybody? Hot stuff! And that Marl Perry, boy, he's some cool customer, that Marl Perry."

*

Betsy was desperate.

At home in South Portland, her parents still seemed so surprised by her engagement to Marl that they didn't know how to act. Away from Marl, Betsy herself had never felt so isolated and insecure. She waited for her parents to object, for somebody to say something. But they didn't speak of Marl at all. Mrs. Thomson's hand trembled over the breakfast things, but she pressed her lips together and smiled. Mr. Thomson, who spent every odd hour practicing with the Portland Symphony Orchestra, shut himself into his music room with his violin and it sobbed. It agonized through one unbearable Beethoven quartet after another, all alone. But nobody said anything.

Betsy wrote letters to Marl, she planned to see him, she went downtown and spent more money than she could afford on summer clothes. As an afterthought she practiced her violin. One day while she was practicing, her mother slipped into her room to listen. "Betsy," she said after a while, "is there music up north, dear—the kind you're interested in? Will you be able to have musical gatherings in Monson?" She went and smoothed the bright hair off Betsy's forehead.

Betsy pulled away. "Mother, I'm old enough to choose for myself!"

Was she? She wrote to Marl and told him she needed to see him. She told him she thought her parents were upset over the engagement, and she asked if she could visit Octavia's Hill. When Marl didn't answer, she wrote to say that she loved him and that she was coming to make plans. "It will be easier for everyone," she wrote, "if we set a definite date for the wedding." As a postscript, she said she was coming right away.

The truth was, she didn't trust herself, didn't feel sure of Marl at this distance, and couldn't wait any longer.

"But, dear," Betsy's mother said in a gentle and truly apologetic way, smoothing her apron and ducking her head as if she prayed before she spoke, "don't you think I'd better write to his mother before you visit? Somehow it doesn't seem quite proper—"

"Proper!" Betsy exploded. "Mother, welcome to the twentieth century! I am twenty-two years old, and I plan to do as I please! And you and Dad will have to put up with the idea that now I intend to be a farmer's wife!"

Mrs. Thomson backed out of the room, hurt tears in her eyes, one hand only twisting back the wings of gray-black hair that never would stay pinned.

That same day Betsy put on one of her new summer dresses. "If I'm going to do this," she told herself, "I'd darn well better wear some becoming clothes." Then, with hardly a word to her parents, she hopped a bus to Bangor. A girl friend drove her from there to Monson. Once in Monson, Betsy had planned to call

Marl, except that she happened to see his truck outside the feed store. She had never kissed him in public in her life, except for that once on graduation day, but today when, angry and scared, she marched herself up those steps and saw him talking to that big, frumpish girl behind the counter, something snapped. Time she laid her claim, she thought. So she kissed him until he had to come up for air.

*

One person in town passed it to the next, and on it went. It made a juicy little tale in a summer of good stories, all courtesy of Marl Perry. For a week Betsy was seen with him wherever he went. She never sat, as country women did, on her side of the truck seat. No, she sat as close to him as she could, and she didn't seem to care who knew it either. Soon people were seeing Marl Perry and his honey blonde on every old abandoned road and lover's lane in the town, and where they didn't see them, of course, they thought they might have seen them, they weren't sure.

"Oh, Amy?" they said to each other. "Just a sidelight, one of Marl Perry's sidelights."

As for Marl, he knew one thing: he was embarrassed. The nice part about Betsy in college was that she hadn't been eager, as most girls had been, to have Marl notice her. The thing Marl had liked about Betsy was that she seemed to lead a life of her own: she was independent, she had her music, her own interests. Then if she made love to him it was an independent choice and therefore exciting. But now something had changed.

She'd given up her life, it seemed, and taken a firm grip on his.

"Don't you want to practice?" he would say to her when she insisted on riding to town with him in the truck. But she would get almost a hunted look in her eye and speak up sharply. "What are you, trying to get rid of me or something?"

"No, no," he would assure her, and she would go with him. Neither one of them was too happy.

On the first and second evenings of her visit it was she who sought him out, although he was dead tired from the first haying of the season. She sat close to him in the dark of the porch after Lucy had gone to bed, put his hand on her breast, and they made love with silent efficiency. Old habit, Marl thought.

Twice during the week she put on a pair of blue jeans and went out across the fields to find him, and once he let her drive the tractor behind his new mowing machine. But the next day she was badly sunburned and the sun made her lightheaded. After that, she was willing to stay on the shady front porch with Lucy.

Marl didn't know just what he was going to do. He didn't want to hurt the girl, and he had asked her to marry him. It was kind of hard to pull out now. But he was trying to avoid her and he knew it. He got up earlier in the morning, went off to do the chores before she was awake, came in for a breakfast that he carried out to the barn to eat with the cows, climbed on his tractor, and off he went. At the end of the day he bathed and sat in his chair and really felt too tired to talk. Soon after supper he fell asleep. Once or twice she tried to awaken him, but all he could do was mumble, "Life of a farmer, my dear, sorry,'.' and go back to sleep.

The worst of it was that his mother and Betsy seemed to recognize each other as allies right away. Betsy's parents lived in Portland, but occasionally went up to Boston for music and books, so Betsy was quite familiar with that city—the Charles, King's Chapel, the Old Corner Book Store—and had moved rather quickly into dead center of Lucy's regard.

Marl guessed his mother had decided that her son would have to get married sometime and could go farther and do worse. Here was a girl with refinement, not some clodhopper, slow-footed, country girl. The devil of it was, Marl thought, that as his mother's isolation in her classroom grew, she had become more and more attuned to what she called the "finer" things. When she heard that Betsy had given up studying in Boston to become engaged to Marlowe, it was just about all she could stand. You could almost hear her thinking: maybe this girl will convince Marlowe to go to law school after all; Harvard . . .

It was enough to make you sick. All Marl wanted to do was

[174]

avoid them both. But this, he knew, made his mother mad and Betsy madder. A young man falling asleep, right in front of his fiancée! And there that poor, gentle, beautiful child sat, for all the world like a little lost lamb! Lucy wouldn't stand for it!

Marl tried to lay low and wait it out.

*

Four days into the week, Marl finished his mowing and returned to noon dinner on that Thursday tired and sunweary but happy. He had hay chaff in his hair and under his belt and in the cuffs of his pants, but he hadn't given Betsy or his mother a thought for several hours, and all told, he was feeling pretty comfortable.

With some pride, he drove his new tractor back up the hayfield and parked it in the driveway by the barn. This tractor was one of the first John Deeres for miles around. Marl had bought it out of mortgage money and it ran like a dream, *put-put-put.* Not purring, he thought to himself, pleased enough to specify, but more like speaking. "I'm tough," that's what his new red tractor was saying to him. "Bring on the work, I can handle anything, I'm tough." Why, it made a man plan ahead, an engine like that. Marl was going to need some hired help around this farm pretty damn quick, he could see that. There was no limit to what you could do if you had the proper tools and this particular tractor! Yes, Marl was happy. Things on the farm were going well. He stopped at the kitchen door and shook what chaff he could out on the mat, then he went inside.

The kitchen was surprisingly dark and cool. Usually it blazed at noon—boiling potatoes, roasting meat or chicken—because, like every other farmer he knew, Marl liked his big meal in the middle of the day. But where was everybody? There wasn't a sign of cooking in the whole damned place, and he was hungry. He hoped the ladies hadn't forgotten to make his meal. He sniffed, smelled nothing at all, shrugged.

Leaning his head over the kitchen sink, he turned on the new faucet he'd lately installed. It still ran only cold water, but it was an improvement over the old pumphead. He bent down, let the cold well water flow over his head and neck, then grabbed a linen towel made for teacups, mopped his red face with it, and flung the towel marked with water and dirt over one bare, tanned shoulder. Again he looked around the kitchen.

"Hey!" he yelled. "What is this, the library? Where's my food?"

There was a rustling and his mother came to the door of the dining room. She was all dressed up and she had a bunch of daisies pinned to her dress.

"Hey, look at you!" Marl said jovially, but his heart sank. "Where's dinner? We got company?"

Lucy regarded her tall son. He was dripping water off his brown-red shoulders and around his hairline was a rim of sweat and chaff. "Marlowe Perry," she said sharply, "is that one of my best tea towels?"

Marl looked down at the rag over his shoulder. "This?" he said and held it out to her.

"Yes, it is!" she cried. "Oh, Marlowe!" She snatched it away. Then she looked at him again, obviously not too pleased with what she saw.

Suddenly Marl felt uncomfortable. In fact, he prickled all over. Chaff, he guessed. He ran a finger around his belt, but that didn't stop the itching. At last he turned his back to Lucy and opened his pants and lowered them enough to scrape at his waist. "Sorry, Mother," he said over his shoulder. "Do we have company?"

His mother answered him in the tight little voice that meant trouble. "We have had company," she said, "for almost a week." Her hair seemed straighter than ever, her mouth twisted more tightly than usual.

"Who?" said Marl, buckling his belt. "You don't mean Betsy, do you?"

"Put on a shirt!" his mother rapped out. "Come to the table! Today we will eat in the dining room! My good linen towel! Marlowe!"

Marl looked around. "That?" he said, nodding at the thing in her hand. But Lucy didn't offer to reply; she turned and walked stiff-backed into the dining room.

Well, he was hungry. He followed her.

On the table was no good meal that he could see, no steaming hot vegetables, no mashed or fried potatoes. On the table was what looked like a mess of salads, with olives on some of them, he saw—he'd never been one for olives. For Chrissake. He tried to smile. "This is pretty," he managed. "Where's the food?"

His mother frowned. She turned and left the room. While she was gone Betsy entered, dressed in a bright blue dress with bare shoulders and a bouffant skirt and a little jacket flung carelessly over one arm. She had daisies, too, pinned to her waist.

Marl gasped. "Good God," he said, "what is this?"

Betsy didn't say a word, her lips were trembling. His mother, reappearing, handed him a shirt.

He took it. "Just dinner," he protested mildly, nevertheless settling it onto his prickling, damp shoulders. Two to one, he was thinking. Outnumbered by females.

"This," Betsy said, "is lunch."

Marl felt beleaguered. "I know," he said. "But we usually eat in the kitchen, hot food." He sat down. The ladies sat. They made him nervous. He began to help himself and eat. After all, he thought, no telling how much of this green stuff you have to have in order to get an ordinary good meal.

He was uneasy. He drained his glass of lemonade and slopped in more and drank that, too. Then he looked up. Neither Betsy nor his mother had touched anything.

He thought he didn't like the way this was shaping up at all. Determined, he shoveled in.

"This," said Betsy, "is our engagement luncheon."

Marl choked on his lettuce.

"It's time," Lucy Perry chimed in, "for us to make some plans."

Coughing, Marl gulped from his glass. Betsy was now staring down at her plate. He could not have known that for her this was a make-or-break meal, that his future lay in how he would handle the following conversation. But that was just as well.

[177]

"Plans?" he managed.

"First of all," said his mother, "we must discuss the engagement ring. A proper engagement calls for a proper ring. Now, I have a plan—"

"Mother!" Marl gasped. "That is between Betsy and me!"

Lucy Perry fixed on him a quelling glance he remembered from childhood. "Do not interrupt me, Marlowe!"

Marl stared at Betsy. "You've put her up to this!" he said.

Betsy didn't say a word. The little jacket that had been over her arm was now clutched in her two hands and wrung again and again under the table. Marl saw it, set his glass down with a thump.

"Marlowe." His mother spoke sternly. "We all know that you have spent a good deal on the new tractor that you like so much and on the cows and on all the other things you needed for the barn and the farm. That's fine. The farm is now yours and you are to do with it as you please. However, I have a plan. You will remember that I, too, earn some money—"

"Oh, no," Marl groaned.

"—and over the years I have saved quite a bit—enough, Marlowe, to purchase quite a nice ring, an engagement ring for you and Elizabeth, which I should like you to have with my blessing. Perhaps we should travel to Bangor together to choose it, or we could go to Portland, or maybe even as far as Boston—"

That did it. Marl had heard enough. "Mother," he said slowly, "drop it."

But Lucy Perry continued. "It is astounding to me that you should allow this poor girl to go without a proper ring while you invest in—in inventions!"

"Drop it!" Marl cried. He looked from her to Betsy. "You two make quite a pair!"

"Marl, I want you to come to Portland!" Betsy spoke up suddenly. "Please! Come to Portland, Marl, we'll make some plans."

"I am not going to leave this farm, Betsy, not ever!" Angry and perplexed, Marl stared at her. "I've told you that before! Weren't you listening?"

Lucy Perry interrupted again. "Perhaps not during haying season," she said, "but—"

"No!" Marl roared. "Never! And as for your buying an engagement ring for me, Mother, you might just as well go down and try to swap for one with Cone Green!" It had slipped out, jumped from some pile of rubble in his mind, like a snake lurking, waiting all this time to reach out and bite. Marl's mother turned white and he was sorry immediately, but he was mad. "The day I let you run my love life for me will be a cold day in hell, Mother, and you will know it!"

Lucy gasped. Marl was shouting at her—that was all she heard, all she would let herself hear.

Betsy flamed: blond hair, blue eyes, blue dress, all hot and electric. "How could you!" she cried. "Why I have never—"

"And you!" Marl turned to her. "Plotting things up with my mother! When you couldn't get to me, you—"

"Get to you! Who could talk to you? Who could say anything to you? You've been out in the barn with the cows."

"Well, maybe it's because cows only need to be milked twice a day!"

Lucy Perry's jaw dropped, her mouth opened. There was a short silence in which Betsy blushed furiously. "Damn you, Marl Perry!" Tears began to run down her cheeks.

Even when he was angry, Marl was a sucker for tears. He began to relent a little. "Look, Betsy, I'm sorry, I don't want to hurt you. Look"—he lifted his hands toward her—"maybe—maybe we should think about this whole thing again."

The end was near, Betsy knew it. Her lips trembled. "What?"

Marl told the truth. "You and I will never work, I guess that's what I mean. You know it, don't you? You're fighting it so hard! I—I have this farm to run, Betsy, and you have your music. You'd never be able to live without it, and I can never leave here."

Hurt and with the feeling, suddenly, that she'd been stranded among the natives of some strange country, Betsy searched for her dignity and found some pitiful remnant of it in anger. "Marl Perry!" she cried. "Damn you! And after I gave you—after you

[179]

had everything from me! Oh, I—I hate you! You can go to hell!"
She dashed the tears from her cheeks, tore the ring he had given
her—his high school ring on a chain—off her neck, and threw
it at him. It bounced off Marl and fell into one of the salads; one
deviled egg eye, she saw, sprouted a pupil. It was the final indig-
nity. She ran out of the room.

By nightfall she'd left for South Portland. Two weeks later she
wrote to say she was glad she had gone. So was Marl.

After a few days of huffy silences Lucy Perry became resigned.

They didn't refer to the Cone Green ring business again, but
after a decent interval had passed, Lucy turned to Marl casually
one night and said, "Marlowe, what did that girl mean, 'after you
had everything from me'?"

Marl studied his *Agriculture Today* and moved uncomfortably in
his chair. "You mean Betsy?" he asked.

"Yes," said his mother. " 'After you had everything from me'
—that's what she said, Marlowe."

Marl shrugged and raised his magazine. "Damned if I know,"
he said. But behind the magazine, he couldn't help it, he had to
grin.

*

Marl had cause to grin. Three days after Betsy left town he went
back to the feed store, but it was Amy's day off. So he went out
to the Trowley farm to see her.

The Trowleys raised horses as well as cows, boarded them for
the summer people who lived along Moosehead Lake. Their
holdings were large and included a stable as well as a barn. Their
land was flat and crisscrossed with bridle paths of hard-packed
dirt that led to woods roads and from there to more woods roads.
Eventually Bill Trowley's land abutted the holdings of Great
Northern Paper, and if you crossed his lines, he always said, you
were on your own in the howlin' wilderness.

Along the northern border of their land was a distant relative
of that same Branch that ran across the foot of Octavia's Hill, fed
in part by the spring in which Marl had tried to take a bath that
time.

The Trowley farmhouse was a long building that stretched from up near the road almost down to the barn, a distance of a hundred feet or more. The front part of it was a Cape Cod cottage built early in the 1800s. Over the years, however, a funny jumble of sheds and back porches had been built onto it and then converted—continually, it seemed—to house the ever-enlarging Trowley family. At the time of Marl's visit there were four genera- tions of Trowleys living at the farmhouse. Amy had four older brothers. Two of the brothers were married and lived with their wives and children in various parts of the house, and the house- hold was just as Marl remembered it—noisy, squabbling, happy. The Trowleys always seemed to communicate best in trivial argu- ment.

"Good heavens, Marl!" Mary Trowley met him at the door, wiping her hands on her apron. She looked just the same, tall, florid, quick-moving. "You come right in. Haven't seen you in a dog's age, how you doin'?"

Marl grinned. "It's this damn farmin'," he said. "Can't get my head above the water! How about you?"

"Good, I'm good." They were both referring to their common loss, Sears, and they didn't need to mention his name to know it. Just being there, looking at each other, was enough.

"You want some dinner?" Mary asked automatically. "We're all done, but we can scare up somethin'—"

"No, no," said Marl. "Just ate, myself. But you know, I'm looking for Amy. She around?"

"Amy?" Mary Trowley was surprised and putting two and two together, he knew it. Well, let her, he thought. He was just as happy. Time they had some better connection than poor ol' Sears; they all missed Sears.

"Yes." He cleared his throat. "If she isn't busy. Like to ask her to go on a picnic or something."

"A picnic?"

Slowly Mary Trowley picked up a stack of plates from the dining room table. Marl nodded at Grandpa Trowley, who was falling asleep in a rocking chair at the far end of the room, and at various female Trowleys, whom he knew to be wives and aunts.

He grinned at all the food. "I guess every day is a little like Thanksgiving around here," he said.

"What?" Now Mary Trowley's eyes were bright, merry, and relieved. She'd decided, he could see, that everything was all right. " 'Cept you never heard so much argument and talk in your whole life, Marl," she said. "Amy is out back. She just about killed herself gettin' this dinner, so we sent her out while we cleaned up. She's mindin' the baby, that's where you'll find her. Go along now." He had her blessing, then.

Marl grinned and Mary headed for the kitchen. "You know where the back door is."

Marl did. He headed out through it toward the shed, which smelled of ripe dust and hot sun, and then down the back steps. There he could see Amy, at a distance. She was sitting under a big old maple in the back yard, beside somebody's baby carriage; it had a mosquito netting over it.

Amy sat in a white wooden lawn chair. On her knee was a pad of paper and in her lap he could see some pencils. She appeared to be writing or sketching. Marl stood by the shed to watch. Now and then, he saw, she would jiggle the carriage comfortably with her foot. It was very sunny and hot and very quiet. Bees buzzed somewhere, stopped. "Come on, boy," Marl said to himself. "Time to move."

Suddenly he did feel like a boy. He felt as if ol' Sears must be just around the corner somewhere. The grass was sweet and green and warm; he knew its feel, although he had on his boots. He knew the feel of the day, too, hot and bleary and still, and somehow as if every movement of his had been foreordained.

Amy continued to sketch; she didn't hear him coming. But this wasn't childhood sober Amy, never allowed into the big boys' business. This was Amy the girl who had cut an outline into him that, he knew now, no one else could ever fit. He got very close to her before she looked up. He could see her sketch, some flowers in a border; they looked real to him.

If she was surprised to see him there, he couldn't tell it. One hand fell away from her work, and she did shade her eyes with the other, although there wasn't any need, she was sitting in the shade.

"Amy?" he said. "Do you remember me?" The question was absurd, appropriate.

She looked at him. "Yes," she said at last, carefully. There was a smudge of ink on her chin—he couldn't keep his eyes off it.

"I wonder," he said. "I'm finishin' up my hayin' this afternoon, not much left to do. Be done by five, maybe. Then chores. But I was thinkin', after, we could go to the pond for a swim, get a hamburger there. If you'd like to."

She kept her shading hand up. "You want me to?"

"Yes," said Marl.

"I'm not ol' Sears, you know." She dropped the hand.

"Don't want ol' Sears," said Marl somewhat gruffly. He thought he knew what was coming next; he felt he deserved it.

"And I thought you had a girl," she said.

"Did have," said Marl. He tilted his head to one side. "Don't anymore."

"Not anymore?" She looked right at him.

"No." Would she believe him? He couldn't tell.

"What time did you want to go?" she said carefully.

Marl stared off into the distance. "Around six, eat afterward? Can you?"

"I might." But she meant yes, yes, she did!

"Okay! I'll be here at six then!"

"You haven't got a girl?"

"No." He looked her in the eye.

She nodded. "All right then."

"Six?"

"Yes."

Marl turned and left quick, before she could change her mind.

Why, it was better and more than he'd expected! Waving at Mary, who now sat out on the Trowleys' front porch, he loped to his truck and started it up so fast the engine hollered. He tore the ten miles to the hill, up it, and into his own driveway, and fairly sprinted to his tractor. Before three he was done his work, having thrown in the last of the haybales as if they were marshmallows. The cows' jaws dropped when they heard his "Hey, Boss, ho, Boss" before four o'clock that afternoon, almost an hour early. But they turned toward him obediently, patiently.

Never did five cows give down milk so fast as that afternoon. They were back into the pasture before five, thoroughly cleaned, milked, and surprised. At five-thirty Marl was taking a bath out in the shed in cold water, too impatient to wait for the kettles to heat. A bath was clearly a waste before swimming, but he took one anyway. Lucy, who had just begun to think about supper at five-thirty, was startled by the six-foot whirlwind that passed her: it reeked of Old Spice, and it called out, "Don't wait up, Mother! I'm going for a swim at the pond, and I'll eat there," on its way to the truck.

"A swim?" Lucy's hands immediately wound into little knots. Her vigilant bird's eyes followed him as he ran. "With all that aftershave lotion on?"

When the whirlwind didn't answer, she ran to the door and called after it, "Marlowe, do you have a girl?"

The truck had already started and turned in the driveway, but Marl stopped long enough to wind down his window.

"Are you taking a girl?" his mother was calling in a little, high, fearful voice. "Do you have a girl?"

"You bet I do!" Marl called back, and he grinned the grin even his mother couldn't resist. "And she's a doozy! Amy Trowley, you remember? Ol' Sears's sister? You know her?" Then he waved and started off in the teeth of Lucy's answer, which was a helpless, dismayed wail that came as if she'd practiced it for years: "Oh, Marlowe, no!"

*

It was ten miles to the Trowleys', over rough back roads, but Marl got there with five minutes to spare; easy street, he thought. Shadows were longer now across the porch, and the hot afternoon had cooled somewhat. He stood by the door and knocked, and from the screened windows he could hear the sounds of noisy conversation: it sounded like about twenty people were talking at once. And that—when he'd met Mary Trowley's clear-eyed, unavoidably honest look and she'd smiled him in—was what, he saw, was happening. Amy was nowhere in sight, but all the other Trowleys—and there must have been at least twenty of them—were seated around the supper table, on which were the remnants of a cold roast, a huge bowl of potato salad, and a platter of corn chewed clean to the cob. All twenty were talking at once.

Bill Trowley, just as heavy as ever, sat in his undershirt at the head of the table. On his face were the remains of a few corn kernels, not bothering him or anybody else, it seemed. He was turned toward his oldest son.

"I'm tellin' you, that just ain't so!" he was saying. "It ain't possible to—" Then he caught sight of Marl.

"Well, Marl Perry!" he yelled. "Come on in! You still like us, do you? You come for some farmin' advice, right? Come to see the expert?" He meant himself. "Set yourself down! Now, Tom here's sayin' they gonna tar a section of the Dunlap road this fall, and I tell him that's a needless expense and we hadn't ought to let 'em do it."

"All's I'm sayin' is," said Tom Trowley, his father's son, short and heavy and loud, "we're gonna have cars and trucks, we gotta have tarred roads. Why, it's a foregone conclusion—"

"Bullshit!" cried Bill Trowley. "You can't—"

"Father!" His wife, Mary, intervened. "Such talk! You take it right out to the barn! And for heaven's sake, will you use your napkin!"

"The barn?" cried Bill Trowley, backing his chair up with a squeak, in a shower of corn pieces. "All right, I will! Bring me my pie, wife, and out I'll go!"

There was a cackle from the corner, where old Grandpa Trowley, now long past eighty, had waked up from a doze. "Damn right!" Grandpa cried, pounding the arm of his rocking chair. "These women! I wouldn't give you two shits for any of 'em!"

"Oh, no," said Mary, sighing. "Now look who you've got going."

"All the children out!" roared Bill Trowley good-naturedly. "Your grandmother says your innocent little ears can't stand this! Take the babies out, for Chrissake! Get them out, out!"

"Father," remonstrated one of the daughters-in-law. Another rolled her eyes ceilingward and began to laugh. The children were all giggling.

Old Grandpa Trowley, in the corner, was busy swearing a blue streak counterpoint. "It wouldn't get past this whole fuckin' crew!" he was yelling—if that trembly sound could be called a yell. "Spend all day takin' care of this shittin' farm, nobody in this goddamn world give a cowshit whether you live to—"

"Bill. Do something," said his wife.

"Good God, Father!" roared Bill Trowley into the old man's ear. "Go back to sleep, will you?"

"Great," said Mary. "That really helps a lot, Bill."

Simultaneously, various mothers and fathers were having discussions with various children about why they had to have their dessert on the porch, and who cared whether old Grandpa swore or not, and what did they mean they had to go to bed early. Meanwhile Grandpa kept up his crackling in the corner. "Goddamn . . ."

Bill Trowley turned to Marl. "Marlowe Perry," he roared over the other noise in the room, "has come to me on business! I will have to take him out to the porch to talk, thanks to all of you." He motioned to Marl. "Come on, young feller, let's we go out on the porch and have some pie. Little peace and quiet."

But his announcement only brought more groans and rearrangements from children and the parents of children who had been ready to migrate to the porch. In the corner, Grandpa had subsided to a kind of quiet undercurrent of sound: "Put my fuckin' elbow out of joint," he was saying to no one in particular. "That was in forty-one. Nobody in this goddamn fuck-or-shit household give a damn—"

But just then old Grandma Trowley came in from the kitchen.

She looked, if possible, more feeble than her husband. "Herbert," she said firmly, "you must stop that this instant."

Her voice was so light, it barely registered among all the other noises, but somehow Grandpa Trowley heard her.

"Oh, for heaven's sake," he said. "Didn't know you was in the room, Harriet. Why, I should never have spoken so." And that old man might have been two people, one a farmworker with a blistering tongue and the other a gentleman of the drawing room, for he took the hand of his little old wife and planted a kiss on her bare, dishwater-damp knuckles.

"There, Herbert," she said gently. "There, it's quite all right."

"Marlowe Perry!" Bill Trowley was still roaring. "Come out to the barn, for God's sake."

Mary Trowley spoke up again. "Marl is not here to talk to you, Father." To add to the confusion, she sometimes called her husband that. "Marl is here for Amy!"

Although there was plenty of noise, Bill Trowley heard his wife perfectly well. "What?" he roared.

"Amy!" his wife said more distinctly. "They're goin' for a swim!"

"A what?"

"He and Amy are going for a swim!"

"Marlowe Perry and our Amy?" Again Bill Trowley had heard perfectly, but he loved a good tease and was quick to scent one. This was his way of announcing that Marl and Amy were an "item": "What the hell for?"

"Bill." Mary sighed, shrugging in Marl's direction. "Don't be difficult."

"I'll tell you what, Mary," said her husband, a twinkle in his eye. "You go up, tell Amy Marl's come out to the barn with me. Hell, they don't need to go swimmin'! It's been some time since I seen ol' Marl . . ."

Marl had by this time begun to be truly alarmed. But Mary Trowley, it seemed, was not. Her husband's shenanigans were merely making her cross. "Father!" she cried. "Please, just this once!"

At that moment, however, Amy appeared at the door. She had on a cotton dress, and in her hand was a bag of swimming gear. The room was so noisy that it made her squint a little as she looked for Marl, spotted him, went to stand at his side. Mary Trowley was still busy scolding her husband. Under cover of these goings-on, Amy looked at Marl, nodded toward the door, and they quietly headed in that direction. They were almost outside when Bill Trowley yelled after them, "You have her in by ten-thirty, young feller!"

"I will!" Marl called back, but Amy detained him.

"I'm over twenty-one, Dad," she said, and stepped out with Marl, letting the screen door slam behind them.

"Twenty-one?" Bill Trowley roared. By now he'd sat back down in the dining room and was enjoying himself hugely. "Mother, she ain't no twenty-one, is she? You ain't twenty-one, Amy Trowley!" he hollered. "Not by a long shot, girlie! Why, just yesterday I was still changin' your—"

"You never," said Mary Trowley succinctly.

But by this time Marl had started the motor to his truck and he and Amy were off.

On the way to the pond Amy kept quiet and kept to her side of the seat, although Marl wished she wouldn't.

Deer Pond was not a tourist spot. There were bigger and better beaches up and down Moosehead. But it was a pleasant little place where the local kids went to cool off, get a hamburger. On the beach there were two changing houses and a small hamburger take-out made of logs. To one side was a forest that marched right down to the water's edge, but the pond itself was all sand on the bottom, a pure white that fell away from the trees gradually in a deep, consistent slope stretching far out into the water. Across the shining expanse of it, the sun was an hour and a half from setting.

"Your family doesn't like to argue much." Marl grinned as they got out of the truck and walked toward the bathhouses. "I remember that now."

Amy shrugged. "I hardly hear them anymore. You get used to it."

"I don't know, but it looked like kind of fun to me," said Marl. She nodded. They separated to change.

Marl put on his bathing suit like lightning and was standing among the trees waiting for Amy when she came out of the bathhouse. She had thrown a towel over one shoulder and looked at him a bit defiantly, he thought, her face tinged with the faintest blush. Her legs were strong, her hips wide.

He held out his hand. "Carry your towel, lady?" He smiled the old, irresistible smile. She hesitated, then shrugged off the towel and handed it to him.

Suddenly he wanted to bury his lips in the firm white where her neck met her shoulder. "You're something," he said.

She looked up at him quickly, as if expecting a joke of some sort, then smiled a little. "Hard to get mad at that," she murmured, almost to herself. Then, turning, she led Marl, slowly and deliberately, down to the water.

Tave

*I*T WASN'T THAT the cellar had been comfortable, it hadn't. It was dusty, damp, and chilly. A hot plate for cooking was not the Ritz, but as long as you had light and heat and water, you could manage. You could get by for a few dozen hours without your family. If you could keep yourself busy you could get by. You could read, listen to the radio, paint. With electricity.

Without it Tave was not so sure. The cellar was very dark. Even if you sat for quite a few minutes, waiting for your eyes to get used to it, you couldn't manage. The windows were blocked off, and she herself had filled the cracks around the door with clay; there was, simply, no light anywhere.

For a few minutes she waited bravely, the darkened flashlight found and in her hand, thinking that the lights might flicker on again, as they sometimes did in a winter storm. Then she remembered the generator and knew that if something had gone wrong with it, she would be without power, now, for the duration. It was enough to make her panic a little. She huddled into a smaller unit on her mattress, finding the button on the flashlight. There was something insidious about total darkness, she thought a bit crazily. It not only surrounded you, it entered your mind. It made winding avenues of black smoke in your brain cells and a black thickness at the edge of every thought. Tave switched the flashlight on.

Only a tiny ring of light, maybe, but light. It gave the black box of the furnace a strange width, a kind of presence it hadn't had before. To one side was the water heater, still warm. Tave stood up and touched it to assure herself that things felt familiar, that they really stayed the same in the dark. Still, she had the feeling that with her sudden loss of power something had changed in the cellar, she wasn't sure what.

After a moment, she stepped up to the workbench and switched on Bob's lantern, discovering with relief that the little bulb gave off a surprising amount of illumination, lighting up most of the area between the stairs, the furnace, and the sink. Beyond, however, the dark looked as soft and complete as a wall colored in with charcoal on a sketch. Walking beyond the sink might be like walking into a wall of soot—you might smother.

By the sharp glare of the lantern she went over her supplies. No more batteries for her hand flashlight, two little batteries for the radio; not new—they'd taken the radio outside a number of times in the early spring, to listen to it while they did chores. The lantern was burning strongly at the moment, but once its battery was gone, there was no replacement. There were the three candles and a box of matches. Once the water tank cooled down, the cellar would be cold, and there was no way to cook.

With shaking hands, Tave fit the batteries into the radio. Suddenly she was desperate for a human voice. But the batteries were not much good. Even with the volume turned way up, she could barely hear Ray Gray.

". . . *in one half hour we shall have an address from the President of the United States . . .*"

Reluctantly Tave shut the radio off. She would wait and listen in half an hour, to hear what the President had to say. Without the radio, however, it was very quiet.

She went to the percolator. The coffee in it was still warm but she had no way of keeping it warm, so she poured the last of it into her cup. Then she sat at the workbench and drank it slowly, just on the edge of panic, trying to get herself organized.

As long as the batteries lasted, she decided, she would listen every hour on the hour, beginning in a half hour, with the President's speech. The lantern, which had no replacement battery, she might use only when the flashlight wouldn't do. But she would have to have some light, she knew, for as long as she could.

Without the radio, the cellar seemed so silent you could hear things and not know whether they were real or not. Tave thought she heard a faint sound, like spiders climbing the walls, maybe; there was a whispering, just at the edge of hearing, and now and then a soft crushing noise, like a beam settling or a small animal eating. Otherwise nothing.

You expected footsteps. Without the radio, Tave realized, she was listening for footsteps, maybe because she had never been down cellar when there weren't feet moving across the floors overhead: the clomp of her father's boots, the steady, thick noise of her mother's sensible shoes, the unexpectedly heavy sound of Lucy Perry in her slippers. More recently, it had been Bob's crepe-soled walk, the lighter noises of Tavia and Billy. In fact, Tave thought, she'd probably never come down into the cellar in recent memory without having an emergency call for her presence somewhere upstairs, someone falling with a crash, or yelling "Mom-mee!"

Once she'd come down only for a minute—she'd had to get up her courage to do it—and upstairs Tavia had broken a glass and the toaster had caught fire and Billy had sat down and bawled at the head of the stairs.

Tave had rushed back upstairs on that particular day, settled Billy under one arm, disconnected the toaster, and thrown baking soda on it and on the wall in back of it. Then she'd swept up toast glowing like coals and the broken glass and thrown it and the toaster out. Finally she'd dried Tavia's tears and handed them each a cookie and sat at the kitchen table utterly dejected, thinking, Good Lord, I can't even go down to the cellar—I can't even do that, can I?

But now that she was down here, all she could do was listen for calamities upstairs—it figured. The truth was that at this moment she would give her eyeteeth to hear just one normally calamitous sound.

Suddenly a normal day was what Tave wanted more than anything. She'd even take that most terrible of times, a morning getting the children ready for school.

Into Tavia's room. "Get up, punkin, time to wake up." Tavia would squint at her mother through a tangle of dark hair, groan, and go back to sleep.

"Come on, now!" With fake cheer Tave would pull up the window shades. Shelves of stuffed animals, shelves of books.

"Oh, Ma, not yet." Tavia would settle farther down into her pillow.

If there was anything Tave hated, it was being called "Ma." She would pause by the bed, equal parts affection and exasperation. "Get up, you!" she would say. "I mean it, now! Don't let me tell you again!" And she would leave Tavia muttering disgustedly into her pillow.

Billy's room. Batman curtains and a Superman bedspread. Tobor, the mechanical robot, lived in one corner. In another was a wobbly worktable with two tree-stabbed kites on it. "Billy? Wake up, Bill."

No movement, of course. When Billy was out, he was out. Tave would have to go to the bed and wiggle one of Superman's feet. "Get up now, Bill!"

But Billy was like his dad, one minute dead to the world, the next wide awake and totally alert. He had Bob's curly blond hair and freckles and he would sit up and grin at her suddenly with his father's smile.

"Cartoons today?" He never said good morning.

"School today."

"Oh, no." He would dive back down under the covers.

Tave would tap her foot. "Billy, come on now."

"Well, I want oatmeal." Muffled in quilts, he could drive quite a hard bargain.

Tave would sigh. "Okay."

"And toast, and juice."

"Okay."

"And celery with peanut butter."

[196]

Or bacon with peanut butter. Or bananas with peanut butter. Tave's stomach would do its customary early morning roll. "You get that yourself," she would say, as usual. "I only make the oatmeal."

From there it was all uphill: breakfast, toast crumbs, slopped milk. Tavia crying the length of the house, "Mother, I don't have any jeans! You forgot to wash my jeans!" Bob peering suspiciously into his lunchbag: "You didn't put bologna in here again, did you? All those nitrites, Tave!" Billy: "Mom, you seen my Batman ring? I got to have it for school!"

It was awful. Even a stay in the cellar couldn't make it look good. Still, she'd almost like to tackle it again—she'd be able to, wouldn't she? She would have to think so.

Tave shut off the big lantern and simultaneously, convulsively, turned on her flashlight. No, she wasn't going to be without light, not for as long as she could, at any rate. If the emergency did last longer than her light sources, well, she would just have to deal with it then. Scared all the time, or scared all at once. Tave chose the latter; if she got lucky it might never happen.

But the trouble with a flashlight was, it would only light one area at a time. If you shone it in front of you, everything at your back and sides was dark. Tave decided to take another look around. For no reason. Exercise. Perhaps to reassure herself, as you reassured a child, that light on or light off, things stayed the same.

She began to move toward the far end of the cellar, flashlight playing along the walls and shelves. Once at the far side, she shone her light along the pile of junk under the bulkheading, forcing herself to stand still and feel the dark—she supposed that was what it was—creeping around her. She didn't like this cellar business.

But after all, none of the junk down here had moved.

No, the only movement was her own flashlight, in her own shaking hand. After a minute she gave a small, tired laugh that sounded more like a sob—she hadn't slept well, she was tired—and turned around. But she forced herself to examine the walls and floors of all the cubicles on the way back to the furnace. She even forced herself to look for holes where mice or rats might come in. She found none; that didn't surprise her. Bob had been proud of his work in the cellar, and it was tight, no sign of small animals anywhere.

"Very well," Tave told herself. "Now, if I can just believe my own eyes and not worry about what I didn't see . . ." By now her shirt was damp with sweat, for no good reason.

On her way back to the furnace area she stumbled over her easel—which she'd set up under the lightbulb in the passageway and forgotten—and knocked it flat, bruising one hip in the process. In the too-silent cellar, however, the noise sounded like a minor explosion, and even though Tave knew immediately what she'd done, she jumped a little and gave a half shriek. The hand that gripped the flashlight felt suddenly cold, slippery.

She knelt on the floor and felt along the wooden frame of the easel to see if it was broken. But suddenly she was at the end of her rope, shaking all over. She bit her lips and tried to cry but was unable to. Crying might have helped, but she'd forgotten how. Too damn scared, she guessed. Or maybe you forgot how to cry. And if you did, why, who the hell was the loser? Handkerchief manufacturers, she guessed. Scott paper. Big deal, hell with them.

"You shouldn't swear," said Lucy Perry.

"I'm over thirty!"

"It is a shocking habit."

"I've got a million of 'em. You should hear—"

That little air, that twist of the chin upward—oh, yes, Tave could see it. As if Lucy were alive.

Tave's lips moved down with the strain of no tears. "Leave me alone, old woman," she whispered.

But Lucy Perry, sitting behind the kitchen stove, didn't answer. Her presence was like a judgment.

Eyes shut, Tave fought the image of Lucy she saw. Flashlight still clutched in one hand, the other wrapped around her ribs, she began to move back and forth on her knees, fighting and rocking. It was like putting anguish to a tune, pounding out pain. Lucy

Perry, she thought, did you ever have a happy moment?

The old woman didn't reply, but of course Tave knew she had. Lucy Perry had had a son who loved her and who had tried to make her comfortable. She'd had Amy to see to everything she needed. And, Tave thought, she had me.

"Hymph," said Lucy: an unimpressed little sniff.

Rocking, Tave ached all over. You get bruises so deep they don't show, she thought. You get hurt so bad that . . .

"I'm sorry," she whispered to the dark, to the hill, her family. "I'm sorry."

She was, deeply. Suddenly she felt she'd never done anything, not one thing, for the future; certainly nothing to help her avoid this day.

"What am I doing here?" she wanted to ask. "Is this what I was made for?"

It was as if the hill were muttering at her constantly: "Remember your father, your mother, grandmother; remember them all, remember me."

"Why?" Tave wanted to cry out. "Oh, I remember, but why? Keep me from remembering!"

Was the hill trying to tell her something it thought she needed? Some vital message that, like the Octavias before her, she'd missed?

Either that, of course, or the hill was just tormenting her. Or the world was. Or maybe God himself turned inside out and became infernal. To prove how small she was, and how piti-ful—

"No!" Tave said.

She said it aloud, and the sound scared her. Shivering violently, she stood up and moved on aching legs back to the furnace area, taking her easel with her and leaning it against the chimney. You couldn't paint in the dark—one of the little ironies of the hill, she supposed.

Now she stood at Bob's workbench, staring at it. It was so sturdy, well planned and solid. On it stood *Ghost of the North*, turned to the wall.

"No!" Tave cried again. She was angry now, not only at the

hill, the family, her dilemma. She was furious with her husband. It was, as usual, a kind of accumulated anger.

There were two realities in Tave's world, or had been. One she called "normal" life, in which you loved your family and your husband as a matter of course, and you did your best to take care of them. For the other reality, however, she had no name. This nameless part she did not explore, and she knew it. In fact, she tried to live away from it as much as possible.

But the further she went to separate herself—cooking, caring, chauffering children, giving back rubs at midnight—the more she acted "normal," the closer a kind of inner blackness came. She would work furiously, even paint furiously, to ignore its approach, but it crept toward her like a stealthy beast, its white face shining out of the dark at the last possible moment, its hands reaching toward her.

And then she would be so scared, so angry, that all she wanted to do was destroy.

Destroy anything. Of course, she didn't. But Bob was her scapegoat. Now she touched the workbench, polished it a little with one finger. A part of her admired this bench. Another part wondered: how could he endure their daily life better than she did? What did he have that she didn't? How could he work down here in the cellar, sometimes for hours, not afraid of a thing? She could hear him down here, the saw, the sander. A little whistle through the front of his teeth.

Standing in this small ring of light, Tave thought of Bob's whistle now and knew she wanted to hear it again. She wanted Bob to stand there and grin at her. She wanted . . . what? His protection? His strength?

She hated herself for having no strength of her own.

She pictured Bob as she had seen him a few nights before, hustling around the bathroom, getting ready for bed. He was not much taller than she, made square and stocky, freckles across his shoulders, waist thickening a little, small square bottom. That night, as on many other nights, when she saw him naked she knew in her fingertips what his skin would feel like, and her hands were homesick for the touch of him. He'd turned to face her, seen her stare, reddened a little, grinned so that he reminded her of Billy. Without a word she had reached out for him.

Not only her hands, but her whole body felt homesick for him. She loved the way he was put together. In a moment they had embraced, holding each other tight, to lock out for a little time at least all the loneliness in the world. Bodies knew to whom they belonged, what love they needed: that night they'd made love simply, their hands soothing, delicate. Bob had lain exposed, waiting, and Tave's fingers had been a cool answer to his heat, making him groan. His hands on her hips, lifting her to him, were warm; they were just what she needed. She'd gasped and wanted to weep.

Yes, Tave thought now, abruptly, staring at the workbench. As long as they were naked they were fine. With their clothes on, however, it was much more complicated.

Her finger on the workbench turned into a fist. She pounded once, pulled a stool forward, sat in the light. Around her it was so very black. For an instant, she decided, she would turn the lantern on. Just to make sure, yes. There. Shelves, mattress, furnace, easel, workbench, and a bit farther away, the sink: this would be her area. She would be all right. Not like Bob, of course. No whistling. But she would manage.

She guessed that was what made her maddest in their marriage —Bob whistled and she barely managed. It was as if she kept falling out of step and he marched along holding her up, waiting for her to catch the stride. Tave had whole days when from morning to night nothing went as it was supposed to. The children fought, there were no more parking spaces at the grocery store, Monson's one traffic light turned red when it saw her coming. Her car broke down, her painting was so bad that there seemed to be no point in going on with it, and then Bob would come home whistling.

"Have a good day?" he would ask cheerily.

A question like that left Tave with two alternatives: slug him or run. If she said no, there he would be toting his load and hers again. It was more than her pride could stand. If she said yes, it would be a lie. Sometimes Tave decided that the lie was worth it.

"I had an all-right day," she would say, and kiss him. But she could tell he didn't know whether to believe her or not.

"Are you sure?" he would say gently, looking at her carefully.

"Of course." She would try to shrug him off while inside, black fury gathered.

"Come put your feet up for a minute," he would say. "Tell me all about it."

And then she would blow her stack. "Why don't you just leave me alone!" she would cry. "I'm fine, damnit! You always expect the worst, you always think something's going to be wrong. Nothing's wrong! Nothing!" As her voice rose, the children melted around corners, taking their troubled, resigned faces with them.

"Good God, Tave, I just asked!" He would set down his papers and books with a thump. "Why are you always so damned defensive?"

"Well, it's hard," Tave would cry, "to live with someone who's so perfect all he's got to do is go around helping his fellow man—"

"Don't do this!" It would be as close to a shout as Bob ever came. There would be a dark furrow between his eyebrows, and his face would be bright red beneath freckles. The hurt brown eyes would suddenly get a dull look, like two cold round pebbles off the road. "I hate it! Why can't you just answer me honestly? If you had a bad day, say so. I don't care."

"That's just it!" Tave would yell. "You don't care! You don't know how it feels—"

"You're not me! You don't know what I feel! Don't make judgments about me—"

"You do it to me!" Now the fight would be in full force. Tave would feel herself courting it, pushing it. No matter what it was about, or how ridiculous or small the issue was, all that was important was the fight. If you could fight, you could win, you might be winning, for a change, over the black and all its accumulations; you might win over your life, prove it was worth something. "It's not too much, is it, to ask for the same privilege?" Words didn't matter; you said anything. You wanted to wash it all away, you wanted to win.

"Tave, damnit—"

"No! I have you there, mister! You know I do!"

Bob didn't seem to need to win, or even to fight as Tave would have liked to. Too soon he would shake his head, his face now pale, one freckled hand reaching up to rub his eyes. "Tave, I don't even know what this is about." Shoulders slumped, he would head upstairs to change.

Tave would send her voice after him, to stop him. "And you don't care!" she would cry—it was like a cry. But it would be too late. The argument would join the rest of Tave's day, and she had lost again.

Bob's turned back frightened her. She needed him and was afraid she would lose him. When he stayed late at work she was afraid—of what? That she had driven him away at last and for good, this another part of the cosmic joke, that she could never hang on to the people she needed? Would he go away, leave her? At those times it didn't matter that she knew he had a teacher's meeting, or a strategy session for the coaches. It seemed to her he had gone, been swallowed up forever.

He would come home tired, and she would be so relieved all she could do was cry at him, "Where have you been, what took you so long?" And finally, of course, if the fight got that far: "You don't love me!"

And then it didn't matter what he said.

"Tave, you must know by now . . ."

The truth was—and now Tave thought this out for the first time, in the harsh light of the lantern—she didn't really believe in love. That is, it was nice, but you couldn't count on it. People changed their minds, they went away, gave up, went crazy, died. You couldn't believe, not if your eyes were open, if the blinders were really off.

Perhaps Bob was like her, inside. Maybe he didn't really know

[203]

what he thought. And what he said today might not be true tomorrow.

"It's the hill you love!" she would cry at him, knowing there was enough truth in this to hurt him. "A family place, plenty of work to do, a place to live—"

"Goddamnit, Tave," he would say softly and rapidly, "why don't you ever give yourself a break?" And then once again turn his back and go.

She would slam pots and pans around in the kitchen late at night—no other reason for her to be there—and then go up to bed. Sometimes they would sleep far apart on the bed. Some nights they would turn to face each other at the same time. He would look at her—she could see his face in the hall light they kept burning every night—he would touch her. She would cry then, sob, and hold on to him like a lost child.

She missed him now! She wanted him to be here, to fight with, and make love to, make this cellar nightmare go away.

She should shut the lantern off, she knew it. She needed it now, however; she would leave it on. Chin on hands, she leaned against the workbench: it had long been a point of contention between her and Bob. One of his passions was for woodworking and tinkering. Soon after they were married he had cleaned up the cellar and put in the cement floor, doing the lighting himself. Tave had hated those times. It was like a physical pain to watch him disappear down those stairs. Crashing noises from the cellar, pushing things—he would trudge up and down with a cheerful look on his face. But when he was downstairs, how did Tave know who it was, moving, pounding, changing things?

As for Bob, she supposed he didn't even suspect her feelings or the depth of her fright, and she could never bring herself to tell him enough so he would understand. His reasoning was that when he had finished, the cellar would be a different place. But Tave knew that no amount of change would relieve her of the burden she carried: the real cellar that never died. Knowing this, she suffered in silence the change she suspected had taken place in Bob; that is, he became to her in some ways like the beast in her imagination. Who else could set up shop in that place?

Up and down the cellar stairs. He had chosen this warm corner by the furnace and built in this worktable and bench, and put up a pegboard to hang his matched screwdrivers on.

"Tave, come down and see," he'd urged her several times. "You won't know the place, it's all different." A pleading in his eyes that turned them dark, almost a liquid brown. They were eager-puppy eyes.

Tave couldn't trust him. She would not be lured into a position of trust, not ever again; it simply wasn't safe. Besides, what man could emerge from the cellar unscathed?

"Come down," he would beg.

"No, thank you," she would say in a miffed, polite little voice.

At last, however, a trip down the stairs to see the new workbench became obligatory, even an issue in their marriage. Bob was so sure he'd fixed the place for good, so proud of what he'd done. Tave felt dread, and below that a kind of sneaking curiosity, a tiny hope. She, too, would have liked to see the cellar made into some different kind of place, where nightmares never happened.

Bob put on all the lights, took her arm, and led her down. He was grinning. "There," he said. "Now then. Isn't that better?"

Finely organized, superbly clean, each shelf and cubicle was just so. Perhaps this wasn't the cellar, after all? She managed a smile. "You've done a lot," she said.

"Router over there, see," he explained, leading her to the workbench. "And all sizes of bits for the drills, the sander . . ." He showed her his wrenches, lined up by sizes, one to a peg on the wall. He pointed out his files, his sanding gear, the special shelf at a distance from the furnace for all his paint and wood finishes. "Look, Tave, look." He was like a kid at Christmas.

Tave fought to respond again, but she couldn't. This light, clean place couldn't fool her for long. It was an overlay, a disguise. Wasn't he afraid? She fought to ask, but she was unable to move or speak. The old cellar crept about her ankles, and she hated herself and refused to give in to what he would surely think was a weakness of imagination.

Bob didn't understand her silence. He got more desperate

each time she refused to speak. At last he seemed to decide that the fault lay in his exposition, so he went over it all again: the router, the drill and bits, the wrenches.

But it was all too far-fetched for Tave. She looked into his eyes and saw the wide pupils, like two circles of black, reaching for her. From somewhere came words that cut like knives; she used them to save herself: "If you wish to spend your time down here, you may," she said. "As for me, I have better things to do."

But he wasn't fooled anymore. His lips tightened. "You're still scared, right?"

"I am not scared! I just don't like it, that's all!"

"Well," he said, "you will. Just stick with me, ma'am."

Repelled and fascinated, she stood still while he came to her and took her in his arms. She sagged against him, almost succeeding in losing herself in him once again.

They'd been married for years now, and still, where the cellar was concerned, Bob played John Wayne to her frightened ingenue. He enjoyed the role, and she let him. But little doubts she still carried with her: his strength consoled her, frightened her, and made her jealous of what he had.

Sometimes these days she caught him watching her, a peculiar waiting look in his eyes. Waiting for their pain to be over, she thought. Waiting for the good times to begin. His weight of hope in her, she felt, was utterly misplaced. Once she spoke to him about it.

"Bob, why do you look at me like that?" Her sharp voice troubled him, she could see. She tempered it as well as she could. "You look like you're—I don't know—expecting something from me."

"That's just your imagination," he began, then flushed. "No. That's not true. There, now I'm doing it, too."

"Doing what?"

But suddenly, somehow, it had turned into a rare quiet time between them. The children were in bed, the room was lit with one lamp. She went to sit on a hassock beside his chair.

He picked up one of her hands, playing a little with the fingertips as he spoke. "When I was a kid and lived with my aunt and uncle, I went for a long time thinking there was no point in anything. My own parents didn't want me, didn't love me enough to—" Bob had spoken of this only a few times. When he was a child his parents had divorced and remarried, each into a new family. They'd fought over him, but not in the usual way: neither parent had wanted him. He'd been shunted from relative to relative, ending up at last with his aunt and uncle, who were kind to him. "Anyway," he continued, "I thought, what was the point? I was one unhappy kid. But after a long time—I don't know how or when—things got better. I thought, you know, good does exist. It's hard to tell you." Tave watched him struggle for the words. She sat very still.

"I don't know how I know about it," he said, running one hand through tight blond curls. "But I know there is something good for us, if we can only—"

"You think so?" Now their hands were clasped tightly together. "If we knew, for sure."

He'd grinned a lopsided grin. "I *do* know it, Tave!" He spoke in a voice that apologized for itself.

On a night like that, Tave thought, you could almost believe him. But people were fragile, they broke.

At the edges of her eyes, the lantern light swam into a million lines of red and blue and yellow and she knew she was again on the verge of tears. Automatically she quelled them and looked about her. She'd forgotten Ray Gray, she suddenly realized, and switched the radio on.

A voice finally came, with a hacking, even desperate edge to it.

" '. . . *classified material,*' " Ray was saying. " '*However, at this time my advisers and I think it best to inform the American public . . .*' "

It was the President's speech; Tave had forgotten all about it.

" '. . . *that the airbase at Lessing, Vermont, was also a secret storage facility for nuclear weapons. Policy in the United States for the last thirty years or more has been to move weapons under cover, to disperse them with all possible secrecy to selected air force bases across the country. What occurred at Lessing, Vermont, is at this moment under investigation. We believe, however, that what happened was an accident and took place during a low-level drill. Certain personnel are always being trained in the construction and function of nuclear weapons, and in their detonation. In general, detonators are not linked with nuclear materials in a way that could cause an explosion. Somehow, somewhere, however, there was a failure in the system. An innocent error of some kind has led to the gravest consequences.'"*

Ray's voice hesitated, began again. " *'Currently, fires are widespread in southern Vermont and in parts of New Hampshire. Electrical lines are down in both states and in the State of Maine, and some further damage to electrical lines in New England may be anticipated. This makes communication and investigation very difficult.'"*

Tave, sitting in her little circle of light, covered her face with her hands. I'm scared, she thought. I'm really scared. Ray's tired voice seemed to go on and on, now whispering, now loud. The sound was like a seesaw, to which she clung.

Amy

THEM'S HENS," said Grandpa Trowley, "and them's bantams."

He pointed at the basket of eggs he'd brought in from the barn. The stout little six-year-old girl with the thick brown braids and smooth round face looked at him solemnly.

Grandpa had said it, she was thinking, and what Grandpa said was God's honest truth. Or was it?

The little girl, Amy Trowley, clutched her pad of coloring paper between her arm and her side; the pad was the length of her arm and it just fit. In her other hand she held her two best crayons, yellow and blue. You could, she'd discovered, draw just about anything with those two crayons: yellow sun, yellow flowers, yellow house. Well, the Trowley house was white, really, but she thought yellow would be prettier. Yellow-haired girls with long blue dresses. Blue eyes. And you could color yellow and color blue and get sea-green grass, trees.

The fact was that all her crayons were lost except the blue and the yellow. She had tried to keep them all clutched in her hand at all times, but they kept dropping to the floor because her fingers were too fat. The crayons that dropped rolled and rolled, and when you got down on your plump knees to look for them, why, they had gone forever. Her mother would have to hunt them up for her on cleaning day, when she moved all the furniture away from the walls.

"Them white eggs," Grandpa was saying, "them thin-shelled little beauties, all hatch to hens, every one of 'em, yessir. But them brown ones, why, hell in a basket! Roosters, ever' one!"

Amy stared at the eggs. She wanted to believe Grandpa, but she knew very well that inside the eggs in that basket were only whites and yolks. Every day Grandpa brought a basket of eggs to the kitchen and every day she watched her mother crack a dozen at a time into a frying pan and scramble them with a fork.

"These eggs is eggs inside," she said.

Grandpa was the excitable type, everybody said so. He meant well, but he got twizzled up awful easy. Now he opened his mouth wide and went down slowly onto his knees so he could look Amy in the eye.

"Why, hell you say!" he cried, putting his fuzzy gray face very close to hers.

Amy's mother often called her "anchor in the storm." When something was so, it was, and that was the end of it for Amy. "These eggs is for cookin'," she said now, sturdily.

Grandpa's face came close, until it was no more than three inches from hers. There was the thin line of his mouth; and there were the thin lips when he opened it. There was another, thinner line between his eyebrows. She wished she could draw his picture, but she knew she never could. She was just no good at drawing people.

"I know that," he was saying. "Shit, I know it! But I mean the eggs that hatch! Brown eggs hatch roosters and white eggs hatch hens!"

It was brown-green eye to brown-green eye, now.

"How do you know?" asked the little girl reasonably.

Grandpa sat back on his heels. His overalls were blue and his underwear was yellowish; that was all right, she was thinking. But that red shirt . . .

"Once," said Grandpa, "they did this scientific experiment, see. Out of the damn eggs come the baby chicks one by one, see, and onto their legs they put little tags, brown for brown eggs, and white for white."

"What for?" said Amy.

"Good God in hell!" said Grandpa. "Ain't you payin' attention to me at all, girl?"

"I am, too," said Amy.

"Well, then. Them brown eggs, see, sure enough, them little chicks with the little brown tags to their legs, they grew up to be bantam roosters, cock-doodling, you know all that." Here Grandpa snickered a little. "But them white eggs, hens, every last shittin' one of 'em!"

"But not those," Amy said, pointing at the basket of eggs, some brown, some white.

Grandpa pounded his hand against his other hand. "No, damn-it!" he shouted. "The ones that hatch, for Chrissake! Don't you believe me?"

But Amy knew how to handle that question. She'd heard all about it on the radio, just last week. "Is it God's honest truth?" she asked.

She didn't know that much about God. There was no Sunday school but the Baptists' in town, and the Trowleys were not and never had been Baptists. No one knew, exactly, what the Trowleys were. But Amy had figured God, she knew what His truth was. When you were telling God's honest truth, you knew it. Otherwise, you weren't telling it.

"God's what?" Grandpa sputtered. "Now where in the hell did you hear that? You been sneakin' down to that Sunday school? All of them son-of-a-bitch holy rollers with their dunkin' people, givin' 'em naked baths right in public—"

Now both Mother and Grandma were listening. They hadn't been listening before, Amy knew, or they would have spoken up about "swearing before children." Amy knew what that was. Grandpa did a lot of it.

"Holy old Hannah!" he was shouting now. "Kids! Don't believe nothin' in this Christly world you tell 'em!"

Amy thought Grandpa hollered an awful lot, but she didn't mind it. She even liked it a little.

"Them goddamn fuckin' brown eggs is bantams!" he was shouting. "Them white eggs—"

"Father!" This was from Grandma. "Don't you swear so in

front of that child. Your language belongs out in the barn! Them's barn words, we won't have 'em in the house! Why, I'm surprised at you!"

Grandma was plump and spry. When she spoke, he listened.

"Why, Harriet," said Grandpa. "Have I offended?"

But "Harriet" wasn't having any. "Offended?" she cried. "Barn words!"

"Barn?" said Grandpa. He had drawn his legs together like a dancing master's. "Why, Harriet! Do you mean, like 'pitchfork'? 'Hay rake'? 'Silo'?"

"You know what I'm talkin' about." Grandma was trying to frown as she moved her plump little body across the room to him. Twig and mushroom, they confronted each other.

"She asked me," said Grandpa, "if I was tellin' her the God's honest truth."

"She did?" said Grandma. "Not a bad idea, considerin'."

"Oh, sure, oh, sure!" The dancing master disappeared; it was Grandpa again. "Churchie-churchie-Sunday school!" he cried. In rare devout moments Grandpa called himself a Universalist. That meant, he said, church every twenty years, without fail.

"Lower your voice," said Grandma, "or they'll hear you all the way to town." Town was fifteen miles away.

"Well, I don't give a damn!" Grandpa shouted.

"Amy," said Grandma, "please shut all the doors and windows. On a day as hot as today, course, it would be nice to catch an early morning breeze, but—"

Amy giggled a little. This was a part of this game she liked. She clutched her yellow and blue crayons and made her way to the big kitchen door. This she slammed shut on its screen. Then she went to the kitchen windows. She did it deliberately—that was how she always moved—but this time, to give Grandpa time to make his escape.

"Wimmen," said Grandpa. "I'll be in the barn!" He opened the door Amy had just shut. "And there's your damned eggs!"

Without another word, Grandma took them up and went back

to the stove, where she and Amy's mother were getting ready to make the usual two dozen scrambled. Grandpa went out, but then he turned and looked at Amy through the screen.

"You gonna grow up like them?" he asked.

"Don't swear!" Grandma shouted at him from across the kitchen.

"Good God, I wasn't!" Grandpa ducked his shoulders as if he'd been hit. This made Amy laugh. For a second he looked at her sourly through the screen, then he grinned and waggled his eyebrows. Amy, on the other side of the screen, waggled her eyebrows back. Then Grandpa moved down off the porch.

"Amy," her mother called over, "stop making eyes at your grandfather and come put these eggs in the ice chest."

Grandma was looking at the clock. "Gosh, yes," she said, bustling from cupboards to table and back. "Only fifteen minutes to Madhouse Time!"

Madhouse Time was when Amy's father and Grandpa and her four big brothers and ol' Sears and Marl Perry would come in from the barn. They'd all be shouting—learned from Grandpa, Grandma said. The four older boys Grandma sometimes called Shout, Squabble, Pick, and Fight. That was what Amy called them, too. Their real names were Tom, Edward, Grover, and Ashley. Tom, the oldest, was twenty-two and engaged to be married. Ashley, the youngest but for Sears, was fifteen. Ol' Sears and Marl Perry were only nine, but Amy knew that didn't make any difference. They still wouldn't speak to her, she knew; they thought she was a baby.

All the Trowley boys were tall and husky, brown-haired, round-faced: this was the Trowley look, Amy herself had it. Back to, in fact, it was easy to call out the wrong name. Amy's mother, who knew which was which right down to the last shirt and sock, would very often call out all the names, or begin to, before she got the one she was trying to call. "I can't reach my big platter," she might say. "Tom—Ed—Gr—Ash—Edward, would you get it for me?"

The son in question would be all ready to help her out before she gave him a name, but of course he could never resist asking, politely, "Who was it you wanted, again, Mother?"

"I want my platter!" Mary Trowley would say, almost yell. In this family it was hard not to. "Now, Tom—Ed—Grov—Ash—Edward, there! You get it for me!"

"Gettin' old, Mother!" Amy's father would call out. This was a joke, too, Amy knew, because her mother was only three days younger than her father was.

"Amy!" That, it seemed, was the only name her mother didn't struggle with. "The eggs, quick!"

Amy, who never did anything quickly, covered the room with all the deliberate speed she could muster and put away the surplus eggs as she'd been asked to do. Her grandma was speeding around the breakfast table now, bread and butter, rhubarb, coffee, milk. Amy watched her mother scramble the eggs in the frying pan, her yellowed fork flying like lightning while the other hand shook the pan to keep the eggs from sticking. God's honest truth, Amy was thinking. Those eggs were eggs. Yellow crayon. And that, she knew, was what made Grandpa so mad.

In the last week Amy had worked it out for herself. The farther away from the truth you were, the more you had to yell. If Tom said he could get fifty bales off that little piece by the barn and Ashley said he doubted it, and it was Ashley who yelled the most, then Ashley was wrong. Just this week, that had happened.

"Big talk!" Ashley had yelled. "Ain't no way in the world you'll get that much hay off there!" And he'd got louder and louder, with Tom helping him along: lots of "We'll see, little brother," and "I dunno's you're old enough to remember."

Finally Ash had stomped out, he'd been so mad. Tom had strolled along after him, quietly. And you just knew that Tom was telling the truth and Ashley wasn't. And you would be right. But Ashley had kept right on yelling until that fiftieth bale turned up in a full round sworl. Then he'd had to shut up.

"A still small voice," the man on the radio had whispered in his funny accent. "God's honest truth, God's holy truth, in a still small voice." Then one of the big boys had come in and changed the station to Country Music, Wheeling, West Virginia. But still it made you think. Amy, who never had anybody to play with, had plenty of time to think. If people were quiet, they could tell the truth, she concluded. If people listened, they would hear the truth.

Grandpa came back into the house first; it was almost seven o'clock in the morning this Saturday, and he did like his meals on time. He stood inside the screen. "Well, wife," he hollered. "We got anything to eat around here?"

"That depends," Grandma hollered right back, "on whether anybody has washed up or not!"

Grandpa announced, "I do not have to be reminded like a small child!" Then he looked at Amy. "Come on, girlie," he said. "I'll help you wash your hands." They were at the sink when Amy's father and her four big brothers came in, followed closely by ol' Sears and Marl Perry. In a moment, breakfast for eleven was on the table, stewed rhubarb, homemade bread and rolls, eggs, coffee, milk. Everybody began to eat and talk, all at the same time.

Amy, seated beside her mother, looked down the table wistfully at Marl Perry and ol' Sears. They weren't talking much except to each other. She wished she knew what they were saying.

She knew better than to ask; they wouldn't tell her anyway. Tom and Grover were arguing with her father about the amount of corn they needed to put in. Soon Grandpa had joined that argument. Mother and Grandma discussed the baking they planned to do that morning. Edward and Ash were arguing about who would use the wagon that day. It was noisy for everybody but Amy. She strained toward the undercurrent of sound between Marl and ol' Sears. "The Branch," she heard Marl say, and saw ol' Sears make a motion to hush him. "Boots," she heard Sears whisper after a while. "A hammer?" asked Marl very quietly, on a rising inflection. But it carried.

"You boys ain't plannin' to use my tools again, are you?" Bill Trowley called out. "Sears! You hear me?"

"Well," said Sears, and fidgeted. "Well . . ."

And then Amy saw the thing about Marl Perry that always fascinated her. Light caught his face. When it happened, she always wanted to draw it, to save it, but she couldn't draw faces. "We need to borrow your hammer, sir," Marl Perry said. He grinned and tilted his head. "We've got a little project going, down at the Branch."

God's holy truth, so stunning that the whole Trowley family sat still for a moment.

"Down at the Branch?" Mary Trowley said slowly. "The water's awful high down there."

"Hell!" cried Grandpa, grinning. "Let 'em do it! They's boys, ain't they? Got to have some goddamn fun, can't fuck around doin' chores all the—"

"Father!" cried Grandma. "Please!"

"Oh," said Grandpa. "Ladies present. So sorry, Harriet, do forgive me."

"Well," said Bill Trowley. He gave the boys a careful, measuring look. "I don't believe you'll drown, do you?"

Ol' Sears began to grin.

"No, sir!" said Marl.

It was one of those times when Amy knew the whole family was thinking the same thing. Let them go, let them have a little fun. That Marl Perry, awful good kid, but stuck up there on that hill all alone, only his mother and all them books. And boys will be boys, have to be.

She'd heard it all before.

"Hell, Mother," said Bill Trowley to his wife, "they'll be all right."

"Yahoo!" said Sears.

"All's I care 'bout, you boys got to bring my tools back when you're done! I go out there to my tool chest, find anything missin' at five o'clock tonight, and oh, my God, there'll be hell to pay."

"William, my son," said Grandpa piously. "Please be careful. There are ladies present, you know."

Into the ensuing chuckle Amy spoke up in as still and small a voice as she could. "I'd like to go down to the Branch, too," she said.

"What'd she say?" said Grandpa.

"No, Amy," said her mother. "You're not old enough. Unless, of course, these boys would take you with them . . ."

"Excuse me," said ol' Sears, rapidly.

"Excuse me, thank you for breakfast, Mrs. Trowley," said Marl, following suit.

Mrs. Trowley nodded at them and sighed. "Go ahead, boys." In one minute they were out the door and gone. And that was that, Amy knew.

"It's good for him," said Bill Trowley to his wife. "He needs it."

They weren't talking about ol' Sears, either, Amy knew. She finished her breakfast. But that little voice, her own voice, whispered and whispered. She could hear it, if they couldn't.

After breakfast she helped her mother and grandmother clear the kitchen. Then they began the baking. It was the middle of the morning before Mary Trowley looked down at the goodhearted, barrel-shaped little worker beside her and nodded toward the back door. That meant Amy was free as a bird. She picked up her pad of paper and drew her two crayons out of her overalls pocket; maybe she would make some pictures. She went out the back door.

But the voice was still whispering.

Just here was her mother's clothesline, and just there the compost heap with its heavy, hot smell. Somehow some squash seeds had found their way into it and sprouted, and now the beginnings of a squash vine ran over the heap of moldering vegetable refuse. Amy walked out toward the flower beds, in which the daffodils and tulips were now gone and little English wood hyacinths grew in neat rows. Her mother always said she had started that shady border with eight small hyacinth bulbs, but this was hard to believe because now it was about two feet wide and eight feet long, thick with the little bell-shaped blooms on their slender stems, with the sharp dark leaves growing together in tight clumps. The hyacinths were beautiful. But they were pink and lavender.

Amy squatted before them. She could, she supposed, draw

them yellow and blue and pretend they were pink and lavender. Some days she might even do that. But not today. It didn't seem like much fun and it wouldn't be real. Amy liked to draw things that were real: she knew the difference between real and pretend, and pretend was a child's game she didn't feel like playing. Her voice was still whispering. What she wanted to do was go down to the Branch.

She stood up and walked past the garden, down to the first fence in her father's fields. The pasture lay before her in a rolling downhill slope. In the distance, about six acres away, she could see a line of trees. Beyond that, she knew, was the Branch. The upper pastures were full of rocky ledge that pushed out through the grass. In the distance, Amy saw her father's cows in a herd. If she went, she would have to try not to attract their attention because once they saw her, they would walk toward her, friendly and curious. Then she would have the whole herd following her as she walked to the Branch. Amy wasn't afraid of cows; she liked them. But a herd of cows walking down to the Branch with her would attract attention. Father or Grover or Ashley or somebody would be sure to see. And she wasn't allowed down at the Branch by herself.

Would she go, though? Yes!

She ducked under the fence with difficulty; it was hard to bend over when you were built so close to the ground anyway. Then she started across the pasture, skirting clumps of bushes and rock ledge so that she wouldn't be seen. Six acres make a long, hot walk, but Amy hardly felt it. She was doing what she wanted to do; she'd go as far as her legs would take her. At last she rolled stomach first in the high grass under the other side of the fence, and she was in the trees. The Branch roared, not too very far away.

The tree floor was a mass of small hummocks, quite swampy and damp underfoot. Here and there mud topped Amy's sensible brown shoes. She made her way steadily toward the sound of the water, but her feet were wet through when she arrived, her overalls were torn, her shirt was untucked, one braid had lost its tie and the hair flowed out from that side of her head in a wild tangle. Her face was sweaty and begrimed. But it didn't matter, any of it. Here she was.

The Branch was high and running fast. Minerals in the water had given a reddish brown tinge to the rocks over which it ran, here in deep pools and there in gravel-bottomed shallows, always through the woods. The water glistened. And there by the deepest pool, Amy saw, were ol Sears and Marl Perry.

She gasped. The boys had built themselves a raft out of logs and planks. Beyond them, on a flat rock, she could see quite a few of her father's tools laid out neatly. The raft was finished; it was about three feet square. They had fastened a rope to one log and had found a place to put two slender poles. At this moment they were urging the raft off the rocks and into the water. The only thing Marl and ol' Sears had on were their rubber boots.

Bare naked those two boys were, pushing the hunk of raft into the water. As they tipped it in, Amy realized that it even had a flag on it, billowy and white and stuck on a stick between two planks. The flag looked suspiciously like a pair of underdrawers. The boys were grinning and their hair was wet. Every so often somebody would slip into the water and then have to stop and empty his boots. The bottom of the Branch was full of sharp rocks, Amy knew, or they probably wouldn't be wearing the boots either. Hanging from a big old wild apple tree upstream was every last item of their clothing—in the sunlight Amy could see it drip. Why, those boys had been swimming! It wasn't fair!

Above the roar of the water she could hear nothing of what they were saying to each other. Their bodies—Marl's slim and white and ol' Sears's white and stout—were tense as they nudged the raft out farther and farther. At last it skidded off the rocks completely and floated in the biggest pool, which was maybe ten feet by fifteen feet, and not so deep that you couldn't see the bottom.

Ol' Sears stood on a flat rock and held the rope in one hand. With the other he urged Marl onto the boat. Marl put one careful, rubber-booted toe out onto the raft, which whirled away from his weight so that he had to pull back quickly. He and ol' Sears hauled the raft toward them again, then they fastened its rope to a rock. At last, after much arm swinging and pointing and discussion, ol' Sears got onto the center of the raft and squatted, holding the planks at the side. The raft tipped a little, held.

Hanging on with one hand, Sears motioned to Marl. Marl tiptoed onto the planks, they swung and whirled; he, too, squatted down and waited. When the raft seemed steady again, he very gently picked up a pole and pushed at the rope until it unfastened itself from the rock. Then they were afloat.

For a minute or so, Amy could see, neither one of them dared to move. She thought they looked funny, jaybird naked, squatting on their little raft, which now floated gently to the center of the pool. But at last Marl stood up with his pole and began to tool the raft from one corner of the pool to the other. Then Sears stood up, too, very carefully. The next minute, tippy but happy, they might have been poling their way up and down Moosehead. Didn't they look proud!

Amy felt it was time to make herself known. With care, she picked her way down to the edge of the Branch. "I want to come, too!" she yelled at them.

At first they didn't seem to hear, too busy calling out orders to each other. But then ol' Sears spotted her. "Holy cats!" she heard him yell. The next minute the raft had tipped both him and Marl into the pool with a splash. Then it whirled away and floated toward the nearest exit, which was, fortunately, at a narrow place in the rocks; there it lodged. First Marl's head appeared above the water, then ol' Sears's.

"You get back! Get back!" ol' Sears yelled at her.

But Amy stood her ground. Here she was and here she was staying.

Ol' Sears, still in the water, shook his fist at her.

That wasn't nice, but Amy didn't move. She stuck out her lower lip. At last both boys gave up motioning her to get back into the woods and they swam ashore, making it up over the slippery rocks in record time and hightailing it for their clothes. Amy didn't know what all the fuss was about, and she didn't care. She had something else in mind.

Pretty soon ol' Sears and Marl Perry came back toward her. Now they had on their trousers and they were looking mad. Amy planted her feet firmly and stuck her lower lip out farther.

"What are you doing here?" Sears cried when he was close enough so she could hear him. "Did somebody bring you down?"

He looked out through the woods.

"No," she said.

"Well, how come you were spyin' on us, then? We fell off that raft because of you, and now our darn boots are down there at the bottom of the water." His eyes were like little slits in his red round face.

Then Marl came up behind him. "Come on," he said to Amy. "I'll take you back home."

"Don't be nice to her!" Sears cried. "She doesn't belong down here and she knows it. Does anybody know where you are, Amy?"

"No," said Amy. "I wanted to come and I came."

"You're a mess!" said Sears. "Look at you! Marl and I have important business! We can't be stoppin' every time some darn little kid wants to come and fall into the Branch—"

"I didn't fall in," Amy pointed out. "You did. I want a ride."

"Oh, for the love of—" Sears raised his eyes and rolled them. "Go home, darnit, Amy, and leave us alone!"

"I want a ride," said Amy firmly. "I won't go home till I have a ride."

"Oh, jeez," Sears said. "You little hellion! Wouldn't you know!"

Marl Perry came up and knelt beside Amy. "You know," he said diplomatically, "that water is awful cold."

Amy didn't say anything.

"If you fell in," Marl continued, "you'd be awful wet and cold. Prob'ly catch a chill and all." He was so nice. Amy began to waver a little.

But Sears cried out, "Don't talk to her!" His face was bright red and he was puffing. "She should turn right around right now and go back up to the house, and she knows it!"

"Well, it was a long walk," said Marl, still on his knees.

"I want a ride!" said Amy. She scowled, and her lower lip stuck out about a full inch. It wasn't nice for Sears to keep yelling at her that way and she was tired of being left out. She wasn't a kid for crying, but . . .

"Cut it out," said Marl in an aside to Sears. "Don't you see she's about to bawl?"

"Well, what in H are we goin' to do then?" Sears said. "Gotta stop everythin' and carry her, kicking and screaming, up the hill."

Marl turned back to Amy. "Now, Amy," he said persuasively, "isn't it time for you to go home—"

"I want to ride!" Amy said. "I want to ride, I want to ride, I want to ride!" She stamped her foot.

"Oh, jeez." Sears hid his forehead in the crotch of a tree.

Marl sighed. "You want a ride on the raft."

"Yes," said Amy. Now she said it very quietly, because she was determined. For a few seconds, all anyone heard was the roaring of the Branch and the overhead patter of popple leaves.

At last Marl nodded and grinned. "Okay, okay. We'll give you a ride. And then you'll go home, right?" Amy nodded. She drew in her lip a little. After all, that Marl Perry was nice.

"Oh, jeez, the things!" moaned Sears to his tree crotch. "The things you have to do!" Then he turned. "But if we give you a ride, kid, you gotta promise not to bother us again! Right?"

Amy nodded. "But I don't want to get wet," she said as an afterthought.

"Course not! Course you don't want to get wet, that figures!" cried Sears. But at a motion from Marl he sighed. "All right, all right, we'll get the raft. But you stay here! Right on the bank! And don't you move till we bring it over, okay?"

In a few moments Amy was sitting in the middle of the raft with Marl and ol' Sears, still wearing their trousers, swimming along-side it. Oh, this was fun, just like rocking in a cradle. The boys kept it level, and she floated easily from one side of the pool to another. It felt fine to do what you wanted! Amy relaxed; she enjoyed the ride. But at last she felt a familiar good feeling in her stomach. "I want to go home now," she told the boys. "I'm hungry."

"Queen of Sheba," muttered Sears.

She didn't care, she was happy. In a little while the boys had set her safely ashore. Then, because it was near to dinnertime anyway, they decided they'd better walk her back up the hill. They would come down in the afternoon anyway, and do some more. As for Amy, she had promised to stay away, did she remember that?

Oh, yes, Amy remembered. Besides, she was tired. She guessed her little voice was telling her to eat and nap and draw, she'd had enough adventure for one day. Halfway up the hill the boys got impatient with her again, her legs were so short. But then Marl had the idea that they should make a chair for her to ride on. So they did, lugging her up the hill and depositing her on the front porch while they skun up the back stairs to put on dry clothes before Amy's mother found out about their wet ones.

Amy heard Sears muttering about her as they rounded the corner of the house, but before they'd made it out of earshot Marl's voice came to her. "Heck," he was saying, "that was quite a walk for her, all the way down there. She's not such a bad little kid." Marl's voice was very quiet. Amy smiled to herself. It must be that Marl Perry was speaking God's honest truth.

*

That was one of the very few times when the "big boys" let Amy into their business, however. Mostly they left her behind, or went where she couldn't go. But after that, Amy always liked Marl Perry. He was somebody you could depend on and trust. For years she wished she, too, could be a boy, and then she could be in on what he and ol' Sears cooked up.

The next year, when Amy was old enough to go to Lucy's school, Marl and ol' Sears already had a favored position, far up in the upper classes. Amy sat in the little kids' corner and, like all her friends, worshiped Marl from afar. When he and ol' Sears left to go to high school in Monson, the classroom seemed very bare and grim. But by the end of her own eighth-grade year, Amy had made good friends of her own. Lucy paid very little attention to her at all, either to praise or to scold.

And she had her drawing. Where she'd gotten her quick fingers for artwork no one in the family could say. Her father liked to make blueprints for little sheds and barns for the farm, and he had designed and built his own silos and stable. Her mother had an eye for color and pieced quilts that were so bright they made you blink. By the age of ten, Amy had pieced her first quilt in a pattern called Butterflies. On each square of muslin you sewed a different-color butterfly, then this was edged with blanket stitch. Each butterfly had two sworls of feelers you did in chain stitch. The squares were sewn together for a quilt top, and that was sewn to the rest of the quilt and tacked again. Amy's tacks and blanket stitches were all blue and yellow. She'd enjoyed making the quilt, and it came out well. But she liked drawing best.

Nobody in the Trowley family saw any harm in drawing. In fact, they said it probably kept the child from being too lonely; there were no friends Amy's age living close by. So in the evenings Amy sat in the center of the broad braided rug in the Trowley living room, trying to sketch this or that. Now and then a new kind of paper would appear beside her plate, or a new set of paints or artist's chalk or charcoal, that somebody in the family had seen in town and thought she might like.

At high school, Amy was a good enough student to get by. In her sophomore year, to her great surprise, she was elected president of the art club. Of course, the club had only eight members, but it gave her some standing in the school. Not, of course, like Marl Perry and ol' Sears. They were in a different league altogether: they were in debating and student government and glee club and plays and whatever else was going on. As in grade school, in high school, too, Amy and her friends worshiped from afar.

At the end of her sophomore year, however, when Marl Perry danced with her, it was for Amy as if the world—which had been looking a bit gray and ordinary—suddenly took a flying leap into Technicolor. She'd seen Marl staring at her from time to time, of course. But he seemed so far above her that she didn't let herself give it much thought. After all, what would Marl Perry, winner of the high school trophy, want with ol' Sears's little sister?

When Marl finally made it across the dance floor and asked her —of all people—to dance, she didn't know how to act or what to say. In fact, she was about to refuse. But somewhere in the back of her mind she could hear his voice from all those years ago saying, "She's not such a bad kid." And she wanted to dance with him.

She wanted to so much, in fact, that it made her catch her breath and act very dignified and solemn. After all, all that was between you and black nothing was this tall shape in a gray suit, that felt under your hand as no gray cloth had felt before. It was Marl Perry looking at you, when you dared to look up. You wanted to touch his face and make sure it was real.

The other thing was, you weren't a child. You weren't some-body's tagalong. You were his choice, and you felt it the length of your body. When he urged you to come close to him, you fit. You were even proud of the fit. You gave up and closed your eyes and couldn't believe your luck.

"Well, Sis." Her father's voice broke into that; it was so abrupt a transition that Amy couldn't bear it. Suddenly she felt she must have been making a fool of herself: she'd lost real time, in which tomorrow Marl Perry and ol' Sears would be going off, once again, without her. So wordlessly she turned and left Marl, almost embarrassed to discover herself among other people after what she'd been feeling for him. She rode home in the back of her parents' car, her face pressed against the seat, her big form numb and crumpled. Silent tears slid down her cheeks in the dark. In the front seat her parents, finding nothing unusual in Amy's quiet, were gay and tired and talked softly. They wouldn't dance again until another spring. And it was a big thing, having ol' Sears and Marl Perry go off to the war tomorrow, a big, sad thing.

Once again Amy was forgotten.

She finished high school. During that time, her share of boys danced with her, but she never allowed herself to be "foolish" again. In her junior year ol' Sears was killed, and Marl Perry, off overseas somewhere, wrote a letter to her parents that made them weep. But he couldn't come home for the service. Everyone was very quiet, very sad. The world was ordinary, gray.

After high school, Amy went off to Portland to art school. It seemed like a good idea; her folks could afford it and wanted to do it for her. Art school was a four-year college, and Amy stuck it out, learning at last that she didn't want to become an artist, or a teacher of artists. A country girl was a country girl, she decided in the long run. Those streets—how could a person think, when one street ran into another all higgledy-piggledy, and you could go for days without seeing one field? The art school, in downtown Portland, was a nice place to be, and she loved Deering Oaks, a Portland park. But it wasn't country, that was all. Some days she was amazed and depressed by the nosing of one building into another and by the jumble of trash that seemed to blow into every unoccupied corner.

It wasn't that Portland was a bad city. In fact, it was fairly clean as cities went, with plenty of good Maine people in it. But the fact that it was a city at all—for Amy, maybe that was it. Or maybe it was that she herself was just not happy. She liked the drawing, but she kept to herself and she wasn't happy. She wanted to feel the way she'd felt that day when she'd decided to go down to the Branch and she'd ended up getting a ride on a raft. Yes, she wanted to feel as good as that, and she didn't.

She stuck it out until graduation, and then she went home.

*

They were in the kitchen at the Trowley farmhouse, Amy and her mother. Amy was polishing the silver knives, a job she loved.

"They look good," said Mary Trowley, coming to sit at the table with a cup of coffee.

Amy smiled a little. "You got a minute?" she asked her mother. "Because we have to talk about my schoolin'." Amy still spoke in her forthright Maine way; she was determined she always would.

Mary Trowley sighed. "I know. You're goin' to get a job off somewheres, teachin'."

"What I was thinkin'," said Amy, "is that I would get a job, but down to the feed store."

"Feed—" Mary Trowley set her coffee cup on its saucer.

"Down to the feed store," said Amy again, firmly. "Louise Holt's gettin' done, I heard they're gonna need someone."

"And stay here? And live here?" Mary was incredulous, happy. "But what about art—"

"It ain't what I want to do, this art business," said Amy quietly. "I don't know just what I do want. But meantime, might's well work at the feed store as anyplace."

"Your father will say it's no job for a girl." Mary Trowley seemed cautious, but in fact she was so glad she felt like howling.

"Louise Holt—" said Amy.

"Your father will say she's no girl," said Mary. "And he's right."

"Still, I can handle myself," said Amy reasonably. "And it's something I want to do."

"Well, it'll be a fight," said her mother. "Oh, I'm glad to have you home! But maybe you could stay here with me and think about getting a job later."

"No," said Amy. "I want to support myself."

There was, simply, no use arguing with Amy once her mind was made up. The girl didn't yell, but she always stood her ground.

After several family discussions in which her father and brothers shouted their heads off and Amy stuck to her guns, Amy had her way. The Trowleys gave the feed store so much business, she pointed out, that there wasn't a day when one or another of the men wouldn't be checking in to see how she was doing. Or, they told her, to break the arms of any male who stepped out of line.

Amy said she guessed she could take care of herself all right.

*

Louise Holt, who was getting done down at the feed store, was a tough old gal who'd been there for years. A chain smoker whose false teeth seemed to start out of her mouth when she spoke,

Louise had long since reached that indeterminate age of women when hair dye has to be false because the lines on the face are so indelible. Her tragedy was that she had been in and out of Eastern Maine General Hospital battling cancer and now knew the battle was lost. This had made her angry and bitter, and she showed Amy the ropes at the store, calling her "deah" somewhat maliciously. But Amy took over without making many mistakes and with no particular fuss.

"Yes, deah," Louise would say, squinting through her cigarette smoke at Amy's adding machine totals or bookkeeping accounts. "Ayeh, ayeh, that's right. Oh, you're good at this, all right, deah."

But before she left the feed store for the last time, Louise felt compelled to make an announcement.

It was near the end of the day, and men had gathered, as they often did, in a little group near the stove. "Now, you men," Louise called out sharply that night, "I'm about to leave for good, and I want to tell you one thing before I go!" One by one heads lifted; when she had their attention, she looked cat-satisfied. "What you got here," she announced, "is a young girl."

At once the men's gaze shifted to Amy, who stood stock still, stunned, for just a moment. Then she turned to go about some task or other, it didn't matter what. But she hadn't gotten quite around before somebody in the dark, huddled-up group whistled.

"Now you cut that out," Louise hollered, "and listen to me! You're gonna have a nice young girl workin' here! An' she don't know nothin'! Do you, deah?"

But before Amy could speak, Louise continued. "No," she said. "You don't. Now," she addressed the men, "I expect you to act accordingly! You got stories to tell, I don't mind 'em! Ain't much I haven't heard! But this here is a young girl, she don't want to listen to a bunch of sh—smut. You got that?"

While it was unbelievably embarrassing, it was also, Amy saw, like a swan song. Louise was leaving, and she wanted everybody to know it. Or somebody to know it.

Then Bud Harper stood up. He was a young man, thin, less than Amy's height.

The thing about Bud Harper, Amy said later when she could laugh about it, was that he was awful good to look at. He had dark hair that curled over his forehead. His eyes were light green, the more startling because his skin stayed tan even in winter and his beard never seemed quite shaven. Bud's eyebrows were thick and dark and legendary: known to be awfully eloquent with the women. The green eyes below them had a pupilless sheen; they were two circles of jade in sockets of dark tan velvet. People said there wasn't a woman in town Bud Harper hadn't undressed with those eyes. And there were, they said, quite a few women who melted out of their clothes, just by the looking.

There are times when you can stare at a man as if he were a bug on a pin and he'll leave off bothering. That Amy almost managed, she would have said. After all, she was a big girl, bigger than he was by a long chalk. And when she turned to find him only a counter's width away and staring at her with the old moving-eyebrow routine, she almost managed to stare him down. Would have, except that Louise spoke up, good old Louise.

"Now I mean it!" Louise said. Her protest was shameless and like tin pans banging. Amy felt her own face scorch. The Harper green eyes ran over her body and it was just like being rubbed down by a rough-round piece of Wedgwood; her mother had one Wedgwood vase, just that color.

"Bud!" Louise was warning him, and she seemed to mean it, too. But under that woman's sallow, helpless skin Amy saw something give in, sickeningly. Louise was looking toward Bud, and Bud wasn't having anything to do with her, that was it.

"So you just take all your dirty stuff out to the warehouse." Now Louise's voice had sunk and came up like bubbles from some thick, boiling liquid.

But Bud still ignored her.

"This is a young girl!" Louise cried, but so softly that someone in the corner muttered, "Guess Bud took the starch outta her underpants," and somebody else gave a startled guffaw.

His eyes still on Amy, Bud spoke to Louise. "What the hell you turnin' into, Louise?" he wanted to know. "A skinny old hen?"

It was cruel. For a second the older woman's jaw trembled and she seemed close to tears. "Why, you—" she began. But then Bud reached over and rubbed his hand over her thin freckled arm, his eyes still on Amy.

If Louise had been a cat she would have purred. Instead she said, "You're mighty friendly, Bud, considerin' where you spend your mornin's." At the house of one of the town shopkeepers, in the arms of his wife; this was well known.

From the stove came another ill-timed snort of laughter, just one, quickly hidden. Nobody wanted to make an enemy of Bud Harper. When he had a fight with you, he solved it too often with your wife. Too often because the women would hide and protect him, and you might hear about it months later, after it was no longer town gossip.

But he spoke softly. "Why, Louise," he said, still staring at Amy, "you must be jealous."

Now Amy, her mouth plain and grim, stared right back at him. He reminded her of one of those little boys who lay under the Grange Hall steps and looked up women's skirts. Then bragged about it after.

Louise stuck her cigarette between her china teeth and squinted at Bud through the smoke. "Someday," she said, "your doormat's gonna reach out and bite you. Hope to God I'm around to see it. Well, so long, gang. Amy, have fun. Anything you want, give me a call."

Amy nodded. Then, with a rattle and a slam, Louise got out from behind the counter and left.

Amy turned to tend to the feed list, but Bud Harper, it seemed, had decided to wait. She looked up to see he was still standing at the counter.

"Yes?" she said.

He leaned on the counter. "You scared of me?"

"Not so you'd notice it," she said quietly.

"Well, good, good," he said. He reached over and placed a finger on the hand she had laid on the counter. Furious, she snatched it away and turned to the accounts Louise had left her

[232]

to unsnarl, making up her mind that if he so much as made a move in her direction again, she'd let him have it.

There was nothing flossy about the manners of the other men who came into the store, but they treated Amy as they might have the women of their own families. By the end of the first week Amy had managed to get some of the accounts in order, and Paul Wright, who owned the place, became her champion. "This girl right here," he always said, "is the best thing that ever happened to this place."

Off and on during those first days, however, Bud Harper would come in and elaborately fail to take notice of Amy. That is, he would look at her until she felt his eyes and looked up, then he would look away, a second too late. Once, as she swept the floor, he put a hand out and steadied himself away from the broom in a way that made his hand travel near her arm. Another instant and Amy, who never moved fast but always efficiently, would have reached up and broken the broom handle over his head, but he moved in time.

Then, just before noontime on the first day of her second week in the store, Bud Harper left the group of men buzzing out in the warehouse and came into the store and found Amy alone.

Her plan that day had been to tack up all the new tool advertisements and feed circulars, and she was on her hands and knees in front of the feed store counter. Her eye had been caught by an illustration of an installation for measuring hog feed; for no good reason at all there she was, reading it and not paying attention, with the largest portion of her anatomy up. She never heard or felt a thing until two hands cupped her buttocks, squeezing gently through her cotton dress.

For one astonished split second she stayed stock still.

Harper, who was used to making time when he could, became even more personal. He leaned over her intently, fingers roaming. "Well, honey," he said. "Honey."

Then Amy was up off the floor, snorting like a mad bull. There were men in the warehouse, but it never occurred to her to call them. Bud Harper's hands moved to take possession again as she turned and hauled off and hit him right in the eye. One precious eyebrow, she was happy to see, rose straight up, twisted, and fell dead. The green eye beneath it sprouted cracks, glued with red glue. Amy didn't hold back. In a blind rage she got ready to swing at him again. The only way to stop those eyebrows was to knock them clean off, and, she thought, she'd better get to both of them while she had the chance.

"Why, you didn't want to do that," Bud said, and grabbed her wrist hard, twisting it.

By now some attention had been aroused out in the warehouse. The men approached the door in time to see Amy break Bud's grasp on her wrist, grab him by the front of his shirt, and push him back to the feed store wall, like a truck plow to a tree stump, somebody said. And there she held him. And—the story went around afterward—she had hardly mussed her hair in the process.

But at that moment the men in the doorway just gaped.

"You ever lay a hand on me again," said Amy quietly, looking at Bud as if she expected to see him slide through her fingers and slither out the door, "I'll put you right through this wall."

Later the men lounged in the warehouse and said things like, "By the Jesus, wa'n't she mad! 'Minds me of her grandfather, back in twenty-two, he . . ." and "Never saw a woman get mad 'thout cryin' and stampin' her foot, did you? Hell, she just hauled off and nailed him! There's a girl you hadn't oughta mess with." Quite a few were glad to see Bud Harper get his. There was a lot of: "Never saw old Bud look quite so surprised, did you?" and "Did you see the look on his face when she . . ."

But at that moment there wasn't a man who moved. They just stood still and looked shocked.

It took Amy a minute or so to realize that Bud wasn't going to fight with her; he'd seen the men in the doorway before she did, and he had a reputation to uphold. Also, she doubted if he was strong enough to. Flat against the wall, he managed a crooked smile that never made it as far as the one cracked-looking green eye.

[234]

"This ain't a woman!" Bud announced with difficulty. "This here is a goddamn gorilla! I'll kiss you, honey," he joked weakly, "but hell, you gotta let me go first."

Amy hardly heard him. She didn't get mad often, but when she did it took her time to get over it. Now Bud Harper might have been the devil himself she held there, or anything that lurked in shadows and hurt people. So she kept right on holding him with one white marble arm until he had become, definitively, a fool in front of the gaping men.

Gradually, however, she did realize where she was and what had happened. And then she felt bad; she felt unclean. Bud Harper was just a little man with a big itch; she didn't want to be touching him at all. When she awoke to herself he was saying, "Jesus, honey, you hard of hearin'? Why do we go on meetin' this way?" and other nonsense, which would have been funny if it hadn't been for her strong white arm. Nobody was laughing, and Bud knew it.

"I don't want you to touch me again. Ever," said Amy grimly, letting go of him.

Then he was gone, the door slammed and vibrating on its hinges.

"Jesus." One of the men took in breath. "Amy, you all right?"

"Why, yes," she said. "I'm just fine."

"Jeez, Amy, we could have helped you—it all happened so fast."

She shrugged and turned back to the counter. "That's all right," she said. "I just don't intend to be handled like public property, is all."

One by one, a little sheepishly, the men nodded at her and left. "That Amy Trowley, boy, you don't want to mess with her."

There was no doubt in Amy's mind that Bud Harper would be back. That evening she kept all the lights on until closing time. Old Paul stayed awake to watch with her until Tom Trowley came by to pick her up. Even then, she hurried the few steps from store to car. As the car headlights swung around they illuminated the warehouse, and sure enough, beside it was a small, swaggering form that turned quickly around a corner of the building.

But whether Amy's story had gone around town like lightning and given somebody courage, or whether the shopkeeper who'd been wronged had finally heard the truth for the first time, Amy didn't have to worry long. The next day, that shopkeeper left his house in the morning as usual and then snuck back and hid in his garage. Beside him he had his hunting rifle, loaded. He waited until Bud Harper arrived and the wife let him in; then he waited a little more, so that when he went inside his house he was in time to catch Bud proving something, the woman under him, in his, the shopkeeper's, own bed.

Then the rifle was raised and fired twice, but Bud didn't die until he'd run, holding himself together, to his car, and climbed in and driven the man with the rifle—who had chased him out —right through his own front window, so that the shopkeeper was killed, too. A few minutes later someone picked up the wife on the road. She was frantic, wearing a bloodstained bathrobe, wandering by the roadbed.

A typical country story: how a bad thing could be tolerated for years, providing something to mutter and mumble about, putting the old spice in the coffee. And then suddenly explode with too much justice for anybody's stomach, so that, for a little while at least, no one knew where to look.

Then after a while that justice itself became the coffee spice and the muttering-mumbling grew and subsided the way an ocean does, retreating to low tide, coming in again. Of course, by then the shopkeeper had been transformed from a determined man with a grievance into a raving maniac, and Bud Harper had made a dying resolution to take as many people with him as he could. The woman, who could never have been right in her head to start with, was lying beside the road taking on all comers while two dead bodies simmered at the other end of her driveway. And wa'n't that an awful mess, though?

As best she could, Amy steered clear of the gossip. She was sorry for the whole mess, and even for Bud Harper. She did her best to pay attention to her job. At the feed store, however, she was lonely. Men made circles around her. Occasionally she surprised a group of them talking, but when she did they immediately fell silent, a thick silence that made it clear she was under discussion. A lot of boys she'd gone out with in high school seemed to get married that June to nice, quiet, little girls. When people looked at her these days, she felt, they were only measuring her muscle.

Marl Perry came into the feed store in the third week of June, but for Amy it was like hearing an old song that could still hurt you. She remembered Marl Perry. He reminded her of Sears, dead five and a half years. And of all those childhood days when she'd wanted to follow the older boys, just to be with somebody; and Marl reminded her of a certain dance, a body memory that had faded to a still, empty place inside her.

She was feeling thick, ugly, strong as a horse, big as a house. So she acted as if she hardly knew him while the old song tore up her insides. Marl Perry's turning up after all this time, she thought, was probably some kind of joke on her. Here she'd had the potential to grow up into an attractive woman, and she'd blown it, somehow, turned into an elephant instead. Marl Perry was probably God's little joke on her, to show her just what she'd become since the last time she'd seen him, all those years ago. The song was a pulsing ache in her bloodstream, but she wouldn't look at Marl unless she had to, nossir. And she'd swing those old sacks of grain like a man, to show him. Only way you could treat this kind of joke, she guessed. When Marl left the store that day, she kept right on working like a man. That night she brushed her hair with her back to the mirror.

But the second time he came into the store she knew she'd been expecting him. In the interval she'd somehow relearned his face, so that when he appeared it was like substance to the image, tanned, blond, light blue eyes, that tilt to the head; he always looked, she thought, as if he expected to hear something happy. Those lines at his mouth, as if he weren't afraid to speak up and say his piece if he had to. And then he did.

"Nothing so good has happened to me since," he said, and

heaven help her, she believed him! It was as if he were restoring in her a feeling she'd lost, the last few days. As if there were a warm, bright place somewhere, a place where God himself wouldn't be ashamed to smile.

So there she was, feeling like a kid at Christmas. And there was Marl Perry, his head on that side the way he did. And he was telling her he'd never forgotten her, in all this time. Inside Amy, lights were beginning to turn on . . .

And then somebody came in wafting perfume and pulled Marl's head down and kissed him. Somebody small and pretty. Someone who had those damn little thin ankles and high heels.

Well, nylon stockings had gone one way and Marl's boots and pant legs had followed. The old ankle socks and brown oxfords went the other; that way was gray, the landscape flat: the dead song, leaving her veins, took good blood with it. It was all a joke, all right, and she'd been caught—her and her grain bags. There was no place on earth she was going to fit, maybe. She wasn't an artist, she didn't have a farm. Just Auntie Amy, beast of burden.

The hell of it was, despite that little blond thing, she still wanted to believe Marl Perry. In her memory he'd always told the truth, God's honest truth; that long-dead phrase came back to her now. She'd not been so blind as to miss the look of horror on his face when he first caught sight of that other girl. It even occurred to Amy that maybe the joke was on Marl Perry, too. Nobody ever really got what they wanted, did they? Oh, God existed, you had to believe that, and Amy did. Happiness and warmth and light— these were real. Just unavailable, that was all. Not for her. What was hope, but rigging yourself up in high heels and earrings and wanting to be something you weren't?

Amy began to work so hard that she didn't need or want to think anymore. During free minutes, she sketched every damn flower in her mother's garden half a dozen times and was starting in all over again the day Marl Perry walked out back and asked her to go swimming with him. Those treacherous lights had begun to switch on again, it was almost more than she could stand. But she was careful! It might still be a joke. So she didn't move until he left, and she didn't let on about anything.

When she was sure he was gone, she jumped up and went to her room and put on her bathing suit, hours ahead of time, and stood in front of the mirror. Floodlights—and fear. She was too big—big hips, bust, thighs. She would have wept, she thought, if she could have stopped grinning.

So when she came out of the bathhouse that night at Deer Pond, she was ready. For protection against the joke she expected, she had thrown her towel across one shoulder and clutched it in thick, blunt fingers while she examined the tree trunks and the space around Marl for what was hidden and ready to jump out and laugh at her. Especially she expected the thin girl, slender and snappy, to come out and grab him and kiss him again. It was a measure of what she felt for Marl, what she was willing to risk; in that moment she knew it, too.

But no girl came. She examined Marl's face. He wasn't laughing.

"Carry your towel, lady?" he said. He was looking at her in a way she had to believe, a steady look, uncertain and a little shy. She went to him and shrugged off the towel, and he said something, it didn't matter what, but it made the sun dazzle on blue —not gray—water. She turned and he followed her, only her, down to the beach, where by common consent they walked to the far side, reserved by long custom for lovers.

*

Amy could swim a breast stroke. It allowed her to watch him as he dove in and out and swam overarm circles. She was learning his body and how it worked. His shoulders and back were brown and a little freckled. His waist tapered down to a pale spot that his work pants covered but his swimming trunks didn't; she wanted to touch that spot.

But when she wasn't watching Marl she was scanning the water.

At last he stopped swimming and lay on his back and floated toward her. "Feels good, doesn't it?"

She nodded.

[239]

"Are you waiting for someone?"

"No, I—"

"Then why do you keep looking out over the water that way?"

Amy stared down at her hands, unreal underwater flesh. It cost her something, but she admitted, "I can't help thinking she'll come back and kiss you again."

"What?" With a splash and sputter he stood up. He looked upset.

Well, she was upset, too. "And you can bet," she said quietly, "that it doesn't make me happy, either."

Suddenly his face changed and he reached out and took her by the shoulders. At first his lips were hard on hers and then very, very soft, fluttering like butterfly wings, as if to begin with she had no choice in this kiss, and then, out of regard for her, he would give her a choice. Amy drew close to him. Then it was all wet bathing suits, his lips nudging at hers, almost playing with them, until she gasped and pulled away a little and lay her face in his neck. After a while, gripping hands tightly, they walked back up onto the beach to their towels, to sit on the big pine roots and stare out into the water.

It was like seeing Deer Pond for the first time: the prophecy of their own lives, children playing, lovers, families, the old couples in street clothes staring who knew where. The last rays of the sun caught a new batch of evening picnickers coming down the beach, and lit them rosy and golden. It was so beautiful Amy shivered.

"Are you cold?" he asked instantly.

"Gettin' chilly. But they look happy down there, all set for a picnic."

"We'll do that," he said. "We'll do lots of things."

Amy nodded.

They went to change and then stopped at the little hamburger stand. Then, carrying wet bathing suits wrapped in towels and munching ice cream cones, they went back to the truck and rode home to the Trowleys'.

It was just after ten when they pulled in. Someone in the house was playing a Victrola and somebody else was talking to a fussy baby, you could hear it through the screened windows. Amy stared down the driveway toward the house and thought she might never go in.

Marl evidently thought so, too, because he began to tell her of his plans for Octavia's Hill—he had it all worked out, it seemed. A one-year plan, a five-year plan, a ten-year plan, and so on, turning Octavia's Hill into a self-supporting farm. Amy liked this kind of talk.

"So," he finished after a while, "that's the whole thing." He laughed a little. "Up to twenty-five years from now, if you can believe it."

"Oh, I believe it."

"But what do you think?"

"Well, it all sounds good to me—"

"Does it?" He was tickled.

"—except that you've forgotten somethin' kind of important."

Marl didn't believe it. "What?"

"You've rebuilt the old barn and built another, you've put in milking machines and sprinklers and a generator, you've plowed and put bob wire and all the rest of it. But where you goin' to live all this time?"

"Oh, that." Marl dismissed it with a wave of his hand. "In the farmhouse," he said. "My grandfather built it, it's plenty big—"

"But it's goin' to need some improvements, keep up with the times."

Marl studied her face in the dark. "Why, it's got a stone foundation, good shingles, two chimneys, tight roof—"

"Oh, I know," said Amy. "Like all the houses around here. If it were me, though, I'd want to have a furnace someday. And a bathroom. And a dry cellar. You get water in your cellar?"

"Need a rowboat."

"Hmm," she said.

"Well, Mother doesn't care, course, and I don't know much about houses."

"Well," she said cautiously, "maybe you should talk to your mother about it."

He lifted his head and laughed. "What Mother would like would be to move to Boston, but she'll never do it now. Deep down, I think, she knows she wouldn't be happy there, either. Nothing will please her. You know Mother."

Amy did. "She's been teachin' right along?"

"Teaching? Earning her living. Hers and mine, too."

"You want to repay—"

Just then, however, the screen door banged. Bill Trowley stood on the front porch. "Amy!" he hollered. "The seat of a truck just ain't that comfortable!"

"Oh, Lord," Amy said to Marl, sighing. "I am twenty-one, Pa!" she called out the window at his stocky form.

Marl snickered.

"Don't care about that!" her father hollered back. "Just want to know your plans, is all!"

"Bill! You come in here this minute!" This was Mary Trowley; her tall silhouette appeared at one of the lighted screened front windows.

"But Mother," said Bill, "you gonna let them stay out there 'till . . ." The rest was a mumble.

"Bill!" Mary Trowley's shocked voice. In a moment she had made her way to the kitchen, then she reached through the screen door and hauled her husband back inside, where the overtones of the argument continued to carry for a moment before subsiding.

Amy sighed again. "Well, I'd better go."

"Look," he said. "I'll come back tomorrow, that's Friday. I'll come earlier if I can get the cows milked. We'll go for a picnic or something, all right? I'll have Mother—"

"I'll make the food," said Amy. In the dark she could see what was now to her the irresistible tilt of his head.

He smiled. "Pick you up at work?"

"Yes."

"All right then."

Amy reached for the door handle, but then she drew her hand away. If this was going to be the end—and it very well might be, you never knew—if this was going to be the only last and best night of her life, she made up her mind suddenly she'd have everything in it she was supposed to have. Quietly she placed her two hands in her lap and waited.

Marl looked at her. If she'd started to get out, he would have stopped her. Now there she sat, dark hair just so, body substantial and cool-looking. He reached one hand toward her; she turned as if she were the lock, and that the key.

After a time he pressed her back against the seat, his mouth on hers, giving and getting consent. His hand was on her breast, which rose in his fingers.

"Oh, God," he groaned. "I want you, you know that."

She couldn't speak, but lay back, waiting. But his fingers grew lighter, then went away altogether. The breast missed him. She laid a hand on his leg. At the same time, however, she worked to put back together the elements of lucidity she knew he needed. "Not the place," she murmured.

He groaned again, took her fingers from his leg and kissed them. "Go. Quick. Or there's gonna be trouble."

Without a word she opened the truck door and climbed out and walked toward the house. About halfway there she paused and reached her hands to her hair. Then she turned and waved, and he left.

*

A sketch half-filled with color, one moment poppy red, the next dust. Time went endlessly, but Amy didn't let on. Late in the next day she left the store to Paul for a few minutes and went out back to the washroom, where she tried to see herself in the cracked, dusty piece of mirror tacked to the wall. As best she could she washed, pinning her hair more neatly. Then she went to the ice chest and took out the basket she'd prepared early that morning, deviled eggs, cold sliced beef, bread and butter, strawberries, cake, a thermos of lemonade. That picnic basket, she felt, was the

[243]

only tangible link between her and what had happened the night before.

Marl Perry was up early that day, too. He'd fed and milked twelve cows by hand and cleaned out their stalls and driven them to pasture by six-thirty that morning. He'd gone into the house, made himself breakfast, and left again by the time Lucy was up at seven. By noon he'd finished the garden work and went back to the house to eat his dinner. Lucy was fretting.

"Where did you go last night?" she wanted to know. "I waited up for you, but these days I just can't keep my eyes open past ten o'clock."

"Deer Pond," said Marl.

"Deer Pond," said Lucy. "And you went with—"

"Amy Trowley," said Marl. "Ol' Sears's sister. You remember Sears?"

"Of course I do," said Lucy. "I remember Amy, too. She was rather round, as a child, but all the Trowleys are. Is she any prettier now?"

"I think so," said Marl.

Lucy sat helplessly, a thin, little, unhappy woman, ramrod straight, behind her thin, little, uneaten meal; she felt as if she'd looked into her son's smile and seen her own shadow. She felt she was coming unstitched when she most needed stitching.

Marl thought she looked small and scared, and for that reason he got up and kissed her and patted her shoulder a little, something he rarely thought to do these days. "Don't worry, Mother. It'll be all right."

Lucy leaned against him. Overnight her son had grown up. It was all a mystery to her, she would never understand it. She waved him away. That Trowley girl, of all people. Tears formed in the fraught, tired corners of her eyes and she forgot to search for her handkerchief, wiping them instead—she discovered later with horror—on her napkin.

By suppertime she had recovered enough to think of cucumber sandwiches and hard-boiled eggs for her son the farmer. But he came in early.

"My goodness," she said, looking at his long, sweating length, "it's not time for supper yet, is it?" He was breathing hard, as if he'd been running.

"Mother, I won't be eating supper here. Amy's making a picnic."

"Amy?" A snail, deep in a shell: a small, hollow voice.

"I forgot to tell you, I'm sorry." His undershirt was in his hand. He mopped it across his sweaty forehead and around his neck. That left ribbons of black on the shirt.

"Give me that," Lucy snapped. "I trust you intend to wash?"

"Amy," said Marl, grinning at his own joke, "will take me as I am."

Lucy left the kitchen.

Marl could see that his mother might be a problem, but at that moment he had other business. He dragged out the old tin tub and took it to the shed, filling it half full of cold water from the new faucet he'd installed, then pouring in the rest of the lukewarm water from the teakettle. He didn't have time to wait for hot.

When he'd collected all his gear and brought that, too, out to the shed and set it on a sawhorse, he stepped into the tub and sat, ridiculously, knees to chin. He'd done this nightly just about all his life, but suddenly he began to study his routine. What, he wondered, would Amy think of it?

Marl looked about him. He'd always thought bathing this way was pleasant in the summer. You could watch flies buzz in and out of the shed door, and it was private, no one around for miles. The sun, and the trees in the distance, blue sky. You could study the clouds.

In the winter he bathed in the kitchen beside the stove in this same tub, sluicing down that part of the kitchen floor when he was done, since the water had always overflowed by the time he'd gotten all of him into it. Winter and summer his mother bathed in her room, endless basins of water, endless sponge baths. But Marl couldn't see Amy, that great big girl, bathing in a basin.

Amy, Marl decided, should have a bathroom if she wanted it,

and hot and cold running water, too. Amy should have everything she wanted. Octavia's Hill would be no good without Amy, no good at all.

Later, barreling down the hill at a dangerous speed, he realized he hadn't given his mother another thought. Oh, well, he told himself, she's a tough old girl, she'll get used to it.

He parked the truck beside the feed store warehouse and swung inside the wide warehouse door. Amy, he saw, was heading back over the threshold into the store at the other end. Lounging in a corner of the area she'd just passed was a group of men. Marl nodded; somebody waved back. But one loudmouth kept on talking.

"Think they raised that girl on bear meat," he was saying. "That Amy, boy, I'm scared to go near her."

Marl was by that time at the threshold of the store, but he paused, turning on his heel, and swung back to the group. A little muscle played along his jaw. He stepped up beside the talker, one Arthur Brown, a short, fat man for whom talk, the next time, wouldn't be quite so cheap.

"What was that?" Marl asked pleasantly enough.

"She's a big girl!" Arthur rolled his eyes and somebody else snickered. It was idle talk, harmless, wa'n't it? They thought so. The end of a day of discouraging hardscrabble work, a little fun, take your mind off your troubles? "I'd like to make friends with her, Jeesus!" Arthur's pudgy hands made circular motions at the front of his chest. "But I don't dare, nossir. Hell, I was here the time she picked up Bud Harper and nailed him to the wall! I dunno, guess he touched somethin' he shouldn't have. Girls that size, he always said, they're the best kind for—"

But suddenly Arthur Brown seemed to grow taller. Mouth still working but with no sound coming out of it, he grew right up out of that little group, down the warehouse, and out the doorframe at the end of it. In fact, if you hadn't seen Marl Perry behind him, you'd have thought old Art had sprouted wings. As it was, he flew through the warehouse door at surprising speed and landed on his ample bottom in the dirt outside, where he sat unhurt but shaking his head half-dazed, as if to say, "What in the hell hit me?"

It was a minute before he spotted Marl Perry, tall and straight and hard-handed, up on the landing.

"Son of a bitch," he whined.

"You wanna fight with me?" said Marl, breathing hard. "If you do, I'll fight!"

But from where Arthur was sitting, Marl Perry looked about nine feet tall. He didn't want to fight. "We got an argument, have we?" he asked.

"You talk anymore, ever, about that girl in there, we do," Marl said.

Arthur stood up slowly and dusted himself off. "Why, holy Jesus, Marl," he said, "if you didn't like it, all's you had to do was say so."

"You so much as say her name—" Marl continued.

"I don't intend to, Marl! Hell, just so's you don't beat me up!" said Arthur. "It was all in fun anyways."

"Hell with that," said Marl.

The short, fat man shook his head and shrugged. "Well, kids and mad dogs," he said. "God deliver us." And off he went, muttering and shaking the dust out of his pants.

Marl waited until Arthur had climbed into his old Ford and roared off. Then he strode back through the warehouse. But one by one the other men had melted out through the store, and he finished his entry to the tune of starting motors and cars rumbling away. Amy was standing by herself behind the counter. Beside her was a picnic basket. And there was, evidently, nothing wrong with her hearing.

"They'll just talk more, you know," she said quietly. "Only now they'll talk about you."

"Well, then, I'll handle that, too," said Marl, still red behind the ears.

"Well, it was good of you to—"

"You weren't mixed up with Bud Harper," he interrupted her.

"No, well . . ." She looked down. "I did shove him against a wall. And I guess I gave him a black eye." Her voice sank. "Don't know my own strength." She braced herself against his inevitable laughter.

But Marl only nodded his head, one sharp nod. "Damn right, too," he said. "Give 'em hell. You don't, I will."

He picked up the picnic basket and leaned on the counter where it had been. Amy still didn't look up.

"Hey, buddy," he said in his gentlest voice, "you goin' out with me?"

When Amy did meet his eye, her lips were trembling. One tear had made a wet path to her jaw.

"I want to if you want to," she said in a broken voice.

He hadn't far to go to touch the tear path with his lips, and the taste of it stayed on his tongue long after they ended up on Octavia's Hill.

*

As he had known they would. Before dark they drove to the little schoolhouse, parked the truck, and took the path past it into the woods, strolling toward the foot of the hill, talking and climbing around its base. Amy told Marl all about Bud Harper, and Marl mentioned Betsy. When they came to an open, grassed-over spot, they sat with their backs comfortably against the trunks of trees, with only the summer air between them.

"When I saw Betsy that day, I thought she must be your girl," Amy said, "the way she kissed you. That gave the men something to talk about."

Marl stared past her. "So they discussed that, too, did they?"

"You knew they would."

"I made love to Betsy."

"You did." Amy didn't move.

"Not just once by mistake either. Lots of times."

There was a silence. "You still want to?"

Marl flushed. "God, no!"

"Then it's all right."

"You don't want to get mad, something?"

"I want to be happy." She smiled a slow smile. "Today is already more than I expected."

"Here today, gone tomorrow—that what you think?"

"Hell." Amy dimpled, staring above their heads at green leaves, sky. "I'm not going to think at all, just gets me into trouble."

After a while they walked again, staying in the forest and strolling to the north side. Then they went up the hill, quite close to the farmhouse, but hidden.

"Enough pasture for forty cows, well, thirty, anyways," Marl was saying to her as they went. "Space down there, by the spring? You see it? Fodder corn, put it to rye for now, till I get the stalls built. Good barn, though. Put out some apple trees, see that? Over there, those six little sticks, poking up, out beyond the barn? Goin' to have two apples this year—big ones! Well, there was an old orchard there, once." Picking up that bit of stone as he walked, touching this tree, gauging its growth potential.

"I want to take you into the house, too," he said as they walked. "See what you think."

But Amy stared out over the darkening hill. "Time enough for that," she said.

Not so much as a twig seemed to obstruct the path they took. When the field was dark and cool they crossed it; newly mown and fragrant, the grass stretched before them in easy, grasshopper-sung silence. By the spring frogs chirruped. It was stillness for country ears, silver and starlit. At the end of the field they stopped to turn and look back up the hill. A light in a window of the far-off house went out. "That's Mother," said Marl. "Goin' to bed."

"Gettin' late," said Amy.

Two strong forms, tall and well made: Marl and Amy moved together and then apart. But now they held the impress of one another, Amy thought. As if they had been made of poured silver, different halves of the same mold, torn apart somehow. They moved down the field, back to the grassed-over place in the woods, missing each other, reaching blindly toward each other, searching.

What no one saw that night but Amy and Marl, who never spoke of it and never felt the need to explain until it was too late, was two bodies easing together with a kind of silver shine. Marl, who knew the more, waited. Amy, gasping and learning fast, moved at first with slow dignity and then with the dignity of delicious speed. What nobody else ever saw, and in the light of day forgot to think about, were these long silver hours between them, of which this was only the first and certainly not the best. But it seemed to Amy to be the best, as over years of encounters, certain silver nights always seemed the most impossibly best, and yet in retrospect nothing beside the silver present.

The first night what they had they treasured between them, so personal they would never share it with another living soul, could never speak of it, not with mother or daughter or friend. Once Marl, his tender waiting stretched to the breaking point, hovering, had entered Amy for the first time and she, gasping, learned how to move and he had come—once Marl had come and stayed and waited for her until her own body arched in a wild, high arch and she sobbed and laughed together—then the lock was shut around them and they were, finally, no one else's. The silver impression left in the woods was for their eyes and no others. And that, in time, was what made their relationship so irrevocable and vulnerable: it belonged to two very private people.

After a while they stood and dressed, helping each other, learning how clothes fit there, or just there. They could never travel by this place again without knowing it for the mirror of what they carried inside them during the days and found again on certain nights, when they made love so quietly they disturbed no one else in the house.

Marl took Amy home, feeling that all the future had been implied and accepted and snatched away from him again as she left him. Amy went to bed with one foot in the silver grave of what had shone so and was now finished, the other reaching for a rung up to the next time, the next place—that was how, suddenly, she needed him.

Much later, in their married life, when Tave was a little girl, she came upon them suddenly and found them in a rare, tight embrace. She heard her father murmur, "There's that place, you know the one." His face was nestling beneath the hair on her mother's neck. "I remember," her mother murmured.

Tave tiptoed out of the room and never mentioned it to a living soul, it was too private.

*

In a month Amy and Marl saw each other thirty days. Lucy said acidly that she hoped he would hurry up and marry the girl so that she could get a look at her son's face again.

Bill Trowley stopped calling out, "What are your plans, Amy?" Now there was only an audible mutter and the slammed screen door.

Amy settled on August 25; by then Marl's haying would be over and they could get away for a long weekend. Marl, who would have taken time off the farm for no other reason, hunted all over town and finally found in this busy time of year young Tommy Green, who was available to come and do the chores. Tommy Green was Cone Green's son, Alden Green's grandson. Sometimes when you went up Octavia's Hill you could see him squatting out by the porch door at the Greens'; he seemed to be counting the traffic. Tall, lanky, dirty, silent as the coming darkness, Tommy was a "good enough worker." By that time both Cone and Tommy were hired all over town, not regularly, but at so much a week, for odd jobs. People said there was something uncanny about that young one and the way he appeared and disappeared outside doors.

Lucy, sick to the heart at Marl's marriage, locked herself into the farmhouse while Tommy Green was there, although Marl said he was harmless, practically a deaf-mute. Lucy said she was having nothing more to do with any Green, ever. It had been years since Lucy had seen Cone, but she hadn't forgotten the shock of seeing her mother's ring again. She supposed that by now it was long gone. All old business. Marl suspected that it wasn't Tommy, exactly, that Lucy was avoiding. It was something between people that she seemed to fear; her son and Amy Trowley: did they resemble too much another couple, about whom she never spoke?

One day during that summer before the marriage, Marl brought Amy to the farmhouse to make the engagement official, and Amy, shaking hands and speaking with country friendliness, invited Lucy down to the Trowleys' on the following Sunday afternoon. There'd be a picnic and she would, she said, show off her ring.

"Oh? I wasn't aware . . ." said Lucy, with a trembling, unnecessary flutter that made Amy think of a sparrow caught in a chicken yard.

"Good gosh," said Marl. He leaned back on his heels and grinned proudly. "I thought you knew."

"May I see?" Little bird chirps.

Amy pitied those sharp sounds. She held out her blunt fingers. On her hand was a ring, a square diamond set between two opals; a heavy silver ring, not elaborate, certainly, but it satisfied Amy. Solid-looking, she thought. Made to last.

"Hay money," said Marl.

"Did you," said Lucy to Amy, "design it yourself?"

As if, Amy thought, a hen might as easily birth a heifer.

"I saw it first," Marl said, "last time I was in Bangor. Friday night we went down and bought it."

"Why, I had no idea," said Lucy.

It was as honest as she was all that day.

But Amy hadn't expected compliments. She knew Lucy Perry; besides, all Amy's life the world had had a tendency to yammer. She wasn't going to let one little woman with a poker for a spine bother her. She and Lucy would never be friends; she didn't commit the grave error of proffering friendship. Lucy could have taken that and twisted it fourteen dozen ways to Sunday.

Amy knew, simply, that Marl loved the hill and that he was indebted to his mother. It never occurred to her to suggest that Lucy should now take an indefinite vacation with the Marlowes in Boston. Instead she held out her ring and let the thin woman

[252]

speak in her brisk, cutting twitter; Amy nodded and hardly heard. That voice would probably be one of the daytime conditions of her life down the patience-thinned years, but in those moments Amy accepted that. She could stand it. And there was always Marl, tall and handsome and loving her, Technicolor days and silver nights. It was worth it. What they had already was worth it.

*

At the Sunday afternoon engagement picnic there were Trowleys and Trowley relations, townspeople, children. Perhaps there were a hundred and fifty people or more; half the county, it seemed, were either friends or relatives. It was a pleasantly hot day. Lucy wore a hat, Amy saw, and sat on the porch and nodded at people if she had to, offering thin fingers to the women to shake, nothing at all to the men.

After a while Grandpa Trowley wobbled out to the porch. He was thin, old, as trembling as one frightened breath. He leaned on his son's arm and offered Lucy his shaking hand. Lucy touched it coolly with the tip of her longest fingers. Then Grandpa raised one everlasting eyebrow and wheezed in a thin-reed voice, "Jesus Christ, woman, can't you do no better than that?"

Amy snorted out a laugh and studied her potato salad until she could stop snickering.

Her father, who had Grandpa by the arm, sighed, and his face got red. "Now, Pa." He tried to subdue the old man. "That ain't good manners! You come set down! This lady's a school-teacher!"

"Well, damned if anybody bother to tell me!" wheezed Grandpa. "Holy old outhouse!"

Amy's father waggled his eyebrows helplessly in the Trowley signal of apology at Lucy, who obviously didn't understand it. Then he got Grandpa off the porch as quickly as possible.

The truth was, Amy thought, that the only cold place on the Trowley farm that day was on the porch where Lucy sat, and the weather didn't have a lot to do with it. The rest was chicken barbecue, slopped soda in the punch, melting sherbet, watermelon, sun. There were kids rolling down hills and kids riding horses and men playing horseshoes and women taking tours of the house and discussing quilts and babies. It was hot and bright. You made an occasional dive, a plunge, really, onto Lucy's part of the porch, and when it got too cold to stand it, Amy thought, why, you got off fast and went out to warm up again.

Marl stood by the fence talking cows and Amy stayed up by the house passing paper plates of chicken. There was no line between them, nothing to connect them, it seemed. Even in this celebration they kept it private. You wouldn't have known who was engaged if it hadn't been for that curious, outlandish silver ring flashing among dishes and cutlery. The engagement party was like any outdoor picnic, only bigger. There was plenty of joshing, even a water fight with buckets and hoses. Old Grandpa Trowley beat at the lawn furiously with a stick and hollered, "Get him! Soak him in the pants! Jesus, boy, ain't you house-trained yet?" Everybody acted up more, Amy knew, for Grandpa's benefit, having seen him fall away and fail so in the last months. Plenty of buckets threatened to soak him, never, of course, allowing one drop of water too near him, to remind his sun-warmed flesh of chill.

Amy glanced from time to time up at the porch. Lucy, she saw, picked at a piece of chicken. Her elbows were in and her knife carefully laid aside all the bright, sweet sauce, a famous Trowley recipe. But all around Marl's mother, people picked up the chicken and chewed it off the bone and acted as if it tasted good. Then Amy's mother went and with sunny, sweating good humor sat down beside Lucy.

"Heavens," Amy heard her mother say, "you didn't get enough to eat, did you? Now you set right there while I go make them fill up your plate better 'n 'at—"

Lucy said, as Amy knew she would, "Why, no, thank you, Mrs. Trowley. I really don't care for any more."

Mary Trowley could hardly believe it. "You sure? Heavens! Round here, picnic like this, we expect people are goin' to eat all afternoon, maybe longer! Little more potato salad, maybe, get you goin' again? Amy made it, two big canners full! One thing your son is gettin' is a girl who knows her way around a kitchen—"

"No, thank you," Lucy said, right out of the deep freeze. "Nothing more."

All those years when Sears and Marl had played together, all the associations Lucy had had with the Trowley family, and she had never made friends with them, maybe never would. Mary Trowley stood up and rowed ashore, as it were, joining her daughter out in the sun. "She's a tough one," she muttered to Amy. "I dunno . . ."

Her mother, Amy knew, was used to making lifelong friends on an afternoon like this. Pretty soon she was cutting a big piece of chocolate cake and taking it up to Lucy, along with a clean fork and a fresh napkin.

"Oh, no, I—" Lucy said, half rising.

"Now don't you get up," said Mary Trowley. "Good heavens, no. You just set right there and I'll pull this table over. We'll put the cake here so's 'twill be here when you want it. Though I dunno's you want to leave it too long, the flies'll be after it." Mary pulled up a chair and sat, a tall, content, hospitable woman in a flowered cotton dress. She had large white earrings in her ears —she'd put them on especially for this occasion. Mary never worried about talking to people; if they didn't like her—and so far just about everybody had, hadn't they?—why, then, that was their problem, and she wa'n't goin' to spend time worryin' it over. But she'd put on this dress and squeezed her feet into her dress-up shoes and put on her summer earrings, and she'd try to make Marl's mother like her. After all, Marl was such a good boy.

Lucy was wearing her best, too. It was a dove-gray suit of summer-weight wool, with a white silk blouse gathered at the neck in high, immaculate ruffles. On her feet were white shoes. A pair of pure white gloves lay in her lap. The whole outfit was probably years old, Amy knew from what Marl had told her, but it looked as if it had been bought the day before. It was a talent to choose clothes that were always in style and to keep them looking so fresh; Amy admired it.

Lucy sat up straight. Her eyes went repeatedly toward her tall blond son, as if to say, "Why have you abandoned me?" But he now stood with his back to her, at the other side of the lawn. He'd long since forgotten her and all women. One foot up on the white board gate, he was listening earnestly to something Bill Trowley was saying. While Amy watched, both men lifted their heads back and laughed and her father reached up and clapped Marl on the shoulder. It was a comfortable sight.

"They do get along, don't they?" said Mary Trowley, who had seen it, too. "Talk by the hour, never a raised voice between 'em. And in this house that's somethin'."

"Oh?" said Lucy.

"Gracious, yes," Mary said. "I've always been grateful we were so far away from our next neighbors—so they couldn't hear the fightin', you know." And she leaned back and laughed.

"I see," said Lucy.

"Marl says your people come from up Boston." Mary Trowley settled her wide rear more comfortably in her chair. "Says you was raised there, though I believe I do remember your father, just. Lived here all his life, didn't he?"

"Yes," said Lucy, "I believe so. I didn't know him well. When Mother died, I was sent to Boston to school."

Mary Trowley had been to Boston twice. Now she searched her mind for slender memories of it; it was work. By this time ladies were usually discussing labors, the personal habits of their children, and family medical problems.

"Well, I was up to Boston several years ago," she said at last. "Bill had a cow convention, and I went. Did some shoppin'. Prob'ly you been there since I have, though, that was ten years ago."

"I have not been to Massachusetts for thirty years," said Lucy stiffly. "All Marlowe cares about is his farming."

There was a short silence. Mary Trowley gave a little laugh. "Well, now," she said easily, "it ain't such a dirty word as all that."

"But he could have gone to Harvard," said Lucy. "All the Marlowe men have gone there."

"Oh, he ain't done so badly, though," said Mary. "One of the few educated farmers around here—only one, I think. Him and Bill, they've already laid out a breedin' plan for—"

"Cows," said Lucy Perry. "I know. If he'd married differently, however . . ." She didn't finish.

Mary Trowley stiffened. There was a limit to what she would put up with, from anybody. "But if there's anybody that's made for each other," she said firmly, "it's those two young ones. We wouldn't let Amy go 'less we thought so. It's a good match, the best. And a good match—nothin' like it. No bed of roses, anyway. Father and I've had our go 'rounds. But Amy and Marl are strong and sensible and a good age for startin' . . ."

Mary's eyes touched at her husband's form for a second, then moved away. She fell silent. There were some things you talked about and some you didn't. Some you couldn't tell if you wanted to. She reached up and batted at an imaginary fly. "Well," she said, "they've found out where I am, them flies! I'm goin' to take a turn around the yard and say hello. You want to come along, Miss Perry? Meet a few more Trowleys, if you can stand it?"

"I shall stay here," said Lucy primly, "until Marlowe can take me home."

For a split second Amy held her breath. Her mother looked totally exasperated, like she wished to God Lucy would be the sort of woman who could dish food and talk along. But somehow Mary managed to keep it to herself. "Well, all these relatives," she said. "Don't know's I blame you. Be back, later on. You eat your cake . . ." This vaguely into the sunlit air as Mary walked away. But it was obvious she'd begun to suspect what Amy already knew, that all her encounters with Lucy Perry would be cut from the same cloth as this one.

A few days later Marl brought Amy back up to Octavia's Hill again. This time she was shown the house. Then Marl said, "Mother, you know, my room will be too small after the wedding. I think, if you don't mind, we might take over the big room at the

[257]

end of the hall. It's got that big bed in it and the two bureaus, and much more space—"

"The big room?" said Lucy. They might have been asking for the moon. "You want to—"

Amy said nothing. She stood there and felt somehow that she belonged in the house. She and Marl had been over it and she felt that it fit her; in spite of Lucy Perry, she would learn its ways easily.

"Yes," said Marl. "I've opened up that bed already and moved my things in. Over the next little while, maybe, we'll put in Amy's clothes. We could bring some over tomorrow."

"Amy's clothes." One of Lucy's hands wrapped itself tightly over the other at her waist. "But I don't think that room is suitable." She said it sharply.

Marl had already turned to go back up the stairs. Now he paused. "Mother, it's the logical choice," he said patiently. "And it's really the only room big enough—"

"No!" A cry, torn out of his mother, almost. "You don't know what you—"

Marl frowned.

"I opened the windows," said Amy quietly, to help her. "We don't care if the room hasn't been used for a while. I thought if you had sheets for the bed, I would use them, whatever you think. Or we have some sheets now, a wedding present. I'll bring them over tomorrow. They're kind of nice, embroidered."

After a moment it did seem to help. "The hall closet, upstairs," Lucy whispered, clearing her throat. But she looked, Amy thought, as if they'd walked over her grave. "Take whatever you need. I—I don't feel very well suddenly, Marlowe. A bit faint . . ."

Marl was back downstairs in an instant. "Why, you come right out here, Mother," he said, taking her arm and leading her toward the porch. "You sit right down. I'll bring some tea."

"I shall go to my room," said Lucy. "Tell her"—"Amy" never made it into Lucy's vocabulary—"to take what she wants. It'll be

[258]

her house soon . . ." She headed for her room and closed the door behind her.

But Amy made some tea—the kitchen was easy, almost familiar, and no one said no—and Marl took it in while she went back upstairs to the hall closet.

Heavy percale sheets, yellowed but whole and good. They need to be laid in the sun, Amy was thinking. They'll sweeten and bleach. But for now they would do. The whole house was that way, it seemed to her. Clean, yes, but not cared for, not loved. Amy itched to get busy. She had made the big bed and was examining the room when Marl came back upstairs. It hadn't been opened for some time, and the air was musty. The curtains were clean but limp; the furniture needed an affectionate polish. There was so much to do! Amy would do it gladly, even make a clean sweep of the house for fall housekeeping. Lucy would be at school and glad of the help, probably. Amy would let in air, sunshine, color. She would put out the warm new blankets and thick towels that had come to her from all over town; she would can applesauce and make pies . . .

Then Marl, tall and blond, was in the doorway. "Find what you need?"

She smiled her answer. "Is your mother all right?"

"Oh, yes. She's not really sick, you know. Just upset."

"I know."

"Can you stand it?"

"It's hard for her, Marl."

"And not for you?"

"Not that much. There's the house, the hill. Marl?"

The look of happiness in her eyes made him kick the door shut and go to her. "Yes?"

She saw in his mind the long silver nights. His hands were on her body. "You like this house?" he asked.

She sighed. "Yes, I do." Then a thought struck her and she moved against him, more for the sake of his sense of humor than anything. "You know that hallway room beyond the closet?" she murmured.

[259]

"Storage room?" He muttered it to her neck as they swayed together.

She grinned into his shoulder. "Make a good bathroom," she said.

There was a snort of astonishment and then a hoot of laughter. "Boy, that's catching me in a weak moment."

Amy nodded. She looked up at him serenely, devil mischief hidden in her eyes. "A bathroom would be nice," she said softly. "Besides which, we might as well talk about that. We can't make love in broad daylight. Your mother is downstairs." But now her hands were moving along his body; she loved the feel of him.

"Lady," he mumbled, "you can have whatever you want."

"Do it standing up," said Amy.

"What?"

"Otherwise we'll muss the bed. She'll know."

"Hell with that."

So they used the bed. And coming home after their wedding and honeymoon was coming home to the silver of that, too; it greeted them and held them until new nights erased the old. But it was never so much the act as their combined need in the act that made it shine.

*

There was something gay about the wedding, something solemn. It was a quiet ceremony in the center of Mary Trowley's braided rug. Amy in a beige suit and an elbow-length antique veil, her hands full of sweet peas and baby's breath picked that morning in her mother's garden; Dr. Locke from Bangor, the distinguished minister of the Universalist Church there, performing the ceremony; Marl tall and handsome in a new dark suit; the living room filled with flowers and shining with polish.

When the time came, the bride walked down the long pine-board hall and out through the living room to where Marl stood. Lucy Perry was the only one of Marl's family to attend, although a number of his college friends were present. The Marlowes of Boston had declined. None of them had ever been farther north

[260]

than Ogunquit and would dear Lucy understand if they sent along gifts instead? The Marlowe silver coffee service was sent directly to Amy's home, and a matched set of books, entitled *The Romantic Poets*, handsomely bound in leather.

During the few simple minutes of wedding service there came to the family gathered a kind of surrender, as wistful as the breath of that day, blowing in gently through all the windows. Amy's low voice, Marl's broken one, the friendly murmur of the minister: these were ceremonious in spite of themselves; promises made where no one pretended to be anything but human and made of dust and promises. It was a ceremony felt in the tentative, unexplored regions of hearts, and more inviolate because of its simplicity—as if the shapes inside a precious locket came alive and merged, so that the locket could not be pried apart, or if it were, both pictures would be destroyed.

Lucy stood straight as an arrow in the Trowley living room, her stiff, unwilling fingers intertwined with daisies and sweet peas still damp from Mary's border. She kept her spine straight despite the dizzying smell of fresh flowers, and she didn't look at her son, now lost to her. She didn't see the kiss, a short kiss that ended in laughter and flower-pelting.

Then it was all country party. All those brick red faces and every last resident in town, it seemed, on hand, grinning and eating. Lucy's pupils and their children who were pupils, a thick white cake she couldn't eat, someone thrust a ground ham and pickle sandwich on a decorated plate into her hand—it was all too much.

She could see Amy's large beige form, her quiet smile, handshakes, kisses. She wondered how, and what on earth, and why. This was so different from what she'd pictured Marl's wedding might be: an awning, perhaps, in some Boston garden, shrimp cocktail, tea, a champagne toast. Dinner served by white-coated attendants. Marl in formal dress, his bride chic in expensive white. She, Lucy, would have worn one perfect orchid.

At the far end of the porch two white-covered picnic tables groaned with wedding gifts, ruffled doilies with homemade crocheted lace in yellow and purple and white, an afghan, quilts, canned goods, aprons, pots and pans, thick glasses for everyday, dishes, serving spoons, measuring cups, cutting boards, a mixer from Amy's mother, a set of frying pans with black cast-iron hooks so they could be hung on the wall within easy reach of the stove. There were garden tools from Bill Trowley, including a scythe and an old-fashioned hay rake, for a joke. And in the middle of it all stood the matched set of the Romantic poets, Keats up, and the Marlowe silver coffee service, gleaming austerely.

"Got an awful lot of good stuff, ain't they?" somebody would say. Or, "Jeez, nice things, wouldn't mind havin' that afghan myself." "Nice glasses. We need glasses?" "Hey, Miss Perry, how much of this do you want me to steal?"

Lucy tried to smile, but the pink sandwich troubled her because there was no place to put it down. She couldn't eat it, and she didn't trust her legs, suddenly, to get her off the porch. Wildly she looked around and didn't see Marl. She panicked; the dish fell and broke, Mary Trowley was at her side.

"You all right?" Mary asked, kneeling to pick up the broken plate and the pieces of sandwich. Then she stood up, a bit pink-faced. She was feeling a little uneasy herself. "These weddings, they do a person in," she said sympathetically.

"As a matter of fact," said Lucy, reaching out to steady herself on the back of a chair, "I am a little dizzy. The heat, probably. I thought I'd missed, that he'd—they'd—gone off and not said goodbye."

"Here," said Mary gently, "you come with me. You stay right by me. No, no, they haven't gone yet. Why, them kids haven't finished doctorin' up the truck. No, Amy's gone up to change and Marl's gettin' her suitcase. Now you come and stand in the shade with me. You'll see them in a minute."

"I'm sorry," said Lucy weakly. "My knees . . ."

"Well, the heat!" said Mary. "And I know just how you feel. It's a real step, ain't it? Here, right through here, you stand with me. That's better. You better now?"

The only thing Lucy didn't want, which was to stand there with her arm through the strong arm of that girl's mother, was the thing she did. "Oh, yes," she said, her lips trembling. "I'm much better now." If only the world weren't so dark, she was thinking. If it made more sense . . .

Mary Trowley glanced at her with a summing-up look. "Not that much, though, huh?" she said. "White as a sheet! Well, they'll be leavin' soon, and then we'll tuck you up and take you home to bed."

"I can take care of myself! There's no need for you to . . ."

But Mary Trowley had turned back to face the truck, to which finishing touches in the form of shaving cream were being added. "There's no need to fuss," she said. "It'll give me something to think about."

There was a little lost note in her voice that Lucy recognized: the mother missing the lamb that would never come back again. But even then Lucy took her arm away and said, "Marlowe's truck!"

Marl's blue truck—Lucy had never been fond of it, but Marl kept it clean and shining—looked very strange. There were sticks with pennants flying from them taped securely along the sides. A long stream of toilet paper had been twisted in a bunting that sagged across the back. Tied to the rearview mirror was a string of old shoes, and a long line of tin cans hung out the back. Several JUST MARRIED signs in differing sizes of cardboard had been attached to the truck, and one of similar spelling now ran along one side of it in shaving cream.

"They're coming, they're coming." A murmur of warning ran along the crowd as the last pebble-filled hubcap was tapped into place and handfuls of rice and flower petals passed among them. Amy came to the porch first, with Marl right behind her. Laughing, she tossed her flowers out into the crowd of females waiting. The bouquet came apart in the air, and many hands caught at the blossoms. Mary Trowley began to laugh. "I hope they don't all decide to get married at once."

In a hail of petals and rice the bride and groom ran to their

[263]

parents, and there was no time for anything but a quick peck in the direction of Marl's chin and a quick laying of Amy's cool cheek against hers. Then they were off into the truck, Amy in and Marl slamming her door and rushing around to his—he knew that amount of manners, anyway, Lucy thought—and when he opened his door two gallons of carefully rigged confetti fell out all over him in a shower, so that he stood in a little heap of it. There was a laugh from the crowd and a new rain of rice. He shook his fists at them, grinning, confetti in his hair and down his collar. Then he was in, and then he was gone, with a wave and a toot.

It was over. Lucy found that her arm was once again in the tight grip of Mary Trowley.

"Well, there." Mary sighed. "I guess we'll none of us forget that for a while. Sorry I hung on so close. Couldn't help myself, I guess."

Lucy quietly extricated her arm, saying nothing.

"Well, we might as well join the party." There was strain in Mary's eyes, but just for a moment. Then she smiled. "All over but the hollerin'. You sure you're all right, now? Stand by yourself?"

"I have been standing by myself," said Lucy clearly, "for a number of years."

And just as straight and dark as a crow in the flowers, too, thought Mary. "Why, yes," she murmured. "That's fine."

"I wonder," said Lucy, "do you suppose there is someone among these people who might take me home now?"

Mary blinked. "Home? We thought you'd stay. At least until . . ." At least until the party's over, she was thinking. At least until I've had a chance to put my feet up and talk it all out. You take my one and only girl up onto that hill and I'm not at all sure you'll make her happy. Marl will. But you—I'd like to make sure we understand one another first.

"I'm very tired," said Lucy. "And the heat . . ."

"Well, if you're sick . . ." Mary Trowley said it reluctantly. Suddenly she feared that she and Lucy understood each other too

[264]

well, and all the talking in the world wouldn't change it.

The oldest boy, Tom, was found to take Lucy home. The next day he went back with the wedding gifts, which at Lucy's direction he placed in the front sitting room. There Lucy left them, shut the door on them, pretended they didn't exist. Nothing existed. Wasn't it better that way?

Four days later she stood on the porch and watched Amy open her own truck door and step solidly onto the ground and wait for Marl to join her, and of course it all existed and it was inexplicable. Amy looked as if she didn't even have to watch Marl to know just where he walked; now why was that? Once up on the porch the girl did no more than incline her cheek toward Lucy. Lucy did the same. Had they been brought up at the Ritz? And then there was Marl's smack on his mother's cheek, like an explosion.

"Mother," said Marl, "here is my wife." Gay and solemn, it was as much a ceremony as the wedding itself had been.

Lucy suddenly felt weak.

"Mother?" said Marl. "You all right?"

It was only a slight trembling, a convenient weakness that wrapped tiny arms around Lucy and protected her: she hugged it to her as if it were her only true child. "I must be ill," she said. "The last few days—a touch of influenza, perhaps."

In Marl's memory his mother had been sick only once: the time Cone Green had showed her that ring. "Maybe a doctor," he said.

But Lucy found herself looking into the level eyes of Amy Trowley, now Amy Perry. "It's nothing," Lucy said. "But I do think I will go and sit down. I planned to get a good supper for you, Marlowe, but now—"

Amy understood. "Heavens," she spoke up, "you go right in and sit down, Miss Perry. I haven't cooked a thing for four days and it's about time I stopped bein' so lazy."

"Mother," corrected Marl. Amy looked directly at Lucy, who made no move to affirm or deny.

"Mother Perry," said Amy. "You go on, Marl, you take her. I can find my way around the kitchen, don't you worry."

[265]

Marl grinned. "Yes, ma'am," he said. "Mother, we have to do what she says."

"Well," said Lucy, "all right then." She began to feel a little better (she hated cooking) and took her son's arm. "Marlowe, you come right in here and tell me all about your trip."

But somewhere above her head she felt rather than saw the eyes of those two meet.

"I can, just for a minute," Marl said politely. "Then I've got to go down to the barn and see how Tommy's doing."

"You and your precious barn," Lucy said. Marl tucked her up on the porch sofa.

"All I'll tell you," he said, "is that the ocean was blue and the sky was yellow and we ate in restaurants three times a day. The rest I'll say after supper, and Amy can help me tell it."

Lucy saw him look again at Amy, who was now standing quietly in the doorway. Then he left. Amy stood still for a moment. "You rest now," she said.

"If you don't find pans to suit you," Lucy said suddenly, sharply, "your wedding presents are in the front sitting room."

"Marl and I'll look at those together later, I believe," said Amy, and turned toward the kitchen.

*

In a brief time, quietly, Amy was running the house and doing it her own way. It was a little like having Jane Sapley around all over again. Lucy's dizzy spells occurred only at home, never at school, where she now ruled the roost in a somewhat frightening way. A trip to Dr. Sapley's revealed only that Lucy was a healthy woman soon to turn sixty. The doctor prescribed mild exercise, so every morning while Amy got breakfast—she was young and strong, so obviously made for kitchen work—Lucy walked the length of the hall, up the stairs, down the stairs, the length of hall again, ten times. Then she sat and ate Amy's good hot cereal and muffins and Marl drove her to school. It was too bitterly cold outside, Lucy said, for a woman of her age and delicate constitution to be walking to work.

As for Amy and Marl, there was never a raised eyebrow between them at these new antics. They simply left Lucy free to do and act as she pleased. Over a period of time, Lucy began to realize that it didn't matter what she did or said or how she worked on this couple, there was something of iron between them, which held their open hearts at a distance from her and seemed to keep them safe.

If Amy had been lazy or given to daydreaming, she might have been insecure enough to worry about the little literate jibes Lucy dished out. "Obfuscate," she would say to Amy in an odd moment. "Now there's a word. But I'm sure that it's not in your vocabulary."

Amy's reply always blended the required humility with the faintest trace of humor. "It's not a word I use much, course, Mother Perry."

Then Lucy would sigh and say, "I thought not." Sometimes the word would be *periphrastic*, or *kyphosis*, or *apodictic*.

Amy kept right on about her business.

Perhaps it was that she and Marl began their married life while Lucy was away at school most of the day; at any rate, they seemed to fit each other's rhythm in a way that Lucy found inexplicable. Breakfast was full of the odd jobs Marl meant to do, to which Amy listened consideringly. The language of tractor and garden, cows coming in or drying up, was common to both of them; these were country words. At supper Marl stretched his stockinged feet under the table and tilted his head at Lucy, but she could tell it was Amy's footstep from stove to table he really heard, Amy's chuckle he courted. At noontime Lucy ate at school, alone in the schoolroom at her desk, while the children ate outside, or behind a book while the children munched with surreptitious giggles around the stove. Amy and Marl ate alone together in the house.

And made love. The fact was that Lucy didn't imagine—couldn't—the other half of the life Marl and Amy led together: when people were around they hardly looked at each other, never touched or kissed, never seemed to want to. When Marl stopped opening doors for Amy, Lucy blamed it on the girl. She didn't know, she couldn't have pictured, Amy hovering in rich, large nakedness above Marl on their bed upstairs, nothing between them but laughter.

"Open the damn door for your mother, if you got to," Amy was telling him, with a throaty chuckle. "Leaves me feelin' I got two left feet."

Marl laughed freely into the corners of the ceiling, but then his eyes were serious, hungry for her in the bright noon light. "Whatever you want," he said, waiting for her white breasts to be lowered, to tease at his lips.

*

In her quiet way Amy saw more color now than she'd seen in all the rest of her life, or so it seemed. She brought warmth with her into rooms: she was happy, she felt strong; she'd been lost and unloved and now was neither. Marl was her life, she was going to have his baby, and oh, wasn't she busy?

After a while Lucy said it didn't matter what they did with the upstairs, she was too delicate to take care of that part of the house anyway. Amy soon picked out one of the unused bedrooms and set to braiding rugs for the floors and thinking about paint and paper. This would be the baby's room, although no one but Amy knew it yet. Another bedroom she put to good use with her sketches and art supplies; she still liked to dabble of an afternoon.

She polished floors and washed walls. In the middle of the fall, Marl found the money for her to have her precious bathroom. They put it in the small room next to the linen closet. A closet in the front sitting room they turned into a lavatory for Lucy, too, so that the house was one of the first in the area to have two bathrooms. The cellar Amy appropriated for canned goods, and Marl put in drains and built shelves for it during the winter.

Lucy worked less and less around the house. In fact, she now seemed to think it was below her station to do anything but go to school in the morning. Amy didn't mind. She was glad to take over the kitchen, and when the plumbing was all done, she had hot water there. And the house was warmer. They cleaned out all the usable fireplaces and installed a small coal stove in Lucy's room, so that that area was always heated with a fine, even warmth. Things shone; there was always the smell of cooking in the house.

Gradually Amy adopted what came to be her job in life: turning a cold and somewhat musty, old-fashioned farmhouse into a home. She did it out of her own new riches: every night when she got into bed, there was Marl. You just had to be happy.

*

Was there such a thing as too happy?

"Seem to you," she began one night—she wasn't sure why, maybe out of sheer wifely perversity—"that we should take a rest from each other?"

Marl was almost asleep. "You tired?" he mumbled.

"No," she murmured. "Not what I mean." She didn't know quite what she did mean.

For some reason she would have liked not to rest her head on his shoulder just then, but how could she resist it? He seemed to need it there, too. She moved close to him.

"What then?" His hand traveled at her side, found a breast to cradle. Some part of her would have liked to pull away even then, not because she didn't like it, but maybe to prove that she could. But there was a kind of hypnosis at the hands of Marl Perry, a drowning. Who could resist him?

"Don't it seem strange to you"—she felt for words to present a thought she hadn't yet formulated—"all's we do is pay attention to each other?"

But the hand stroked. She moved to meet it.

"That's what we're supposed to do, honey." He gathered her as close to him as he could. Through the length of his body she could feel his need of her. It was that, she guessed, that scared her a little sometimes.

"But if anything should happen to me," she said, feeling foolish, "what would you—"

He nibbled her ear, moved to her shoulder. "Better take out some insurance."

"Marl, I mean it!" she whispered, half laughing. "If anything should happen to me, I'd want you to go on and—"

"Well, okay," he murmured agreeably. "I will. But if you could hold off until I've seen somebody in town—"

"Marl!"

"Nothing's going to happen!" Now both his hands were on her, and his lips. "Except this. And, maybe, this . . ."

*

"You know," Marl said, one night before they dropped off to sleep, "the hill is awful quiet."

"Middle of the night."

"Be serious."

"Well, then . . ." She was very sleepy.

"It used to talk to me, you know."

"The hill?" Fighting to stay awake.

"Ay-eh." He exaggerated this.

"Come on, it's late."

"No, I mean it. I'd hear it, sometimes—thought I did. I'd think it was telling me what to do, you know kids."

"I know lonely kids."

"Yeah."

"You don't need the hill talkin', maybe that's it."

"You think so?"

Sleepily Amy reached over and touched his face. "You got me," she said. But the tone of her quiet voice was almost an apology, and he knew it. They went to sleep holding each other.

*

That first winter Amy began naming cows and going out to the barn to talk to them so they could learn their names. She'd put on one of Marl's cast-off jackets, ripped in the arm, and an old pair of jeans—long before blue jeans went underground and came out stylish—and a pair of Marl's barn boots. Soon she was making Marl's breakfast in blue jeans and a flannel shirt. Lucy was furious. "I have sometimes seen a resemblance between country women and their cows," she would say acidly. Amy never seemed to notice.

One night they were getting up from the supper table and Amy had begun to clear the dishes. Marl steered Lucy into her comfortable chair. Amy had placed a little rocker by the stove so that Marl's mother could sit in the kitchen and be sociable if it pleased her; Lucy sat, regally.

"You come over beside me, Marlowe," she said, meticulously straightening the folds of her Shelton Stroller, beautifully laundered by Amy.

But Marl went to the sink to help his wife with the dishes. "Well," my dear," he asked loudly, "how's Blossom today?"

Cow talk, thought Lucy, sniffing with a little wet sound: "Hymph!" Marl had set a shelf by her chair and now she took from it some papers to correct. That was how it happened that she didn't see a round face bent over the dishpan redden.

"Oh, Blossom?" Amy said casually, running a fingernail along a stubborn spot. "She's just fine."

"Getting fatter, isn't she?" said Marl, grinning broadly.

"Not so you'd notice it, I believe," said Amy firmly.

"There is entirely too much cow talk around here," said Lucy. She didn't look up from her papers.

"How long's she been expectin' now?" said Marl in the same loud voice, with that same telling grin.

"I'm not sure." Amy, steamy.

"Deliver when?" said Marl; it was almost a shout.

"Marlowe, please," said Lucy. "What is going on here?"

Marl hooted. It was Amy, rinsing the last pan and setting it on the stove to dry, who said, "Never mind him, Mother Perry. He thinks he's bein' funny. I'm expectin' a baby. Four months along, the doctor says, and doin' fine. Due date is May fifteenth."

Lucy gripped her papers. "Good heavens," she said. "Good heavens!"

Marl threw his head back and laughed. "Is that all you can say, Grandma?"

"Are—are you quite well?" Lucy said helplessly to Amy after a moment.

"Oh, yes," said Amy.

"It seems so—so soon, so sudden—" Lucy fluttered.

Amy said nothing at all. She didn't need to; her face was placid.

Pleased with herself, thought Lucy. Pleased with the whole procedure, no doubt. "Next time you have something to tell me, Amy," she said then, in fine short chirps, "perhaps it should be in terms of people, not cows."

"Your son's fault," said Amy, smiling.

But Marl looked hurt. "Aren't you glad to be having a grandchild?"

Lucy stared at him and suddenly she felt quite old, quite tired and defeated. "I couldn't be happier," she said slowly, and kissed them both.

It was Amy who took her to her room then, and fixed the damper on her nice new stove, so that she'd be comfortable all night long.

*

Despite Amy's care and Marl's good laughter, things weren't going at all well for Lucy. The anger that didn't register at home against the happiness of her son's wife Lucy took to school; in fact, it became a crucial weapon in her arsenal. For a lady, she found herself doing some frightening things. Oh, she would start the day on a perfectly polite level, she was pleased to say. There would be the Lord's Prayer and the Pledge of Allegiance and "America the Beautiful." She would appoint the paper-passer, the board-cleaner, the bathroom-checker. (In a recent year, the townspeople had put in two flush toilets, and it was up to the bathroom-checker to make sure that these were flushed. There were some children who had no reason to have learned this habit.) Everything would be in order, the schoolwork would begin.

But then something insignificant would happen, a little whisper, perhaps, or a dropped pencil, and suddenly Lucy would find herself enmeshed in a net of anger.

"Arthur Timberlake!" she would cry in a voice so dangerous she herself hardly recognized it.

"Yes, Miss Perry?"

She never knew precisely who the wrongdoer was, but that didn't seem to matter. More often than not it was the little tremble of an innocent voice that awoke something vicious in her.

"Have you completed your reading assignment?" Now she would be up and around her desk and off her platform, stalking the small child. Pupils no longer went to her for coldly meted rational punishment; now she went to them.

So angry that she saw the child as if down at the end of a tunnel. He would answer her, his eyes closed in fear. "No, Miss Perry."

"And why not?" She would use an ugly voice she didn't recognize, low and thick with hate, and he wouldn't dare to speak again.

She was helpless. She would make the child stand up in front of the class, holding his outsized geography book and trying to study standing, until, flushed and dizzy, he began to weave on his feet. But these days she didn't wait for him to take his place. Instead, with desperate cold hands she hardly knew were hers, she would drag him from his seat and shove him to the front. She would snatch his book from the floor where it had fallen and shove it into his chest and cry, in that strange, strangled voice, "Now, young man, you stand there, and you work!"

It was a reign of terror. Too many gentle souls became immune to learning; they were scared to death.

Lucy knew it; she frightened herself. At home she felt—excluded, was that it? As if she were missing something? But at school, by the time her grandchild was born, Lucy had pulled a handful of hair from a pupil's head with a hand that seemed detached from her body; and she had sprained the arm of a frail little girl who couldn't stop lisping on demand.

The new central school in Monson was now nearing completion and teachers in one-room schoolhouses all over the area were receiving new contracts. But not Lucy, although technically she had tenure. Lucy didn't fight it; she was too frightened, scared of herself.

A retirement dinner was held in her honor. After all, at the age of sixty and without even a college degree—could you imagine? —she had taught in the same one room for thirty-four years. Charitable people said: "Wa'n't that somethin', wa'n't that a record?" Those parents and town officials who could still bear to look at her came to the schoolroom with their covered dishes and set up tables. There were speeches and tunafish casseroles, sweet Jell-O with sour grapes suspended in it, desserts of fruit cocktail and marshmallows. There was a gold watch. From now on the children would attend the new "learning plant" in the center of town.

*

John Sapley did little more than pat Amy's stomach and take her blood pressure, squinting at the gauge from the length of his arm, when she appeared in his office for her prenatal visits. It wasn't necessary to do more than that, he chuckled, leaning over her, breathing his peppermint breath; John was always eating these days and then needing something to eat, to settle his stomach. At the age of seventy-five, he weighed 260 pounds. Those Trowleys, he'd delivered babies for the Trowleys for forty years or more. Never had trouble with their babies and never were sick a day with them, either.

"You've got a good country face," he would say, patting Amy's knee and squinting at her. "You'll do, girl. You'll do."

And he never measured Amy, as Marl had learned to do for all his cows.

But the birth canal was very small, and Amy's labor in the front sitting room went on for thirty-three bone-stretching hours before Tave was born. Amy bled heavily after the birth and was whisked in the middle of the night all the way to Eastern Maine General Hospital, where she recovered quickly enough with the aid of transfusions, although she would never be able to conceive again.

While she was in the hospital, however, it was Marl who suffered. Day after day he was up early, did his work, went to Bangor to stay with his wife for as long as they would let him visit. The look of him worried Amy.

"Marl, are you all right?" His face was thinner, the light in his blue eyes scarcely flickering.

"Are you all right, that's the question," he would reply brusquely.

But this was foolishness to Amy. "You know," she said gently, "even if I'd died . . ." His face became grim as a stone mask; she couldn't continue.

On the day she came home from the hospital she told him, "You haven't missed me that bad, have you? I bet Mother Perry just loved havin' her kitchen back, her whole house back all to herself." She even laughed at him a little as they bumped home in the truck. But he didn't smile.

"Burnt oatmeal for breakfast," was his comment. "She never did learn how to make oatmeal." In spite of herself, Amy felt strangely pleased at this little-boy answer.

It was a cold day for May. The flowers around the house bloomed and shivered. Amy had put in daffodils and poppies from her mother's garden, but they looked cold. She was worried and glanced down at the baby in her arms quickly. But little Tave, in her warm cocoon of blankets and comforters, hiccuped gently and went back to sleep as they pulled into the yard.

Inside the house Marl took the baby and put her in Lucy's arms; it was the first time Amy ever saw Lucy look, softly, happy. "Octavia," said Marl, "meet Octavia."

Lucy gasped, but she was pleased. "Thank you, Marlowe," she said. Her arms, with their skinny elbows and sagging muscles, tightened around the bundle that was Tave. "Well, there," said the old woman, whispering into the bundle. "There, there." She smiled.

It was worth it to Amy just to watch. That night, however, she learned how desperate Marl had been. "We need you," he kept saying. "Hell, Amy, you are this hill."

"Foolish talk!" She pounded the bedcovers. "Be serious, Marl! The hill is somethin' else."

"The hill is us two," he said firmly. "You and me. I don't give a damn! I mean, we got Tave. We got her and we'll keep her." He grinned a little. "Mother will keep her, I guess, if we don't. But we're the hill! Amy! When you're not here, I can't seem to give a damn."

"You tend to the animals?"

"Sure, who wouldn't?" He leaned over her in the dark; she could feel how he loved her. "But we go it together, from here on in, and no funny business, no close calls, no nothin', okay?"

Amy sighed. "Okay," she whispered. "It's all right with me."

*

Over the summer the baby, Tave, was nourished to happy fatness at Amy's breast. Amy nursed in private, where Marl often joined her, after that first time, nursing in front of Lucy. Sitting up in bed, Amy had casually opened her nightgown and pressed the baby's mouth open, pushing her reaching brown nipple between those narrow, moist little lips. But Lucy, who had been visiting the baby at the time, looked a little sick and left the room quickly to the sound of Tave's contented smacking. "Just like a cow," she'd fumed to Marl later.

Amy and Marl giggled a little at his mother in that summer milky-haze of happiness. But Lucy sat alone, straight-backed on the porch, during feeding times. She would have taken the baby over altogether if it hadn't been for her distaste of all its creature functions. Lucy would settle with little Tave on the porch, but as soon as the baby was wet or hungry she would hand her over to Amy—that was how high class she'd become since her own son's babyhood.

There is a private pleased look that passes between mothers and their children, a faint but proud and loving look different from any other. Lucy saw it and was envious, but there was nothing she could do.

Amy wasn't a silly mother, not even demonstratively affectionate. There was only this look, and a gentle laughing voice that caressed the baby and nudged it, saying, in effect, stand on your own, little one. Be my companion.

"Oh," Amy would say, picking up Tave and settling her on her lap. "Strained pears. This is going to be good!" And sure enough, it was good.

When the baby ate, her lips not quite closing over mouthfuls and food dribbling on her chin, Amy only laughed gently. But Lucy, as helpless as the baby, would go to the front porch and rock in her chair. "This is the poor bare-born human creature," she would pronounce to herself, "who hasn't learned to think or act on its own." Back and forth her chair would go, creaking a little painfully, wood on wood.

Tave

*T*HE LANTERN SHONE without wavering; it was the voice that flickered. Ray Gray had finished his transmission of the President's speech and now commented on it steadily, but the radio batteries were weak. Also, Ray was no longer broadcasting in the usual sense; his voice was a tired whisper.

"*. . . may mean we can expect nuclear warheads have been placed not only at silos in the West, which have received the publicity we all know about, but also at bases in other parts of the country. A tactic, a strategy—*" The whisper rose, broke off.

Trying to sort it out for himself, as well as for his listeners, he continued: "*Some of the silos we know about may be dummies. Like the military installations at Calais in the Second World War. Not even de Gaulle knew about that one. How should we be any better? They put empty tents, inflatable tanks, up at Pas de Calais, fighting for time, fighting to outflank the Germans! Now we seem to be playing old war games with something new, something so destructive—*"

Once again his voice broke. He took an audible breath. "*I'm hoarse, I've been talking too much,*" he said. "*Am I crazy? The world is crazy! Don't take me seriously.*"

He must be exhausted, Tave thought. There was a rattle of papers and then his voice continued: "*Is there anyone listening to me? Maybe not. I've broadcast everything I have here that can be helpful; some things I've said twice, three times. But now what I have in my hands is a map of the United States issued by civil defense headquarters and filed away among all the other material this station has chosen to—to ignore. I wish I could draw this map out for you over the air! It's entitled High Risk Areas, and blotted out in black ink are not only military installations in the West, but every military base in the United States. I don't need to tell you there are blacked-out portions in every state. But now we should begin to assume, maybe, that any one of these blacked-in areas could be the site of—of nuclear weapons.*"

A silence. It lengthened. Had Ray had enough? Or had the radio died?

Tave grabbed it with cold hands, shook it. In her mind's eye, suddenly, she could see that map with its spots, like a disease. Or like a big polka-dotted bosom, alive until a dot exploded in a welter of blood.

Ray's whisper came back again, sharply. "*. . . a man in a crawl space, raving,*" he said. "*That's all I am. Maybe you should ignore me for a few minutes, while I let the President's speech shake down, till I calm down.*" He paused for a moment, then continued, as if he couldn't stop.

"*Haven't we been ignoring this long enough?*" he whispered. Tave suddenly felt as if he whispered to her alone. "*Too painful? Too frightening? Madness—keep away from it—that's what I've thought! Cannot be contemplated! Somehow the human race will avoid it—that's what I've thought! All the while, right next door in Vermont, our soldiers were playing war! And somewhere, somewhere protected, Pentagon intelligence has been working out—strategies. It says here that the Soviets believe a nuclear war is survivable—*" But this ended in a harsh sound, the phlegmy cough of the overworked throat.

Tave frowned. She would have to be cool and precise, she thought. Poor Ray Gray was going a little crazy. And he probably would regret what he was saying someday, when the FCC got ahold of him and things got back to—normal. Normal. Was that a word she understood anymore?

But she didn't reach for the dial, not yet. Some part of her was fascinated: a radio personality was being himself and not a professional, smooth voice, full of machine-made charm.

"*We shouldn't ignore the nuclear question anymore,*" Ray was whispering now. *"It's real. We should be doing two things. We should be trying, in every way we can, to find a way not to need nuclear weapons—any weapons! And we should be learning to live with the weapons we've already got. Because me, I want to survive."*

Silence.

Tave shivered. Once again she shook the black box with chilly fingers.

"Come on, you," she whispered, but there was no sound.

"Ray!" By now she was trembling with cold, but she deferred going for a blanket. Anxiously, she took the batteries out of the radio and replaced them, fitting the terminals with exaggerated care. It seemed to help. Gray's voice, so tired it was barely audible, came back again.

". . . from Lessing via WLBZ are that fires still rage in an area of approximately one hundred miles in circumference. In a circle of up to nine miles across, all around the site of the Lessing blast, all creatures in the open at the time are dead or are at present suffering from serious burns. Lines are down, and fallout is at a dangerous level, making it difficult to reach victims and treat them—"

Tave's hand darted out. She shut the radio off. There was just so much, she thought suddenly, a person could stand.

Shaking, she sat for a moment in her little ring of light. It was quiet, the kind of quiet you ran from, did anything to avoid, a silence that inquired softly, "Now I have you, how much can you take?"

But she wouldn't turn the radio back on, either; the suffering in Lessing scared her worse than the quiet in the cellar.

She stared out into the dark, eyes straining for—what? Some kind of answering light? But there was none, only the soot wall of black. Would it, too, explode? Was it like the black on Ray's map?

Of course not. Tave fought for balance. She was a little like a drunkard pretending to be sober, she told herself. She wanted to keep her equilibrium, set one foot in front of the other on that straight, white, hopeful line, but . . .

It was cold; she would get a sweater. And somehow, she

thought, everything would be all right. It would have to be. This nuclear thing was only one accident in a big world. She would live through it and then get back to—

Normal? Did she really want everything to be, only, normal?

It was another thought to avoid.

From the stack of clothing on the shelves she pulled out a sweater and put it on. She was at a distance from the lantern but turned to face it, daring it to waver or grow dim. Expecting the worst, she knew. But in the shadow of the dark shelves, the worst seemed plausible, even reasonable.

She was trembling with cold. The sweater gave warmth but not enough, never enough. She reached for another and then realized that the furnace, although out, was still warm, that this chill she carried around inside her. She should, she knew, shut the lantern light off, conserve, spend some time in the dark. For a second she closed her eyes, to try it, but even that much was more than she could bear. Well, she would have to leave the light on, for a little while!

She found herself staring at her food supply. Without electricity she would not be able to cook. What would she eat? Cold canned vegetables? She guessed she wouldn't eat cold canned vegetables unless she had to. There was a bunch of fruit. She reached for an orange, held it in her hand for a moment mostly for reassurance; it was real, whole. She kept her eyes on the lantern, some part of her daring it to go out. The orange was cold, she realized after a moment; she put it down. Her hands touched a shelf as she did so. It, too, was chilly, even damp. There were corners of this cellar that never got warm, she thought suddenly. There were places down here on which moisture condensed and never dried. In the dark, would she feel along clammy stones, never knowing what she might encounter, blind, while things that lived in the dark reached for her—

No!

She would have to keep the lantern on, for as long as she could.

Now Tave tried to swallow; her throat was so dry it hurt, its parts rubbing against each other thickly. She needed water, but the sink was in the half-dark. Shakily she walked to the lantern —you walked an imaginary white line, pretending that the hill didn't swing under your feet—and grasped it with her two hands, carrying it to the sink, where she set it down. She pumped water, which came rusty, then clear.

Her father had always said that the old well water, coming as it did unpolluted from some deep underground source, was better than the water they used for the farm. But in summer there wasn't enough of a reservoir of it to serve both house and barn.

"Could have made a mint," he used to joke, "if I'd bottled that well water instead of milk. Especially with the damn Maine Milk Commission the way it is . . ."

Tave's mother, Amy, would smile indulgently at his mutterings about the commission. "Drink of that water once a day," she would say, "keep a body regulated for life."

Tave took a sip; it was cold, but clean and good. It steadied her. Glass in hand, lantern under one arm, she headed for her mattress, pulled out a stack of magazines, fumbled to make herself a cocoon of blankets, and climbed into it. "Me, I want to survive," Ray had whispered.

Tave wanted to, too, very much.

After all, she told herself firmly, she wasn't what her mother would have called "real bad off." She still had light, blankets, water, food, magazines for distraction. You had to concentrate on yourself, on your own needs. You had to forget everything else, everybody else, all that suffering, even your own danger. You had to, to survive.

With a kind of waiting room concentration she began to flip through the magazine pages, and it wasn't until somewhere between the fifty hairdos and the ten ways to make over your living room that the full horror at last caught up with her.

The delay came, perhaps, from hearing firsthand reports of all the crises of the world on a daily basis. Murders, explosions, wars, assassinations—insulated in her own bad dreams, Tave had always managed to keep the nightmares of the world at arm's length, in as much reach as, say, the record player, or the toaster.

Somehow she had always been in control of world problems; she could shut them off if she wished. As she had shut Ray Gray off, a moment ago. When it got to be too much to stand: click.

So it was not until the flicker of a page, that instant when she was not looking at one picture and not at the other, but at the wavering sharp edge between them, when at last she could hold the nightmare at bay no longer.

First she saw her own house. She felt she was measuring it, room by room, every window, every door opening, every mop board and molding she had at one time or another touched, dusted, taken for granted. Every inch of it was unutterably dear to her. But in Lessing, houses as much cared for as hers had been taken up in a ball of fire and hurled out in broken, flaming pieces, to start fires in other houses. In every one of those homes, it occurred to her suddenly, had been rooms made by hands.

People's hands. People who, yesterday, had finished lunch and gone back to work as usual, or maybe to a nap in a sunny room. Who had left the dishes, saying, "They'll still be there, waiting for me, when I come back." Who had gone out for a walk on the streets of Lessing and lifted face to the sun, thinking, "Guess it'll leaf out, after all."

New leaves: Tave saw them frizzled and scorched in their cupped buds. While she watched they crackled, crumpled, fell among dead bodies—poor burnt corpses covered with killing dust. Somewhere people were still dying from burns, unable to see, or speak, or reach for help, their hands burnt; ugly bloodless ulcers, white bone . . .

Agonized, still-breathing bodies, illuminated in red, she could see them! Angry faces, cheated out of their lives, out of their work, out of spring; faces haunted, lips and eyes moving help-lessly, pleading, crying the same cry—her cry: is this what I worked all my life to get?

All those muscles and limbs Tave had learned, painstakingly, to draw, picked up by the blast, strewn about, cooked brown. Some woman lay in Lessing, she was Tave's double, like a warn-ing, and she was horribly burnt, a gutted, moving husk with a skeleton hand that reached for what empty eye sockets could not see. That's me, Tave thought. That could be me.

Tave felt she could draw it all, in anger, in agony. Draw from her own vomit those bodies, fires, flames, licking from mouth to seared mouth, eye to sightless eye, finger to evaporating finger, house to house and out, endlessly, over leveled hills! She could feel the flames in her own hands; she could hear their sound, like a low roar.

Or maybe, from this distance, more like dark laughter? One huge horrible joke, is that what this was, playing itself out in square miles of gray slash and desolation? And the final lash of the dragontail this: that the flame could be put out, the strewn limbs and pitted torsos gathered up and buried, but the dragon's breath stayed aloft, to kill with strange ugly diseases, when you thought you had escaped.

Was this the blinder joke again? That the more man discovered, the more self-destructive he became? Was evolution only the path to destruction, a vast colorful arc of creation, like a rainbow with a lake of fire at its end?

She could paint that! And the bodies, their flesh cooked to bursting.

Convulsively she reached for the glass of water, watching her own hand, fascinated by its quiver of pulse: an intact hand. It did not reassure her.

She tasted the water, not daring to drink because suddenly she felt sick.

Ray was right, she thought. How could they all have ignored this? Had they really believed it couldn't happen? Fire was in the blood, wasn't it? Maybe it was in the plan. Like living on Octavia's Hill with the Greens somewhere just outside. You knew they were there. You felt them counting your comings and goings. And what did you do? Nothing. You ignored them. Yes, you told yourself, they would go away, nothing bad could happen. But underneath you knew that sometime it would be time for you! Then there would be no pretense. Then there would be—what?

A body, lying broken in the dark?

"No," she whimpered. Black was eating at her brain cells, maybe; for a second she felt faint.

She would have to fight, she told herself. There was nothing else to do, to survive. She would have to smash any Green that tried to come near her. She would have to be tough. The earth could be split like a flea and discarded like a sloughed-off cell; you didn't sit around shaking. You didn't faint or cry. Not even if you felt on your own body those swollen juicy limbs, or the hollow where a womb should have been. Not even if you found on your own face that ugly grimace born of the knowledge of fear, the suspicion of fraud.

She wouldn't give in. She would have to live, if only to paint the destruction she saw. Someday, maybe, somebody would see her work and realize that Tave Perry, at least, had not been fooled. She would paint until the paintbrush burnt in her hand.

Or until the lights went out.

One of the ironies of the hill, she supposed. Another of them, maybe: you couldn't paint in the dark.

Hell, hadn't she been painting in the dark for years?

And every time she'd begun to believe in the light, every time what she'd painted seemed cutting and good, then the lights went out. Each of her paintings had at some time or other looked as *Ghost* now looked—uneven, pretentious, a little silly. Laughable, if it hadn't hurt so much.

Angry paintings, all that fire, but never quite enough light, no. She would try and try to—what? Make something out of nothing? Or maybe that wasn't quite true. There was always something to start her: some curve, some color she couldn't resist. She'd work and work and finish up what looked like a great painting, and then some little thing would happen and she would be mad again and in the dark again, with nothing to show—no, less than nothing. A poor painting, and a minus quantity of confidence.

It was like being buried alive. Doomed to darkness and the everlasting angry groping to dispel darkness, the only light the human creature burnt by, maybe. Man the victim. And her meta-

phor for this had become the hill, Octavia's Hill. In her paintings
the hill was God, and he acted like the very devil.

Proof? The cellar.

You didn't cry; maybe you couldn't. You tripped on laughter
and fell into endless pain.

It was almost like a prophecy, as if the hill said to you, "You
will paint and paint nothing, so that even painting will be like
nothing. The light you go by will be angry, flickering, malicious."

And was that, really, the only light of which a human being was
capable?

Tave clutched at her magazine. The pages in her hands
shuffled to the end and back. Helpful hints for the woman's
world, a springtime of house plans, how to compute the insurance needs of the modern housewife. Ashes.

Her breathing was jagged, her hands shook. She stood up and
immediately felt sick, but fought back the nausea, which subsided
to a kind of controlled interior lurch.

You have to be practical, she told herself. Keep busy . . .

At last she collected her water glass and moved with it, a coffee
cup, and a spoon to the sink.

There she clutched the cold pump handle, swinging it up and
down until water gurgled, splashed. As she did so she found
herself muttering, "Please, let it close its eyes when it comes to
me, let me escape this—not me, not me."

A pitiful little mutter and she knew it. The water splashed, its
sound drowning out her voice. Tave stared into the dark, which
fell in a sharp edge too near the sink, and realized she'd forgotten
the lantern.

Immediately she retrieved it, holding the little wire handle in
clammy fingers. Back at the sink again, she discovered she'd
forgotten the soap, too, and took the lantern with her to the shelf
to fetch it, finding some comfort in the light and some, even, in
that feeling of extraneous motion that comes of using an unfamiliar kitchen. Then she stood at the sink sideways in order to face
the lantern and sloshed the dishes through the cold water very
slowly, one at a time. The water was so cold she had to rest her

hands from it as she worked. She took a very long time, moving with great care. But somehow the spoon still managed to shake itself loose as she set it to drain. It fell to the floor with an ugly clatter.

Tave tensed against the noise, stooped into the shadow to pick up the spoon. As she did she noticed a spot on the cement and touched it; it was dry. Paint? Had she spilled some? Or had someone cut themselves down here and not run through the house shrieking bloody murder for a Band-Aid?

The spot was dry. She stared out into the dark. She knew no one was there, but a worm of fear wiggled up her spine and touched the edge of her heart before it exploded. Her thoughts ran suddenly into a mad jumble, and she left the dishes and stumbled back to the workbench, the lantern swinging in a wild arc: what she needed was another human voice.

She turned the radio on, shook it, placed it on its side, fiddled with the antenna, but nothing seemed to help. At last Ray's voice came floating out; he seemed to be moving far away from her, out of earshot. *"Plume of radioactive dust,"* he whispered. *"Now gone out to sea . . ."*

Silence. Tave shook the radio. One more whisper floated back: *". . . not to come . . . out of shelters . . . until notified."*

He was gone. Once again she took the batteries out, put them back. But this time, she knew, it was no use. The radio was completely dead.

Like a death in the family. Reasonable voices, always going away from her, over some distance she couldn't cross and didn't understand.

And it was cold, very cold. "Breathe," Tave told herself. "Don't forget to breathe." In cutting gasps, she did. The corners of her mouth drew in with the effort. This was going to be very much harder than she had expected, she suddenly knew. And maybe somewhere a malignancy was growing, getting personal, counting her up, getting ready to pluck her flesh from her bones and find out what she was made of.

For a long time she lay still, unable to move, her face against her arms on the workbench. The wool of her sweater irritated the skin of her cheeks and forehead, but she didn't care.

At last, for lack of anything else to do and in lieu of crying, she stood, went back to the sink. Automatically she rinsed her three dishes once again in splashing water.

"Don't wash those with that!" It was Lucy Perry, gesturing. "Where is your glass cloth, Octavia? And cold water? Is that how your mother taught you to wash dishes? I wouldn't put it past her! From now on this will be our kitchen, yours and mine, and we will do things properly!" Lucy pressed her lips together and looked forbidding.

Tave moaned like a little girl. She had heard those words before, long before. "Good God, you never give up, do you?" she whispered.

"I don't know what you mean, Octavia!"

Tave took a deep breath. Ghosts were all part of the miserable joke—you had to remember that, weather it. She searched for some reply that would put Lucy Perry out of mind forever. But all she could come up with were words that felt as if they'd been said long before. "You leave my mother out of this!" she cried. "And it isn't your kitchen, it's mine!"

But it seemed to her that the whole hill was shaking with the joke of that.

Tommy Green

TOMMY GREEN WAS SLOW, but he did have patience. Patience was a quality he cultivated early, sleeping in his bureau drawer. There was no longer any bureau; it had been chopped up for wood one winter before Cone came home with money from the ring he'd sold. That winter, business had been slow for Tommy's mother and for Cone, and there wasn't another stick of wood in the house. Lying in his bureau-drawer bed, Tommy learned not to cry for his mother—she would as soon slap him as look at him—but to wait for his grandmother, who would feed him from a soda bottle with a nipple jammed on the end of it. As early as five months old, maybe earlier, some instinct for survival told him that it was better to drink five soda bottles of canned milk and water in the hours of the night, tucked up half-asleep by Grandmother's snoring chin, than it was to utter so much as a whimper during the days, when the old woman was not there and the darkened bedroom was filled with strange smells and shapes, the noises rhythmic and otherwise, the giggles and whispers, occasionally a slap or a cry.

By the age of one year Tommy had learned that inopportune sounds from him always ended in pain—a slap if his mother was otherwise occupied, a blow if she was not. Until the age of three his world was one of sharp contrasts: pain and the absence of pain, desperate fear and his grandmother's desperate cuddling. A sharp pain to the head would mean a stunning, white, agonizing flash, but then a slow sinking into blissful dark.

At three, Tommy finally learned to walk on his own, during the day while his grandmother worked and his mother was busy. By that time his bureau drawer had been moved out under the kitchen table in the other room, not the place where his mother slept. From his bed in the kitchen Tommy had seen the passage of many kinds of booted legs and had learned not to stir; either you lay still or you were kicked. But when his mother's door was shut, he would crawl out of his drawer and pull himself up with a table leg until he had learned to stand and, eventually, to walk. At night he still slept with his grandmother, but now when she was comatose, in the beery sleep of the elderly drunk, he would pull himself carefully, slowly, out of that moldering velvet embrace and slide quickly by his mother, who was the source of all fear and power. In the nights, too, he began to discover the house for himself.

It was only two rooms and a porch. The floor was crooked and slanted and urged you to go ever downhill or ever uphill, downhill to the bureau drawer, uphill to the cupboards. It was dirty, although his grandmother did try, occasionally, to clean it. But she was tired. She spent her days cleaning houses and public buildings the length of Monson's one main street. Often she was too tired even to feed Tommy; he was always hungry.

Tommy didn't care about dirt. His grandmother brought him clothes; these were just as dirty. Until he learned to control himself he was constantly wet, his bottom and penis covered with angry, purple-pink burns that must have caused him pain; but he never cried, it wasn't worth it.

Three fourths of the year it was also cold and damp in the house, with smells that Tommy in his prowls learned by heart and understood in all the depths of their meaning. Rotting food—rotting before his eyes when he was hungry—that he did care about. Now and then he ate it anyway, and if he was ever sick, in his general misery he hardly noticed. Discarded empty bottles—he cared about these, too, because they meant nowhere to hide from drunken adults. Even lying flat down in your drawer you could be hauled out and flung against a wall, you could lose the baby teeth that came in rotting anyway. It didn't matter what you did, but you had to learn to be still, very still.

Somehow by the age of four Tommy could just about take care of himself, and then he refused to be embraced by his grandmother any longer: she'd begun to lean on him in her sleep. He learned to stay out of the way of both women, the pain-angry witch his mother, and the old sour-thick lady who had once cared for him. He learned to feed himself and stay dry. He learned to look forward to the arrival of Cone.

Cone could have been Tommy's father, it was all uncertain to Tommy. There were times—Tommy knew them in the night—when Cone came heavily up the stairs and his mother turned and twisted, fighting, until brother and sister were a tangle of bare limbs and hate, while the drunk grandmother snored in her corner or huddled fearfully out of the way. At last the struggle would give itself up, and then Cone would pull on his pants and leave and Tommy's mother would whisper, "You son of a bitch, you goddamn—" Hate whispers, but Tommy knew she loved to whisper them. As for Tommy, he was always on Cone's side, cheering him on without words; his four-year-old brain didn't know many words. "Get her, Cone, get her good, hurt her hard." And when Cone did, why, that was a satisfaction worth waiting for.

During the daytime Tommy walked silently about the upstairs, looking for food to eat, but the one certainty in his life was that he was to make no noise. Opening a bread wrapper under those conditions became a terrible and delicate procedure. Tommy learned patience, he practiced it. Long black fingernails worked the cellophane open a centimeter at a time, dirty fingers sank into that soft white loaf and eased the slices out a bit at a time, slowly. No matter how hungry you were, you tucked the bread in your shirt for later, because you knew you would be hungry all day. Even though it might earn you a shriek and a cuffing, you braved the continual tiny rattle your hands made and sank your fingers gratefully into the fluffy white with the smell, the heart-catching smell, of fresh store bread. You put them—however many slices you dared; what you ate shouldn't be missed, after all—underneath your shirt, next to your skin, where nobody could see them. Then you closed the loaf and put it down, so carefully, and found canned milk and opened it.

This operation had to be performed outside in the yard, it was noisy. Open the door an inch at a time; move outside with slow stealth; close the door, no matter how cold you were, behind you. A knife and a stone. Far out of earshot you banged holes into the top of that can, that one can with the rich, thick milk inside, that you got by being quiet. You drank it outside, for fear the sound of your swallowing might awaken your mother, who now beat you not with her hands but with bottles or belts or firewood, while the thick old woman sat and wheezed and whimpered for a beer, as if a change of subject would fix everything.

Then back into the house. Standing beside the paper bag, ever so cautiously you pulled from it cool, smooth, grocery-wrapped slices you knew were bologna, and then you began the patient operation all over again, and the meat also went inside the shirt: gobbling on the spot led to inattention and that, Tommy already knew, to catastrophe. He was patient; he had to be. Then, if it was winter, you went back into a corner and there you took breakfast, lunch, and dinner, morsel by slow morsel, from beneath your shirt. You never chewed quickly and swallowed: it might make a noise, it might take you off your guard. No, if you were awake, you had to be totem-still. So you sucked slowly until your mouthful was a paste of bread or meat. Only then did you allow it to slip, bit by bit, down your throat. But swallowing was dangerous. The food had to slide by itself.

By the age of four Tommy was capable of sitting for hours at a time and doing nothing at all, staring off into space so intently and without movement that he might have been a profile on a coin. Thus he sat for all the long cold months, escaping punishment.

The next summer he moved outdoors into the sun, ranging over the hill, always keeping himself out of the sight of Lucy or Marl, who was by then about fourteen years old and out every day working on Octavia's Hill. Tommy would see them come and go, watch them pass his house every day. But never once, that whole summer, did he make a sound heard by another human ear, and he didn't move so that anyone could see him do it. He didn't want to. It was enough that he was free.

One morning in the early fall he walked out of the house at dawn, with his shirt full of food, only to find that the light had been deceptive and the rest of the sky was full of thick brownish-gray clouds. It was thunderstorm weather. He knew that if he went back into the house, his food would be found at the first crack of the storm; his mother hated storms. He would be blamed and beaten as if the lightning were all his fault. Big drops of water began to fall as he stood there, dampening his shirt and the food beneath it. This was a vital hurt: all he would eat that day he cradled next to his skin.

Slowly he moved down the steps, a small boy with the Green legacy of soupy, blank blue eyes and expressionless face, too-big clothes, no shoes, dirty; his ankles were elephant-gray with grime that had been lived in and never scrubbed. One foot at a time he went down the steps, feeling the rain soak into his shirt and looking about with desperate deliberation. And then for the first time he looked, really looked, at the panel under the porch: it was partially open. At last, blinking against the dark, he crept inside.

No one there, dark, the floor was dirt. But it was warm and dry. An inch at a time, Tommy moved toward the source of the warmth, a stove made of an oil can set up on bricks. Even the dirt floor around it was warm. Tommy went to a corner beyond the stove and began, methodically, to eat, the food sliding sound-lessly down his throat, and to wait for the light to clear from his eyes so that he could see.

After a while he saw that this place under the porch was orga-nized in a square around a central chimney. To the left was a large opening, shut now, through which, he knew already, Cone Green drove his tractor and its attachments in the summer. The rest of the year, Tommy knew, Cone tinkered. The side hill was loaded with motors and parts that Cone put together in unlikely combinations and took to nearby fairgrounds for stock car racing.

On the other side of the square space was where Cone lived. There was a heap of blankets on an old cot across from the stove, a makeshift table with a lantern on it, and a bucket of water beside it. Along one side was a set of bricked-in shelves on which were placed utensils, tools, and bits of motor, neatly separated into compartments. The floor was uncluttered. It went downhill toward the tractor end, but in Tommy's corner, if you were as tall a man as Cone, you would have to kneel or bend over.

Tommy looked about and let his food slip down his throat one tiny piece at a time. It wasn't until late afternoon, while the steady rain—which had followed the thundershower—poured down, that Cone came home. Cone backed his tractor into the opening and shut the door tightly. Then he went to the stove and took his thick boots off, splaying his feet out into the soft-powder dirt. He opened the cut-out lid of the stove, stuck a piece of wood in it, and by this red light caught sight of Tommy, who sat so still and pale, a few feet away, that he might have been made of porcelain.

Cone said nothing for a moment. He fit the tin cover back on the stove and went to sit on the bed with his hands between his knees. Tommy didn't move.

"Who you?" Cone's voice was dark and soft, like the dirt under his feet. Tommy knew much, but few words. He did know his first name.

"Tommy." He spoke in a hoarse voice; he never learned to do much more than whisper.

"Wha's that?" Cone rubbed a hand over his face and looked toward Tommy.

"Tommy," the boy said again.

There was a short silence. "You come down by yourself?" Cone was watching him now. Tommy could see his eyes, like two dark holes, staring.

"Yeah."

"That bitch didn't send you?"

"No."

"That old woman didn't send you?"

"No."

Cone paused. "Then what you doin' here?"

But Tommy had no words to describe what he did. He sat and was silent.

Cone scowled through the dark. "You gonna steal my things?"

This was a longer conversation than Tommy had ever had in his life. But he knew *steal* from his grandmother, who held him sweaty-tight and whispered, "Don't steal food, boy. Wait for me to feed you. You'll go to hell if you steal."

"No," said Tommy.

"You a good boy, then?" said Cone.

No answer.

Suddenly a thought seemed to occur to Cone. He gestured with both hands.

" 'Cause I like good boys," he said. "You a good boy, you can stay with me. I could teach you things; I like a good boy. Got only one bed though." Cone grinned. Tommy saw it, but he didn't move.

"You want to sleep with me?" Cone asked, still grinning.

Tommy said nothing.

Cone looked him up and down.

"C'mere," he said. "Come right over here, le's see what we got. Le's see what the bitch sent me."

When Tommy was standing before him Cone scratched a match, held the flame to Tommy's still face, and then lit a lantern he took from a shelf.

"That all you got to wear?" he asked.

Tommy nodded slowly.

"Don't fit you so good."

Tommy looked down at the ragged shirt and the baggy, rope-tied pants. *Fit* was a word he didn't know.

"Well," said Cone comfortably, "le's we take 'em off. Le's we see what we got here."

The man began to unbutton Tommy's shirt, but in a surprisingly gentle way. In a moment Tommy stood naked. Cone breathed in.

"Yes," he said. "Yes."

[301]

Tommy stood still as a statue. At least it was not unpleasant standing there: no blows yet, no screams, no beating. You stood and felt the air on your body and watched Cone, who, in all your memory, was the only one who ever paid that bitch your mother back. And he watched you.

"You'll find," the man said after a moment, " 'at I'm a little fussier than 'em fuckin' women. First, you got to wash. Christ. Jesus." He still looked Tommy up and down. Then he reached over and laid a finger near the spout of Tommy's penis, on his bare stomach. It was not an unpleasant feeling. Tommy's stomach quivered a little, but still he stood almost without breathing.

Cone's voice, now as soft and dark as a hot night wind: "I'll wash you, yessir. Yes.

"You lay right down," said Cone. "Don't need those old clothes, do we? Just you lay right down . . ."

He put Tommy on the bed and pushed him back till he lay small and naked against the wood sides of the foundation.

And if what began then with a washing, and continued at intervals right on up through Tommy's adolescence and manhood, if that was wicked or bad, it was the least painful thing that had occurred so far in his life. He learned to lie still with his bent back toward Cone, and he was patient.

*

Never was a child born in Monson, however, that some woman of the town didn't know about it somehow, and with the school so close and Cone gone about his business most of the day, it was inevitable that Tommy Green should be hunted out and told to go to school, which he did do, more or less, at Lucy's school, until age thirteen. Like Cone, Tommy only went as far as the third grade, sitting like a mountain among little girls and boys who came to school with clean faces and clean clothes, and full lunch-boxes. Tommy was tall and thin, his uncut hair shagged in strange directions.

But it was somehow pleasant to Lucy Perry to have this blank-faced boy right where she wanted him. And that was usually

standing up in front of the classroom with a book in his hands
—no matter that he couldn't read it. It was perhaps a mercy for
everyone that Tommy didn't bring his lunch with him. Most days
at noon recess he would light off home and, depending on the
warmth of the day, would come back or not, as he pleased. Lucy
let it alone. He was a rough-shorn beast, silent, and as he grew,
dangerous-looking.

Tommy didn't learn books, but there was something shrewd
about him, almost uncanny. In a crowd of children he could
fade until you hardly knew he was there, then disappear. At
other times he would suddenly appear, standing behind you, or
in a corner of the cloakroom, turning up when you least expected him. You would turn, and there he would be, watching
you. Always so silent. He could sit in the classroom for half a
day and not move, and yet you had the impression that nothing
got by him, that on some primitive level everything that happened got placed on scales, counted up, and weighed in. Sometimes Lucy had the feeling that her punishments of Tommy
were something he took personally and kept track of, but he
never said a word. If she asked him a direct question, he simply
stared at her. As he grew, he reminded her more and more of
Alden Green, and she questioned him—and punished him—
less and less, breathing a sigh of relief when he left the classroom for the day.

If you had told Tommy that he hated Lucy Perry, he would
have stared at you, too, until you bit your tongue and got, uneasily, as far out of his way as you could. But he did hate her—
and all women. During the years he spent sitting in her classroom, staring at her, or off into space while her sharp little voice
chirped and pecked pockmarks in his hide, she became a kind of
adjunct to an anger present since his birth and daily nourished
by Cone Green's soft, "Over, Tommy, boy. Over, yes, yes. We'll
show those bitches. Move, Tommy, yesss, yes . . ."

At first he had thought Lucy was some different type of animal,
neither man nor woman, and that the other children were some
kind of useless unidentifiable species. Their speech was high and

bright and sharp, fast as knives; he didn't understand them. Coiled to run, he'd sat without stirring where Cone Green left him in the school and let the blur and buzz go on around him; he'd been incapable of more than his name.

But as days passed, then years, he began to see the school as a jail and a woman as the jailer. His eyes sharpened, focused, became accustomed; he started to look over her contours. She was another of the type, all right, not the sagging pink and the pimpled slack face of his mother, nor that old snoring, smothering, fat woman, his grandmother. But in time Tommy Green, more perhaps than any other child in the history of the school, had an accurate picture of what Lucy looked like with no clothes on: white, skinny-shanked, sagging girlish nipples, gray hair. Watching her, he sometimes wished for a night like those when Cone had come up the stairs, fought his mother, and won. Meanwhile he sat, forced to his hard chair for hours on end, or forced to stand at the front of the classroom, big and awkward and ugly, while this woman ridiculed, demanded, and punished.

*

It was lunchtime in the schoolroom on the day before Tommy would be allowed to quit for good. Lucy sat at her desk on the platform. There were children eating inside at their desks and outside on the doorstep—it was a lovely day. Gradually the children finished and left the schoolroom for noon recess. After a while Lucy went outside to join them, but there were no children in sight, and it was very, very quiet.

Lucy didn't cry out. Experience had taught her to creep up on children and catch them red-handed. She walked out across the gravel and soon saw them all sitting quietly in a circle behind the lilac bush at the rear of the school building.

"Children, what are you—" Then she saw Tommy Green, sitting at an angle to the circle. In one hand he held a chunk of firewood, which he dropped to the ground when he saw her. In the middle of the circle stood one pigtailed little girl.

"Why, Tommy," said Lucy, "what is going on here?"

Of course he didn't answer. The girl in pigtails spoke up: "We had to do what he said, he made us."

"You have to do what he says?" said Lucy stiffly. "I doubt that. I doubt he even talks. Now, all of you, run to the front of the schoolyard and play as usual or recess will be over!"

Not a child moved.

"Go on!" Lucy cried. "Do as I tell you! Run!"

It was a question of the greater evil. One by one, the children rose and walked away. In a moment or two they were playing in front of the school as usual.

"Now, Tommy," Lucy began.

But suddenly Tommy stood up, and he grinned.

It was the only time Lucy had ever seen him respond in any way and she thought it made him look like Cone. It frightened her a little. Before she could say another word, he had looked her over slowly and carefully from head to foot. Then he winked.

"Chicka-chicka," he said softly, in that dark, powdered-dirt voice he'd learned from Cone. "Here chicka, here chicka."

Lucy's mouth fell open.

Tommy eyed her again and laughed Cone's laugh, the one that brought kitchen knives and old boots and howls and shrieks of wrath from Tommy's gap-clothed mother. He pursed his lips and made two kissing sounds into the air between them. It was an act of aggression. Then he was gone.

Lucy was, simply, astonished. The boy, she thought, was unhinged.

Tommy had disappeared in his own way, up the road to the shack. Cone and him, he was thinking. Some night. Not this dried-up bitch—what good was she? But they would have themselves a woman to torment, to take things away from. The strongest, juiciest bitch they could find.

*

Once out of school for good, Tommy became a member of the community. He spent a lot of time in the Green front yard, sitting so still you weren't sure you saw him at all. But somehow you knew he was watching. Although farmers' wives wouldn't have the Greens near their houses for some reason they could never quite put a finger on, farmers hired them and Cone's tractor, by the week, day, or hour, to do "jobs of work."

"Old Cone, he's all right," they'd tell their wives. "And that kid, hell, he's harmless, don't even talk. Two of 'em just like wind-up toys. Give 'em work to do, they do it."

Plowing was the best of what they did. For the rest, it was cleaning out barns, digging sewage ditches, building fences through the swampland. When they were done at the end of each week, they had a little money, and they used it to come up with a car that would run. In fact, together Tommy and Cone built the first demolition derby jalopy in that part of the county and ran it at the current champion, Wildcat Joe and his fighting "Mo" (for "Motor"), at the Bangor Raceway. "Mo" burst aflame and crumpled into dusty pieces of metal. It felt good! Tommy drove and did what Cone told him to. It was like spilling himself all out at Cone's hand, unbearable excitement and relief.

When Tommy was fourteen, Marl Perry was married and that summer hired Tommy to work for him. Lucy did as all the country women did: she avoided the barn, and Tommy. If she saw him trudging up the hill in the morning, she stayed indoors until he was out of sight. If in the afternoon she glimpsed him driving cows to be milked, she waited to take in her laundry until he'd disappeared into the barn. Tommy didn't see her once during that four days.

When Marl and Amy returned from Bar Harbor, Marl decided to keep Tommy on for morning and evening chores and to help him build the henhouses and barn stalls he knew he would require. Over the years Tommy worked on the hill quite steadily, and Marl came to take him as much for granted as he did his number three milking machine.

All that while Tommy watched and waited.

He never had a quarrel with Marl Perry; men he tolerated. But from time to time he lay flat in the barn loft and watched the man-dressed Amy Perry come in and walk among the cows, speaking gently to them and petting them. He wasn't fooled by Amy. Here was a bitch in man's clothes, big-chested and strong. He couldn't tolerate her big hands on the cows nor her feet in the barn. Most women stayed out of Tommy's way, but she walked up and down the barn, day after day, year after year, as if she didn't care what he thought.

If he happened to get caught out in the open and Amy nodded or spoke to him, he ducked his head and ran.

Once he heard her laugh at him to Marl. "Scared o' girls," she whispered into Marl's neck. "Could use a little more of that around here."

Amy was a daily annoyance, and inside Marl's house was that other bitch, the old one, as well as a little girl. But for years Tommy had plenty of outlets. With successively more souped-up cars that he painted with licking flames—their tails dragging, doors tied shut, trunk and hood wired closed—Tommy smashed up Shenandoah (from Calais, Maine), Steeple Jack (Portland), Grand Am the Pirate (Biddeford), Fearless Freddy (Oxford Plains), as well as a number of lesser lights. He became the feature attraction at state fairs. Nobody ever talked to him, of course, but they did watch him, even brag about him, and bet on him in a hurly-burly of slopped beer and mad yelling. Cone made the arrangements, Cone did the talking. Tommy did the riding. Men hanging over fairground fences told each other happily, "That guy don't have no feelin's atall."

Then Cone Green contracted some kind of stomach ailment. It began with diarrhea so draining that all he could do was lie on his bed and howl at the cramps; the space under the porch began to reek of the yellow-brown liquid that squirted from him. He grew very thin, in fact, seemed to shrink, so that Tommy towered over him.

Dr. John Sapley had died some time before of a heart attack, leaving a large rural area of the state with no medical help at all. He was mourned by the whole town. With no doctor, they were obliged to wait for emergencies and then make the wild ride clear in to Bangor to the hospital there. Dr. Sapley had left in trust enough money to send a qualified student from Monson to medical school, but at the moment there was no one to take over his patients. Personally Dr. Sapley had been a reassurance to a great many in the town, and his death "left a hole," as townspeople said.

A doctor at one of the raceways prescribed something for Cone, and Tommy's care for him was quite simple: whenever Cone woke up, he was given medicine. Cone spent two weeks drugged. Then, on his last day in the dark, drugged and reeking, he opened his eyes only once and looked at Tommy, dug deep into his quilt with what was left of his bottom, convulsed, died.

Tommy sat very still for a long time, looking at Cone. At last he got up and went upstairs. His grandmother had long since died; that was his only other experience of death. There'd been no funeral for her, only a quick burial in the town plot, but that had cost $75. Death cost you.

That time Cone had gotten most of the money from Tommy's mother in a fight that had progressed from shrieks to blows to rhythmic grunts and crying. The rest had come out of Tommy's demolition derby money.

Silently Tommy entered his mother's bedroom and pulled her current caller off her, throwing him out the door with his shoes clutched in one hand and his pants in the other. Tommy was very strong, his hands cold and deadly on the fellow's neck; the man didn't argue. Tommy went back to the bedroom to find his mother huddled fearfully in a blanket. He reached for her, too, grasped her shoulder, her arm, dragged her downstairs where he held her so that she could see Cone was dead. For a second she stood so that her dirty blond hair fell into the corpse's face. She looked, gagged, pulled away, shaking herself out of Tommy's grasp and dragging the blanket more closely around herself.

She glared at Tommy. "You think I'm forkin' over the money for this one, you're wrong," she said. "I ain't got no money. He cleaned me out the last time."

Inside Tommy, anger suddenly flowered. Out of control at last it bloomed, large and red and fiery, like some exotic plant that had been pinched back until it couldn't help itself and had to burgeon into huge blossom. He moved toward this huddled female with her big red mouth and dragged-down hair. He remembered her, oh, yes. He was stiff with anger. "Chicka, chicka," he muttered softly, his cold hands fighting through her hair, finding her neck.

"What're you gonna do, what're you—" He held her at arm's length for a moment and stared. That big wet mouth. He flung one arm back, slammed his open hand into that mouth hard, and again, and again, until it bled in a mass of bruises and the woman didn't struggle anymore.

Now she knew she was fighting for her life. Into her eyes came a challenge, like a glaze of hope. Blood ran down upon the blanket she clutched about her. With a gesture she dropped it and stood before him utterly naked.

Tommy saw only fire, so hot it burnt, blooming and blooming. He grabbed at his mother's bare body, dragged her to the garage at the end of the cellar.

"Bastard!" she screamed through a mouthful of blood. "You fairy fag—"

Tommy slapped her. He held her up and slammed his hand against her face again and again until at last he was satisfied. She no longer made a sound. She no longer had a face. Then he let her go. She fell in a heap at his feet.

It was almost enough. No. Not nearly enough. The flowering inside him whispered, begged, burnt for more. In a moment he had flung open the trunk of his fire-licked car and shoved her into it. He was breathing hard. Somewhere, he thought, Cone whispered. "Yes, Tommy. Yes."

In a few seconds he had driven to the edge of the road over which he and Cone customarily disposed of junk cars and parts. He drove as if to a derby, leaping out at the last possible moment, falling, landing, turning to watch. The car plunged deep into a woods gully and exploded. It was rigged so that even then a person in the driver's seat might have crawled out and walked away from the blaze, but of course a person wired into the trunk

[309]

could not. Tommy watched. He could still hear Cone breathing, "Yes, Tommy, yes." Tommy's own anger was flinging sparks like petals before his eyes; he ran into the house and found his mother's money and wrapped Cone in the soiled quilt he'd died on and put him on the tractor—now the only vehicle on the place that would work—and took him into town. He left Cone's body and the money on the back doorstep of Al Holt, the undertaker.

Storekeeper by day and only in the business—as he told his wife over and over again the next morning, recovering from the shock—because somebody had to do it, Al found Cone's body the next day. It was enough to make you die puking, he told her, shaking his head feebly. That Tommy Green, he said. Probably wouldn't even show up for the burial. Well, somebody had ought to do somethin' decent, he said. Call up the police, maybe, somethin'.

Later that morning, when he'd cleaned up the rubber-blue body covered with its own stinking mess, Al did call the police. Cone seemed to have died of natural causes, but you couldn't tell. And somebody, somewhere, had to make this right, somehow, he felt. Because it wasn't right as it was. So he called then, but it was too late.

*

Tommy's car, down in the sharp gully where it wouldn't be found for years, had burnt, smoldered; the fire had died out to wisps of smoke that blended with the early morning mist on Octavia's Hill. What it looked like was just another wreck in a gulch full of old car parts and rusted trash. Eventually there grew over it a tangle of blackberry vines and hardhack and Queen Anne's lace. Not one of the men who knew Tommy's mother ever thought to inquire where she'd gone to. After a while they took their trade elsewhere.

*

At that time Octavia's Hill supported forty head of dairy cows. Marl worked constantly to improve the stock. At night he and

Amy pored over charts of genetics, breeding in short legs, broad chests, wide udders, and rich milk, and all-important disease resistance. Morning and evening they supervised the feeding of the heifers: this was an art. They produced prizewinners by the careful addition each day of just the right amount of feed to the grain trough. Each day they fed the heifers just a little more, not so much as to cause digestive problems, but maybe even a handful more at a time, just enough to make each day count toward the optimal growth that brought blue ribbons, high sale prices, and the reputation you needed to make it in the dairy world.

The day after Cone's death, Tommy did chores as usual until Marl left for the feed store. Then he took up his old post in the barn loft, to watch for Amy. He was seeing sparks, he was burning.

Soon enough she came all right, walking directly below him. "Ho, Mary, ho, ho, there's a girl, Ella, how are you, hold still now."

The bitch went from stall to stall, Tommy could hear her talking in that low rumble. By this time the cows all knew her voice and would come to her full, strong calling: "Hey, Boss, ho, Bossy, come on now, come on!"

She was at the far end of the barn when Tommy jumped silently out of the loft and squatted at the end of the stalls nearest the door to the shed and the house. After a while Amy turned, went toward him, slowly nodding in his direction. Tommy stood, blocking the door.

"Well, Tom," she said briskly, "what is it? Marl's gone down to the store, but he'll be back."

Tommy stood very, very still.

But this wasn't unusual. Amy, who had never had a real conversation with him, took it to mean he had nothing to say and, frowning slightly, reached past him for the latch to the shed door.

But this was what Tommy had been waiting for. In a second he was on her, behind her, his hands raking her shoulders, grasping her neck. And he was grinning.

"Tommy, what—" Amy's knees began to buckle, mostly from

surprise. As his cold hands closed about her throat, however, even while she sagged, she collected herself. When she made her move, it was slow but thorough: with one strong wrench and back-armed swing she let him have it in the side, catching him just under the ribs, so that he groaned and his hands loosened at her throat. Then she hit him again, hard, in the same spot and he bent over, his wind knocked out. In three strides she was through the shed and into the house. A moment later she had barred the doors behind her with whatever she could find, and by the time Tommy had recovered enough to come after her, the whole house was shut tight.

*

Even with his fury in full flower within him on that day, however, Tommy was patient. The bitch had hit him hard, but he would make her pay. He was making her pay, wasn't he, with the old glass clattering over that big body? He was making that glass cut into her face, cut off her tits! He was heaving them rocks, dancing around the house, racing around and around and breaking windows. Scare her, by the God, scare all the lousy bitches to death, all three of them in there! He'd have them so they'd want to die, so they'd beg to get out of that house and off the hill. He'd have the hill for his! By God, he'd cut them up with glass—it was a promise. It said, "I'm comin' to get you, and when I'm done, you're gonna look like a busted window! They're gonna scrape you up with a dustpan and a big broom, all the little pieces and slivers, they're gonna scrape you up."

Tommy was in this wild state, running and heaving stones, when he heard the cars at the bottom of the hill. Then, quick as lightning, he fled to the back of the house and lit out across the field, so the men in the cars would see him going. Then he turned and circled back, after the men in the cars had begun to search toward the woods. When they were out of sight, Tommy went to the back of the farmhouse and found a broken cellar window, one he'd kicked in himself. "Yes, Tommy," he heard Cone whisper, "they can't lock us out, not ever." Then, inch by inch, Tommy lowered himself down into the cellar.

It was dark, but he was used to that. It was chilly, but he'd been overheated, running in the sun. His skin adapted like a lizard's. He stood still as a statue, hearing the high-pitched hum of excited voices above him; what they were saying he couldn't hear. He looked from one side to another with a peculiar, slow, sharp twist of the neck, as if he had no peripheral vision. If he'd had a reptile's tongue it would have been tasting the air. His feet, dressed in a pair of Cone's cast-off shoes, rummage sale dress shoes you bought for a nickel, began to move with delicacy and resolution: they might have been moccasins, or webbed, or no feet at all, but a method of scaly locomotion that fit itself to every curve and hump in the dark cellar floor. This floor, too, was dirt, like Cone's, but not powder dry. Damp, hard-packed clay, full of lumps and unevenness.

The voices upstairs quieted; there were sounds of persons leaving or beginning to move furniture, pick up glass. Heavy footsteps, a low-pitched voice: the big bitch who'd hit him. Light footsteps: the daughter, a kid. A sound like someone dropping into a chair, and then the big bitch's voice again: "How are you now, Mother Perry?"

Tommy seemed not to move, but he moved everywhere. Past Marl's shelves, past all the Perry claptrap, back into the little space under the bulkheading.

The bulkheading remained banked winter and summer; Tommy himself attended to that. On the outside it was a long set of double doors at the back of the foundation, laid at an angle almost flat to the ground. When the skinny little bitch, Amy's daughter, was old enough to toddle around, Lucy Perry had made a fuss about those doors, one of the few fusses the big bitch had listened to. From that time the doors were kept covered with a wall of plain wood, on top of which the hay bales were piled. No one, Tommy knew, had entered the cellar from that direction in years: the area underneath was a jumble of storage.

An inch at a time, as if he were a shadow moving with the motion of the sun, Tommy made his way into that bulkhead space. An old toboggan bristling with nails, dining room chairs up on end and held together by their glue of dust and spatters of old food, legless tables, cot beds ready to cry out with the clangor of moist, rusted metal, two overstuffed chairs, pictures in ornamental frames, pots and pans, old tarps, an oil slicker, pieces of a stove—all these were tangled together so personally that only one who had acted like furniture for most of his life could make his way into it noiselessly, and this Tommy did.

Upstairs, conversations came and went. Gradually the sounds of the cleanup ceased; no one offered to search the cellar. At one point men's feet were visible at Tommy's window, but he was too far away from it by then to see. But he heard the voices.

"Goddamn shame," said Bill Trowley. "What a mess."

"Oh, we'll fix it up," said Marl. "We'll fix him, too. Don't know what got into him, but we'll fix him."

"Damn right," said Trowley, and there was the whipped sound of landing spit. Then the feet moved on.

That night in the dark, when all he could hear was the sway of the house on its beams, Tommy pulled himself out from behind the furniture and began to prowl. He was hungry and thirsty. It was pitch black in the cellar. That didn't matter to him. One by one he took the cellar stairs. Quietly he lifted the latch on the cellar door and then he was in the kitchen. He stood, a black intruder, in the center of the kitchen floor, listening.

From the front sitting room came the rhythmic guardian snores of Bill Trowley and his son Ashley; they'd decided to stay the night, just in case. To one side was the little, dry shuffle-breath Tommy knew would belong to Lucy Perry. Upstairs was the quieter breathing of Marl and Amy. The child made no sound at all. But she would, Tommy thought, if he made her. Yes.

Tonight the house was full of men. He would have to wait, he would have to be patient, do it in a way that no one would suspect. He would have to wait until the Trowley men had gone home and the Perrys weren't listening, as now he knew they were, in their sleep.

Although he'd never been in the kitchen of this house before, Tommy had often smelled the food smells from it, and the odor of soap and floor wax. Tonight there were lilac smells through the broken windows as well. Instinctively he knew where the food would be kept, and training from childhood had taught him how much he could steal from the loaf of bread, the piece of cheese, before it would be questioned. He could see which apple leant no support to the others in the bowl. He took what wouldn't be missed, or what would be noticed in a suspicion so brief it was nameless, sliding the food into his shirt and then gliding back out of the kitchen and shutting the door noiselessly behind him.

He was halfway down the cellar stairs when he realized that all along the wall to one side and at the bottom were shallow shelves containing tinned meat and vegetables that Amy bought on sale by the case at the new supermarket in town. At the end of the stairs, at the foot, the shelves contained Amy's canned goods: jars of new peas, pink and golden chicken pieces succulent in a jellied sauce, jars of spinach and early chard. Last year's preserves were not quite gone, and a few jars of different kinds of fruit left from the year before were still on the shelves.

Saliva washed the underside of Tommy Green's tongue: he wouldn't go hungry while he stayed here. Noiselessly, he made his way to the end of the cellar, and while everybody slept he set up housekeeping under the bulkhead, moving furniture silently, pulling up one of the overstuffed armchairs. In the hours before morning he made the only sounds he would make for three days, the sounds of chewing, and the tiny click of the throat that meant he was swallowing.

The next night Tommy knew as soon as he was in the kitchen that Ashley Trowley had gone home but that Bill still slept in the front room. That night Tommy made his way deep into the house, breathing the unfamiliar smells of furniture polish, clean curtains, washed bodies in repose. The smells made him uneasy, but he moved quietly, learning which boards in the floor complained, learning the protests of old wooden thresholds and the whispering of the stairs.

By the end of the second night he was familiar with every room in the house and could move by a fluttering curtain without interrupting the flutter. He was familiar with the upstairs hall and all the doorways in it, how far ajar the doors were likely to be, at what time of night Marl reached for Amy. He knew how their little bitch, named Tave, slept in her bed, and when she turned, how she settled her cheek against the pillow. He had stood for long minutes at the end of her bed, watching, breathing with her, willing her breath to come with his; and all the while, within his body, the fire still licked and burnt and whispered, with Cone's own whisper: "Yes, Tommy, yes."

During all three of these days Tommy slept and listened and slept, hardly moving a muscle, in his overstuffed chair. He came to know mealtimes and cleaning times and napping times. When Tave and Amy sat on the sofa together in the afternoon sketching, Tommy somehow knew it, as if he heard even the scratch of charcoal on rough paper. On the second day, too, Amy took up her canning of peas and beans, and began filling jars with strawberry preserves. Tommy knew that she left the strawberries outside in the sun in shallow wooden bowls, strawberries mashed with honey and covered with a mosquito netting, to simmer down into a delicious sweet mass he had often seen but never dared to touch. Then, in the late afternoon, she would take the bowls inside and he would never see them again. What happened to the strawberries? It had long been a mystery to Tommy how so much produce could disappear into the farmhouse at Octavia's Hill, never to be seen again. What did they do with all that food? Now he learned that the big bitch took it. The female hoarded it in jars and thought it was hers.

She thought the cellar was hers, too. He watched her—and only her—go up and down his cellar stairs repeatedly on the second and third days with her baskets full of jars. Invading his territory, hiding food in it. Those square, straight shoulders, and that wide ass, and the thick legs in their white socks and brown shoes, set so firmly on the stairs. She thought the stairs were hers, too, but Tommy knew better.

On the third night he took a toolbox from underneath those stairs. From it he took a hammer and a small hand drill.

Tap! Tap! Sounds so soft they imitated house sounds. No one stirred; he knew that in his skin. Hammer claws on nailheads. The old stairs, with the jiggle in their treads that came from comfortable use, gave up their nails easily. The nails hardly cried out. The hand drill sank down, ever down. When it was finished the nail would barely hold, hold nothing. Two hours of work made sweat on a cold forehead; when it was finished, Tommy had stairs that no one would ever walk down again, only slide down, ever afterward stumble and fall down.

It was what he needed, he felt. He was the wrecker, come to unbuild while people slept in comfort. Cone whispered with an echo of Green voices and Tommy heard it: "Yes, Tommy, yes."

The voices called, he was ready. He replaced Marl's tools and went up the stairs one last time—but he knew where to step. He ate and drank from Amy's food supply and waited while the house swayed uncomfortably on its sills. Then, having given all the warning it could to the sleepers inside, it settled back down on its foundation.

When the house had ceased, Tommy began.

With a knowledge so sharp and complete it was almost instinctive, he started down the quiet hall. Bill Trowley had gone home, the Perrys were alone, it was time. Explosions of anger like hot acid began to burn in his belly. At Lucy's door he paused. Lucy slept with her door shut and always had, but now he opened it, knowing just where the latch would click and what amount of pressure on the door would keep it from doing so.

Did the old woman dream he stood there? He hoped she did. He wanted her frightened. He watched her as she lay, her mouth open, her lips moving with a muttering sound. Even in her sleep she was scolding, in some garbled, complicated vocabulary. White hair, white pillow. Had her breakfast with the little bitch upstairs. Her voice was different then, quite changed from the angry weapon of the schoolroom, a precise chitter of doting. She used it on the little bitch, nobody else.

He stared at the old woman and knew he could break her easily;

she was already half dead, already full of bad dreams. She was useless to him, not worth rousing the house over. He let her mutter, stepped back out into the dark hall.

The air was close with the smell of old wood, lemon oil, and sleep. The smells poked at him; he knew he didn't belong. Still, he began his tortuous way down the hall and up the stairs to the bedrooms.

Amy's mother had made a rectangular braided mat for each stair. Tommy didn't wear shoes for his nighttime journeys into the house, and now he carefully planted one foot on each braided mat, feeling the smooth wool bump and ripple of it and the solid oak beneath it, knowing the heart of the oak and placing his toes just where that heart was least able to defend itself with a cry. Not a stair creaked.

"You was given nothin', Tommy," Cone whispered. "You got to take. Yes."

Now he was up the stairs. He knew the plan of the rooms and what they looked like by dark. There were six doors off the hallway, all solid wood. One of these had a modern knob, not a latch, and a smell of Babo and bathroom tile and glass cleaner; it was a humid little room where in the night everything you touched was damp from night baths: damp porcelain, damp towels, occasionally a pile of cast-off clothing. It was a peculiar room. It held, among other things, a straight razor. Tommy picked this up.

Another of the gray-dark doors opened only to shelves of sheets and towels, and another to a little room turned into a storage closet full of coats. There was also an extra bedroom where no one slept. This was beside the bathroom, a peculiar still room, with chests of extra blankets in it and the made bed covered with large sheets of paper and canvas, the pictures the big bitch laid out to look at, the ones she painted.

Suddenly Tommy knew a use for the razor. He entered, feet playing on the wood floor until its music was silenced. He leaned over the bed, his face white, almost shining. His dark hair lay in bristling, sweaty points about his face. His lips had split apart; in the agony of his excitement, he was smiling. Meticulously he began to slice through the sketches again and again, cutting the mattress under them, cutting and cutting again, until he found he was breathing in small explosions, like the spitting of a flame. Then, out of breath, out of tune with the dismayed house which once again seemed to whine and settle, his razor embedded among coil springs so that his sweating cold hands couldn't loosen it, he paused, closed his eyes, and waited for the house to become still.

In time he could hear the sound of even breathing from Marl's and Amy's room. He could go to their doorway, he knew, even to their bed, and they would not hear him. They heard only each other in their sleep. He could hang over their bed and grab the big bitch. But as long as Marl was beside her he didn't have a chance of getting away. And Tommy Green must live.

Fire blossomed again. But he was careful, listening so as to hear past sound. From downstairs came Lucy's constant chuffle and whisper, and from the room of the little bitch, no voice at all. But there never was, he told himself. He knew that she slept silently, breath passing in and out of her body with only the faintest stirring of the bedclothes. Tommy listened, and then, leaving the razor in the bed, he walked slowly and delicately out of the guest room, leaving behind him pictures of flowers, like ash spots, tattered, on the bed. He walked, each toe alive as the tentacle of a sea plant, over the long pieces of polished wood, down the hall to the little bitch's room.

Tave was not asleep. He didn't realize it until he was about two feet from her bed. Then, in the gray-dark, her eyes suddenly loomed at him, black as two burns in a sheet. In a moment he was on top of her, but before he could get his hand across her mouth she had shrieked, a loud, long shriek.

She struggled on the bed, knocked over her bedside lamp with a crash, and then the big bitch was behind him: "What are you doing?" Her voice was low, but it had the carrying power of a car horn. "You get off her."

She dragged him off the bed and dumped him in a heap on the

floor. By this time he could hear Marl Perry coming down the hall. Tommy was up and off, fast as a snake. He whipped past Marl's knees and was down the stairs and out the door before Marl could catch him. Marl wasn't far behind.

Tommy could see in the dark; Marl couldn't. Both knew the hill. Amy had thrown Tommy down with such force that he had cracked a bone in his arm and so he ran leaning over, half-crippled. Suddenly, as he was about to shy off into the woods, he felt himself tackled, hurled forward. He struck his head on a stone and knew nothing until he found himself in a Bangor jail two hours later.

*

When Tommy came back to Octavia's Hill he'd done nine years in prison, not just for attacking Tave, but for what some people in town called murder. He'd been put away first on a breaking and entering charge, then tried and convicted of manslaughter. People said nine years was far too short a sentence, it was a sin, but what could you do?

In prison Tommy survived, mostly in the same way as he had living with Cone. He even earned enough money making crafts to finance the buying of another wreck of a car, once he was out. When he first came back to town he wasn't at home much; maybe that was why people in town and up on the hill tolerated him. He was busy making a name for himself at state fairs once again. In a few years he had earned enough money to buy himself a real car. This he parked outside the Green shack on the rare occasions when he was home. It was incongruous there: a fancy, out-of-date white Cadillac, with push-button windows and air conditioning, beside the crumbling Green house. The boards around the porch opening had long since given way, leaving the little shack sitting up ridiculously on high posts. It was whispered in town that Tommy lived in his car and used his shack for an outhouse.

Tommy knew the people on the hill hated him. Now and then he was at home when Tave, now all grown up, passed the shack in her rattletrap. He saw how she deliberately turned her eyes away from him, his house, his car. He felt nothing at all. He was busy wrecking cars and building them to wreck. That was what Cone told him to do.

*

The night before the air raid alert, however, Tommy Green was in a crackup to end all crackups. He'd taken a bet that he could drive a two-ton truck cab off a ramp and over six station wagons. This he did, to the senseless delight of about a thousand spectators. He revved the truck to sixty miles an hour, hit the ramp doing seventy, and flew out into the air, clearing the station wagons just fine.

However, the truck still had to land. Tommy was thrown forward against the windshield and tossed back against the seat. The truck rolled over and over, spurting fire. Tommy was thrown free. A moment later the truck smashed into a concrete wall and stopped flat, belching smoke and flame, while in the distance fire engine sirens wailed and the crowd screamed.

The main thing was, of course, that you had to get up and walk away from a wreck. It was Cone who told you to do it. "Get up and walk, Tommy, yes, yes," Cone breathed into Tommy's ear, and Tommy, in great pain, managed to do just that: got up, took off his helmet, and walked away while the crowd roared approval. He collected his money and left, stone-faced as usual to all the slavish admiration, not a mark on him, it seemed. No one even suggested that he might need a doctor.

But Tommy did. He had broken something, he knew; his whole side was turning purple-black. Still, he didn't cry or give in to it. He knew that after pain came pleasure, and so he was patient with his pain. Occasionally it would be very bad and he would swirl away, far away, and come to again much later. When he did, he heard Cone's voice calling him: "Come back, old Tommy, come on now." And then Tommy would come back and it would be painful, but the pain, he knew, wouldn't last.

The next afternoon—the afternoon of the air raid alert—he bounced his Cadillac back up to the shack and parked it. He had the radio on. *"Take cover immediately,"* he heard it say. *"Take shelter."*

Tommy was half out of his head with pain, and it seemed to him that the voice on the radio was Cone's voice. "Take the hill," the radio whispered. "Do it now!"

He hadn't been up to the summit of Octavia's Hill for years, since he'd gotten out of prison. But when he shut the radio off it continued to speak: "Take the hill," it whispered with Cone's voice. "Get that bitch."

When Cone spoke, Tommy moved. At once he pulled the car out of his driveway and headed up the hill, gasping as he bounced the Cadillac down a little woods road he remembered out in back of the big house. He drove until the car got stuck in the mud. But it was in the trees, invisible. Then he got out and began to walk. It was all he could do to get to the house.

He was standing in the kitchen on Octavia's Hill when he saw Tave's rattletrap station wagon drive in. His vision was not clear: it looked like there were two people in a variety of cars. But he couldn't tell how many, and he couldn't take chances.

He turned and, leaving one drop of blood behind him, started down the cellar stairs. Unerringly he made his way over the new, stone-cold cement floor, past the new shelves Bob Martin had put up. Like a wounded beast finding his way to his lair, Tommy huddled down into his old spot under the bulkheading, found one of the overstuffed chairs still there, and sat in it.

The pain was very bad. Cone was speaking to him: "Get the bitches, yes, Tommy, yes, yes."

Then the stiffness in his side became an agony. His mind was like a purple bruise that rose to a head, popped, drained blood deliciously, and melted, leaving a limp and puckered, empty skin. Sitting far back in the furniture and junk he fell away, swirled out into that emptiness, that pleasurable blackness in which nothing was real. Sitting so still that for more than a night and a day he might have been dead.

Tave: Early

*I*T WAS SATURDAY. Tave and Lucy Perry were eating breakfast together in the dining room. Marl and Amy had breakfasted much earlier, but Tave acquired Lucy's habits in the summer: they were ladies. They used the fine china for their creamy oatmeal, hiding chunks of brown sugar in the bowls: if Tave had acquired her manners from Lucy, Lucy got her sweet tooth, she said, from Tave. They used cloth napkins carefully "done up" by Lucy; it was one of the few chores she did around the house. Tave was thirteen; Lucy was seventy-three.

Tave and Lucy were eating breakfast at a table covered with what Lucy called a "morning cloth" of pink linen, and their napkins, also pink, were about as smooth and shiny and flexible as concrete: but they did scrape your face clean, and they smelled pleasantly of the hot iron Lucy used on them. There they sat, having their breakfast, Lucy for real and Tave playing a fond game. She was fond of this helpless old woman with her short, straight white hair pinned to the side and her sharp nose and thin-pointed chin. Lucy helped herself to extra brown sugar from the little silver bowl in the middle of the table. "If your manners are elegant," she'd always told Tave, "you can eat whatever you want, and no one will notice." Lucy's manners were elegant, all right, but Tave could count.

"That's three, Grandma," she said. "And not good for your teeth, if you please." And she smiled the Marlowe smile, sweetly.

"Octavia," said Lucy severely, dropping the little silver sugar spoon. "It is very bad manners to comment upon what others ingest."

"Yes, Grandmother," Tave said, and smiled again, still more sweetly. "Please, pass the sugar."

"When you ask me as nicely as that," said Lucy with a sigh, "how can I refuse?"

Tave put three heaped spoonfuls of brown sugar into her bowl. She buried them, her mouth watering in anticipation of the warm brown wells of sweetness they would make.

"The lilacs are out," said Lucy politely. "I do love lilacs."

Tave took one spoonful of plain oatmeal and ate it sugarless; the best was yet to come. "The poppies are budding, too," she said mischievously; there'd been some bad feeling when Amy planted those beside the doorstep, and Tave was just old enough to remember it.

"Hymph." This was Lucy's favorite little wet sniff. "Garish."

Just then Amy burst in from the shed. With one swift movement she shut the door behind her and dragged the kitchen table in front of it—the table groaned as it was dragged.

"Now, who is that?" Lucy inquired of Tave primly. "Is it your mother?"

Now Amy was dragging the big hall dresser against the kitchen door to the porch. Still in her barn boots and jeans—an outfit that rarely made it past the kitchen—her face flushed, she brushed past the dining room breakfast table and propped a chair under the door to the porch. The next instant she was in the front hall. None of the doors on Octavia's Hill had ever had locks or bolts on them, it simply hadn't been necessary. There was hardly a house in Monson that even in the 1960s was locked up at night. Tave jumped up and joined her mother in the hall. "Mom? What are you doing?"

But Amy only picked up a wooden settee and with Tave's help slid it against the front door. Then she rested, staring at Tave for a minute, her hand searching along her shoulders, touching her neck. "Collar's ripped," she said.

"Mom?" Tave and her mother looked at each other. It was

almost like a wavelength that they reached simultaneously, excluding everything else.

"Looks like Tommy Green's on a rampage." Amy's usually calm face was flushed and puzzled. "He grabbed me."

"He did?" This from Lucy, now standing in the doorway. She reached for the doorjamb to steady herself.

Amy still looked at Tave. "I gave him a good shove and got away. Dunno where he is now, but—"

"Tommy Green?" Tave couldn't believe it. It was like having the garden hose turn and bite you.

Amy nodded. Little beads of sweat had gathered on her upper lip. She wiped them off. "Silly, I guess, to get upset. Just he scared me so—"

"Oh, my!" Lucy still clutched the doorjamb. She was watching them out of the corner of one eye and waiting for their sympathy and attention. But this time she would have to wait.

"Where is he now?" said Tave. She was certainly not used to protecting her mother, but now the large round shoulders seemed frail, somehow, even defenseless. With her bare hands, Tave decided, she would kill Tommy Green, or anybody who harmed Amy Perry. "Is he—out there?"

The first glass, in the window over the kitchen sink, broke then. Tave and Lucy cried out; Amy jumped.

"By the gods, if he thinks he's coming in here—" Then Amy was down the hall and into the kitchen, where she picked up a broom from behind the hall door. It looked as if she thought Tommy would be climbing in; she held the broom by the thick end, ready to clout him a good one if he did.

"Mother Perry, you stay in the hall," she called in a low voice, clipped and precise. "Tave, you stay with her."

It was like her mother to assume the whole job, but suddenly Tave wanted to be with her, to do her part. "No!" she cried. "I want to get him! I want to—"

There was a crash of breaking glass in another part of the house—somewhere upstairs, it sounded like, or in the front sitting room.

"Damn him anyways," Amy muttered, passing through the hall again, broom in hand. "Tave! Phone the sheriff!"

As Tave went to the living room to phone, she could hear her mother moving furniture in the front sitting room. Then there was another crash, this time in the glass in the hall door, then another, upstairs. With a quaver Tave spoke to the sheriff's wife. "Hello, Didi? This is Tave Perry. Is Roger there?"

The town didn't have a full-time sheriff, there'd never been a need. Today, as always, Roger had gone to work at the lumberyard. Didi would call him there. What was the trouble?

There was the sound of more breaking glass, this time from the living room. "Did you hear that?" said Tave. "Tommy Green's gone crazy—he's breaking windows—I think he's after my mother." And she tried to explain. Didi said hang on, she'd send help.

Now Lucy stood by the phone, holding on to a chair and not saying a word. Tave could see she would have to tend to her grandmother. But first—one second more and she was on the phone to the Trowleys. There was Grandpa Bill's warm voice, his instant reaction: "You sit tight, Tave. We'll be right over."

Crashing glass, moving furniture. Lucy was quivering all over.

"Grandma," Tave said, "you sit here. Come on now." She led her grandmother to a chair in the protected hallway. "You take these pillows, in case glass begins to fly."

It now seemed that the very house was breaking: the sound of smashing glass came again and again, and after each crash, her mother's hurried footsteps, chasing the break. In the next moment Amy was back down the stairs.

"Tave," she yelled, "you watch the kitchen area, I'm going to the front rooms. If he decides to climb in, it won't be through the upstairs. Anyway, he's broken most of the glass up there. I don't know what else he can do. You watch. If you see anything, even the least little shadow of a thing, you sing out, all right? You holler!" Amy Perry was no longer shaken, Tave saw. She was mad, clear through. Her voice was a bark. "Did you call the sheriff?"

[328]

"Yes. He wasn't home, gone to work; Didi will send help. Then I called Grandpa Trowley. He said they'd be right up."

"Good girl. You watch, now." Even in an emergency like this, Tave and Amy were a team, they understood each other. Tave nodded; they took up their positions.

The really frightening thing was that now the crashes of glass came intermittently; between these noises Tommy's stillness was all the more treacherous.

For years, ever since she was a baby, probably, Tave had seen Tommy without really seeing him; he could blend into backgrounds, that was it. Now it was hard to know what to look for, he could be any shadow. Tave, standing on the kitchen threshold, developed a routine of shifting her eyes from window to window, examining each sash in turn for the sudden creeping irregularity that would develop into Tommy's profile. After a while the sound of breaking glass stopped altogether. The women waited.

It seemed like a long time before they heard voices, Trowley voices and the anxious calling of Tave's father: "Amy? Amy, you all right?"

"Mom!" cried Tave, suddenly limp with relief. "It's Dad and Grandpa, they're here!"

When they were all together in the kitchen, Marl was very pale and very angry. "But what got into him?" he kept asking. "I don't understand it! Of all the crazy—"

"Cone Green's dead," said Bill Trowley. "You know that?"

Tave's father shook his head. "He never said a word! Came to do chores as usual."

"Seems Tommy took Cone's body and left it with Al Holt, sometime in the night. Al was up to the farm this morning, looked some shaken up. Scared him 'bout to death, he said, findin' that body by his back door. Said Cone was an awful mess. Them Greens, I dunno, crazy . . ."

"Marlowe," said Lucy, who had not stopped trembling, "I am feeling weak. I believe I would like to go to my room."

"There's glass all over, Mother Perry," said Amy. "You come

in and sit down, I'll clean it up." Her eyes met Tave's father's briefly. Then she took Lucy back to her room.

"Roger's coming in," said Bill Trowley, at the window. "Now we'll see if we can find Tommy."

"Probably lit out by now," said Marl. "But if he hasn't, we'll get him. Tave, you all right?" She'd been standing under her father's arm all this time, her face hidden in his shirt. She wanted to be a grown-up, and would have been, except that she couldn't control her voice. "He's not going to hurt us, is he?"

"No," said Marl, stroking her hair. "No, not now."

"But he grabbed Mom, she said he—"

"I know, but now he's gone off. Don't you worry, Tave. We'll find him."

They didn't.

Tave and her mother spent the day picking up glass.

It was all the worse, Tave thought, outraged as she worked, because Octavia's Hill was such a good place. When you came down to it, she loved every inch. She loved the old boards and fireplaces, thick door moldings, cast-iron latches and hinges. She loved how you could get to the front porch from both kitchen and dining room, and how the front door faced west, so that the last thing in the afternoon, you could sit on the stairs and look out the screen and there you would be, with a whole sunset right in your lap, and the hallway and stairs turned red-orange. Everything glowed then.

Tave had said once that she loved that red color, and Amy, who'd been sitting beside her in the hall, sketchbook forgotten on her lap, had gotten that humorous look on her face and said, "Color of poppies, Tave," and then they had both thought of Lucy—and known it without saying so—and laughed.

It was a sturdy house, made to be kept beautifully, as Tave's mother kept it. There was lots of solid, dark woodwork waxed by Amy to a rich, dull polish. There were expanses of wall that seemed built especially to fit the old-fashioned furniture. There was comfort in this house, even when Tave's grandmother criticized it and longed aloud for some long-dead Boston relative. It was home. Tave sometimes thought of her great-grandfather, Lucy's father. She thought that before he built the house he must have stood on the hill and said, "From my upstairs windows I will see this, and from the front sitting room, that."

It was he who had set the glass for the windows in the house. It was old glass, some of it with ripples in it, some of it the faintest shade of gray-green. Tave's father went over the sashes from time to time with putty and paint, but until today most of the windows had kept their original glass. Tave, staring at jagged openings, then pulling out the shattered antique pieces with gloved hands, could not understand. It seemed to her suddenly that there were forces that worked against the good people did, and she was angry for the house. You had to watch, you had to be on your guard.

Tave and her mother were sweeping up glass in the kitchen when Tave said, "What I don't get is, why would Tommy want to do this?" She dumped a last dustpanful of glass bits into the trash. "It doesn't make sense! Haven't we always been good to him? What did we do?"

Amy shook her head. Gloves on, she was picking the last sharp pieces out of a window frame. "With some people," she said, "you don't have to do nothin', I guess. All's you have to do is be alive, that's how they are. I guess he lost his—" She stopped, at a loss to describe the relationship between Tommy and Cone. "His uncle last night, and you know what his mother was. He didn't have anybody or anything."

"But he's weird! And crazy! He grabbed you!"

"And I hit him some good ones and he broke a few windows," said Amy. "Not so much. It's all over now. Windows'll fix. Some people, Tave, you have to let 'em alone. You can't get all mucked up with 'em or things get worse and worse. I doubt the men will find him. He's long gone by now." Amy sat, wearily, at the kitchen table. "What your father thinks is, best thing would be to forget it."

"But what if he's out there?" Tave said. She grinned a little, so as to take the scare out of it. "What if he's just waiting to—"

"I dunno," said her mother. "He might be. But sometimes if you let these things alone, they go away, fix themselves. I'm not goin' to waste my time worryin'."

"He wrecked the house!"

"No," said Amy. "Few windows, that's all. You'd have to go pretty far to wreck the whole house. Come on, let's forget it, get supper."

But there was something funny in her mother's voice and Tave looked up to see tears in Amy's eyes. She and Tave stared at each other, and for the first time Tave saw her mother bewildered, even helpless. That look gave the lie to everything Amy had been saying. The look said we are innocent and I don't understand, all my life I believed in good and did it, I believed in being comfortable, that was all, and now—this.

"Mom?" said Tave.

"Supper!" said Amy resolutely, and turned to the stove. But the question was left between them, and they both knew it. Would Tommy Green go away? Could you ignore him?

But she would like to see Tommy Green try to touch her mother again! She would like to see him try! She'd fight him, kill him if she had to, she, Tave Perry! Suddenly she hated him and knew that if he ever touched one hair in the shining dark crown on her mother's head . . . Maybe the grown-ups could ignore him. She would not.

The men searched for him all day. At last they agreed that he had let off a little steam and then run away. They did stake out his shack at the foot of the hill, but no one thought he'd come back. That night Bill and Ashley Trowley stayed up on the hill. Bill was just mad enough to skin the feller, he said, if he ever got ahold of him. The next night, although both Trowleys went down to their farm during the day, Bill came back up to stay again that night. By the third night, however, the windows had been redone and there was still no sign of Tommy. Roger Mason, the sheriff, had alerted the State Police, and they were on the lookout. There really didn't seem to be much more that anybody could do, so on the third night Bill Trowley stayed home, and everything was very quiet on Octavia's Hill.

Was that why Tave woke up? Or perhaps—as she sometimes thought afterward—she somehow heard and identified the rattle of cut papers, or perhaps the hill itself warned her. The house rafters moved uncomfortably and she was, simply, awake in the dark that night: a vague feeling of quaking half-horror, which she'd ignored since the window-breaking, was fully upon her. She had thought of herself as a grown-up for years. This was easy to do, as the only child in a houseful of competent, forthright adults. But they had somehow taken the windows and Tommy's disappearance in stride. Nobody would talk about it. They got that look—the same one Amy had had: outraged righteous innocence —and changed the subject. The less said about Tommy Green the better, they seemed to feel.

Tave tried to be adult, she tried not to think about it. But there she lay, alert and listening. If you had asked her what she was doing, she couldn't have explained it. It was silly to be lying in your bed without even a weapon, keeping watch with the house. But there she lay without moving her head, staring at the dark doorway of her room. Her hands were cold in the bedclothes, her eyes wide and staring.

And then she saw his profile against the white door of her bedroom.

She had time to inhale and give one shriek before her mouth was enclosed in the dirty palm of Tommy Green and his fingernails were digging against her ear and the skin of her face. It was Tommy: at once she recognized him, the dark hollows around the blank eyes. But this was a Tommy she'd never seen before. On his face was a cheek-splitting grin.

It was then that her mother came, and then her father. That night Tommy was taken into custody. The next morning Amy led the pale, sleepless Tave to the dining room table. "Sit here," she said. "We'll have pancakes and my new jam. You'll feel better."

Her father had stayed in that morning to be with Tave and to be by the phone in case there was news; the State Police had taken Tommy to Bangor.

"Oh, boy, new jam," he said, and tried to grin. He and Tave

sat together at the table while Amy tied an apron over her jeans and then opened the cellar door and started down the stairs.

*

A cry, the sound of falling wood, of a body falling. A crash, a second crash, the sound of falling shelves and splintering jars.

"Oh, my God," said Marl as he ran for the door, down the cellar stairs, half falling himself. With superhuman effort he tore at the shelves he had built, pulling them off the queerly sprawled body of his wife. "Amy?" he cried. "Amy?"

Tave stayed at the top of the stairs, clinging to the door frame. Her father had gone down, but the stairs had broken, they were falling. "Don't come, Tave!" he called. She hardly recognized his voice, the crawling horror in it.

Lucy Perry had come running.

"Mother?" he cried.

"What is it? Oh, Marlowe, no!" She, too, almost started down the stairs, then drew back. She saw what Marl had not noticed, that the three upper treads were completely missing, and that the fourth was loose—the stairs were in pieces. Tave was hanging on to the wall beside the cellar door. Now and then it slipped away from her, slanted on its way to a fall. Then Tave would grab at it, pull herself upright again. Everything was falling away; the world was breaking.

"Don't come down!" her father cried. "Mother, get Bill, he's in the barn. Tave! Get away from the door!" Now he was trying to protect Amy from the light. But Tave had already seen her body, peculiarly heaped up among the broken glass jars and spilled food. Tave had seen the spouting forehead, the blood in a pool, the twisted neck. It was all frighteningly ordinary and helpless, pitiful, that crushed body. She began to shriek, to awaken her mother. "Mom!" she screamed and screamed. "Mom! Mom!"

Bill Trowley came running into the house. "Why, Tave!" he said. His face was bright red from running. Behind him came Lucy Perry, her face pinched and sharp and suffering. The wall fell away; Tave grabbed it. She was still shrieking.

[334]

But her grandfather ran past her, looked down through the cellar door. "Oh, God," he said quietly to Lucy. "Call the ambulance."

"No!" said Marl Perry, but not to them. It was a long, keening whisper. Tave heard it in the midst of her own shrieking, which seemed to go on and on, like a mechanism out of control. "No!" her father whispered, like a cry. "No!"

Lucy whimpered. "Is she—"

Tave couldn't bear to hear it. She turned, ran through the house with her hands over her ears. She was shrieking and shrieking. This, she decided over the sound of her own voice, was how a crazy person acted, but she couldn't help it, she didn't care. She ran as if her heart were on fire, ran from one room to another. Now Lucy Perry was behind her, trying to catch her. Again and again, still making those impossible high sounds, Tave eluded the old lady's grasp and fled from her, ending up upstairs, ending up in the little bedroom where the paintings and sketches, all her mother's work and Tave's own, lay cut and slashed. There, seeing them, Tave threw body and soul into shrieking, now crying out on every breath. It was almost like breathing, and automatic.

At last Lucy Perry, tears running down her gray cheeks, reached out and with every ounce of her long-forgotten schoolteacher's iron, slapped Tave twice, hard, once across each cheek.

Then the screaming stopped and the room, the house, and the hill were very still.

For an instant Tave was grateful.

Then, there were all those ripped pictures.

She fell among them and she sobbed; Lucy Perry cried along with her. The pain on Tave's bruised face sang out. She wanted to call for her mother right now, as she had when she was a baby, and have Amy's footsteps sound through the house as they had then, in that slow, comfortable way. She wanted her mother to come and set the world to rights as usual, put it all back together. It was all in pieces, somehow.

After a long while Bill Trowley came wheezing up the stairs and found Tave and her grandmother sitting together, weeping. His usually red face was now quite pale. "There," he said, his thick lips trembling. "Al just took her to the—the hearse, on a —a stretcher. She's—gone, Miss Perry. Marl's down with Al now. She's gone, Tave. There was nothing anybody could do." Bill's forehead wrinkled, his eyes blinked tears, but he kept himself under control. "Tave," he said slowly, "you want to come home with us? Just for a little while?"

"No," said Lucy, more sharply than she meant to. The Perrys had always been private about their grief. Or the Marlowes had. "My son will want to stay here."

Bill Trowley looked at them steadily for a moment, but then his upper lip began to tremble. "Don't I get anyone?" he said in a barely audible voice. "Won't anyone come with me?"

It was the loneliest voice Tave had ever heard, it sounded like her own. "Oh, Grandpa," she sobbed, "I'll come with you. Don't worry, don't cry."

Together they stumbled down the stairs.

Tave's father came in from the car. He was a strange, white-faced man.

"Daddy?" Tave whispered.

But her father's face had sunken in on itself, the nose too sharp and hooked, the chin suddenly weak. "I'm going to town with Al, Tave," he said brokenly. "For the ride, to be with her . . ."

Bill Trowley cleared his throat. "Marl, you know Al won't have any use for you, once he . . ." But then his unsteady gentle voice trailed off.

Tave had the sudden wild impression that she had been forgotten, maybe that she wasn't even standing there. "Daddy?" Now there was a frantic note in her voice. She slipped under his arm. "Daddy, I—" But he patted her automatically.

"If you would come to Al's, pick me up later," he said to his father-in-law.

"Why, yes," said Bill. "But Marl, she don't—she won't know. And Tave, little Tave, she's been through a lot."

"I'll know." Marl stared down at his daughter. Tave felt that she could look right through his eyes. They were blue, with little black spaces in them, and on the other side of those spaces nothing, nothing at all. "Now, Tave, you stay with your grandpa, and I'll be back in a little while."

Had he loved her only when her mother was around? "Daddy, I—"

"You'll be all right," said Marl. "Go with Grandpa now." Then he broke away from her and was gone.

Didn't he know she needed him? Didn't he love her, didn't he care? The floor opened up and Tave fell through it; it closed over her and she was scared. It was black, black, it was the cellar and she couldn't get out, her mother was dead, her father dying, someone was holding her, someone was keeping her away from them. She fought, awoke to smelling salts. Then she and her grandpa left Lucy with the Trowley brothers and rode home to Grandma.

Tave lay in the back seat under a car blanket, shivering although it was a bright summer day. From time to time she saw her grandpa's thick neck redden as he drove slowly down the hill. Then one pudgy hand would fumble, would bring out an old handkerchief, and he would mop his eyes. And Mary Trowley knew, the minute they came in the door they saw that.

"She's gone," said Bill brokenly. "Fell down the cellar stairs, the damnedest thing. Al said he thought her neck was broken. They'll have a doctor look at her."

Mary's face got a hard look, as if someone had hit her and she hated them and wouldn't cry. Then she saw Tave and that look fell away, broke off. "Lambie," she said, holding out her arms. "Don't worry. We'll be all right."

*

They cried for the sturdy child with her handful of crayons, the quiet girl going to Portland and then coming back to stand behind the feed store counter, the woman who blossomed in love and became a wife, a mother. They wept and then finally stopped weeping. You couldn't cry this loss away, Tave found. It lived with you, an ache that never left, while you amended your life and tried to learn how to live without her.

For Tave it was as if half her house had suddenly fallen away and disappeared. All the little routines she'd learned, all involving one big, handsome presence: simple things like buttering toast, or putting on a kettle, or mixing yellow ocher and a dash of green, just so, knife in paint. None of these were the same. No one made sure you had butter or handed you a potholder and moved, just at the right instant, out of your way. No one squinted at your paints and nodded. Everything stopped working in its customary way, and all around there were Amy-shaped shadows.

On the day of the funeral, Grandma Mary Trowley took her own flowers in her own vases into the living room, and that was where the service was held. Tave didn't hear much of it. She only saw her grandmother Mary Trowley, caught standing in a door-way with a vase of red flowers in her hands when the casket was brought up the steps to the Trowley farmhouse. Her face had a look that said, "Oh, Lord, my pain goes on and on and I'm not strong enough to bear it."

And then somehow she was strong enough, and she turned calmly and followed the casket into her living room, as she had others, and set the white vase of red flowers beside it.

Dr. Locke, who had married Marl and Amy, read from Revelations: "He showed me the river of the water of life, bright as crystal, flowing from the throne of God and of the Lamb, through the middle of the street of the city . . ."

Tave stared at the casket as she listened. It was closed. She was wondering how her mother could stand being shut up in that box. She was thinking how cruel it was, to put people in boxes, bury them.

"There shall be no more anything accursed," read the minister. "God will be their light, and they shall reign forever and ever."

Around Tave people were weeping, the house was full of weeping and flowers and food. Tave had had enough crying; it didn't seem to help. Now she was angry. She stood beside her father. He was pale, his face almost gray. His skin looked slack, he seemed twice as thin as usual. "I know a place," Tave had heard

[338]

him murmur into her mother's hair. And Amy's quiet, low laugh.

He seemed to see no one. His control was superb, as if there were nothing to control. Tave shook so, trembling in the warm sun, that she could hardly stand during the service. One of the Trowley cousins stood behind her. Tave leaned against the woman, who was weeping, and then, although she had cried and cried, she felt slow tears creep down her cheeks once again. She was sorry for everyone, sorry for herself and her father and her grandparents, for all the weeping people who stood there listening and watching that still, shiny box. It stayed shut, it was locked shut. Her mother would never come out of it.

*

Although Lucy Perry came to the funeral, she had stayed alone on the hill; she preferred that to staying with the Trowleys. After a few days Tave went back up to be with her.

There was the house that Amy had kept beautifully. Now every shining room was empty. There was the hill, rolling away from every window and off into the distance. Tave thought she could draw them, all those fine vistas, once again. She thought she would draw her mother's flowers, as they returned during the weeks following. But she found she could not. Instead she drew faces, bereaved, bewildered, angry faces.

And she never slept in the dark again.

Lucy Perry and Tave began to share the chores. Tave's father came in and out of the house. He was quiet and gentle but somehow removed from them. He took care of the animals, but Tave took care of the garden. Bill Trowley came up and did the haying and his sons did the heavy chores. Weeks passed in which their rearranged life often stumbled and faltered, but Tave knew they were all waiting for her father to pull himself together, pick up somewhere near where he'd left off. After a while it became apparent to everyone that he wasn't going to.

Ashley Trowley, rooting through the cellar one day after he'd repaired the stairs, came upon an overstuffed chair under the bulkheading and said it looked to him as if Tommy Green had set up shop there. "Don't know's I'd have looked in at all," he told Marl, " 'cept I saw that old toboggan sticking out, all them nails, and I thought, Jesus, somebody comes down here, they're gonna rip their clothes on it, or worse. Well, one thing led to another. Marl, there that chair sits. Looks to me like he lived down there! Pieces of food. And in the corner, he—" But Tave was listening and Ashley was too delicate to explain just what he'd had to clean up in the corner. "Wouldn't surprise me if he'd monkeyed with them stairs, neither."

Tave's father didn't say a word; he simply turned white and bit his lips. After a moment Ashley touched Marl's shoulder and was gone. They'd all been sickened by Amy's death. No one wanted to bring it up and belabor it in front of Marl.

Marl did nothing. Bill Trowley tried to argue with him about it. "Get somebody up here," he said, "have 'em look around. There ought to be some way to prove . . ." Even the town talked.

Marl just shrugged, pale and shaky, and walked away.

Finally Bill found a Bangor attorney and discussed the case with him. "Anything's possible, Mr. Trowley," the attorney said. "We'll talk to the police."

Marl Perry was perfectly polite, but Tave thought it was the kind of politeness that buried screaming. He let the police in, the attorney in, the reporters, whoever wanted to come. Six months later the case came to trial. It turned out that Ashley, meaning to do a good deed, had put up new stairs and cleaned up all the evidence. Tommy Green was put away for nine years, manslaughter.

Tave's father lived through that, too, but none of it really seemed to make much difference to him. He was deep in mourning; nothing would bring Amy back. Tave went to school, but she often avoided her schoolmates. Lucy Perry stayed on the hill, puttering around, doing some fussy housework, leaving the rest. It was a lame household, it limped.

The farm, too, suffered. After Tommy's trial, Bill Trowley came up the hill one night to talk with Marl, who sat gray-faced at the kitchen table and hardly answered him. Lucy sat in her old place by the stove; Tave was scrubbing dishes at the kitchen sink. Her grandfather talked along for a while, but her father seemed hardly to hear him; Tave wondered if anyone would ever touch her father again, or wake him up.

Finally Bill turned to Lucy. "Miss Perry," he said formally, "I'm going to talk straight to this boy here, and it may involve some swearin' and settin'-to. I'd be just as happy if you didn't hear it."

"Now, he's been under a strain," said Lucy. "You have to remember that, Mr. Trowley."

Tave's grandfather shut his eyes, opened them, nodded. "I do remember," he said with dignity and waited for them to leave.

Later Tave heard his voice through the hot-air grate in the floor of her father's room.

"Ella?" her grandpa was saying. "Jesus Christ, Marl, you sold her off a month ago! Good cow, too! Oh, I heard about it, I hear these things! Now what are you up to up here? I want to know!"

"Nothing." Tave's father's tense shrug was audible.

Bill Trowley exploded: "Nothin'! Why, shit, man, look! I know you're sick over Amy's death! We all are! But you got to pull yourself out of it! Why, you got hay, layin' out there in the field right now, and it's no goddamn earthly good to anybody—"

"Let me alone, Bill." Her father's low, shaken voice. "Please."

Her grandpa's voice, rising: "Amy's dead! All right, so be it! But you gotta get busy! You got pigs, you got a barn looks more like a manure shed! Now I been out there, I saw it! Jesus, Marl, Harry comes out here"—Harry was the milk inspector—"he gets one look at that, you're dead, you're off his list! And then what the hell you gonna do, where you gonna sell your milk?"

Still Tave's father said nothing. Her grandpa pounded the table. "What about your mother? Your daughter? *Amy's* daughter?" But here his voice broke.

Tave wanted to call down through the register, "Let it alone, Grandpa, it's all right," but she couldn't.

Now her grandfather spoke again, quietly. "Marl, what's goin' on? Jeez, you was a kid, nothin' you wouldn't do for this hill, nothin'! Why, you told me once—you remember it?—the hill

[341]

says, farm! Well, I remember it! You wa'n't very big, either! You was standin' right there, lookin' at me just as solemn, an' ol' Sears, why, he was standin' there, too." There was another silence, then the sound of Bill Trowley, blowing into his handkerchief. "That big old garden," he said. "That big old garden, Mack, all to your lone . . ."

Mack, Tave knew, was the name her uncle Sears had called her father by. Then, without another word, her grandpa left.

The next day her father was up early and had the chores done before her uncle Ashley got there to help. After that he seemed to pull himself together a little. He didn't talk and he didn't smile, but he did work, hard. He kept at the farm, deriving some comfort, it seemed, from being too tired to worry or think.

But the hill failed to flourish. Marl Perry's timing was off. Cows died, hay got rained on, pork prices bottomed out. He was so tense that at the end of a long day he would sit in his chair and shake. Tave wanted to yell at him, "Daddy! Go ahead and scream! Get it over with! Then let's get on with it!" But Lucy and Tave could do nothing. In a year's time Marl had had a massive heart attack that kept him confined to the house afterward. Money was tight. By the time Tave was finishing her sophomore year in high school, the only thing left to do was to sell off the livestock, which they did, squeaking by on the proceeds from the sales. Many of the cows brought high prices; they'd been well selected and carefully bred. The Perrys sold the farm equipment, too, and emptied the barn.

It was Tave who did the last sweeping and shoveling. Marl came in and tried to help, but was soon dizzy and had to be led back to the porch to sit. Tave didn't mind. She wasn't very big, but she was wiry and strong, the strongest of the three on the hill now, she knew.

It was strange to stand in that big empty barn. It had once been so full of life, warmth, plans for the future. Now the future itself had changed; Tave thought it had been taken from her. She couldn't make plans, she felt. No one could. No one dared, because the future could reach out and grab you and break you. She and her mother had done a lot of pipe-dreaming together: how

Tave would go to a good college, then on to art school, and someday, maybe, in a bright golden haze, she might become a good artist, even a great one. "Don't know what we'll do for money," Amy had said, "but we'll scare it up somewhere. The artist you get from me, maybe, that good brain from the Perry side. Got to plan ahead, get the best we can for you." And she'd smiled, but Tave couldn't bear to picture that smile anymore.

Life's special child was what she'd felt herself to be, for a while. But now the future was like this barn, a dusty, cavernous, empty place. Tomorrow—what use was it? No more use than today.

Lucy carried on in her increasingly dotty way about Tave's taking the college course at the high school, but in her junior year Tave realized that once graduated, she would be her family's only cash crop. Without a word to anyone she dropped the college course and took Business Math and Typing instead.

She brought home her rank card at the middle of the year, hoping her father would sign it without really looking. But it was Lucy who saw it first, snatching it out of Tave's hand.

"The Marlowes always have such good grades," said Lucy, turning the card over to look at it. But then she frowned. "Octavia Perry. Hmmm, they have given you the wrong card, child. B in Typing? B in Business Math? Shorthand? My goodness, somewhere there's a child bringing home A's in Literature, French, Latin. Look, Marlowe, this child has brought home the wrong report card! Hymph! That never happened in my school, did it?" She handed the card to Tave's father.

He stared. "But Mother, these new courses have been typed in on Tave's old card."

Tave could stand it no longer. "It's not a mistake," she said. "I changed the courses myself. I'll need them, to get a job."

"A job?" Lucy Perry sat down in her rocking chair. "What does the child mean, Marlowe?"

Marl's face was ashen. He stared at his daughter. "I think it means her father and grandmother can no longer support her," he said.

Tave felt bruised all over, inside and out. She stared back at her father, head up to keep the tears from splashing. Marl spoke:

"We never meant you to give up everything, Tave. We want you to have what you want. It's your right—"

"Your birthright!" cried Lucy sharply. "There are scholarships! You can do whatever you want. You'll want to paint."

Tave found it within herself to pity them. How could you reach out and make anything so anymore? Wasn't it like sweeping dust motes in an empty building? You had to put away hopes and plans and live in the real world! But how could she tell them that, two broken people. They were her children now. She would care for them.

"Grandma, I haven't painted a thing for months," said Tave. "You know that." She stood up straight and did a Marl Perry imitation, a charming grin, head to one side. "Besides," she said, "why should I want to go away and leave you?"

"But, Octavia." Lucy Perry closed her eyes, shook her head. "Just like your father! It's the Perry in you! The Marlowes would never . . ." And she began to argue with herself, muttering difficult, half-audible phrases, her eyes far away.

Tave hadn't grown up as an only child without knowing how to handle Lucy, handle them both. She went to her father. "We got to be practical, Dad." She stood, feet firmly planted. It was, perhaps, more of an imitation of her mother than she realized. "Painting I did," she said. "That's not my whole life. The hill is. Like you and—" "Mom," she wanted to say, and couldn't. "I want to get a job. I want to stay here. I can paint anytime—after work, on weekends. With a business course I can find a job, I know I can! And painting, it's not the same now . . ."

Marl held up one shaking hand, to stop her. "It's all right, Tave," he said. "Just so you know you can have anything"—he cleared his throat—"just about anything you want."

Tave didn't have the time, money, or inclination to do much at high school except attend as required. She settled down to getting B's, not A's. A's were asking for trouble. If you were too good, you'd get hurt, she felt. It was all survival, without much knowing why. She did chores and took care of her father and made decisions about money, clothing, food; neither her father nor Lucy, who was losing touch with reality more and more these days, could. She had few leisure moments, very few in which she wished to paint, but when she did, it was still the angry, bereaved faces that made it onto paper. She threw these paintings out. It was all a tremendous waste, she felt. Better to get on with real life—who knew why?

She had to grow up, somehow. In her senior year she watched the other girls and imitated: this hairdo, that lipstick. When you went out on a job interview, the school guidance counselor told them, you had to look your best. One afternoon the business course girls were ushered into the home economics rooms, and a long discussion ensued about how short dresses should be, how thick-heeled the platform shoes. Tave listened. She had "assets," she learned, gray eyes, pretty dark hair, good features. The nose was a little long. You put white foundation here, and dark there, though, and that fixed that.

Tave experimented at home. It was a little like painting yourself a face. Through the school, a job interview was set up for her at an insurance office in town, and a few weeks later she learned that she and two other girls had been hired.

She went home and told her father and he smiled his gentle smile. "How very nice," said Lucy Perry. "How charming."

That summer Tave began to work. She was neither happy nor unhappy precisely. She was in a state of suspension of feeling in which she only knew she had to stay on the site of her mother's death, to care for the survivors. It was not she who was insecure, they were. Without her to hold the household together, it would crumble away and leave nothing. Daily she passed the door her mother had opened before she fell. Daily she fought back the picture of her mother's crumpled body until it went away; she had consciously suppressed it. Then it only appeared at intervals, and she fought, fought it hard, until it went away again.

She remained deathly afraid of the dark.

*

She met Bob Martin at the office one day soon after he took his teaching job at Monson High. He came in to inquire about car insurance rates and left with a date with Tave for the following

Friday night. After all, there weren't that many eligible girls in Monson, or that many men, either.

By that time, on the outside at least, Tave had turned into a pretty secretary. Small and straight and well made, she wore her lipstick and her good dresses to work. She smiled when she was supposed to, she looked and acted—and felt—normal. Gradually her life had become a routine. Bob called her up about once a week, and they went to the movies every Friday night, all fall. A movie and a cup of coffee, comfortable as old shoes. You kept your head down, you survived.

Bob was nice-looking and pleasant to be with, even handsome in an engaging kind of way, tightly curled blond hair, freckles beneath which the color came and went. He was quiet company, perfectly agreeable. Sometimes Tave thought she saw in his brown eyes what she had been looking for for a long time: a regard that saw her for what she was and cared about what happened to her. But it was the slowest courtship in history. Bob waited for something from her, she didn't know quite what.

And he never talked about himself. Tave didn't realize how little she said about herself, either. Bob seemed so sure of himself, so confident, that his refusal to speak about personal subjects began to seem to her like an insult. After all, if he'd listened to anybody in town he would by now know everything about Octavia's Hill, and about her, Tave Perry.

It was as if each waited for the other to make the first move. It was wearing.

All fall they went out every Friday night, and in the town of Monson they became an accepted "item"; that was easy to do. All you had to do was breathe in someone's direction and gossip linked you forever after. Their relationship was all show, however. At least Tave began to think so. A few friendly, deferential kisses. It was, she thought a bit grimly, like being married without any of the fun.

Finally, one Friday night she'd had enough. She climbed in beside Bob and they went to the movies and she didn't say a single word.

"Popcorn?" he asked. He's a big dumb bunny, she was thinking.

They sat silently on cushioned seats and waited for the movie to begin. Sooner or later, she thought, he'll have to talk.

But he didn't. After the movie began he put his arm around her shoulders. She shrugged it off. He pulled into himself in his seat, his chin settling into the collar of his parka, and didn't touch her again.

"Something bothering you?" Bob asked her in the car on the way to the coffee shop. Tave didn't bother to reply.

They went to their usual table. They sat. Bob studied her face, color rising in his. After a moment in which nothing happened, he stood up and went to the counter and came back with the usual, coffee.

Tave thought, this is crazy.

"You big idiot!" she hissed at him. "Sit down!"

He blinked, he sat. Nervously he ran one hand through his hair, opened his mouth, shut it.

Furious, Tave grappled with air. "You never even asked me if I wanted coffee!" she exploded. "You never said, 'Coffee, Tave?' or anything! Did you? You don't care whether you talk to me or not!" she cried. "And now you just hand me this cup of coffee?" Her voice was audible, probably the length of the restaurant. She didn't care.

His lips pursed and a line appeared down the center of his forehead. "You—you didn't want coffee?"

"Oh, come on! That has nothing to do with it! *Talk* to me! You never talk! Tell me, don't you find that a handicap in your line of work? I mean, really? A college graduate, for God's sake, that's more than I am!"

"Are you mad at me?" he asked.

"I don't believe this!" said Tave. "I can yell at him like that, and that's all he says? 'Are you mad at me?' 'Mad at me?' Peachy!" She glared at Bob. "Just peachy! You can't even fight!"

"But I don't want to fight!" He seemed, of all things, shocked.

"You don't talk much about yourself, either, Tave. I thought you didn't want to! I like you and I—"

Tave never even applied the brakes. "You do? You like me? How'm I supposed to know that? And another thing—what are you thinking about all the time? And, and—" She searched for some way to make herself understood. "What do you do to your hands, they're so rough."

She picked up one of his hands—nice hands, she thought, big and square, and she liked them—and shook one blunt finger before his eyes. "What did you do here? You've got a hurt place, you see this?" She showed him the scratch. It was about an inch long, quite deep, now healing. "But if I'd asked you about it, you would have shrugged it off! 'Oh, yes,' you'd say. 'Accident.' Accident! 'Oh?' I'd say. 'Tell me about it.' And you know what you'd do? You'd lift up your shoulders and shake your head. 'Nothin' much,' you'd say."

But now they were holding hands. "Maybe that's our problem," he said. "I want you to talk about yourself, too. But you don't say anything."

"I don't? I?"

He didn't let go of her hand. That look was in his eye, the look she loved and craved. "I guess," he said, "I just figured it was off limits or something. I knew there was trouble in your family before and I thought maybe you didn't want to talk about that."

"Is that why you—"

"I mean, my childhood was bad, but under the circumstances, it seemed silly to monopolize the conversation with that, and when you didn't talk about your own . . ."

"I can't talk about it, not very well."

"I know the feeling. I should have spoken up before this, I guess."

"We were getting into a rut."

"But I thought you didn't really . . ."

"It wasn't that, exactly, but I . . ."

They left the restaurant. He turned to her. "Do you mind if I don't take you home right away?"

"No, not at all."

A kiss in a parking lot, middle of nowhere. The more tempting because it was over before it began, leaving her soft-lipped and hungry for kisses.

"Us quiet types," he said into her ear, kissing it, "we always know what we want. We just have a hard time asking for it."

Over the years, it never got any easier.

*

On July 12 of the following summer Tave came downstairs, not as she had planned, in the nice blue dress she wore now and then to work, but in a white dress with a soft overskirt of some light, flowered material. It was pretty and she was glad to wear it on her wedding day, but she had bought it because of Lucy Perry.

Lucy's mind had begun to slip. She had times, frightening times to her, when her loss of memory was so complete that she didn't know where she was or who she was. Then she would sit and mourn, weeping and rocking, for something lost, but no one knew what and she couldn't say.

Tave's father, himself a semi-invalid, stooped and pale at the age of forty-four, blue-lipped at walking across a room, was very kind to his mother at these times. He would sit by her as she wept and hold her hands and whisper, "Look, now, Mother, what is it? You tell me."

But Lucy would continue to weep until she'd cried herself out. Then she would sleep, sometimes for a day and a night together, and wake up hungry and full of plans, her memory completely restored.

"Octavia," she had said to Tave just a week before, after one of these crying-sleeping spells, "tomorrow is Saturday, I believe."

Tave stared. "Yes, Grandma, it is. Don't you want to sit down?"

"Oh, I will," said Lucy. She stood upright, her back ramrod-straight. "But you must promise me that you will buy a new dress tomorrow."

"A new—"

"Yes, indeed, Octavia," said Lucy. "The wedding is only a week away and you have nothing to wear."

"But I'm going to wear my blue dress, Gram," said Tave patiently. "You remember, we talked about it days ago."

"No," said the old woman huffily. "Certainly not! I will not allow it! Most upsetting! A granddaughter of the Marlowes, without a new dress for her wedding? Why, what will people say?"

"That we are living within our income," said Tave drily. "Besides, I don't really care."

"*I* care!" cried Lucy. "It is a matter of appearances!"

"But, Gram . . ."

Now Tave caught sight of her father, who had come to stand in the doorway. He winked at her and made a little motion with his hand. By tomorrow, the motion said, she will have forgotten all about it. Humor her. Tave sighed. "All right, Gram," she said. "You're right. Tomorrow I'll go shopping and—"

"Good," said Lucy. Then she looked distrustfully at what Tave had on that day, a brown flowered shirtwaist, nondescript but comfortable. Nice enough, Tave thought. Lucy's thin lips pressed together; her nose went up. "I believe I shall go with you," she said. "Just in case."

Beyond her grandmother's dignified, small frame Tave could see her father. He had tilted his head to one side and was giving her a little blue smile, the ghost of the old Marlowe grin. Tave sighed, shrugged.

"Okay, Gram, whatever you say."

Saturday marked the beginning of a bright period for Lucy, so bright that they were unprepared when forgetfulness came again. She was up early on Saturday and ate a big breakfast. By nine o'clock that morning Tave found herself starting up the rattletrap for a trip clear in to Bangor, at Lucy's insistence.

Once in the city, Lucy trotted in and out of stores with amazing vigor: she was looking for just the right dress. It was long past lunchtime and Tave was dead tired before her grandmother at last found a dress that suited. Lucy sat in a chair outside the fitting rooms and watched critically as Tave walked by, modeling.

"Now stand up straight, Octavia," the old woman prodded. "You're marrying a teacher, you know. Let's see. Yes. I believe this one will do."

"You're kidding," said Tave wearily. "I don't believe it."

"Don't be flip," said Lucy. "It's a very nice dress."

"Good. I was beginning to give up hope."

But Lucy was eyeing Tave's feet. "You will have to have shoes, of course."

"Damn," muttered Tave.

"Octavia Perry!" her grandmother whispered sternly. "That will be quite enough!"

"Yes, Grandmother." Inspired, Tave tilted her head to one side and grinned.

"And don't you use your father's smile on me, either!"

"Yes, Grandmother." Tave smiled sweetly. She wasn't above turning on the old charm if she had to. "Shall we find a place to eat before we shop further?" Silently she was hoping that there was somewhere in Bangor where they still used linen napkins at lunch.

Lucy melted. "Very well. You're a good girl. Now pay the bill, and we'll go."

"Yes, Grandmother."

The following week Lucy supervised everything, right down to where the minister should stand in the front parlor. Tave went along with her grandmother's arrangements, expecting from moment to moment that this bright spell would be over. But at last even she became too busy to remember those times when she had found Lucy turned into a huddled wreck who whimpered piteously, "I cannot find my bed. Where will I sleep tonight, where will I sleep?"

Then you would have to lead her to her room and soothe her, and no doubt she would look around with the air of a very rich woman being shown the best the hotel has to offer. "Why, yes," she would say. "This is quite nice. I believe I may have slept here before, in fact."

*

Neither Bob nor Tave was prepared when Lucy did lose her memory again. After the ceremony and the small reception, which were held up on the hill, he and Tave ran upstairs to get their luggage for the wedding trip. Lucy was standing in the upstairs hall. "Yes, yes," she was saying. "Must change."

Tave kissed her midflight; the old lady seemed fine.

A few minutes later, Tave and Bob were standing in the doorway of the farmhouse, ready to make a run for their car. Bob looked down at his new wife and grinned. "Well," he said, "you ready?"

From behind them came the sound of weeping, and there was Lucy Perry, crying. "Aldair? Where is he? Aldair, I can't find you."

She pushed past Tave and Bob as if they were strangers and stood on the porch in her nightgown. The front of it was unbuttoned, revealing her white, sagging chest. "Aldair?" she cried.

For a moment nobody moved. "Grandma," said Tave, "what are you—"

Tears ran down Lucy's withered cheeks. "I don't know you!" she cried. "Where is Aldair? Why is he hiding?"

Ashamed and loving, Tave reached out to the old woman, wiping tears off the wrinkled cheeks with her fingers. "It's okay, you're all right."

Marl Perry stepped forward. "Come with me, Lucy Perry," he said with gentle dignity. "Come. We'll leave these folks alone. I'll help you find Aldair." Nodding to Tave and Bob to go ahead, he left the room with Lucy on his arm.

Tave leaned against Bob for a minute; he held her. Then she smiled, at first a little tenuously, as a sign to the guests that the festivities should continue. "She'll sleep," she told them. "She'll feel better. Dad wants us to go, so—"

They ran to the car, greeting everyone's recovering smiles with their own, pelted with rice and good wishes, and it wasn't until she and Bob were far down the road that Tave wiped the tears off her own cheeks.

*

Soon after they returned from their trip, Marl Perry suffered the series of small heart attacks that at last ended his life. He was mourned and missed by Tave, but not with the degree of passion or anger with which she had mourned her mother. Marl had died, in so many ways, years before. Still, Tave had come to count on his frail good humor, and now it was gone. Lucy never mentioned her son. In fact, Tave began to wonder if Lucy even knew she'd had a son, or a son who had died.

Tavia was born and then little Billy. Sometimes Tave thought it was a part of the general cosmic joke that what you wanted and got turned out to be what you didn't want so much after all. She'd wanted to support Octavia's Hill, and yet when she was able to, there was nothing less satisfying than her typing, filing, phone-answering job. Not that she had ever actively disliked it, but that the novelty soon wore off, and she was glad to quit when her children came along. There were two sides to having children, too. On the one hand you loved them, craved the look of them when they weren't around, worried over them, and defended them against all their enemies—from unappreciative teachers to the common cold—but the children created as well in Tave a restlessness, an urge to extricate herself, as if the hill were burying her in domesticity, as if her family were doing it to her, or someone was.

"You realize I've never been off this damned hill?" she would cry at Bob after a long day at home. "I've never been anywhere! I've never been to Boston, for God's sake! And you like that, don't you? It's what you want, isn't it?"

Bob, innocent, would look troubled and say, "No! No, Tave. I want you to have what you want! I really do!"

Rarely, Tave would look into his anxious face and believe him and touch his cheek or cry on his shoulder. More often, she was angry and confused. "What I want?" she would cry. "I want something besides changing diapers and keeping decent clothes on a crazy old woman! I want—I don't know! I want to go and —But no! You like it here! You keep me here!"

He would shake his head, eyes murky with her trouble. "Tave, go if you want. That's fine! But where does it leave us? Where does it put Tavia and little Billy?"

"Damn the children! Damn them and you!" Of course she didn't mean it, but it was all that was left to her to say. Then he would turn away and quietly pick up his latest project and go to work. Once finished, there forever after the project would be—bookshelves, the hobbyhorse, even her wooden easel—to remind her of how wrong she was, how confused, how much he cared.

What Bob wanted was a nice life on the hill. He wanted every day to be predictable, with its own quiet satisfactions. This was due, in part, to his own mixed-up childhood, she knew. He loved the hill for the very reasons that made Tave restless: here was family, history, a small town, a home begging for love.

He didn't talk easily; neither did she. He always thought the work of his hands would speak for him, and Tave knew this wasn't enough. She wanted more talking, fewer projects. But she was never able to tell him so.

One night before they were married she'd shown Bob the house, and they'd argued over the cellar. Since Amy's death it had been the neglected spot in the house. Tave, showing the kitchen to Bob, had indicated the cellar door with a too-casual wave of the hand. "Cellar," she said. "That's about all. Coffee?"

"Sure," said Bob, "but we might as well finish the tour first." He opened the cellar door and peered down into the black hole of it.

"Oh, you don't want to go down there," said Tave. "Nobody does. It's—it's an awful mess."

But Bob had shrugged and grinned. Obviously he'd forgotten for the moment how her mother died, and suddenly Tave didn't feel like telling him again.

"I've been in messy cellars before. Is there a light?"

At that time there was not. "No," said Tave. "You have to light the lantern, there, on the hook. But really, Bob, I—"

By this time the lantern was lit and he was beckoning from the door. "Come on, now."

Angry with him and at herself for her silence, Tave went with him down the steps and into the dark. She tested each riser carefully before she put her full weight on it, and walked past the place where once there had been shelves, now only a few wooden beams with gouged-out places. Nervously she stood beside Bob, looking down the length of the place by the light of the swinging lantern. At that point the floor was still dirt, and because no one had been down there for years to put the place in order, it was incredibly piled with things that had been brought as far as the cellar stairs and then, as often as not, heaved out into the dark. Together she and Bob surveyed a waist-high pile of rubble. Tave was trembling.

"Bob, I want to go up."

But he dived into the junk, leaving her to stand just outside his circle of light. It was like drowning. "You've got some great stuff down here," he said. "Did you know that?"

"Bob!" she cried. "I want to go up! Now!" Stumbling she ran, fell on the stairs, climbed up them madly, and landed at last, bruised and hurt, in the kitchen. He followed her. "Tave, are you all right? What is it?"

"Go home!" she cried. "Go home! Don't talk to me!"

"But, Tave, what's the matter?"

"My mother . . ."

"My God, I'm sorry, Tave. You should have said something."

"It's not my fault! Go home!"

He tried to draw her into his arms. She could feel herself trembling and felt that she did it on purpose, to impress him with her fear and anger.

"Look," he said, "I don't blame you. Maybe what we need to do is clean that place out, fix it up."

"It's an awful place."

"Tave," he said, "you know there's no one down there. You know that, don't you?"

"Of course I know that!" she cried. And then startled herself by dissolving in his arms, weeping like a baby.

Soon after they were married, he'd gone to work and cleaned the place out. "I won't have you frightened anymore!" he'd said when she'd protested. And he did turn the cellar into its present state of storage, transforming it, really, except for the hopelessly tangled area under the bulkhead. He'd been so full of pride in his work that Tave felt doubly caught, once by her fear and once by Bob's pride. She could not explain to him that cleaning it out had nothing to do with her fear, that they would have to sort out more things than were in the cellar in order to do that.

Times of silence, times of noisy argument—they alternated in their marriage. Rare quiet conversations became all the more dear because they were so hard-won. You had to fight to get them, Tave found. Mostly, it was easier to act normally, to keep herself to herself. Bob would do the same, until the next argument. During "normal" times it was possible not only to love one another but to live comfortably. Everything was possible if you could ignore your wounds; they never seemed to heal, beneath sewn skin.

*

At the age of eighty-four Lucy Perry died in her sleep. Going in to dress her one morning, Tave found her very cold and quiet on the bed, her hair spread out on the pillow like so much tangled string. Tave backed out of the room and flew to call Bob, left a message—they hadn't yet arrived at school that morning—then called the new doctor in Monson and the undertaker. Then she tiptoed back to Lucy's bedroom.

Her grandmother lay as if peacefully asleep on the bed. The thin nose and the sharp chin looked much as usual. She had, Tave decided, a faintly inquiring look on her face, as if she had discovered something unexpectedly pleasant.

Tave, studying that face, found herself remembering a time just after Billy was born when she went into Billy's room to get him up from his nap and found Lucy there, in a rocking chair, holding the baby. The old face over the small body slumped in sleep was then as it was now, peaceful, lost in hope. Lucy was murmuring something unintelligible to the baby. As Tave stood watching, she heard Bob and little Tavia come into the kitchen, home from town with groceries, and knew she must break this moment for Lucy, feed Billy, and go.

"I'll take him now, Grandma," she said gently. "Is he a good baby?" She reached for him.

"What? Oh, yes." Lucy stirred, gave him up reluctantly. "Do you want to sit here?"

"No, don't move." Tave carried the baby to an armchair and sat in the shadow of the room; Billy came to her curled and mewing. She suddenly anticipated his feeding so strongly that her blouse dampened in two spots, one above each nipple, and she moved uncomfortably, settled Billy to her breast, ran her fingers over his soft hair. Caught as she was, tangled and happy with the baby, she did not at first hear Lucy's question, chirruped from the other side of the room. Lucy was standing at a window; she would never watch Tave nurse her children.

"Do you know why I call you Octavia?" Lucy asked.

Tave answered without thinking, they'd been through this before. "It was a Marlowe name," she said.

"That's right," said the old woman. "And for whom did your mother name you?"

"For you." Distracted, Tave was watching Billy.

"But who else, who else?" Lucy, impatient.

"My great-grandmother Perry. I know that, Grandma."

"Octavia Marlowe, yes." There was a short silence while Lucy stared out the window. Her face was lit in the sunset, runneled and furrowed and full of light. "And that little girl," Lucy asked, "what is her name?"

"No, no," said Tave. "This is Billy."

"Octavia!" Lucy said it triumphantly.

Tave gave up.

"Octavia!" said Lucy again. "And I address you as Octavia to —to remind you! There's another life besides this one."

Tave, lifting Billy to burp him, felt her love for the baby and her secret knowledge that her grandmother was right, and despaired. How could it all be reconciled?

"Grandma," she said, "come on out with me. I want to change Billy and see what the others have bought."

Lucy went to her and grabbed her arm. "Octavia, I call you! So that no matter what happens—"

"Grandma," said Tave soothingly, "you come out. You sit by the stove."

Just as abruptly, Lucy let go. "Yes, but you take after her, too." "Her," Tave knew, was Amy Perry. "Octavia!" Lucy cried, as if she had lost something precious, and then she sat again and began to rock, refusing to budge, even for supper.

After that incident, clarity and craziness had become so intertwined in Lucy that looking after her was like taking care of another child. And now the child lay, covers pulled up to her chin, that peacefully curious look on her face. No one would ever erase that look again!

Tave didn't weep for her grandmother. Lucy had been so troubled at the end of her life, forgetting to dress, or taking her clothes off in front of the wide-eyed children, weeping through the house at night in a flannel nightgown that flapped open from neck to navel, no matter how securely Tave tried to fasten it with impossibly knotted strings and pins. Bare, down-pointed breasts lifting for Aldair. It had been plain—Lucy was looking for the lover she'd lost. Pitiful. Hopeless. Tave would put her back to bed in the middle of the night and then go and crawl in beside Bob, muttering, "Bare to the hips. Not even sense enough to know it's cold."

Sorry, but not burdened with grief, Tave blinked back tears and reached over and settled the covers, kissing the old face softly, as she had every night, putting the old lady to bed.

But then, on horrified impulse, she pulled the covers back. The body of Lucy Perry was stark naked.

Tave's hands went up, covered her eyes. "If the ambulance comes, if they find you like this— Oh, Grandma!" Then she pulled the blankets up again in an unnecessary attempt at modesty and began to search for Lucy's latest nightgown. She found it tucked into a corner, ripped from neck to hem.

"Oh, Gram," whispered Tave. She went to the drawer, found a clean gown, and dressed Lucy, tucking her in with care for the last time. When the ambulance arrived, nothing could have been more proper than the look of Lucy Perry in her bed. The ripped nightgown had already gone out with the trash. Appearances had been preserved, for Lucy, to the last.

*

With the house just to themselves after Lucy's death, and the awful drain of caring for her at last over, it seemed for a while that Tave and Bob might find themselves. They had lived through Marl's death, the coming of children, and Lucy's death. But somehow their marriage had settled and seemed to replay the old pattern: silence, argument, lovemaking, silence. Only during lovemaking were they their unguarded selves. In spite of what the magazines said about good sex as the basis for a good marriage, neither Bob nor Tave was happy enough to believe it.

It was in retribution for Bob's projects as much as for anything else that Tave threw herself back into her painting once both children were in school. She painted, insisting loudly on its importance, attending art exhibits and hating it when she saw them clinging to old patterns. In her own work she became more and more radical until no one who saw her painting cared for it, and each canvas became a self-fulfilling prophecy of separation and despair.

Tave

SOME PEOPLE GOT CLOSER to knowing a reason for living than she ever had, Tave was thinking. Some people had a reason and didn't believe in it: that was her great-grandfather. He had made a beautiful house on this hill and then what? Given up housebuilding? Despaired? Why wouldn't Lucy Perry ever talk about her father?

Some people were lucky to begin with: Tave's father had started out like one of these. He'd wanted to farm and he'd known it. He'd come into it so easily. He'd only had to fight Lucy Perry and she had never been strong.

Perhaps her father and her grandmother were more alike than she had realized: they'd never fought hard, either of them, for themselves. Maybe Lucy had been maimed from the first. But Marl Perry had simply forgotten how to fight. He'd given himself up to happiness with her mother and lost, the way unprotected soil banks are eaten away by lapping water.

If Tave had learned anything from her mother's death, it was that you had to be on your guard. But, guard against what? Tave didn't know why she was alive. She could mutter platitudes about being the mother of children, but the truth was she needed them as much as they needed her. What was she good for? She didn't know.

For a long time that morning she sat on her mattress envisioning destruction. In Vermont, in Maine, to the hill; for she found herself searching the hill in her mind. She wondered if it were raining out, or sunny. She couldn't tell, the cellar was so dark. She listened for the sounds of rain but heard nothing.

She imagined the hill as it looked on summer mornings, mists coming up off the Branch in the distance, the dark green of spruce, the lighter greens and yellows of new leaves. She saw the swing of the road as it came up toward the house and somehow it caught her heart. Gray dirt, in an eye-sweet curve, with a long stone wall on either side of it. There were stone walls at the edges of all her father's fields. There was moss in the lee of those rocks; there were bushes growing between them that you recognized by shape and smell without knowing their names, willow, alder, others smaller, dusky, and just as strong.

There was a wild rose that grew near the foot of the hill. Tave wondered if that would be blooming today. Five fine pink petals and a center crown of gold. And a scent so sweet, unlike any other smell, certainly unlike the decadent rich variety you purchased in a flower shop. You couldn't pick these wild roses; they lost their petals and died. All you could do was sit on the stone wall and smell them. And wish there was something, anything you had in your possession, as fine and rich as one of those flowers, so you could carry it away with you and keep it, have it to show, take it out when you needed it and be comforted.

Tave sat on her mattress in the strange white light from the lantern and tried to imagine those pink petals salted with fallout, but it was too ugly, almost harder to bear than the idea of radioactivity on human skin.

She found herself recalling her seventh-grade classroom, her first brush with the horrors of the nuclear age. She could remember that day, an afternoon in early June just before school let out for the summer: new green fields in all the open windows. Mr. Howland, their science teacher, had passed out bomb shelter plans in a little pamphlet put out by civil defense. Nobody had been alarmed. Air raid drills meant huddling and giggling under your desk with your head tucked down. It was easy, and you could smell your knees, which was unusual and somehow pleasant.

But then some child asked, "Could radiation go through windows?"

Mr. Howland nodded. "The reason for the shelters, with their thick walls, is for insulation. Radiation works on the same principle as the laser," and he launched into a lengthy scientific explanation.

With one ear they listened to him; they were more interested in the afternoon waiting for them outside. Except for one child, a boy Tave's age. "Can it go through houses?" he asked when Mr. Howland had finished. "Can you see it? What does it do to you?"

His voice was not alarmed, exactly, but troubled and fascinated. Suddenly Tave began to pay attention.

"No, you can't see it," Mr. Howland said. "It can cause . . . diseases."

The boy persisted. "What diseases?"

"Cancers," Mr. Howland admitted. "Blood disorders, leukemia."

"But can you die?"

"Well, yes."

"How?"

"You get sick. People don't know exactly."

The smudged afternoon a fear that lodged in your bones, as radiation itself might do. Tave had taken the shelter plans home and showed them to her parents. Somehow it seemed right that they, too, should be awakened, frightened.

"Well, let's we look now," said Marl agreeably. Tave's mother sat at the kitchen table darning a sock. Her forehead was as clear and smooth and shining as the marble on a statue in an art book. Tave's father looked through the booklet, pushed it to her. Then Amy put down the sock—when she mended a sock, you wished the whole thing were made of her darning—and looked the booklet over, too.

Tave stared at her mother, expecting some shock, maybe even an exclamation. But at last Amy only closed the booklet and picked up the sock again. "Well, if this means," she said slowly, "that you're going to cement in the cellar, then I wish you would."

"Oh, boy," said Tave's father. He began to grin. "Snookered into it."

"But you don't understand." Tave was disappointed at their reaction and glad, too.

"Tave," said her mother softly, "we know you're scared. And we can build a shelter. Maybe we will. We can put the food down there, or anything you want. You can go down and live like a king and be safe from everybody. Or maybe you'd be miserable."

"That's right," said her father, and heaved the little booklet up onto a high shelf, where it stayed for years.

And now Tave knew, of course, that all the bomb shelters in the world couldn't have made her mother safe. A cement floor in the cellar would have snapped her neck all the more quickly. How long, she wondered, would she have to fight at that picture, put it out of her mind: the twisted body, the head spattering blood? She knew if she went over to the foot of the cellar stairs, there would be nothing there to remind her of it; she carried it around in herself, that was all! And couldn't get rid of it! She shook her head, thinking, I must be the ugliest person in the world.

She shivered, drew her knees up on the mattress. When had' she ever felt so low? She was cold, yes. And worried. And this cellar . . .

Didn't it seem, suddenly, that something in the cellar was . . . alive?

"Hello?" she called out into the dark. Silly, even half of a joke. She knew no one was there.

But perhaps the cellar itself had a presence, say, like a big-black-box-shaped monster just now beginning to breathe, to lift itself and prepare to prowl.

"Hello?" Tave called again. This time it wasn't so silly.

The lantern still shone: a steady, peculiarly white light. Tave couldn't face sitting still anymore. She stood up and got ready to paint, preparing her colors and setting up a canvas almost automatically, with no particular subject in mind.

As she worked to get ready her ears were listening for the cellar, for strange sounds in it, because it suddenly seemed so real to her that the cellar might be alive. Well, she was at the end of her rope, she guessed. She was scared. Defenses breaking down; maybe they hadn't been too good to start with. After all, what was she made of? Angry words, probably, and bad paintings.

Without any particular conscious volition, certainly without a plan or a cause, almost unaware that her brush was full of pink paint, she began. She was painting from nowhere, from fright, from listening to the cellar, hardly recognizing the form her fingers gave to the thing on the canvas. It was almost like a doodle: your fingers worked, you let them.

But after a while she was painting with all her energy, for the pure act of it, a way to forget the cellar pounding in her ears. And then she began to paint with heightened perception a thing she would not allow herself to give a name to, as if categorizing it could squeeze it, change it, take it away from her. And at last she forgot to think or to guard against thinking. She was letting the picture grow; it was as if she were only the tool.

She painted all that day, having forgotten for once the cellar, the radiation, the family horrors, all of it, even that she was painting by lantern light. She didn't know how long, exactly, she spent painting; when she looked at her watch, it had stopped. She had been working with a spirit that whispered through her, or so it seemed. And it was so easy, nothing easier. You had only to be still and to let yourself go, and there it was.

But what Tave was painting she finally did give a name to. By then it was the middle of the afternoon, she thought, and she was tired. But what was on the canvas was unmistakable. She stepped back to look at it. There were the pink petals, and there the gold crown. You looked through them, almost, and there was the stone wall on which the flower grew. The stones were in a heap, like some ancient tumbled altar where a man had sacrificed to a false god. Beyond the wild rose stretched the hill, and on the summit a small plain farmhouse with tiny windows. Each window glowed like a jewel, red-gold, poppy color. It was a beautiful place. It was Octavia's Hill, and the sun was rising.

It was a good painting.

"Ha," said Tave. "Give it time."

"Get it up into the real light," she told herself meanly. "Then we'll see what we have, all right."

You painted what would be snatched away, part of the big joke.

She was bone-weary. It seemed to her that the lantern light was a little browner than it had been before, hours before. She had been in the cellar for at least twenty-four hours by now, she guessed, but the time span meant nothing to her. She went to the radio and turned it on, wasn't surprised to find that there was still no sound but a little faint static; the batteries were completely dead. *"Plume of radioactive dust,"* Ray had whispered before, floating away from her. *"Out to sea . . ."*

Surely this wouldn't last much longer! The phone call would come, Bob and the children would be back. They would try to do better, this time. They would try to have a good life.

She ate tinned meat and bread and oranges for supper, quite cheerfully and hungrily; she'd been so engrossed in her work that she'd forgotten to have lunch. Then she went back to the painting, surprised to find that even by the light of the lantern it still pleased her. Oh, it wasn't finished, not in any way. There was plenty to do with it. It might be days, even weeks, before the painting could be finished properly. But there was something about it . . . She was tired, but she began to paint again.

She worked for a long time, then washed her brushes and crawled into the blankets on her mattress. By now the lantern light was quite brown, and the prospect of another night near the now-cold furnace was not very inviting. But she was tired, and in a short time she was asleep. She left the lantern burning deliberately: even in her sleep she had to have a light. She'd convinced herself that the phone call from an authority—Bob or John

Manders, probably—would come soon, and that there might be no need to conserve light. Besides, leaving the lantern burning was like making a fire in a wilderness: it kept wolves away. She slept.

*

Far down the cellar, beneath the bulkheading, Tommy Green's tongue moved silently between his still lips and tasted blood. He had swirled up at last through the dark to a chair and now his hands felt along its frayed material. Beneath one palm was a hole stuffed with straw. He tried to reach farther, but then pain caught up with him, tore at him; it was like wrenching his upper body from his lower. His feet, he felt, were made of weak, layered stone. If he stood, they might crumble under his weight.

His eyes scanned the dark, the pilings of junk around him: the iron bar of a cot, some knobbed wood, a discarded tabletop, the cupped legs of an old kitchen stove. Then he saw a light, a faint gold ring, quite far away.

But hadn't Cone said this cellar was his? Instinctively Tommy listened and Cone whispered to him from everywhere, nowhere.

"We'll get the bitches, Tommy," Cone whispered. "Head down, now, go on, move."

Obediently Tommy bent his head, slid forward, and stood.

"Yesss, Tommy." It was Cone's hand that pressed against Tommy's side. Blood ran, forcing its way through Cone's fingers, soaking Tommy's matted, blood-dried clothing.

That faraway light, the bitch's light, was in his eyes! With one shredded, arrested scream of pain he moved forward. Slowly, silently, while Tave slept, he began to make his tortured way the length of the cellar.

But when at last he came to that light the first thing he saw was water, a basin half full of clear water beneath the pumphead in the sink, and suddenly he was very thirsty. Dimly he could remember stopping beside this sink once before, when he first entered the cellar. Then there had been no water. Now it was all his. He looked about, spotted the roll of blankets on the mattress, gauged its breathing, lowered his head, and, like a shaggy animal, started to lap.

But his dry tongue hovered above the surface of the water: the woman had moved. He knew who it was, all right. The little bitch, Tave. He'd had his eye on her for quite some time. She was owed to him, he felt. Well, he would get her first, then he would drink. He left the water, moved one thick foot at a time toward her.

But halfway there the brown lantern light winked once and went out.

The body on the mattress moved convulsively, a flurry of arms and legs that shocked him. "Who's there?" a voice cried.

Tommy hovered over the twisting blankets. He put out one hand to reach into them, but as he did so something inside his chest rippled and popped, and an agony began that stopped him. His hand opened and closed on nothing. He hovered, waiting.

He was patient.

*

"Who's there?" Tave cried again, trembling. Where was the flashlight, where had she put it? Then she remembered: last night she'd been so bemused by her painting that she'd left the flashlight up on one of the shelves beside the mattress. Now she would have to reach up and get it. She raised one hand into the air, then pulled it back. Suddenly she didn't want to feel around in the dark! She had a kind of skin-aware feeling, as if there were someone close by. "Who's there?"

For a moment she sat still, listening to nothing.

Then she chided herself: "Hysteria!" And then she was up at once, scrabbling along the shelves, knocking things down—cans, aspirin, bandages.

Silver metal. Her hands slid along it, they recognized its color before she found the button. She wrenched the flashlight on.

But after all there was no one there! She played the light about her, dipping it madly along every wall and surface. Despite her feeling of warmth in the air, of a vacated space, however, everything looked as usual. Had her feeling been part of a dream? Some remnant of interrupted sleep?

The lantern was dead; she'd been expecting it. The flashlight was not very strong. It moved feebly over distant walls and shelves while Tave tried to reassure herself once again that dark or light, things stayed the same.

It was no use: the eerie feeling would not leave. Was there someone out there?

"Are you—are you hungry?" she called, coaxed, really, a little crazily. Then she searched along the shelves for an unopened loaf of bread. "Look," she called, "I've got some food."

She was awake, but inside a dream, an illusion that someone watched her. As if sleepwalking, she took one step after another down the corridor of dark, holding the bread high in one hand, her light a valiant, ribbed orange spot in front of her. "Are you hungry?" she coaxed in a child's voice, almost a whisper.

Two thirds of the way down the cellar she stopped: no one had reached out for her, there was no one down here, how could there be? She set the bread down. She would leave it here anyway. On the floor. She wasn't quite sure why. For insurance, maybe.

Then she tiptoed back to her mattress so as not to disturb anyone. And then laughed at herself. And then stared about her. Not a shadow moved.

The blankets were still warm. She climbed in and pulled them up to her chin, leaving only her flashlight hand free. She would stay awake, she told herself. She would watch. Again and again her light fingered the cellar walls, slid along shelves: nothing. The skin of her neck crept along her collar: no sound anywhere. Well, she thought, she would watch.

For a long time Tave remained awake, frightened and vigilant, but at last she began to believe that she must have been suffering from some kind of midnight madness, some dream paranoia. She wasn't doing anyone any good by refusing to sleep, she thought. The blankets were warm, she could, at least, lie down.

She drifted off, drugged by exhaustion into some unreal state in which she dreamed of watching, listening.

*

When she awoke, it was once again to the utter dark, and this time the hair on her head lifted and stood out from its roots. Instinctively she reached for the flashlight, found its little metal button, and pushed at it wildly although she knew it was already on. "Please," she whispered. "Please."

The cellar lay upon her like a big, black-cloud mantle, dragging at her shoulders, feeling for the delicate places about her throat. She fought the dark for lucidity: candles, where were they? On the workbench, of course. Shivering violently, she stood up. She felt like an addict looking for a fix. The air about her teemed with possibilities for harm.

"Leave me alone," she said, on a timid, rising inflection. The words seemed to stop abruptly, midair. As if they had been absorbed. Heard.

She mustn't think so.

Carefully, hands out a little in front of her but not too far— she didn't want to touch anything like peeled grapes or warm ketchup—she moved one foot at a time in the direction of the workbench. It was more than a dozen steps to get there, thirteen, fourteen steps into the swirling black. When at last she reached it, she clung with both hands and, breathing as if she'd run a great distance, she found the candles, snatched at them, lit one, and lifted it high.

There was no one there. Why, the cellar hadn't changed at all. It was all just the same. "Good God," Tave whispered to herself. "The things you can dream."

Suddenly she was weak with relief.

For some reason, she held her light to the painting she'd started on the day before. She was prepared more than ever to hate it, have a good laugh, or a cry. The colors would be wrong, of course, she thought. The conception would be silly. Still, she held the candle up.

Then her lips in their grim straight line softened. Her eyebrows, drawn into the remnants of a frightened frown, lifted. She took a step forward, a step back. A small sound escaped her, a tiny "Oh" of recognition and pleasure.

Of course it was only candlelight, she was tired, and she'd been scared. And the painting wasn't finished, not anywhere near, only outlines here and there, that pink, that poppy. And it wasn't so much that it seemed good. But it pleased her.

"Why, there," she whispered. "There."

Only by candlelight, of course. In the light of day she guessed she'd see something else.

But suddenly a dozen subjects for painting occurred to her, a hundred, too many to count. Hills of fourteen shades of green, farmhouses in mist, in ordinary light and in dying light. Flowers, all the endless flowers she and her mother had once planted and painted together. Oh, they'd loved to—

At once she drew her eyes from the painting and laughed at herself. After all, she knew what painting flowers meant. It meant flowers ripped to shreds, torn to bits, slashed with a razor.

Well, she would go back to her mattress. And when the call came from John—it would have to come soon, wouldn't it?—she would carry the painting up the stairs and there it would be seen, no doubt, for what it was.

Tave took the candle to her shelves, found a dish, allowed wax to drip, and fastened the candle upright. Then she laid it on a shelf by her mattress. Beside it she put a second candle, for a back-up. It was like parsing out sanity, she thought a little ruefully. How dependent she was! She stared into the dark. Soon, she thought, she and Bob would be together. She would talk to him, yes. They would talk and talk, and she would try to be honest, so he could understand what she was feeling. Perhaps they would even be laughing at what she did now. Wax and string and a little flame! "I actually thought for a minute that someone was there," she would tell him. "It was so real to me." They would smile and understand one another and sip their coffee.

If only the candles would last until then.

She reassured herself: the furnace, the workbench, the sink. All familiar: perhaps she was even becoming accustomed to the cellar? Once again she made herself comfortable and dozed fitfully for perhaps an hour, maybe more.

*

Tommy had limped toward the bulkhead and slipped inside it in time to faint. When he came to again it was to a pain so harsh he didn't recognize himself. Training his eyes into the dark, he saw the bitch's light, still shining, far down in the cellar, and knew only that he'd failed Cone. He wouldn't fail again. He stood; now he was numb with cold, thirsty, and ill. He moved forward, hesitated, moved. One bloody hand felt along his face. Oh, yes, he remembered. He was Tommy Green. His foot struck something. The bitch had left him some bread.

But he could not bend over to pick it up. The loaf was there, he could feel it with his foot, push at it a little with his toe. A picture came to him, dimly perceived, of the sweet soft whiteness of that bread inside its wrapper, how good bread felt to his hands, how it kept him alive . . . He groaned.

*

She woke as if to some sound and Tave thought immediately of the loaf of bread, down there on the floor in the dark.

"I'd better go pick it up," she told herself.

Candle in hand, she moved down the dark corridor between cubicles that seemed to breathe and reach for her to where she left the loaf. She picked it up. And it wasn't until she'd carried it, still wrapped in its cellophane, back to her shelves that she found upon the wrapper a red spot, still warm. Blood.

At that moment her first candle guttered.

With shaking hands Tave lit the second one, held it over the bread. One small wet spot. Blood.

Then she heard what sounded like a laugh.

A tiny sound, short-lived, hollow. From someone stuck far down a well, or deep within some closed-in space.

Tave gasped, listened again, heard nothing. She cross-examined herself. Had she laughed, had she? No, she didn't think . . . No, she hadn't at all.

After a moment she cleared her throat, but this made a loud sound that frightened her: the skin behind her ears moved and tightened. She was scared, she realized, of being overheard.

As if there were something—or someone—in the cellar with her.

She heard herself take a deep breath and whisper, "Hello? Is —is anybody there?"

There was no answer.

Of course there was no answer, she told herself. Hadn't she searched the whole area and come up with nothing? Why, she'd looked everywhere, she thought, staring down at the blood-stained cellophane. She'd looked into every little cubbyhole!

Except she hadn't looked under the bulkheading.

But nobody could search in there, she argued with herself. Nothing in there but junk; she'd seen the junk, hadn't she? Yes. She'd looked everywhere she could!

Unless somebody was right inside that junk.

Somebody who could stay so still for long periods of time that you didn't even know he was there. Someone who came into your room in the dark to hurt and frighten you, to maim your life and kill your parents and make you so hatefully angry and afraid you knew if he ever got at you again you would kill him! Yes! As he had killed you! Your life! You were scared; you wanted him dead! You would get yourself a knife, a hammer, anything, and tear his eyes out, slit his throat, disembowel—

"My God," said Tave aloud, carefully. "I must be going crazy."

After all, it might only be a small animal, trapped somewhere. That would make sense, something small and frightened and bleeding.

At once she was mad at herself; damned if she were going to stay in one place and be scared of nothing. She peered off into the dark, picked up her candle, and began at once, grimly, to search the entire cellar. She went methodically to each cubicle, holding the candle well in front of her. One after another, she lit each musty, dark corner she came to. No one. But each successive corner seemed harder to search, hungrier somehow. She visited them all: it was an act of bravery on her part and she recognized it as such. All about her as she moved she felt a queer, just-vacated warmth, as if she were on the verge, always, of detecting something, something awful that lurked in the dark.

At last she reached the jumbled storage at the far end of the cellar under the bulkhead and stood in front of it. So very quiet. Now she was uncertain. Should she pull the junk all apart, or be content with passing her light over it slowly?

She held her candle up, perplexed, and then heard something new. It was not a laugh, more like a gasp or an explosion of breath. It came again, came regularly, faintly. It came from deep within the bulkhead junk.

*

Tommy had seen her light begin to move. He had slunk into the shadows and waited, and there she was in front of him. She'd picked up the bread as if she owned it, taken it away.

His bread! His cellar!

He muttered a little under his breath, stopped: her candle was coming toward him again.

"Let her, Tommy," he'd heard Cone whisper. "She'll find you, all in good time."

It was Cone who led him back inside the junk. Tommy moved only where the bitch's candle couldn't find him. The junk place was the best.

From there he could watch her and wait for his chance.

"Yes," he heard Cone whisper. "Yes, Tommy." Now her light flickered toward him maddeningly, it was very close. His fingers began to move intimately amid the Perry junk. He could see the bitch's face and he couldn't help it, he began to breathe hard. Her mouth opened. Her eyes bulged. Then, with one painful wrench, he pushed forward. The whole pile of junk shifted, the wall of it heaved, tipped. Everything fell. Somewhere he heard Cone, squealing for joy.

*

Iron gashed Tave's shoulder, a wicker chair slashed at her cheek. She dropped the candle dish; it shattered, the light went out. Tave shrieked and tried to run but things chased her, knocked her over, fell about her and on top of her, an avalanche of cast-offs. On her knees she crawled, sobbing, trying to fight loose of them. The spring of a bed entangled her feet; she wrenched away, got up, ran, bumping into shelves, knocking things down as she went. She ran full tilt into the sink and spun from it to the furnace, where at last she stopped herself. Tommy Green—it had to be! He meant to kill her! Explosions of his breath—she heard them again. She whimpered, fumbled for matches, a weapon.

Tommy Green! She was scared. And below that, suddenly, she perceived something new in herself, something very old, reaching up through her like a subterranean plant with freely springing tendrils: fury. Tommy Green meant to kill her, did he? As he had killed her mother? And now he thought to take what she had left? She would have to kill him first.

In the dark she felt among the bones on the workbench— Bob's tools—and came up at last with an ax-and-hammer combination, and the matches. Then she lit her last candle. Oh, she was furious, all right. She made her plan. In a moment she went back to her mattress because it was protected by the furnace and the shelves. This would be the corner she'd fight from. She sobbed a little and tried to listen. Explosions of breath approached her: Tommy. Carefully Tave set her candle on a high shelf and gripped the ax.

*

Hunched over with pain, Tommy searched hungrily. He was bent, angular, and faded from one piece of fallen furniture to the next, invisible, part of each castoff. But at last his head came up: that bitch was still alive. Once again, down the length of the cellar, her little brown light flickered. She had escaped him.

Pain made him moan; he could hardly breathe, he was bleeding. One side of his body was a massed bruise from shoulder to hip and he dragged that leg a little, used it as a prop, otherwise it was no good to him. His mind was dazed, but he knew that light. It was female and ugly to him, the source of all his pain. Suddenly he was a little boy again. His mother had hit him, thrown him against the wall, had she? His mother had laughed at him, offered to kill him?

He heard Cone's voice: "Kill the bitch, Tommy! Now!"

Well, he would, once and for all. Ugly, power-and-pain—he would get her. He would prove that he, Tommy Green, was stronger than she was. He rubbed his bloody hands together, scrubbed his face with them, and slowly began to make his way down the cellar toward the light. It was nighttime in his mind and he was moving from kitchen to bedroom, he was planning how he would kill her. Cone had told him to do it.

*

In her corner by the stairs, Tave Perry heard Tommy approach: a queer little shuffle, an explosion of breath, a silence. She stood quietly. In one hand she gripped the ax-hammer. She would wait until he was in the light. Maybe she would die. But she vowed to herself that somehow she would stay alive long enough to kill him first. Fear was far away from her now. Tave was resolved, quiet. For what he had done, she promised herself, the death he deserved.

One toe, in a scuffed brown boot, appeared at the edge of her ring of light.

"Come on," she whispered to him. "Come on, you—"

Suddenly the whole of him, rough-shorn and ragged, stood before her. Raising her ax, Tave faced him. Her arm tensed, ready to strike him the minute he touched her. Trembling, she stared him in the eye. It was Tommy's inherited color, dark violet blue, blank and hateful in a horribly stained face. The eye promised her death. He stood hunched over for a moment, staring at her, then lifted one arm, reached. His fingers, too, were covered with blood.

Tave shrieked: a battle cry, ripped from her. His bloody arm raised, Tommy stepped closer. Her eyes searched his forehead for the place she would have to strike. She prepared to swing the ax.

Another step. His fingers curled like a blood-rusted claw. He swiped at the air near her face. Madly she shrieked again.

Then his eyes shifted, as if he had heard something—not her shriek, but some awful interior noise. His knees buckled and he fell with a groan, his face smearing blood along her blue jeans. Helpless, he collapsed in front of her. Delivered to her.

He lay face down at her feet for a moment, the bloody hands clawing at nothing. He seemed to be begging for her to strike. When she didn't he raised himself up and reached for her again, a promise in his glazed eyes: I will kill you.

"Murderer!" Tave hissed. It was going to be easy now: in her anger she saw how she would bring the ax down on his head, break it as her mother's head had been broken, raise the ax again and lay open his neck, crack it as her mother's had been cracked. She would chop at his ribs and let out the heart, as her father's heart had been taken out of him! She clutched at the weapon with white-knuckled hands; she would need two hands to do this, murder the murderer, for her mother and her father and all those lost, frightened years.

The last murder. She took a breath, ready to swing.

At that moment the house moved, or settled, or called to her. She thought she heard it tell her something. "Tave," the beams whispered. "Wait," the hill called. "Not this."

Ax raised, arms tensed, Tave saw suddenly how Tommy's hair grew, in matted, shagged triangles all over his head. She saw his torn coat, made of some kind of cotton, light-colored except where it soaked into a dark red stain. She saw the side of his face clearly; it, too, was covered with blood. Had he scrubbed at it with his bloody hands?

Then she knew: she wouldn't hurt him, couldn't. She was a

Perry. She was the hope of the Perrys. She was not a murderer. She could fight, yes. Defend herself. Survive. But not murder, no.

She lowered the ax and threw it into a far corner.

"Tommy," she said, "you're hurt."

Her voice surprised her. It was a quiet, free voice.

Into Tommy's eyes came a look of shock, almost like a question. He moaned.

Down in the pit of Tave's stomach something blossomed and grew, panic under control but still very much alive. She had a hard time forcing her lips to speak what she meant to say. Juices were flowing into her mouth, the kind you taste before vomiting, sour and sweet.

"Tommy," she said, shaking and close to tears, "if you want me to, I'll help you. If you won't hurt me . . ."

Then she stood still. It was a question to which, she felt, she had to have a reply. She was entitled to know whether or not she would be hurt, wasn't she?

But the bloody hand only tore its way toward the blankets on her mattress. He was breathing in gasps now. Beside him on the floor was a tiny dark drop: blood. She stared at it, recognizing it, and what Tommy did or would do didn't matter at all. What she was made of, that did matter. She had not been made only for anger. She knelt, touched the cotton-clad shoulders.

"Tommy," she said, trembling and scared, but suddenly resolute, "if you will roll over, I'll try to see where you're hurt."

But he was helpless. She supported him until he could roll. Then he lay with his arm against his maimed side, the other hand knotted in blankets.

"All right," said Tave shakily. She could see he was in great pain. "Are you thirsty?"

The questioning look was still in his eyes. He didn't answer. She stared at his blood-sodden jacket. "First," she said, "we'll see how you're hurt. Then I'll get you a drink of water. It's very good water, piped in here in my great-grandfather's time."

Injured, one body is very much like another. Tommy lay still while she unzipped his jacket, raised his shirt, and gasped at what she saw there. Even in candlelight, the massive purple and black bruise was horribly raised and colorful. A small piece of bone that looked like a rib stuck through the skin of his side, oozing blood every time he breathed. No, he wasn't going to hurt her. He was dying.

Rapidly Tave began to pack the bruise with cold, wet pieces of blanket, she didn't know what else to do. Then she moistened his lips with the water and sat beside him. "Don't worry," she said. "It won't be long before someone will call, and we'll get out of here, get you a doctor."

Tommy lay very still. His face, lips and all, was drained of color. Each breath he took ended in that little explosion of pain.

*

"Beware," someone said. "Beware Tommy Green." It was Lucy Perry.

"Grandma." Tave sighed a little to herself. "Are you still here?"

The old woman frowned. "Beware, Octavia!" she cried.

Tave shook her head. "The trouble with you, Grandma," she said, "is you're too damn scared to die." Then, as Tave watched, the old woman smiled an unexpected smile, lost in love, and slowly faded. At last she was gone.

*

Tommy didn't move. Tave sat beside him on the mattress, changing the cloths on his side from time to time. But until the last of her candle burnt down and gave out, he stared at her steadily with that puzzled look that never left his eyes.

The candle did burn down, then it was dark. Tave had been expecting it, but now the dark didn't seem to matter. Beside her the faint explosions of breath continued, although Tommy didn't move. She waited with him in the dark. At last the explosions began to come faster and faster, there was a moan on the mattress, a tightening, a stiffening. "Tommy?" she whispered.

The explosions stopped. It was utterly quiet. Tave reached

over and felt for a pulse, finding none. Then she covered the body as best she could and waited quietly in the dark.

After a long while she went to sleep.

*

A distant ringing. She woke, blinked, heard it again, stumbled up from the floor, up the stairs. Then her fingers were tearing at the wedged clay, pulling the door open. And there she was in the kitchen and it was bright with sunlight, so bright her eyes had to squint; then she was racing to the phone.

"Honey, are you all right?" Bob's voice, human, blessed. He loved her—she was ready to love him.

"Yes!" she cried. "Oh, yes! Bob, are you okay? Are the kids— Tavia? Billy?" Speaking their names, her eyes filled.

"All okay!" he said. His voice, that hitch in it. "We've been fine. A little scared. Luckily we missed the fallout. This time, anyway. I was worried about you, all alone in the cellar. You were all right? You were warm enough? Did it get dark?"

"The generator went off," said Tave shakily. "But I was all right. And I wasn't alone."

"Someone was there with you?"

"Come home, Bob! Come home! I'm fine, the house is fine! Please."

"We're on our way," he said. "I'll be right there. We love you, Tave." He hung up.

Tave replaced the phone. Slowly she moved through her house.

Why, it *is* a beautiful place, she thought. What a beautiful place I live in.

She passed from one room to another and loved them, each of them: the bedrooms, front sitting room, living room, porch, kitchen. They were hers: suddenly they were like a gift. From every window she could see the hill. Somebody had done something right, because there was the hill.

Sunlight flooded the kitchen. It must be almost noon, she thought. The kitchen shone. Amy's poppies, on stove shelf and table, were a little wilted. She emptied the vases; soon she would pick more. Her mother was dead, but that didn't hurt any longer. Lucy, Marl—they too were dead. But they were pleased with her, she knew it. What they'd given birth to, it was alive and it was good. It had a chance. Just like the hill. She had a chance.

Now the whole house was hers. And the cellar.

She went back and looked down the stairs. Then, slowly, she went down to Tommy's body. He was a lump under blankets. That was all. She couldn't be afraid. She knelt and pulled the covers back so that she could see his face in the light from the door. His eyes were wide open. He looked, she thought, as if someone had stopped him midquestion, as if he'd left his body and gone to another room to answer it. Tave felt for his eyelids, unexpectedly soft and vulnerable, and closed his eyes. Then she covered him again.

She looked around the cellar. Well, it wasn't the Ritz, was it, but it wasn't that bad, either. She supposed they'd continue now, outfit a real shelter down here. You couldn't ignore the nuclear age; you lived in it. You had to know how to live in it.

Suddenly Tave's eye caught her painting, the pale pink shells of the rose she'd tried to paint.

"All right," she said to herself. "Now we'll see."

She brought it up the stairs and set it on the kitchen table. She didn't expect much. After all, the light in the cellar was all wrong, probably the colors were bad, it was all bad, not worth going on with. Then she stepped back and looked.

Sure enough, here and there were things in the painting that were quite wrong. Shadows would have to be amended; the stone wall, for example, seemed unnecessarily light-colored up here in the sunlit kitchen. It didn't matter, there was plenty of time. She suspected that underneath the little errors, the painting might be good, very good. But even that didn't matter. It occurred to Tave that you had to be listening and maybe even a bit scared to paint the things you loved. But they would last, good or not, because you loved them.

She was pleased. She was almost content.

In the distance she heard the labor of Bob's Scout as it came up that final incline on the road. She ran to the porch door to watch the Scout work its way up, so full of gladness that she flung the screen wide and laughed as the Scout finally slammed open with the force of her family's eagerness. Then she was running toward them: they looked well, they looked real!

"Why, hello!" she called out in a coming-to-tea polite voice, not Lucy's but her own, brimming with laughter and love. "And what brings you up Octavia's Hill?"

And then they were in her arms.